Engaging with Fashion

At the Interface/Probing the Boundaries

Founding Editor

Rob Fisher (*Oxford, United Kingdom*)

Advisory Board

VOLUME 112

The titles published in this series are listed at *brill.com/aipb*

Engaging with Fashion

*Perspectives on Communication,
Education and Business*

Edited by

Federica Carlotto and Natalie C. McCreesh

BRILL
RODOPI

LEIDEN | BOSTON

Cover illustration: art direction by Rochelle Lambourne, photography by Darren Black. Used with kind permission.

The Library of Congress Cataloging-in-Publication Data is available online at http://catalog.loc.gov
LC record available at http://lccn.loc.gov/2018039459

Typeface for the Latin, Greek, and Cyrillic scripts: "Brill". See and download: brill.com/brill-typeface.

ISSN 1570-7113
ISBN 978-90-04-38242-8 (paperback)
ISBN 978-90-04-38243-5 (e-book)

Contents

PART 3

Educating

PART 4

Communicating

Figures

Notes on Contributors

Claire Allen

is a Postgraduate research student in fashion identity at Sheffield Hallam University (UK). Her PhD study is an investigation of fashion identity references, emotive visual memory prompts and how they can be mapped for improving care and support for women living with memory dysfunction. Claire is a former Senior Lecturer in Fashion Communications, programme developer and Course Leader for BA (Hons) Fashion, Communication and Promotion and a Top up degree in partnership with the University of Huddersfield (UK) and a Hong Kong franchise.

Deidra W. Arrington

is a seasoned fashion professional with 20 years experience as a department store apparel buyer and divisional merchandise manager. Deidra joined the Department of Fashion Design & Merchandising at Virginia Commonweatlh University (USA) in 2004. Her areas of research include fashion economics, the luxury market, and fashion show production and its impact on worldwide economies. Deidra Arrington earned a Bachelor's of Science degree in Business Administration at Jacksonwille State University (USA) and a MBA at Virginia Commonwealth University.

Naomi Joanna Braithwaite

is a Senior Lecturer in Fashion Marketing and Branding at Nottingham Trent University (UK). She is an experienced ethnographer whose research interests focus on visual and material culture in the context of fashion and shoes. Before undertaking her Doctorate which was ethnographic study of creativity in shoe design, Naomi managed the international sales for a designer shoe brand.

Jill M. Carey

is Curator of the Lasell Fashion Collection at Lasell College, Newton, MA, (USA). Most recently Jill was promoted to the title of the Joan Weiler Arnow Professor '49 in Historic Fashion, a three-year endowed position awarded for excellence in teaching and community impact. Her curatorial efforts regarding the Lasell Fashion Collection have resulted in grant awards such as a National Endowment for the Arts while also being recognized as 'Best College Collection' by *Boston Magazine*.

Federica Carlotto

is Course Leader of the Art of Luxury at Sotheby's Institute of Art and cultural strategist for businesses and consultancies. Her research and consultancy activity focuses on the social meanings and practices underpinning the production, branding and consumption of luxury and fashion.

Karen Dennis

is currently a designer and pop-up retail manager working for a children's hospice charity. As a fashion designer she has worked internationally with agencies such as OXFAM, Intermediate Technology Development Group and The British Council in the delivery and evaluation of development projects in India, Nepal and Zambia. Karen also works in academia as a Senior Lecturer in Fashion, specialising in sustainable fashion.

Doris Domoszlai-Lantner

is an historian and archivist in fashion, dress, and textiles. Doris holds an MA in Fashion and Textile Studies: History, Theory, Museum Practice, from Fashion Institute of Technology, New York (USA), and a BA in History and East European Studies from Barnard College, Columbia University (USA). She has worked as an archivist for various notable private clients and brands, including the luxury jewelry house, David Webb.

Lindsay E. Feeney

graduated with highest honours earning a BA in Fashion Communication and Production from Lasell College, Newton, MA (USA) in 2014. During her undergraduate years, she and Professor Jill M. Carey collaborated on several projects while curating an exhibition titled *Sixty Years of Nursing History Uniforms and Style* at Brigham and Women's Hospital. Lindsay is currently working in the fashion industry.

Nádia Fernandes

is an Orthoptist in Topcare Clinic and a part-time Lecturer in Orthoptics at Lisbon School of Health Technology (Portugal). Currently, she is a student of Jewellery Design at Lisbon Jewellery Centre. Her longstanding interest in fashion and her work with vision-impaired people motivates her research.

Jacque Lynn Foltyn

is Professor of Sociology, National University, La Jolla, California (USA). Jacque Lynn is a cultural critic, social theorist, and media expert, shaping discourse about the body, fashion, beauty, popular culture, and death and dying. She served as editor-in-chief of *Catwalk: The Journal of Fashion, Beauty and Style* (2011–2016), her fashion books include: *Fashions: Exploring Fashions through Cultures* (ed); *Crafting Allure: Beauty, Culture, and Identity* (ed); and *Fashion-Wise* (ed).

Alessia Grassi

is a Ph.D candidate at the University of Huddersfield (UK). She is a Teaching Assistant in Fashion Marketing. Her background is in business management and accountancy.

Christopher R. Jones

is a Senior Lecturer in Social and Environmental Psychology at the University of Surrey (UK). Since gaining a Ph.D from The University of Sheffield (UK). He has been actively engaged in research into environmental attitudes and behaviours.

Lan Lan

is Senior Lecturer at Beijing Institute of Fashion Technology (China). She received her MA in Womenswear Design at London College of Fashion (UK). Her research and writing is devoted in fashion education.

Peng Liu

is Assistant Professor at Macau University of Science and Technology (China). He received his PhD in Visual Art at Curtin University (Australia). He is a practicing artist working with a wide range of mediums and writes academic journals papers and book chapters in the field of Cultural Studies and Visual Culture.

Mario Matos Ribeiro

is Assistant Professor of Fashion at the Faculty of Architecture, University of Lisbon (Portugal). His research and writing is about fashion curating and the creation of relationships between fashion and the web. He is currently working with Ines Simoes on *A Guide for Fashion Designers*, a book focused on alternative approaches to project.

Natalie C. McCreesh

is an academic consultant and Senior Lecturer in Fashion Management and Communication, at Sheffield Hallam University. Since gaining a PhD from The University of Manchester she has been actively engaged in fashion education and research. Current research interests include tattoos and the female body, appearance and identity and the future of fashion education.

Alex McIntosh

is Business and Research Associate at the Centre for Sustainable Fashion University of the Arts London, London College of Fashion (UK) and is experienced in the development and delivery of industry focused projects. Alex splits his time between his work at CSF and his role as Managing Director of Christopher Raeburn.

Alice Morin

is currently working on her PhD at Paris III-Sorbonne Nouvelle (France). Her work focuses on fashion photography's tendency to over-stage ethno-racial, national and gendered representations, making them into *tableaux*, emphasizing or encouraging their trespassing of 'mainstream' norms. She previously studied Art History at the Ecole du Louvre and American Literature at Paris III.

Noly Moyssi

has a PhD in Traditional Culture from the Department of History and Archaeology of the University of Cyprus. Her current research focuses on the traditional Cypriot dress.

Maria Patsalosavvi

is a Curator at The Leventis Municipal Museum of Nicosia (Cyprus). Her current research focuses on the entertainment during the Byzantine and Medieval period in Cyprus.

Laura Petican

is Assistant Professor of Art History and Director of University Galleries at Texas A&M University-Corpus Christi (USA). Her research is centred in social history of post-war and contemporary Italian art with a focus on its relation to theories of national identity, cultural inheritance, baroque historiography, and the intersections of art history and fashion studies. Her research has been awarded by the Social Sciences and Research Council of Canada and the Center for Faculty Excellence at Texas A&M University-Corpus Christi.

Jennifer Richards

is a Lecturer in Fashion Communication at Manchester Metropolitan University (UK). Her research interests examine the Gothic mode in visual communication with a particular interest in fashion, stage and screen. She co-convened the Gothic Manchester Festival 2017 which focused on the exploration of Gothic Styles. She has published work examining the rise of mysticism and witchcraft in popular culture and the digital realm. Jennifer is currently working on book chapters examining *Fashion and Performance,* and the *Aesthetics of Beauty and Ageing.*

Susanne Schulz

has been a Lecturer in Sociology at Queen Margaret University (Edinburgh) since 2005. She lectures predominantly on cultural sociology, interaction and social order. Susanne has conducted research on fashion forecasting and selection processes of UK high-street womenswear retailers. She has published papers on the role of the customer image in fashion selection and strategies used by fashion practitioners to cope with demand uncertainty.
Susanne is currently working on two projects: Discourses of Creativity and Colour Forecasting.

Ines Simoes

is Assistant Professor of Fashion at the Faculty of Architecture, University of Lisbon (Portugal), and Coordinator of the BA in Fashion Design. Her research and writing is about the paradigms in the representation of the body in pattern design. She is currently working with Francisco Silva on *A Guide for Fashion Designers*, a book focused on alternative approaches to project.

Helen Storey

is an award winning British artist and designer. She is Professor of Fashion and Science at the Centre for Sustainable Fashion, University of the Arts London, London College of Fashion (UK) and Co-Director of The Helen Storey Foundation.

Steve Swindells

is a Professor in Creative Practice at the University of Huddersfield (UK). His research has two strands: public engagement and curation in art and design, and sculptural thinking in fashion.

Stephen Wigley

is in the Fashion & Textiles department at the University of Huddersfield. His research interests incorporate the function of fashion brands, international fashion retailing, and luxury marketing.

Gaye S. Wilson

is Shannon Senior Historian at the Robert H. Smith International Center for Jefferson Studies (USA), the academic branch of the Thomas Jefferson Foundation. Prior to joining the Foundation in 1993, she worked as a theatrical costume designer and taught history of dress in the Theater Department the University of Texas, Austin (USA) and later served as an adjunct for the Theatre Department at the University of Virginia (USA). She is currently working on her forthcoming book, *Jefferson on Display: Attire, Etiquette, and the Art of Presentation.*

Cecilia Winterhalter

is an independent researcher in contemporary fashion sociology, who teaches on the construction of new identities through fashion, trends, consumption, luxury, innovative products, religion and food. Employed at the Swiss Ministry of Culture, she has also held several jobs in the luxury sector (Christie's Int. SA., BVLGARI). She has lectured at the Fashion Institute of Technology, Florence, Italy the University of Pisa, Italy the London College of Fashion (UK), LUISS University (Italy) and the Accademia di Costume e Moda, Rome (Italy).

Introduction

Federica Carlotto and Natalie C. McCreesh

The Editorial Journey: Fashion and Fashions
Federica Carlotto

Editing the 20 papers for this volume has been a reflective practice on Fashion, a journey that eventually brought us to critically engage with its epistemological value.

At the beginning, the editorial process appeared to be a straightforward case of project management, i.e. something divisible into tasks, stages, stakeholders, internal and final deadlines *etc*. As editors, we could clearly envision the path ahead: collate the papers, propose and discuss amendments with the contributors, harmonise styles and contents in alignment with the editorial requirements, organise the final material into chapters and sections. Whilst we discussed thoroughly the details of all the above, we tacitly assumed that Fashion was to be the umbrella construct, the harmonising principle of our work.

When we actually started engaging with the papers – with their content, methodology, language, sources – a much more complex reality emerged. Not unexpected and yet still fascinating, we found ourselves immersed in a vast variety of topics: from the 'slow fashion' in Chinese design education, to the 'wear-again' strategies of the British royals; from the fashion plates of Rudolph Ackermann, to the way visually impaired people experience their own style; from the iconic imagery of shoes and models in *Vogue* and other fashion magazines, to the temporal dimensions of the fashion system. We had papers venturing to explore the intersections of fashion with visual arts and music, gastro-trends and sustainability. Issues of gender, social class, cultural appropriation, and mediated representation were debated.

In alignment with the contents' diversity, the papers relied upon a different mix of research approaches and strategies. Some of them were theoretical in nature, with concepts drawn from the extant scholarly literature, and woven into arguments. Some others were more descriptive, and were supported by a rigorous analysis of original sources and documents. Others capitalized on the empirical knowledge of fieldwork, content analysis, in-depth interviews and exploratory practices.

© KONINKLIJKE BRILL NV, LEIDEN, 2019 | DOI:10.1163/9789004382435_002

Finally, each paper had its own narrative, with a specific tone of voice, pace, and structure. In certain cases, the narration was flowing naturally – a stream-of-consciousness, while in others it was logically structured in building blocks.

In confronting with the strong individuality of each of our papers, we realised that editing was something more than the systematic act of putting different elements together. Rather, editing called for curation, i.e. a deeper and active enquiry into the papers' significance, individually and collectively. In other words, editing entailed us to link the papers to each other so that they maintain their original scope, while at the same time acquiring new meanings by virtue of the links and resonances they established with one another within the book.

In turning those papers into chapters and in grouping them in different sections, we first followed a well established path, that of the disciplinary categorization: it was 'easy' to label the evolution of dress in 19th century Cyprus and the allotment of slave garments in 18th–19th centuries Virginia as historical chapters; it was 'easy' to bring the chapter on the strategies of high-street fashion production, and the chapter on the creation of a retail network for up-cycled fashion, under the business category.

Soon enough, however, those boxes felt both too comfortable and too constrictive. It felt to us that by choosing mainstream epistemological categories we were already imposing a simplistic interpretive reading on the papers. We did not want the complex cross-cultural dynamics behind the change of the Cypriot dress, or the clothing allotment in US slavery plantations, to be flattened by their being 'historical'. We did not want the elements of 'waste' and 'novelty' behind fashion production and up-cycling to be lost through a business approach.

We hence decided to step out from those categorical boxes, and start afresh by questioning, without any preconception, what was the original message of the chapters to us: were the chapter on Missoni and 'Arte Povera', and the chapter on the art foundations of luxury brands, really about art? Is the chapter on pose more art- or body- related?

We also enjoyed 'playing around' with the chapters, experimenting unusual combinations, in a 'what if?' explorative mood. And there, other thematic links started to emerge: fashion design, for instance, was a theme underpinning the chapters about fashion education in China and Portugal – which considered, respectively, the relevance of cultural roots and collaborative work in fashion creativity – and the chapter documenting the cultural inspiration behind Jean Paul Gaultier's Russian Constructivist Collection in 1986. Sustainability was another compelling theme, running with different emphasis through several chapters, and establishing interesting resonances between them: if one chapter highlighted the paradox of contemporary consumers, torn between ethical thinking and fashionable behaviour, another proved how this gap can be reduced by raising public awareness through workshops and other out-reaching projects.

While turning papers into chapters, putting them in order, and grouping them into sections, we ended up establishing an epistemological dialogue with Fashion. We realised, in other words, that the way we were going to shape the book was also going to be the way we addressed the following question: what is Fashion then? Can we legitimately know about Fashion through the individual fashions the chapters address? As it normally happens with edited volumes, we were confronting with the epistemological gap between Fashion as a macro-construct, and the fuzzy reality of fashions, as emerging through the papers.

By acknowledging this gap, we somehow also shifted our editorial perspec-tive. Rather than aiming to close the gap between Fashion and fashions, trying to define what Fashion is, we became somehow comfortable with showing the ways through which we can approach Fashion. This is actually quite a contem-porary feature of our relationship with knowledge: when the reality is mixed and 'augmented', it is getting less important for us to define what reality really is, it is more about how we experience and understand it. Through the differ-ent chapters, we aim to provide the readers with an 'augmented knowledge' about Fashion, as emerging by assembling and de-structuring layers of mean-ings, different perspectives, and a network of links. In other words, we shift from the denotative idea of Fashion as a 'what' to appreciate the connotative aspects of Fashion as 'how'.

Finally, the content has been organised in six sections: (i) Marketing; (ii) Consuming; (iii) Educating; (iv) Communicating; (v) Embodying; (vi) Posi-tioning. Some of the terms are straightforward and conventional; some others might be less obvious. The choice of verbal forms as section headings, however, is meant to remind us of the dynamism between Fashion and fashions as well as the imperfect epistemology of research, trying to address Fashion through fashions. Consider these sections as the result of our personal editorial jour-ney. We invite now the readers to be curators themselves, and to create their own 'augmented knowledge' of Fashion, by reading this books' fashions.

Section Summaries
Federica Carlotto & Natalie C. McCreesh

Marketing
This section addresses fashion as a human economic activity. The term 'mar-keting' is commonly used to refer to a specific discipline in business studies

and, within it, to the communication and promotion of goods and services. Here, the term has been used in its continuous tense form, to indicate production as the very first action through which companies reach out to the market.

The chapter by Susanne Schulz ('Copying to Be Unique? – An Analysis of High Street Retailers' Product Differentiation Strategies') explores fashion production by questioning the actual fashionability of the fashion designed by high-street retailers. Drawing from the classic literature on fashion diffusion, which rests on the dialectic interaction between distinction and emulation, Schulz divides high-street retailers in 'design-led' companies, with a strong emphasis on innovation and originality, and 'buying-led' companies, which rely on the ability to capture and assimilate the trends of the market. These different approaches, Schulz explains, translate into almost opposite organizational and operational stances – corporate structure, planning and design, timing of production *etc.* Ultimately, the analysis of Schulz stretches to question the same meaning of 'stylistic originality' in a system where novelty has become systematized.

Federica Carlotto ('The Fashion "Timescape": Historical Evolution and Contemporary Features') delves further into the production of 'novelty' by linking it to time as a social and cultural construct. From this perspective, fashion is defined as a desirable change that is regularized in time. Carlotto goes back to analyse the birth of the fashion system, which was facilitated by the quest of Western societies for novelty, and stretches the analysis considering its recent evolutions. The chapter portraits the time of fashion as a cluster of different temporal dimensions: the acceleration of the production; the cyclical time followed by sustainable companies; the meaningful moments created by fashion brands on their social media; the strategic use of past and nostalgia as marketing tools. The chapter thus accounts for the complex dynamism characterising the fashion business' timescape.

Alessia Grassi, Steve Swindells, and Stephen Wigley ('The Art Foundations of Luxury Fashion Brands: An Exploratory Investigation') consider the highest tier of fashion, i.e. luxury. The chapter documents the first stage of the study on the increasing involvement of luxury fashion brands – such as Prada, Hermès, Louis Vuitton, Fendi – into art. In addressing the topic, Grassi *et al.* posit that art foundations and the sponsorship of exhibitions and artists are part of a specific business strategy. As the preliminary qualitative and desk research point out, luxury fashion brands need to exude a certain aura of exclusivity as part of their luxury code. Hence, they cannot rely on the continuous production of new items or on brand extensions to retain their relevance. The support to the arts becomes an effective way for luxury fashion brands to connect with a well-educated demographics of consumers, while at the same time capitalizing on the arts' democratic promise of public engagement. From this perspective, we may think of art sponsorship itself as a 'branded product' of the luxury fashion companies.

Consuming

With the recent evolution in the way we shop and how fashion is indeed presented to us, a section on consumption had to follow that on marketing. The very way in which fashion is now available 24/7, at the push of a button, ensures we are constant consumers. Constantly connected, constantly being prompted to think about and make the next purchase. As Deidra W. Arrington discusses in 'Ethical and Sustainable Luxury: The Paradox of Consumerism and Caring' cheap clothing has changed the way consumers perceive value. We are faced with a society of quantity over quality. This sentiment has been transferred from the garments to those who make them, with the knowledge that garment workers are often forced to work in dangerous conditions to ensure retail prices are kept low – Arrington questions, do we value human life as little as a £2 t-shirt? The paradox deepens when research suggests 70 per cent of consumers are influenced by ethics – yet consumption patterns suggest otherwise. Arrington suggests an alternative in 'Lux-Anthropy' expensive, luxury items with a positive environmental impact, yet ultimately it will be consumer actions that will make a real impact.

Another alternative to excessive consumption is explored by Karen Dennis who presents us with a retail movement of charity upcycling in 'Martin House Makers: Exploring Modes of Upcycling and Make within the Charity Retail Sector'. This chapter uses practice-led research to explore the issues with consumption patterns in the current fashion system. The stigma of austerity continues to plague recycling practices, which perhaps begs the question – do we need to revaluate our very definitions of 'sustainable', 'ethical' and 'luxury' altogether. This is what makes Martin House Makers unique, they attempt to engage the community, who are essentially the consumers, in production rather than just engaging them in emptying their pockets.

Perhaps then we need to look at consumption in relation to how it forms part of our lives, as activity, as hobby, as socialising, as status affirming – in this respect it is more than the procurement of garments. Claire Allen explores this in 'The Borrowing of Emotive Connotation Between Fashion and Music' where the authenticity of both fashion and music is explored in relation to commercialism. Here consumers drive consumption by demanding visual expressions of the zeitgeist of the time (today or as it was in the past), and external expressions of their emotions through both music and fashion combined. The powerful bond between music and fashion make them both important in how we structure related memories and thus can be used as memory retrieval triggers. In this respect Allen discusses self-identity in the here and now, but also in our past.

As our tastes in fashion and music grow and evolve so too can our tastes in food, as we grow older, our pallets refine as we welcome new taste sensations. Food does not escape the influences of fashion trends as Cecilia Winterhalter introduces in 'Recent Gastro-Trends: Food Surfing on the Streets'. Taking theories from Ted Polhemus' Streetstyle writings Winterhalter considers recent trends in gastronomy and how we shop the 'supermaket of style' in more ways than one. Similar to fashion clothing style we now combine the past and present, different ethnic and global flavours in our food. It isn't just what we consume but how we consume it – the fashion for street-style and street-food is at an all-time high. Winterhalter uses food to explore how eating habits can influence not only lifestyles but also personal relationships in the importance of gathering around the dinner table – or queuing up at the food truck.

Educating

The very nature of fashion involves keeping up with and even forming part of the zeitgeist. Yet teaching methods are often the same as they were 100 years ago. This is challenged as we move to Education, covering both the education of university students but also the general public. Ines Simoes and Mario Matos Ribeiro ('Collaborative Learning in Fashion Education') discuss Fashion design education practices in Portugal, which often takes similar format across the globe due to the 'Bologna Process'. The BA Fashion Design course was outlined to focus on the experience of the user i.e. the dressed body, and overall favour experimental creative processes. Finding disappointment however with the current taught design process of the individual student designing a full collection, Simoes and Ribeiro tackle pedagogical experimentation and introduced group design to their curriculum. The main goal was to engage students 'in a coordinated effort to solve a problem together'. Here teamwork was explored through collaboration, cooperation and problem solving. Through working in this new way students were faced with compromise and group responsibility, helping them grow as both designers and individuals.

In China Lan Lan and Peng Liu ('Clothing and Body: Case Studies in "Slow Fashion" in Fashion Education') tackle the role of responsibility in education from an ethical standpoint. The aim is to align Chinese societal values of slow-fashion with pedagogical approach. Here the historical and cultural relationship between inherited notions of the body were juxtaposed with the 'performative aspect of self' to allow students experience of developing their own design identity through slow-fashion, reflecting on traditional culture whilst remaining current. This reflects the economic climate in China and the market graduates will go on to work in. Moving away from overly Western influences, manufacturers are focusing on designer-driven product as a reflection of the 'creative economy', where 'Designed in China' takes the place of 'Made in China'.

Natalie C. McCreesh, Christopher R. Jones, Alex McIntosh and Helen Storey ('Making it Real: Engaging the Consumer in Sustainable Fashion Consumption') set about tackling sustainable consumption from an educative knowledge-transfer standpoint. Engaging retailers from both the fashion industry and utilities (such as electricity and water), in conversations about how they could aid their customers in socially responsible behaviours. Energy retailers are legally required to promote sustainability through energy-efficiency schemes and whilst this is not the case for the fashion industry many retailers have been keen to engage their consumers in sustainable practices such as in store recycling schemes, therefore a knowledge-exchange between both retail industries seemed logical. The project set about communicating responsible consumerism concepts to the general public through a series of public workshops, installation and fashion film. The aim to raise awareness, promote mindfulness and create a dialogue with consumers regarding their shopping habits in light of sustainability. While it often takes more than raised awareness and the formation of good intentions to affect change opening up the conversation and educating people is a good place to start.

Communicating

Fashion, in its very nature is fleeting as we constantly seek out the next trend. How we communicate fashion, through varying media, decides the fate of some trends as fads whilst others endure into iconic status. Doris Domoszlai-Lanter discusses political communication and fashion in 'Fashioning a Soviet Narrative: Jean Paul Gaultier's Russian Constructivist Collection, 1986'. Influenced by the zeitgeist of the time the demise of the Soviet Union was explored through numerous designer collections. Domoszlai-Lanter posits that Jean Paul Gaultier's pieces were the most expressive of what was to be termed 'fashnost'. The designer used Constructivist iconography such as Cyrillic letters and numbers in block type, linear and geometric forms, and photomontage in a manner provocative to their audiences. Exclamation marks and arrows were integrated to draw attention to the accompanying text. This fashion collection has remained iconic not only for its contribution to design but also to Soviet history.

'Fashion, Fantasy, Power and Mystery: Interpreting Shoes through the Lens of Visual Culture' by Naomi Joanna Braithwaite explores the iconic status of the high heeled shoe. Braithwaite does this using pop culture – fairytales, film and fiction, as conduits for shoes that are vessels of transformation. Focusing on fashion photography and the work of Guy Bourdin the chapter questions the semiotics of adverts created for Charles Jourdan, and discusses how fashion photography can be used to disseminate meaning.

Jill M. Carey and Lindsay E. Feeney in 'Fashion Plates: Rudolph Ackermann and Paul Poiret. The Relationship Between Classical Revival and Feminist Expressions' also address hidden meaning, in the 17th century fashion plates of the Ackermann Repository. Rather than study the fashion trends depicted within these woodcuts and engravings alone, they delve into the lives of women they display, women on the threshold of civil liberties. The investigation moves forward 100 years to designer Paul Poiret and his liberating, feminist approach to design. A supporter of illustration he commissioned a number of artists to depict his work, a keen way to advertise and entice people into his fashions when sent out as catalogs to customers. Studied together the two different types of illustration retain many similarities, especially those which allow comment on the evolution of classical revival and feministic expression.

Alice Morin ('Fashion Icons in Photography: American Magazine Turning to Iconic Representations From the 1960s On') focuses on how certain women or montages of idealized women became iconic. From the *femme fatale* to Jackie Kennedy, there are certain images that are repeated and constantly reinterpreted in fashion communication. Used to construct narratives and ultimately dream worlds and fantasies for readers of the magazine to idolize, the use of these figures limits readers. Rather than display a wide range of models a small selection of 'accepted' versions of women is instead presented, Morin suggests this sets new norms and unattainable ideals.

Embodying

The relationship between clothing and the human body has many levels. Considered in their materiality, both clothes and bodies are self-contained and finite. Yet, the body is mutable, tridimensional, imbued with agency; clothing is inanimate, bidimensional, produced. What happens when human bodies interact with clothing items? The chapters by Jennifer Richards ('Transcending the Traditional: Fashion as Performance') and Nádia Fernandes ('Visual Impairment and Fashion: Breaking Barriers') explore the osmotic interplay between fashion and the body, by considering specific epiphanies.

Richards focuses on the pose, considered as the moment where embodied fashion becomes a performative act. Through the analysis of specific examples of works on the catwalk, in shop windows, or on stage, Richards captures the rich reality behind clothing manipulation. Hence, for Daphne Guinness

(*Remembrance of the Things Past*) the act of dressing and undressing ritually evocates people and memories. For Viktor and Rolf, it becomes an aesthetic and political act. In the *Russian Doll*, the items of the collection are added on the body of the model, turning into the layers of a living sculpture; in another fashion show, undressing frees the clothing items from their utilitarian role. Finally, the trilogy of performances created by Oliver Saillard and featuring actress Tilda Swinton reminds us of the intimacy of this relationship: in *Eternity Dress,* dress-making is re-discovered as a process through which the body and the material gets familiar to each other – in stark contrast with the production process, where clothes are produced for the body but *in absentia* of the body; in *The Impossible Wardrobe* and *Cloakroom Vestiaire*, the items of clothing are considered as repositories of the bodies who wear them, as well as available canvas for human expression.

Fernandes brings us back to consider clothes as embodied realities in our daily life. Specifically, the chapter explores how visually impaired individuals address fashion, and the role that technology can play in bridging the gap that a sensorial limitation opens between body and clothing. As the field research reveals, visual impairment enhances even more the individualistic quest for self-expression through appearance, with the interviewees considering it more important to find their own style rather than being fashionable. In addition, the insights provided by visually impaired women show that technological devices, which are meant to re-establish contact between clothing and the body, do not usually solve the equation: especially in social settings, the use of devices seems to emphasise even more their visual impairment. Between psychology, social acceptance, clothing materiality and technological innovation, Fernandes invites us to reflect on the several features characterising the relationship of fashion and body.

Positioning

As mentioned in the first section, fashion emerges and unfolds along the mechanism of emulation and distinction. As a matter of fact, distinction and emulation are contextual acts that mirror, challenge, or question the structure of a certain social aggregation as well as the position that individuals occupy within it.

Jacque Lynn Foltyn in 'Sustainable Kate? Wear-Again Anne? – The Recycled Fashions of the Duchess of Cambridge and the Princess Royal' explores the institution of the British royalty, as defined through the readership of tabloids. The chapter makes the move from two articles of the *Daily Mail* reporting on the 'wear-again' habits of Catherine Duchess of Cambridge and Princess Anne. Through the content analysis of the readers' comments, Foltyn highlights the different semantics surrounding the looks of Kate and Anne, with Anne's 'wear-again' being sanctioned as an aristocratic touch of eccentricity, while Kate's stylistic recycling triggers mixed feelings, in that it becomes a painful reminder of her middle-class origin. This leads Foltyn to question the permeability of the British class system in normalizing social achievers.

Appearance as a tangible social barrier is also the interpretive lens adopted by Gaye S. Wilson ('Clothing Issued the Enslaved on the Monticello Plantation'). In her chapter, Wilson considers the clothing allocation system for the enslaved community of Monticello plantation, property of Thomas Jefferson, during 18th–19th centuries. The analysis of documents and accounts shows that the possession of fabrics and items – in terms of quantity, quality, and style – directly reflected each slave's distance or closeness to the master. The application of this Veblenian principle thus drew a line between house slaves, field slaves, and tradesmen. The system also displayed a certain flexibility: although still confined in a condition where 'fashionable' choices were not available, some slaves could alter their appearance, by virtue of the evolution of their personal and professional relationship with their master or his family. Here the term 'fashion' is examined as a representation of Veblen's definition of 'men of esteem', i.e. plantation owners, using fashion to communicate status, power and wealth rather than that of personal style choices.

What happens when a certain society has to confront with external forces and foreign influences? The chapter by Noly Moyssi and Maria Patsalosavvi ('The Metamorphosis of Dress in Cyprus During the British Period') explores the evolution of dress in 19th century Cyprus. Drawing links with the political, social and cultural changes the isle experienced first under the Ottoman Empire, then under the British rule, and finally in its struggle for the independence, Moyssi and Patsalosavvi document the *bricoleurship* of Cypriots in styling their appearance. By mixing and matching Ottoman items and Western elements, by creating a traditional dress, Cypriots were able to discuss and negotiate their own identity, positioning themselves in between independentism and cosmopolitism, in between 'us' and 'the others'.

Fashion production can be also considered socially, as a principle organising workers in hierarchies and strata depending on the role they play within the production. Within fashion production, fashion creation appears as the highest role, which positions the designer well above the other artisanal workforce, but which also traditionally separates the designer from the actual manufacturing process. Laura Petican ('Process and Mani Sapienti: Arte Povera and the Default to Order') reflects on the aristocratic narrative of fashion creation, which is usually perceived as the demiurgic effort of one individual. Petican here takes a different stance, and highlights the silent and unnoticed work of *mani sapienti* or *petit mains*. While this work has been recently praised by couture *maisons* such as Dior and Chanel, Petican focuses on Missoni's 'industrial' and machine-mediated work, drawing parallels with the artistic stances, works, the philosophy of 'Arte Povera'. As 'Arte Povera' brings back the dignity of the humble materials, the unknown hand, the repetitive work, Missoni has been able to elevate the anonymous and mass production of the machine and their monotonous zig-zag patterns to fashion statement and brand motif, thus bridging the gap between low production and high creativity.

Engaging with Fashion
Natalie C. McCreesh

Whilst reading through the first draft of papers for this book I was reminded of a conversation I had with designer and activist Vivienne Westwood around 5 years ago. It was one of those chats over the washbasin in the ladies loos and I happened to be wearing one of her dresses that had her hand drawn Family Tree printed onto the front. She explained that she had wanted to have big posters made of the print to give people when they came into one of her shops, because the message it contained was so important. Based on James Lovelock's Gaia theory on climate change – that the planet is a self-regulating life-system, within Vivienne's Tree 'Gaia' or Mother Earth goes hand in hand with science. On the right hand side of the tree is her vision of the world as we live now, a world destroying itself. She highlights as key issues, consumption, media propaganda and our view of progress – which is often detrimental to the Earth. On the left hand side is her holistic view of what society could be, in an ideal scenario: health, art, learning, human progress, purpose, commerce, cooperation, stability are all listed as key factors. What we spoke about that day was how she had placed quantity on the negative side and quality on the positive, something I would return to time and time again as I worked on sustainability projects.

As discussed in the preluding section it would have been easy for us to lump many of the papers together under a 'sustainability' heading, but it has become a word so carelessly thrown around it has lost its impact, it has lost its power. Whilst working on sustainable issues I was often met with the view that sustainable fashion is 'boring' or 'uncool'. On the project (detailed in my chapter in this book) we were met with stiff opposition from many retailers who declined to work with us on such a 'risky' subject. We changed tact in our wording of emails and how we broached conversations, once we stopped using the word 'sustainability' we were met with a more welcoming reception. Many retailers were so afraid of being branded 'unsustainable' that it appeared easier to bury heads in the sand on the subject rather than be transparent and engage in conversations. Yet when sustainably runs throughout most chapters of a book it cannot be ignored, it cannot be ignored in the fashion system as a whole.

Speaking on why she chose to leave prêt-à-porter to focus on haute couture, designer Iris van Herpen explains,

> [t]he reason I am in fashion is not to make yet another jumper or another coat. Couture is where there is space to change; I don't feel that I can change a system by going along with it. I really need to focus on the combination of craftsmanship and innovation to change the methods of making fashion before it goes mass and that can be an inspiration for Ready To Wear brands.[1]

Fellow Central St Martin's alumnus Stella McCartney would agree that sustainability may need big names to gather momentum but there is no reason why it must stop with luxury brands. Her collection for Adidas followed her namesake company's strict ethical guidelines,

> [f]or the collection we looked closely at reducing waste in fabrics and materials when cutting and constructing garments which ensured 95 per cent of fabric used created the final product, with the remaining five per cent recycled or repurposed. We monitor the manufacturing process and try to be as eco-friendly as possible. We also use organic cotton, recycled yarn and dry dye pieces in the range.[2]

With the launch of DyeCoo[3] for example, the first commercial dry dyeing machine that uses supercritical carbon dioxide instead of water, over eight years ago, the industry certainly has the technology available to become more sustainable, yet it holds back. The fashion industry, an industry focused on newness is resistant to change.

> 'Fashion has to modernize. It has to challenge its history and question the process'. The designer continues to explain 'At Stella McCartney we

---

1 Pers comm. Originally interviewed by Jamie Huckbody for *Harpers Bazaar Australia* (2018), transcripts used with kind permission.
2 Ibid.
3 'DyeCoo: Waterless dying', *DyeCoo*, 2010 <http://www.dyecoo.com/pdfs/colourist.pdf> (Accessed 15 February 2018).

try to push every angle with technology, manufacturing, fashion and try to be as forward thinking as possible. Technology doesn't equal having to forfeit tradition; I have great respect for the history and the craft of what I do. But the way things are done, the fabrics used – they haven't changed in a century! There's a resistance to innovation'.[4]

Van Herpen points out,

[p]eople focus on technology but what is often missing is the connection to traditional methods. When I collaborate with people I try to connect new techniques to traditional techniques because that's when really interesting things start to happen.[5]

She continues,

[i]t doesn't work by simply throwing out 'the old'. I am in-between two worlds: the fashion world which is a very fast, short-term thinking world and then the world of architects and scientists on imagining what's to come and how we can improve things, and developing materials and techniques that takes a long time. The techniques as we know them today won't change the world, or change fashion, but used in hybrid we have the potential.[6]

One of the key reasons fashion, as a whole, doesn't connect with sustainability is because it doesn't connect with people. It keeps garment workers and consumers at more than an arms distance. It divides consumers into groups and sub-groups whose attributes may be relevant to part of a brand – but not the whole person. The move towards holistic lifestyles and wellness trends have highlighted more than ever the need for fashion brands to see their customers as people and not just consumers. Wellness goes beyond the popularity of lux-casual wear; it connects mindfulness, mental wellbeing, the environment and our interactions within it. It is a life-style combination, the Hygge styled living room, the yoga class, the barefaced make-up, the clean eating blog, the trip to Copenhagen, that delivers the whole lifestyle package and results in the decision to buy those sustainable yet fashionable Nike Fly-knit running shoes.

---

4   Pers comm. Jamie Huckbody for *Harpers Bazaar Australia* (2018).
5   Ibid.
6   Ibid.

Van Herpen posits,

> I see it in the new generation they are more conscious of how they con-
> sume. So it comes not only into what you eat or your lifestyle or how
> you get from A to Z, I think people are starting to be more conscious in
> general.[7]

The fashion industry is at loggerheads within itself, those who recognise the
slow-wave of demand for more holistic ways to shop in contrast to the 'see-
now-buy-now' that has become 'the cutting edge' of technology use. How the
industry utilises new technology is interesting, as we have discussed it can be
used to explore new materials and sustainable practices, in contrast it can
be used to create and feed consumer demand. Whilst the 'see-now-buy-now'
movement has remained in the luxury sector with brands such as Burberry and
Tommy Hilfiger making garments available to purchase hot off the runway, it
begs the question if it is causing just as many sustainability issues as the High
Street's 'pile them up high, sell them cheap' mentality. In the 'State of Fashion
2017' report,[8] *The Business of Fashion* conclude that cut-price shoppers make
up 75 per cent of apparel purchases and many retailers now have more outlet
stores than full-price shops. With the ability to price-compare available at the
touch of our iPhones, consumers have forced brands into price transparency and with it discount wars. When sourcing from low-labour-cost countries,
or more efficient manufacturing techniques, have been exhausted companies
have been forced to look elsewhere to keep costs down to account for slow
sales. Burberry, Sonia Rykiel, Roberto Cavalli, Ralph Lauren, Marks & Spencer
have all undertaken restructuring, job cuts and shutting stores to stay afloat –
hardly a sustainable business model. Calls of designer plagiarism (thanks to
cult Instagram account Diet_Prada) are at an all time high with designers being pushed to take influence from buying and merchandising teams to recreate
what is selling, rather than risk predictions of what might sell in their own
designs. With designers putting out six to eight collections per year the fashion
cycle is only gathering speed.

The current turn over of creative directors for luxury fashion brands including Christian Dior, Lanvin, Calvin Klein, Saint Laurent, Givenchy, Louis Vuitton and more is unprecedented. Yet Christopher Bailey, former chief creative

---

7   Ibid.
8   I. Amed and A. Berg, 'The State of Fashion 2017', *The Business of Fashion*, 2016 <https://www.
    businessoffashion.com/articles/news-analysis/the-state-of-fashion-2018> (Accessed 15 Feb-
    ruary 2018).

officer and chief executive of Burberry, protests this isn't a result of too much pressure on designers citing it 'an incredibly patronising argument'.[9] He protests, '[w]e designers are not stupid; we do have brain cells and we're not constrained by timings. We will find solutions to these problems'.[10] Yet Bailey recently announced his departure from Burberry showing his final collection Spring 2018. The reasoning given in a brand statement 'to pursue other creative projects' does not fit with his earlier assertion or perhaps after 17 years at the brand he is just seeking some down time?

Perhaps these are signs that the fashion system is ready to change, in a world where anyone with a food truck can become a Michelin star chef [11] and anyone can become artistic director of a luxury fashion house – as we see the appointment of Virgil Abloh to Louis Vuitton.[12] With no formal fashion training, choosing to study architecture and civil engineering, Abloh picked up enough skills from his seamstress mother to secure an internship at Fendi alongside friend Kanye West in 2006, going on to launch his own brand Off White in 2013 – he took an opportunity and ran with it.

Many of the authors of the chapters you will find in this book are not only researchers in fashion and its related disciplines but educators too. As a university lecturer I find myself repeating to students (who are mostly of the Millennial generation) the constant need to slow down. Focus on the process and not rush ahead to the final outcome, stop focusing on grades and actually enjoy the opportunity to play around with creativity. In a world of overconsumption surely the new luxury is time – time to be creative, time to be mindful, time to dream. Isn't that why we all fell in love with fashion in the first place, the opportunity to step into a dream world? My first memories of fashion were clonking around in my mother's high heels, rummaging through her wardrobe for hidden treasure. Jump forward a good few years and it was getting lost in the pages of *Vogue*. Iris van Herpen reminisces about her relationship with her beloved 90-year-old grandmother:

> [s]he has a big fascination for fashion and garments, when she was younger she collected all kinds of historical costumes and also modern pieces.

---

9   Ibid.

10   Ibid.

11   S. Kim, 'Singapore Street Food Stalls Get Michelin Stars', *The Telegraph*, 25 July 2016 <https://www.telegraph.co.uk/travel/destinations/asia/singapore/articles/singapore-street-food-stalls-get-michelin-star/> (Accessed 15 February 2018).

12   N. Bach, 'Meet Virgil Abloh: Kanye West's Creative Director is Louis Vuitton's Newest Designer', *Fortune*, 26 March 2018 <http://fortune.com/2018/03/26/virgil-abloh-louis-vuitton-new-menswear-designer/> (Accessed 26 March 2018).

She didn't really do anything with them. She just sort of collected them. I grew up in a very small village that had no connections with fashion so my very first insight to fashion was through my Grandmother's attic. I dressed-up a lot in those clothes.[13]

As I look back on my own journey with fashion and my own *bricolage* career that has taken me from ancient Egyptian style, historical footwear and reconsignment retail, I wonder if we are loosing connections with fashion? Will anyone save their piles of Primark for their grandkids to dress up in? Will I find myself curating a collection of mass-produced fashion in the future?

There are many ways in which we can engage with fashion; we hope that this book will serve as an interesting perspective on a vast array of topics from communication, education and business with common themes running throughout such as sustainability, feminism and the embodiment of fashion. Fashion is multifaceted, its history just as important as its future. With growing awareness of the problems we have seen in fashion past and present, we can learn to better connect and engage with the clothes we make, sell, wear, study and curate – to become more mindful of our interactions and actions with fashion, to see the benefit within partnership of traditional and modern techniques. As Vivienne Westwood says the success of the future relies not in the isolation, but in the marriage, of science and art.

Acknowledgments

The editors would like to thank The Faculty of Arts, Computing, Engineering and Sciences, Sheffield Hallam University (McCreesh) and The Faculty of Business and Management at Regent's University London (Carlotto) for their support in this project. Bram Oudenampsen, Assistant Editor, Philosophy and Jennifer Pavelko, Senior Acquisitions Editor, Philosophy at Brill for their guidance throughout the editing process. Rob Fisher and Jacque Lynn Foltyn, Interdisciplinary Organising Chairs for Fashion: Exploring Critical Issues – The Fashion Project, 8th Global Meeting, Mansfield College, Oxford 2016 where this publication was first realised. Finally we would like to thank all contributing authors for their dedication throughout.

With thanks to Rocelle Lambourne and Darren Black from allowing use of their image for the cover.

---

13   Pers comm. Jamie Huckbody for *Harpers Bazaar Australia* (2018).

PART 1

Marketing

∴

Copying to Be Unique?: An Analysis of High Street Retailers' Product Differentiation Strategies

Susanne Schulz

Abstract

Based on empirical data from 20 semi-structured interviews with designers, buyers and merchandisers of UK-based multiple womenswear retailers, this chapter examines the variations in retailers' working practices with a particular emphasis on their product differentiation strategies. The theme running throughout this chapter is that of differentiation and similarity – a topic of enquiry commonly associated with Simmel's essay on fashion.[1] This discussion of the womenswear retailing industry demonstrates that, more than one hundred years after Simmel published his work, the dualistic tendencies of similarity and differentiation continue to fuel the modern fashion system.

Keywords

fashion retailing – Simmel – imitation – differentiation – UK fashion industry – fashion design

1 Introduction

Traditional sociological studies of fashion, such as Simmel for example, argue that fashion satisfies central human needs of differentiation, competition and stratification on the one hand, and the equally essential desire for expressing uniformity, conformity and belongingness on the other.[2] Indeed, Finkelstein maintains that for Simmel imitation and differentiation are the oxymoronic principles that guide all human conduct and that are present on both the individual and societal level.[3] Simmel accords great significance to the interplay

---

1 G. Simmel, 'Fashion', *The American Journal of Sociology*, vol. 62, no. 6, 1957 [1904], pp. 541–558.
2 Ibid.
3 J. Finkelstein, *The Fashioned Self*, Polity Press, Cambridge, 1991.

between them and argues that these forces can never be satisfactorily united in one single institution, law or the like, because imitation

> ... represents the idea of generalisation, of uniformity, of inactive similarity of the forms and contents of life; ... [differentiation] stands for motion, for differentiation of separate elements, producing the restless changing of an individual life.[4]

In order to reach an approximation to the ideal, constant changes are necessary. An expression of this can be found in the rapidly moving cycle of fashion which is fuelled by fashion's unprecedented urge for presentness and newness:

> ... [f]ashion dogmatically rejects the fashion which preceded it, its own past; every new fashion is a refusal to inherit, a subversion against the oppression of the preceding fashion; fashion experiences itself as a right, the natural right of the present over the past...[5]

Fashion confers a sense of group solidarity and security to its followers. Indeed, imitation intensifies existing social bonds as it is a careful and calculated act which presupposes the identification of the contents of a particular fashion, as well as the acknowledgement of an approved fashion elite which one sets out to imitate. By imitating others, the individual transfers their own responsibility to a certain extent onto them, while at the same time being able to experience a feeling of relative security and belongingness for they have become part of a larger group:

> [i]mitation ... gives to the individual the satisfaction of not standing alone in his actions ... the individual is freed from the worry of choosing and appears simply as a creature of the group, as a vessel of the social contents.[6]

Spencer differentiated between 'referential' and 'competitive' fashion imitation, with the latter form of imitation fuelling the adoption of fashion in modern societies.[7] Spencer argued that competitive imitation springs from the

---

4   Simmel, 'Fashion', p. 542.
5   R. Barthes, *The Fashion System*, trans. M. Ward and R. Herward, Hill & Wang, New York, NY, 1983, p. 273.
6   Simmel, 'Fashion', pp. 542–543.
7   H. Spencer, *Principles of Sociology* (vol. 2), D. Appleton & Company, New York, NY, 1898.

motive to assert equality with those perceived as superior and this claim of equality is being made by quickly adopting the latest fashions in order to be classed among the elite.

Fashion cannot exist in seclusion but needs a stage for public display where the roles of performers and spectators are constantly reversed. Fashion needs to be seen – it has to gain approval, which is an essential prerequisite for any form of differentiation.[8] Fashion can function as a barrier to exclude and separate groups by setting standards that are only attainable by some. This makes fashionable individuals conspicuousness, because they are part of a larger privileged elite which adhere to the same standards.

> Distinction, if it is to function effectively by making conspicuous ... must be associated with something that is accepted by the community as a distinctive feature. Every distinction must therefore also be ... accepted by the rest of the community ... distinction from and forming part of a social group do not rule each other out.[9]

The individual hence deviates from some norms but thereby conforms to others: they stand out without standing on their own because they have the approval of the larger social group. Having the support of one's group is essential in Simmel's account, it determines an individual's behaviour. The individual is carried by a feeling of solidarity which enables her/him to deviate in a way that is approved of and that erases feelings of shame or embarrassment.[10]

2 The Importance of Being Different: Life-Style Retailing and Branding

While people's desire to achieve social distinction through clothing is as old as fashion itself, the concept of life-style consumption only properly emerged in the 1980s and was echoed on the retailing side in the 'retailing revolution', which saw the rise of the new retailing concept of 'life-style' or 'niche marketing'.[11] The term 'market niche' refers to the relationship between consumption

---

8   R. König, *The Restless Image: A Sociology of Fashion*, trans. F. Bradley, George Allen & Unwin Ltd., London, 1973.

9   Ibid., pp. 112–113.

10   Simmel, 'Fashion'.

11   P. du Gay, *Consumption and Identity at Work*, Sage Publications, London, 1996.

patterns and consumers' age, income, occupation, lifestyle *etc.*[12] An important step in the realisation of 'niche marketing' was retailers novel use of own-brands. While retailers previously used own-brands as a way of communicating their price consciousness, retailers began to use own-brands as a means to add value to their products – this repositioning of own-brands in retailing significantly challenged the established manufacture-retailer power relationship.[13]

Life-style marketing encompasses more than the tailoring of products to a specifically defined customer group; it includes the overall shopping experience – store image, visual displays, music, sales staff *etc.*[14] By offering the complete 'image package', retailers encourage consumers to transform themselves into the consumer 'types' on offer in store. In addition, window displays can persuade or dissuade potential customers from entering the store and are semiotic strategies to filter customers.[15] This observation is shared by Crewe and Lowe who argue that clothing retailers' particular differentiation strategies are related to the demographics and lifestyle perception of their target customer group.[16] Retailers who cater for a young market, for example, will build their retailing concept around a strong image and brand name, while retailers who are targeting an older market may do so with 'understated, quality classics'.[17]

Indeed, today's customers desire distinctiveness. Murray for instance, has argued that consumption is no longer emulative but has come to resemble a striving for distinction.[18] This point is also made by Bourdieu, who looked at the interrelationship of economic and cultural capital, which he

---

12   P. Braham, 'Fashion: Unpacking a Cultural Production', in P. du Gay (ed.), *Production of Culture/Cultures of Production*, Sage Publications, London, 1997, pp. 121–165.

13   C. M. Moore, 'From Rages to Riches – Creating and Benefiting from the Fashion Own-Brand', *International Journal of Retail Distribution and Management*, vol. 23, no. 9, 1995, pp. 19–27.

14   T. DeNora and S. Belcher, 'When You're Trying Something on You Picture Yourself in a Place Where They Are Playing This Kind of Music: Musically Sponsored Agency in the British Clothing Retailing Sector', *The Sociological Review*, vol. 48, no. 1, 2000, pp. 80–101.

15   Ibid.

16   L. Crewe and M. Lowe, 'United Colours? Globalisations and Localisation Tendencies in Fashion Retailing', in N. Wrigley and M. Lowe (eds.), *Retailing, Consumption and Capital: Towards the New Retail Geography*, Longman Group Limited, Harlow, 1996, pp. 271–283.

17   Ibid., p. 277.

18   R. Murray, 'Benetton Britain: The New Economic Order', in S. Hall and M. Jacques (eds.), *New Times: The Changing Face of Politics in the 1990s*, Lawrence & Wishart, London, 1989, pp. 54–64.

used as markers for mapping 'tastes and preferences which correspond to educational level and social class, in short ... a model of class life-styles'.[19] According to Bourdieu, people who share a similar class of conditions of existence are united by taste, while at the same time their standard of taste distinguishes them from those with different experiences/ background. In his analysis of the field of fashion production and consumption, Bourdieu shows that the fashion industry satisfies consumers' need for social distinction on both a synchronic level and diachronic level, by fulfilling consumer's desires in any given season with garments that differ from season to season.[20]

Having outlined the importance of branding and lifestyle retailing on a general level, it is now time to turn to the data in order to look at interviewees' descriptions of how their companies strive to survive in the market. In order to do this, we will first look at how retailers can be grouped into 'design-led' and 'buying-led' companies depending on their internal organisational structure and working practices.

3   Sample

Through Internet research, more than 30 womenswear retailers (with 10 or more retail outlets and headquarters in the UK) were identified and contacted by telephone to obtain the names and contact details of their designers, buyers and merchandisers. It proved challenging to recruit interviewees for this project – at times the researcher could not get past the switchboard operators who often assume the role of gatekeepers to ward off unwelcome intrusions from outsiders.[21] In the end, 20 semi-structured interviews with designers, buyers and merchandizers of 13 UK-based multiple retailers of womenswear were conducted. The interviews were between 45 and 80 minutes in lengths, were audio recorded and professionally transcribed before being subjected to rigours thematic analysis.

3.1   'Design-Led' and 'Buying-Led' Retailers
The sample was divided into participants' occupational group (e.g. designer, buyer or merchandiser) and the organisational type of company they are

19   R. Jenkins, *Pierre Bourdieu*, Routledge, London, 1992, p. 138 (original emphasis).
20   P. Bourdieu, 'Le couturier et sa griffe: Contribution à une théorie de la magie', *Actes de la Recherche en Sciences Sociales*, vol. 1, 1975, pp. 7–36.
21   P. Baines, C. Fill, and K. Page, *Marketing*, Oxford University Press, Oxford, 2010.

working. Companies were divided into 'design-led' and 'buying-led' companies; the labels attached to each company follow respondents' own explicit or implicit definition. The preface 'design-led' and 'buying-led' points to organisational differences between companies and is testimony to the varying levels of influence these two occupational groups exert in the shaping of a company's range of clothing.[22] This can be clarified by looking at some concrete examples. In companies that have been categorized as 'design-led', it is the designers who are most influential in determining the characteristics of the product range, while buyers and merchandisers are less involved in this process. In Tanya and Eric/Tim's companies, for instance, although the design teams merely consist of two designers each, the balance of power is biased in favour of the designers and all or at least the great majority of these companies' garment ranges are designed in-house. Indeed, in some companies the designers create the entire range as Sarah, a designer of a 'design-led' retailer, states: '100 per cent of the range is done by four designers and that goes through from coats, bags, shoes – we do everything'.

Kate, on the other hand, is the only designer in her company and though she supplies some of the design ideas, the bulk of the range is based on 'bought-in' designs, i.e. manufacturers' sample garments, chosen by the buyers. As, Kate's position in relation to her company's buyers is weak her company has been classified as 'buying-led'. Kate observes that '[w]hen I was a student, I always thought the designers had the say ... they sort of control it all ... but actually it's quite different. It's the buyers!'

Indeed, the most significant difference between retailers lies in the percentage of in-house designs that are used to make up a collection. Designers in 'design-led' companies create most of the range in-house, while garment ranges of 'buying-led' companies are predominantly 'bought in', i.e. built from buying samples that buyers collect from suppliers and during shopping trips. Thus, while 'design-led' companies value designing ranges from scratch, 'buying-led' companies range building is centred around the adaptation of buying samples that are picked from a multitude of sources. The differences in methods can be highlighted in the following quotes from Sophia and Kim:

> ... we do a lot of sketching ... I start with a blank piece of paper, whereas some people tend to start with a bunch of garments and they kind of piece them together. ... I went straight from college to Italy, where you

---

22   S. Schulz, 'Our Lady Hates Viscose: The Role of the Customer Image in High Street Fashion
       Production', *Cultural Sociology*, vol. 2, no. 3, 2008, pp. 385–405.

do design very much ... the first few years in my career I didn't see people's garments to copy. You get to have to create everything. And I think
it probably has made quite a difference ... a lot of people ... build a mock
range and they do variations...

SOPHIA, DESIGNER, 'DESIGN-LED' RETAILER

(Researcher: How do you put the range together?)
... I see a lot of suppliers, I will have been round all the stores and I see
what's happening and it's very much, you know 'That's good from that
supplier and that's good from that supplier. We haven't seen any of this or
we'll ask them to make this for us'. You know, basically you just pick bits,
and bits that are missing you kind of put in yourself [or] ... you ask them
to make it for you or you send them a sample of something you want
them to make for you.

KIM, PRODUCT DEVELOPER/BUYER, 'BUYING-LED' RETAILER

Thus, the pre-fix 'design-led' has been applied to retailers who largely rely on
their own in-house design teams to create the style and brand image of the
company, while the description 'buying-led' indicates that it is the buyers' selection of products that establishes the companies' looks. It is therefore the
combination of the percentage of the range that is designed in-house, and
the power relationships between designers and buyers, that determines the
organisational set-up of a company and its classification into 'design-led' or
'buying-led'.

'Design-' and 'buying-led' companies can be further differentiated with regards
to the consumer age groups they cater for and the market price level they are positioned at. For example, 'buying-led' companies cater for customers in the 15-30-
age bracket and are positioned at the middle-cheap end of the market, whereas
the age span of 'design-led' retailers' customer ranges from 20–70+ years with a
mid-higher market position.

Following this categorisation into 'design-led' and 'buying-led' companies, the
sample consists of seven 'design-led' and nine 'buying-led' companies with nine
and eleven respondents per group respectively.

4   Differentiation and Fashionability

Retailers' relative position on the fashion/non-fashion continuum can be as-
sessed in relation to their overall fashion forwardness, which has an impact
on the company's set up and working practices. Fashion has traditionally been

associated with class distinction[23] and the impact of 'prestige personalities'[24] as fashion leaders and trendsetters. Indeed, designers have become modern-day priests and philosophers of culture[25] and the data suggest that the work of elite designers still serves as a yardstick for fashionability against which interviewees assess their companies' and their customers' level of fashion forwardness.[26] Moreover, for Tseëlon elite designers' catwalk shows also serve as

> the quintessential self-referential ritual of the fashion world where the top designers showcase their new collections to a carefully chosen and well-connected privileged and limited audience of fashion editors, fashion buyers and distinguished clients. The cycle of competition, prestige, ingratiation and glamour that is set in motion by such events testifies to its ceremonial qualities and signifying function ...[27]

Interviewees primarily measured the level of fashionability of their company with reference to top designers, i.e. how quickly and to what extent a company or consumers follow catwalk trends. In the case of respondents from 'buying-led' companies reference was also made to other prestige personalities (musicians and other celebrities) and occasionally with reference to a specific high-street competitor. It is interesting to note that even interviewees whose companies do not follow these trendsetters, they were nonetheless used as points of reference for assessing their companies' fashionability. Tseëlon shows

---

23   See Simmel, 'Fashion'; T. Veblen, *The Theory of the Leisure Class*, The Macmillan Company, London, 1908; P. Bourdieu, *Distinction: A Social Critique of the Judgement of Taste*, trans. R. Nice, Harvard University Press, Cambridge, MA, 1984.

24   König, *The Restless Image*.

25   K. Jacobs and T. Kalman, 'The End', in S. Yelavich (ed.), *The Edge of the Millennium: An International Critique of Architecture, Urban Planning, Product and Communication Design*, Whitney Library of Design, New York, NY, 1993, pp. 26–41.

26   Individuals display varying degrees of the desire to be different from others depending on the reference group that they compare themselves to. Brenninkmeyer believes that, in general, innovators of fashion have a greater need for differentiation, while fashion followers have a more pronounced need for similarity. According to Snyder and Fromkin, a moderate level of similarity generates the highest level of acceptability on the 'uniqueness identity dimension'; the level decreases in relation to the decrease or increase of an individual's perceived similarity relative to others. See I. Brenninkmeyer, *The Sociology of Fashion*, P. G. Keller, Winterhur, 1963; C.R. Snyder and H.L. Fromkin, *Uniqueness: The Human Pursuit of Difference*, Plenum, New York, NY, 1980, p. 33.

27   E. Tseëlon, 'Jean Baudrillard: Post-modern Fashion as the End of Meaning', in A. Rocamora and A. Smelik (eds.), *Thinking Through Fashion: A Guide to Key Theorists*, I.B. Tauris, London and New York, NY, 2015, pp. 215–232, p. 228.

that this stance is reminiscent of Baudrillard's conception of fashion as for him 'even resistance to fashion is still defined within the order of fashion'.[28] Rita, for example, a fabric buyer for a design-led retailer, argues that her company is not very fashion forward because 'catching those trends ... isn't important to us or our customer'. While, Sophia points out that being too fashion forward has adverse effects for a company:

> ... we have made a few mistakes on fashionability, where we thought as a label we could go fashionable and it hasn't worked ... the brand is too established ... on that nice level that the fashionable person doesn't want.
>
> SOPHIA, DESIGNER, 'DESIGN-LED' RETAILER

On the other hand, Faye points out the influence of top designers on her 'buying-led' company while Alicia clearly acknowledges that her company is perceived by other 'buying-led' retailers as a fashion leader:

> ... we spend a lot of time looking at Versace and Gucci ... when the catwalks head down ... those are the kind of looks that we take our inspiration from...
>
> FAYE, DESIGN MANAGER, 'BUYING-LED' RETAILER

> ... a lot of people see us as quite high fashion ... [as having] it in the shop not much after the catwalks have been on.
>
> ALICIA, BUYER, 'BUYING-LED' RETAILER

Similarly, though not a manufacturer of high-fashion clothing, Carla maintains that her company has very successfully used inspiration from top designers within their own clothing ranges:

> ... [catwalk fashion] is hard to decipher or take down to our level [...] [but] Stella McCartney ... whatever she does ... we are still doing versions of that...
>
> CARLA, DESIGNER, 'BUYING-LED' MANUFACTURER

Retailers' degree of fashion forwardness not only influences when, or indeed whether or not, a company follows the fashion lead set by prestige personalities, but also has an impact on the split of retailers' ranges, and the in-shop

---

28   E. Tseëlon, 'Fashion and Signification in Baudrillard', in D. Keller (ed.), *Baudrillard: A Critical Reader*, Wiley-Blackwell, Oxford, 1994, pp. 119–131, p. 129.

lives of their garments. The companies in the sample break down the fashion cycle of garments into three different stages. This is illustrated in the following quote by Vivian:

> [i]f you look at the life cycle of it [fashion] ... you can break [it] into ... trend, ... newness ... [or] contemporary and then you've got kind of core, which is just like high volume stuff.
>
> VIVIAN, DESIGN EXECUTIVE, 'BUYING-LED' MANUFACTURER

Following Vivian's definition 'trend' refers to garments with high fashion content, while garments of a moderate level of fashionability are described as 'newness' or 'contemporary'. Clothes of a minimal or no degree of fashionability are characterised as 'core' garments. This category of clothing is also often called 'basic' or 'standardised'. Not all companies use the same terminology to describe these different degrees of fashionability. In Sophia's company, for example, garments are divided into special (fashion), interest (newness) and basic (core):

> [w]e do our basic range, we do our range that has a bit more interest, so you put a little bit more newness in and then we do what is our proposal for special, the special end.
>
> SOPHIA, DESIGNER, 'DESIGN-LED' RETAILER

Despite these differences in labelling, Sophia and Vivian's division of garments and garment ranges according to their level of fashionability is remarkably similar. Looking at the overall distribution between fashion, contemporary and core garments, it becomes clear that the extent of companies' fashion forwardness determines the mix of their product range. However, whilst all companies in the sample grade their ranges similarly and interviewees share the same points of reference in terms of assessing their companies' fashion level, when looking at the garments in store it becomes clear that what is rated as 'fashion' within one company's range may merely be classified as 'newness' in another's. The overall degree of a company's fashionability, as opposed to outside standards of fashion, appears to act as the point of reference in the internal grading of garments and clothing ranges. This means, for example, that a company with a moderate degree of fashionability may classify a garment as 'fashion' even if it captures a trend that has first appeared on the catwalks more than a year ago. On the other hand, a more fashion forward company may label a garment as 'core' which less ardent followers of fashion may perceive as 'newness'.

Also of significance when comparing companies' levels of fashionability are the differences in their 'seasonal lead-times'. 'Seasonal lead-time' refers to the time between the initial trend forecasting and the arrival of garments in the shops. The data shows that 'seasonal lead-times' vary significantly between 'design-led' retailers and 'buying-led' retailers. On average, the 'design-led' retailers in the sample start planning their ranges just over one year ahead of the season, which means that the initial forecasting and design stages are even further in advance; whereas the lead-times for 'buying-led' retailers range from five months to four weeks. The differences between 'design-' and 'buying-led' companies' lead-times and the connection between lead-time and retailer's degree of fashionability can be clearly seen in the following two quotes:

> ... we are kind of working, one year to two years ahead. But for us, because we aren't an overly fashionable company, ... we can work that far in advance, you know, it's not like we are picking up what's in stores, what the designers are showing, although our colours ... we use colour palettes that are presented as being on trend for those seasons, the fabrications and styling isn't going to be, you know, fashion led as such. So ... yes we do work very much in advance...
> RITA, FABRIC BUYER, 'DESIGN-LED' RETAILER

> ... a lot of people see us as quite high fashion ... [as having] it in the shop not much after the catwalks have been on.
> ALICIA, BUYER, 'BUYING/DESIGN-LED' RETAILER

> ... quite often we've seen things on the catwalks and we've had them in like the next three weeks. Our quickest lead-time is two weeks...
> LISA, ASSISTANT BUYER, 'BUYING-LED' RETAILER

These examples clearly show the connection between a company's level of fashionability and their working practices. Thus, Rita argues that her 'design-led' company does not follow fashion other than in terms of colour and that they can consequently work much further ahead of season than, for instance, Kate's company which targets a younger, more fashion forward market.

There are also significant internal variations in lead-times between different departments and product types. This explains the great variation in lead-times from months to weeks found within 'buying-led' retailers. Alicia explains this as follows:

> different departments have different lead-times. Generally we start, sort of about 6 months before ... just looking at where we think it's going. But

my department [jersey] itself can turn stuff round in 4 to 5 weeks. So we can work very quickly ... but knitwear, for example, have already booked the whole season so ... the design teams run on two kinds of speed, one for us which is really quick and now and the other one where they sort of look quite far in advance.

ALICIA, BUYER, 'BUYING-LED' RETAILER

Knitwear and tailoring are generally placed the furthest in advance not only because they are less likely to be subject to quick fashion changes but also because the more complex designs, sophisticated cuts or finishings make these garments more labour intensive and hence placing them with offshore instead of local suppliers will keep costs down. It follows that through these practices 'design-led' retailers' lead-times are not only much longer than those of 'buying-led' retailers, but it is also more difficult for them to repeat garments from within their own range or to react to emerging trends, as Tanya and Tim point out.

(Researcher: Can you repeat garments that sell really well?)
It depends. Obviously when we place fabric, if there is something we feel very strongly and we think 'I know this is going to be really good', we place additional fabric and therefore if that's in place the sort of turn around for manufacture is 6 to 8 weeks ... However, if we haven't got the fabric, that does prove harder for us because we then have to go back to the mills and see if they've got anything left to be made up. So it's really only on styles that we have cloth available.

TANYA, UK MERCHANDISE CONTROLLER/
BUYER, 'DESIGN-LED' RETAILER

We can't do a great deal of it [repeat orders], because a lot of our goods are actually quite heavily hand worked and so the lead-times are too long basically. That's why our range tends to be quite broad, we don't actually do a great deal quantity-wise per style, but we make it up by putting more in, by more frequently changing things.

TIM, BUYING DIRECTOR, 'DESIGN-LED' RETAILER

We have thus established that there are variations between 'design-'and 'buying-led' companies in terms of their overall level of fashionability and that this has consequences for their working practices. The next section examines the relationship between a company's fashion level and their product differentiation strategy.

5   **It's Difficult to Be Different: The Quest for New**
        Ideas from Similar Sources of Inspiration

The importance of offering consumers something different that allows them to assemble 'a lifestyle (or lifestyles) through personalised acts of choice in a world of goods and services'[29] is keenly felt amongst industry practitioners. However, despite the realisation of the importance of a strong brand that provides customers with a distinctive product range, interviewees' commented on the fact that many mid-market womenswear retailers offer very similar ranges of clothing.

> I think a lot of people want to elevate themselves away from the high street. They want that difference, they don't want to look the same as all their friends ... I think ... personally, that the middle market is saturated, there are too many different retailers in there and I think some of them will get wiped out.
>
> SEAN, ASSISTANT MERCHANDISER, 'BUYING-LED' RETAILER

This criticism of the high street is echoed by Faye, a designer for a large 'buying-led' company, who maintains that 'everybody is just chasing the same end and ... the differentiation between different brands is hardly noticeable'. Indeed, though almost written two decades ago, Robinson's claim that 'many retailers remain merely sellers of brands without their own distinctive handwriting'[30] still appears to hold true.

As mentioned in Sean's quote above, the lack of differentiation is particularly evident amongst mid-market retailers – a segment of the market dominated by 'buying-led' retailers. Indeed, when looking at the sources of inspiration that this group of retailers draws on can see a close overlap between companies not only in terms of what sources are rated as particularly important, but also in terms of how information is actually procured. Thus, the main sources of inspiration for this group of retailers are forecasting agencies (for catwalk trends and colour predictions), fabric shows, and other UK womenswear retailers.

All but two of the 'buying-led' companies used the same forecasting agency, in four cases this provider was used exclusively for trend and colour information, while only one of the 'design-led' companies subscribes to this service. Indeed, of the 'design-led' companies who use dedicated forecasting services

---

29   P. du Gay, *Consumption and Identity at Work*, p. 100.
30   P. Robinson, *Marketing Fashion: Strategies and Trends for Fashion Brands*, Informa Retail & Consumer, London, 1999, p. 20.

all employ a different one, while three companies do not employ any outside forecasters.

All interviewees stated that they attended *Première Vision*, which is the key fabric show for the industry. Fabric shows provide the starting point of the forecasting process for 'buying-led' retailers, while for 'design-led' retailers *Première Vision* 'is sort of at the end' of the forecasting cycle (Leah). Since most retailers within this group obtain their initial sources of inspiration for fabrics and colours directly from mills which start developing new products well in advance of the first fabric shows. In view of the long lead-times of 'design-led' companies, it is not surprising that they should take advantage of the earliest opportunity for seeing new products by visiting fabric mills. This gives them the opportunity of starting their forecasting and planning cycle at least two months ahead of *Première Vision* and other fabric shows.

> ... we tend to start the new season by going to Italy and we go to Milan and we'll do the shops. Then we'll go to Como, Lake Como where the majority of our print mills are based and this will be maybe two months before Première Vision, which is the fabric show in Paris, and at that stage they are all getting prepared for the PV shows, but they, being in that business have all the forecasting books and ... you know, there are ... the Italian Council for Silk and, you know, they've got a lot of information at their fingertips very, very early in the season. Whereas we would have, if we didn't go there, we would have to wait for our fabric forecasting books to come through and the shows, basically. But we tend to get all that information about 6 to 8 weeks before it's possible to get them from any other source really. And from that we tend, if we go around say 8 mills, we tend to know when we come back which are the predominant colours that everyone is going for.
>
> SARAH, DESIGNER, 'DESIGN-LED' RETAILER

While the data suggest that the 'design-led' retailers in the sample find fabric shows useful for finalising and consolidating their decisions, fabric shows may be less useful for 'buying-led' companies or, at least, for certain departments within this group of companies. Alicia, for example, points out that for her jersey department fabric shows are only helpful in terms of colour selections, whereas 'other departments get lots out of it'.

Interviewees across the sample also mentioned going on directional (trend) buying trips to many of the same North American and European cities. While retailers use buying trips abroad for inspiration, UK-based shopping trips have a different significance for retailers, depending on whether they are 'design-led' or 'buying-led'. Although all interviewees stated that they visit the competition to do comparative shopping, i.e. to gage their own price level against that of their competitor, interviewees from 'buying-led' companies openly admitted using the competition for directional (trend) shopping too, i.e. with a view to buying garments in order to rework or copy them. This is an important factor when it comes to assessing the variations in companies' differentiation strategies and will therefore be discussed in detail in the following sections.

6 Designed to Be Unique: Design-Led Retailers' Pursuit of Difference

In order to clarify the divergent differentiation strategies employed by 'design-led' and 'buying-led' retailers, we need to closely look at retailers' use of UK-based competitors as sources of inspiration as it is here that 'design-led' retailers' differentiation strategy becomes most obvious. The data suggest that, because 'design-led' retailers are less concerned with following the latest trends they seek to establish their own specific market niche by developing a unique style.

> [i]t's unique ... 'designed to be individual' ... it's our corporate phrase ... when you buy a [garment from us] it really is individual and original and that's where our strength lies...
> ERIC, SENIOR MERCHANDISER, 'DESIGN-LED' RETAILER

This emphasis on developing one's own stylistic handwriting is at odds with the method of directional shopping because any real individuality in style cannot be achieved by copying or reworking buying samples. It is thus not surprising to find that 'design-led' retailers tend to look at their competitors for price comparison rather than inspiration. This can be clearly seen in Tim and Leah's statements below. Interestingly, Leah argues that at times it is difficult to lay claim to an idea as original, since high-street retailers share similar sources of inspiration and hence fairly similar ideas may be picked up by more than one company. Exposure to similar stimuli and the fact that retailers do not exist in a vacuum, i.e. they need to look at their competitors so that they do not lose touch with the market, mean that a certain amount of interchange of ideas is inevitable. However, like Tim, Leah is very clear about the fact that her company does not intentionally go around to competitors' shops to copy ideas for their own use.

> (Researcher: Do you look at your competitors at all?)
> Competitors, yes of course, it depends in which context you take it ... we don't look at our competitors to extract ideas, it's more to

actually make sure that we are competitive within the same competitive set...

TIM, BUYING DIRECTOR, 'DESIGN-LED' RETAILER

I think we are constantly aware of what other people are doing ... because they are competition so you need to constantly check. I think that we try very much not to copy, well everyone does, I mean it's very difficult to know where the idea came from in the first place sometimes, because it's gone round and round the houses, [but] I wouldn't say that we would go into any of our competitors and pick something up and say 'Oh, yeah that's nice – let's do a version of it'.

LEAH, BUYING DIRECTOR, 'DESIGN-LED' RETAILER

There is a strong rejection of the practice of 'copying others' and interviewees' own emphasis on uniqueness, which transpires in the above quotes. Although a certain cross-fertilisation of ideas is undoubtedly inevitable since everyone in the fashion industry is exposed to similar stimuli, all interviewees who work for 'design-led' retailers rejected the idea of copying others, even though Francis, who works for the youngest and most fashion-forward of the seven design-led retailers, concedes that if everybody else is following a certain trend, her company should get on board. However, she also stresses that:

[this company] ... is slightly different to the high street. We won't go out necessarily and copy what's in the stores. I mean it basically comes from design ideas ... from, you know, [our own] designers themselves.

FRANCIS, BUYER, 'DESIGN-LED' RETAILER

While Francis realises the importance of following general trends for her company, she makes a clear distinction between the copying of garments from others and her design colleagues' interpretation of trends. Here, we see again the interplay of the dualistic and paradoxical forces of uniformity and differentiation that Simmel saw at the very heart of fashion – on the one hand, 'design-led' retailers strive for uniqueness. Yet on the other hand, they recognise the need to follow broad trends and to adhere to the currents within the larger fashion system. It is this system that defines what fashion is so to produce fashionable garments is not possible without reference to the trends set by the system.[31] Nonetheless, 'design-led' retailers' emphasis lies on differentiation and one can now understand why this group of retailers tend to design their entire range, or at least a large

---

31   Simmel, 'Fashion'.

percentage of it, from 'scratch' in house, and why designers hold greater power *vis-à-vis* buyers than they do in 'buying-led' companies. This organisational set-up allows 'design-led' companies to achieve greater exclusivity by only minimally relying on suppliers for design ideas; this practice also makes it easier for them to develop their own stylistic handwriting and a more coherent brand image.

7   Copying to Be Unique? – The Tragedy of (Pseudo-) Differentiation

While the previous section has shown that uniqueness is the overriding differentiation strategy for 'design-led' retailers, this section explores how 'buying-led' retailers seek to differentiate themselves by intentional and speedy adaptation of fashion trends set by top designers and fashion forward competitors. In contrast to 'design-led' retailers who intentionally divert from or lack behind fashion trends to achieve a level of uniqueness, 'buying-led' companies seek distinction through the fast and accurate production of copies. Baudrillard points out the inherent paradoxical nature of differentiation through re-production by stating that in:

> ... the industrial production of differences ... differences are all arrayed hierarchically on an indefinite scale and converge in models, on the basis of which they are subtly produced and reproduced. As a result, to differentiate oneself is precisely to affiliate to a model, to label oneself by reference to an abstract model, to a combinatorial pattern of fashion, and therefore to relinquish any real difference ... This is the miracle and the tragedy of differentiation. ... instead of marking a person out as someone singular, they mark rather his conformity with a code, his integration into a sliding scale of values.[32]

Indeed, the importance to quickly conform to a 'new code', as Baudrillard put it, [33] is epitomised in the quote below:

> ... the high street, very young high street fashion, works very close to the season. So we don't plan so far ahead ... we see things and 4 weeks later they will be in the shop ... very, very quick ... we lift a new trend ... we immediately go and get something like that sampled and put it in the shops. So we respond very quickly ... this end of the market, is very much a case

---

32   J. Baudrillard, *Consumer Society: Myths and Structures*, trans. by Sage, Sage Publications London, 1998, pp. 88–89 (original emphasis).

33   Ibid.

of getting the thing in first [...] It is a bit of a rat race, it is a bit [like] "Who is going to be first?"

> KATE, DESIGNER/TREND CO-ORDINATOR,
> 'BUYING-LED' RETAILER

... most of the work we do is based ... straight off the catwalks ... we're so close to the season it's totally catwalk driven.

> FAYE, DESIGN MANAGER, 'BUYING/DESIGN-LED' RETAILER

... Stella McCartney ... whatever she does, ... we are still doing versions of ... that.

> CARLA, DESIGNER, 'BUYING-LED' MANUFACTURER

While the above statements are clear testimony of the link between differentiation and affiliation to a model as theorised by Baudrillard, none of the respondents reflected on the implications of this kind of pseudo-differentiation, i.e. the fact that straight conformity with the fashion code encourages product sameness. It is exactly the self-referential nature of fashion,[34] i.e. fashion as endlessly reproduced from models, that Baudrillard critiqued.[35] This is also echoed by Finkelstein, who argues that following fashion can only ever confer a false sense of uniqueness onto its followers as adhering to fashion integrates the individual into the fashion system – thus making them more common, conventional and easier to interpret.[36] Fashionability, Finkelstein states, is no solution to the problem of identity and individuality, but is rather an expression of the modern individual's feeble sense of identity and of the degradation of identity in contemporary society.[37] While Baudrillard and Finkelstein's comments relate to fashion consumers, they are also applicable to the producers as fashion as the following quotes from respondents testify:

> ... some ... are very much like 'Oh, this is the sweater to have – copy it!' And that mentality to me is: what's the point! Because everybody else is going to be copying it...
>
> SOPHIA, DESIGNER, 'DESIGN-LED' RETAILER

---

34   E. Esposito, 'Originality Through Imitation: The Rationality of Fashion', *Organization Studies*, vol. 32, no. 5, 2011, pp. 603–613.

35   Baudrillard, *Consumer Society*.

36   Finkelstein, *The Fashioned Self*.

37   These observations stand in contrast to Simmel's assertion that fashion confers a heightened sense of individuality onto its followers. Though Simmel does not reflect to what

[y]ou can go to Oasis and buy a black pair of trousers and you've got identical ones in Warehouse and then you go to Topshop and there's a more
or less identical pair in there ... you've got three shops where you can get
exactly the same pair of trousers ... it's a bit pointless! ... I think it's lost its
individuality, the cheaper end of the market.

SARAH, DESIGNER, 'DESIGN-LED' RETAILER

Sophia and Sarah's statements not only highlight their belief that it is important for retailers to develop their unique style in order to distinguish themselves
from other retailers, but they also allude to the inherent problem of product
sameness found among high-street retailers who seek to copy rather than
design unique garments. Moreover, by employing speed rather than uniqueness 'buying-led' retailers cannot establish customer loyalty and continuity of
sales in the same way as strong branding can.[38] In the absence of a unique
style 'speed to market' can help to reduce demand uncertainty. The ability to
buy closer to the season, once trends have been determined from the forecasting stages, reduces the risk of missing fashion trends or selecting the 'wrong'
garments.[39]

8 Conclusion

What has become clear throughout this chapter is that fashion companies
oscillate between the poles of sameness and differentiation, which gives
rise both to greater security and increased competition. The findings thus
bear a resemblance to Simmel's interpretation of the function of fashion in

---

extent this may be a kind of pseudo-individuality, he nonetheless makes a distinction
between those who gain social distinction through their 'calling or profession' and others who are denied access to this source of individuation and power. 'In a certain sense
fashion gives woman a compensation for her lack of position in a class based on calling
or profession. ... Fashion ... supplements a person's lack of importance ... by enabling
him to join a set characterised and singled out in the public consciousness by fashion
alone. ... The personality as such is reduced to a general formula, yet this formula itself,
from a social standpoint, possesses an individual tinge and thus makes up through the
social way what is denied to the personality in a purely individual way'. Simmel, 'Fashion',
pp. 551–552.

38   G.T. Lau and S.H. Lee, 'Consumers' Trust in a Brand and the Link to Brand Loyalty', *Journal
of Market-Focused Management*, vol. 4, 1999, pp. 341–370.

39   S. Schulz, 'A Question of Order: The Role of Collective Taste as a Strategy to Cope with
Demand Uncertainty in the Womenswear Fashion Industry', *Creative Industries Journal*,
vol. 8, no. 1, 2015, pp. 58–72.

society, which he describes as a paradoxical force that creates a sense of uniformity and differentiation at one and the same time.[40] Like Simmel's followers of fashion who negotiate their dualistic need for belongingness and individuality through their choice of clothing, the companies in the sample are torn between their need to conform to the standards of the fashion system, i.e. by drawing on similar sources of inspiration, and the necessity to employ differentiation tactics, either through a uniqueness of style or quick response to new trends, in order to strengthen their competitive position in the market.

Indeed, it can be argued that at the high-street level differentiation can only ever take on the form of pseudo-differentiation, as fashion practitioners need to pay homage to the fashion trendsetters. As Schulz states fashion cannot be judged objectively, it assumes a self-validating nature where 'the only "proof" of its existence lies in its acceptance amongst a group'.[41] That this is so can be clearly seen in the differentiation strategy used by 'buying-led' retailers both in terms of the practise to copy others and the emphasis on speed in doing so. Yet even 'design-led' retailers, who emphasise claims of uniqueness, cannot operate outside the parameters set by the fashion elite as doing so would effectively mean to leave the realm of *fashion* production. In that sense then, fashion always is about following a code and differentiation can subsequently only ever be by degrees.

Bibliography

Baines, P., C. Fill, and K. Page, *Marketing*. Oxford University Press, Oxford, 2010.

Barthes, R., *The Fashion System*. Trans. M. Ward and R. Herward. Hill & Wang, New York, NY, 1983.

Baudrillard, J., *Consumer Society: Myths and Structures*. Trans. by Sage, Sage Publications, London, 1998.

Baudrillard, J., *For a Political Economy of the Sign*. Trans. C. Levine. St. Louis Publishers, Telos, 1981.

Baudrillard, J., *Symbolic Exchange and Death*. Trans. by Sage, Sage Publications, London, 1993.

Bourdieu, P., 'Le couturier et sa griffe: Contribution à une théorie de la magie', *Actes de la Recherche en Sciences Sociales*, vol. 1, 1975, pp. 7–36.

---

40   Simmel, 'Fashion'.
41   Schulz, 'Our Lady Hates Viscose', p. 69.

Bourdieu, P., *Distinction: A Social Critique of the Judgement of Taste*. Trans. R. Nice. Harvard University Press, Cambridge, MA, 1984.

Braham, P., 'Fashion: Unpacking a Cultural Production', in P. du Gay (ed.), *Production of Culture/Cultures of Production*. Sage Publications, London, 1997, pp. 121–165.

Brenninkmeyer, I., *The Sociology of Fashion*. P. G. Keller, Winterhur, 1963.

Crewe, L., and M. Lowe, 'United Colours? Globalisations and Localisation Tendencies in Fashion Retailing', in N. Wrigley and M. Lowe (eds.), *Retailing, Consumption and Capital: Towards the New Retail Geography*. Longman Group Limited, Harlow, 1996, pp. 271–283.

DeNora, T., and S. Belcher, 'When You're Trying Something on You Picture Yourself in a Place Where They Are Playing This Kind of Music: Musically Sponsored Agency in the British Clothing Retailing Sector', *The Sociological Review*, vol. 48, no. 1, 2000, pp. 80–101.

du Gay, P., *Consumption and Identity at Work*. Sage Publications, London, 1996.

Esposito, E., 'Originality Through Imitation: The Rationality of Fashion', *Organization Studies*, vol. 32, no. 5, 2011, pp. 603–613.

Finkelstein, J., *The Fashioned Self*. Polity Press, Cambridge, 1991.

Jacobs, K., and T. Kalman, 'The End', in S. Yelavich (ed.), *The Edge of the Millennium: An International Critique of Architecture, Urban Planning, Product and Communication Design*. Whitney Library of Design, New York, NY, 1993, pp. 26–41.

Jenkins, R., *Pierre Bourdieu*. Routledge, London, 1992.

König, R., *The Restless Image: A Sociology of Fashion*. Trans. F. Bradley. George Allen & Unwin Ltd., London, 1973.

Lau, G.T., and S.H. Lee, 'Consumers' Trust in a Brand and the Link to Brand Loyalty', *Journal of Market-Focused Management*, vol. 4, 1999, pp. 341–370.

Moore, C.M., 'From Rages to Riches – Creating and Benefiting from the Fashion Own-Brand', *International Journal of Retail Distribution and Management*, vol. 23, no. 9, 1995, pp. 19–27.

Murray, R., 'Benetton Britain: The New Economic Order', in S. Hall and M. Jacques (eds.), *New Times: The Changing Face of Politics in the 1990s*. Lawrence & Wishart, London, 1989, pp. 54–64.

Robinson, P., *Marketing Fashion: Strategies and Trends for Fashion Brands*. Informa Retail & Consumer, London, 1999.

Schulz, S., 'A Question of Order: The Role of Collective Taste as a Strategy to Cope with Demand Uncertainty in the Womenswear Fashion Industry', *Creative Industries Journal*, vol. 8, no. 1, 2015, pp. 58–72.

Schulz, S., 'Our Lady Hates Viscose: The Role of the Customer Image in High Street Fashion Production', *Cultural Sociology*, vol. 2, no. 3, 2008, pp. 385–405.

Simmel, G., 'Fashion', *The American Journal of Sociology*, vol. 62, no. 6, 1957 [1904], pp. 541–558.

Snyder, C.R., and H.L. Fromkin, *Uniqueness: The Human Pursuit of Difference*. Plenum, New York, NY, 1980.

Spencer, H., *Principles of Sociology* (vol. 2). D. Appleton & Company, New York, NY, 1898.

Tseëlon, E., 'Fashion and Signification in Baudrillard', in D. Keller (ed.), *Baudrillard: A Critical Reader*. Wiley-Blackwell, Oxford, 1994, pp. 119–131.

Tseëlon, E., 'Jean Baudrillard: Post-modern Fashion as the End of Meaning', in A. Rocamora and A. Smelik (eds.), *Thinking Through Fashion: A Guide to Key Theorists*. I.B. Tauris, London and New York, NY, 2015, pp. 215–232.

Veblen, T., *The Theory of the Leisure Class*. The Macmillan Company, London, 1908.

CHAPTER 2

The Fashion 'Timescape': Historical Evolution and Contemporary Features

Federica Carlotto

Abstract

In 2016, several fashion houses decided to adopt the 'see-now-buy-now' scheme, by which the clothing items displayed on the catwalk are made immediately available for purchase. This has triggered an intense debate among operators and the general public on the nature and possible consequences of such a change in the fashion calendar.[1] While the press has welcomed the formula as revolutionary, Kering Group has strongly opposed it, pointing out that temporal availability kills the luxury dream. In any case, this can be seen as the last phase of a longer process, that of the fashion industry gradually compressing its cycles of production and distribution.

With this backcloth, the chapter aims to provide an analytical overview of the relationship between time and fashion, with a focus on its recent development. Drawing from the extant scholarship on the socially constructed nature of time, the chapter profiles the different temporalities that are clustering in the fashion 'timescape'. From the 'neophilia' linking fashion to 'present-ness', the chapter will move to consider the speeded-up reality of the current fashion system, with its dysfunctional approach to novelty. Within this scenario, three major temporal features emerge: a quest for deceleration; the appreciation of the (digital) moment; the multi-dimensional reclamation of the past. All these temporalities account for fashion as the space where cultural stances about time are shaped, negotiated, and practiced.

Keywords

fashion – timescape – modernity – capitalism – 'neophilia' – slow fashion – vintage – digital

---

1 C. Fernandez, 'French Fashion Excess Vote Against "See Now, Buy Now" Schedule', *Fashionista*, 23 February 2016 <http://fashionista.com/2016/02/see-now-buy-now-paris> (Accessed 26 September 2016); L. Hall, 'Gucci's Owner Kering Rejects See Now Buy Now … but for How Long?', *WGSN*, 22 February 2016 <https://www.wgsn.com/blogs/guccis-owner-kering-rejects-see-now-buy-now-but-for-how-long/> (Accessed 26 September 2016).

1   Introduction

At the beginning of 2016, Burberry announced the synchronization of their men/women runway collections, together with a three-month compression between the items' presentation on the catwalk and their availability on the retail platforms. With minor adjustments, this was also the strategic stance explored by Tom Ford, Vetements, Alexander Wang, Courrèges, and several premium fashion brands.[2]

In explaining the rationale behind this unprecedented alteration of the fashion calendar, Tom Ford highlighted the gulf separating the 'immediate' satisfaction demanded by the market, in opposition to the 'antiquated' timetable of the luxury fashion brands, which still rests on the purposeful deferral of purchase.[3]

The time seems quite right, therefore, for reassessing the time of fashion. Historians, philosophers, and sociologists have extensively explored the relationship between fashion and time, taking modernity as its conceptual and historical origin.[4] This chapter stretches the analytical reach to include the very recent evolutions in the temporal architecture of the fashion system.

Rather than considering time as the neutral canvas where fashion evolves, time and fashion are here approached as 'social productions'. Fashion, in other words, becomes the material and sensorial mirror that reflects both human agency upon time, and the cultural meanings time is consequently drenched in.[5]

To this purpose, the paper will make use of the concept of 'timescape' as operationalized by Adam.[6] Adam considers time as a cluster of different temporal features, namely: time frames (seconds, days *etc.*); temporality (process,

---

2   L. Indvik, 'Fashion Week Transformation is Already Underway', *Fashionista*, 8 February 2016 <http://fashionista.com/2016/02/fashion-week-overhaul-burberry-tom-ford-vetements> (Accessed 26 September 2016); L. Sherman and K. Abnett, 'Hugo Boss Unveils First See Now, Buy Now Product', *The Business of Fashion*, 14 September 2016 <https://www.businessoffashion.com/articles/news-analysis/a-guide-to-fashion-immediacy?utm_source=Subscribers&utm_campaign=ab82523603-&utm_medium=email&utm_term=0_d2191372b3-ab82523603-418057225> (Accessed 26 September 2016).

3   H. Pike, 'Tom Ford Shifts Fashion Show to Match Retail Cycle', *The Business of Fashion*, 5 February 2016 <https://www.businessoffashion.com/articles/news-analysis/tom-ford-shifts-show-to-match-retail-cycle> (Accessed 26 September 2016).

4   A. Van de Peer, 'So Last Season: The Production of the Fashion Present in the Politics of Time', *Fashion Theory*, vol. 18, no. 3, 2014, pp. 317–340; L.Fr.H. Svendsen, *Fashion: A Philosophy*, trans. J. Irons, Reaktion Books, London, 2006; G. Lipovetsky, *The Empire of Fashion: Dressing Modern Democracy*, trans. C. Porter, Princeton University Press, Princeton, NJ, 1994.

5   S. B. Kaiser, 'Place, Time and Identity: New Directions in Critical Fashion Studies', *Critical Studies in Fashion & Beauty*, vol. 4, no. 1&2, 2013, pp. 3–16.

6   B. Adam, *Time*, Polity Press, Cambridge, 2004.

irreversibility, impermanence); tempo (pace); timing (synchronization); time point (moment, instant, juncture); time patterns (rhythmicity, cyclicality); time sequence (series, cause and effect); time extensions (duration, continuity); time past, present, future (horizons, memory, anticipation).[7] Depending on the case in exam, these features interact differently with one another, determining different outcomes. In this regard, 'timescape' is a suitable analytical construct, in that it allows us to embrace the multidimensional nature of time in its inter-action with space, matter and context.

2   Fashion and Present-ness: The Modern Neophilia

In defining fashion 'the celebration of the social present',[8] Lipovetsky points at two relevant traits characterising the relationship between time and fashion: the 'present-ness' of fashion, and its socially constructed nature.

And indeed time manipulation lies at the very core of the phenomenon of fashion. As such, fashion refers to the variation of clothed appearance throughout time, where the occurrence of change is artificially maintained constant. Besides being regularised, change in fashion is also socially legitimised, and sought after as a desirable novelty.

While the human *penchant* towards novelty and the diachronic evolution of style are cultural universalities,[9] the phenomenon of fashion originated within a specific geo-historical context. It is generally agreed that fashion started in Europe in the late medieval period, further developing throughout the following centuries, and crystallizing as an industrial system by the second half of 19th century.[10] This occurred alongside a revolutionary shift in the way Westerners came to perceive and interpret time.

Medieval societies used to live within the time of God: with the doomsday looming, life was considered as a transitional period towards the divine (i.e. eternal) bliss or damnation.[11] The individual existence thus unfolded along the natural cycle of seasons and the agricultural rhythm on the one hand, and

---

7   Ibid.
8   Lipovetsky, *The Empire of Fashion*, p. 4.
9   R. König, *The Restless Image: A Sociology of Fashion*, trans. F. Bradley, Allen & Unwin Ltd., London, 1973.
10   C. M. Belfanti, *Civiltà della moda*, Il Mulino, Bologna, 2008; Svendsen, *Fashion*; Lipovetsky, *The Empire of Fashion*.
11   J. Martineau, *Time, Capitalism and Alienation: A Socio-Historical Inquiry into the Making of Modern Time*, Haymarket Books, Chicago, IL, 2015; R. Hassan, *Empires of Speed: Time and the Acceleration of Politics and Society*, Brill, Leiden, 2009.

the perpetuation of a predetermined social order on the other. Appearance reflected this immutable hierarchy, with sumptuary laws protecting the decorous society from any subversive attempt against it. When voluntary, change and novelty were symptomatic of disorder, disruption, and sacrilege.

Modern individuals were able to open a breach in the eternal circularity of the medieval time. Already during the Late Middle Ages, courtiers had started discovering the present dimension of time. As Sombart points out, courteous love carved out a private space where individuals could fully appreciate life *hic et nunc* in terms of sensual and material rejoice.[12]

Time secularization was further promoted by the 'new nobility' and the bourgeoisie, the classes who were seeking social recognition through their consumption patterns. Between 16th and 19th century, the expanded trade networks, the acceleration of the manufacturing rhythm, and the establishment of capitalistic enterprises provided them with tangible opportunities for gratification.[13] Exotic goods and the latest craft products flooded the markets, enticing consumers' to crave the next new thing. In addition, Barbon, Mandeville, Hume, and Smith placed endless consumption at the centre of their liberalistic stances on national wealth and trade balance. The quest for novelty was thus granted its moral and economic entitlement,[14] which lead to the emergence of a specific social ideal: 'neophilia', or the inclination to novelty *per se*.

Roughly in the same period, Enlightenment thinkers started deconstructing the eternal time of God in a sequence of unfolding dimensions: past, present and future. They also charged those dimensions with connotations of value: past came to be rated as 'old' and 'useless', while present and future were singled out as 'a qualitative transcendence of the past'.[15] While adopting the linearity of time, individuals started also to faithfully '[opening] up towards the future rather than repeating the past'.[16]

In its emergence, fashion fully epitomised the modern spirit of 'neophilia'. Depending on the historical circumstances, being fashionable would become a matter of distinction in terms of status, purchase power, taste, or geographic location.[17] Fashionability, i.e. the quality of being fashionable, however, would

12   W. Sombart, *Luxury and Capitalism*, trans.W.R. Dittmar, The University of Michigan Press, Ann Arbor, MI, 1967.

13   Ibid.

14   C.J. Berry, *The Idea of Luxury: A Conceptual and Historical Investigation*, Cambridge University Press, Cambridge, 1994.

15   P. Osborne, *The Politics of Time: Modernity and Avant-Garde*, Verso, London, 1995, p. 11.

16   Van de Peer, 'So Last Season', p. 321.

17   G. Simmel, 'Fashion', *The American Journal of Sociology*, vol. 62, no. 6, 1957 [1904], pp. 541- 558.

always retain the same 'temporal benefit': through their 'New Look(s)', trend-setters and groups *à-la-page* would aim to stay current while drawing a visible line between them and those who were physically coevals, yet stylistically allochronous.[18]

While ritually acclaiming for the emergence of a new colour, style, or shape *in the knowing* of its due disappearance, the mechanism of fashion ended up transcending the specific look of a specific present, to embrace the eternal iteration of 'present-ness'.

3   The Fashion System: From the Discipline of 'Neophilia' to Its Postmodern Implosion

Montesquieu expressed his frustration towards the effects of 'neophilia' in his *Lettres Persanes* (1721), lamenting how the restless change of style prevented him from capturing French fashion in writing:

> [w]hat is the use of my giving you an exact description of their dress and ornaments? A new fashion would destroy all my labor, as it does that of their dressmakers, and, before you could receive my letter, everything would be changed. [19]

As the philosopher highlights, this was also the frustration of those operating in the fashion business at the time: milliners, *marchandes de modes*, shoemakers were certainly keen to profit from the market demand for novelty, but they were also wary of the whimsical instability that this entailed.

In 17th century, Louis XIV and Jean-Baptiste Colbert decided to discipline 'neophilia' by synchronising the change of fashion with the cyclical time of the natural seasons. At the beginning of the 20th century, fashion developed a calendar of its own, with the haute couture collections of Paris fashion week saluting the New Year.[20] From that moment on, the fashion system started following a specific temporal pattern, which was based on the planned dyschronia between the creation and the consumption of 'present-ness'.

The tempo of fashion production, however, harmonised soon with that of capitalism. Capitalism detaches time from any specific content or context,[21]

---

18   Van de Peer, 'So Last Season'.
19   Montesquieu, quot. in K. Chrisman-Campbell, *Fashion Victims: Dress at the Court of Louis XVI and Marie-Antoinette*, Yale University Press, New Haven (CT) and London, 2015, p. 17.
20   Van de Peer, 'So Last Season'.
21   Adam, *Time*.

and treat it as any other resource. Similarly to capital, machines, and work-force, time is 'handled economically',[22] i.e. it is measured, managed, opera-tionalized. From this standpoint, speed is the tempo of saving and optimizing time: by producing quicker, we save resources and therefore increase our prof-it; by innovating faster, we gain competitive advantage on the market.[23]

The tempo of speed is particularly compatible with the fashion business, whose value proposition ultimately resides in the timely offer of fashionability. In its prêt-à-porter version, fashion needs to further 'up the game' by combin-ing velocity with market reach. In other words, fashion needs to be available quicker and quicker to a vaster number of consumers.

In the contemporary post-Fordist economy, however, the tempo of speed has dramatically shrunk, almost draining the spring of fashion production: in-novation. As the time to capture revenues on the market is too short, the cost of the creation got too high.[24] Rather than satisfying the customers' 'neophilia' through original design and styles, high-street brands have cut on the creative phase. Zara, Mango, H&M and others are content to get a 'quick grasp' of the trends on the catwalks and on the streets, and they rather focus their attention on the rapidity of supply by compressing the output cycle in a two-or-three-week span. This has been made possible thanks to just-in-time business mod-els that rely on organisational flexibility and the ICTs-mediated integration of the operations.

Luxury companies are following suit. While strongly advocating the timeless-ness of their aesthetic codes, luxury and premium brands conform to the mass fashion pace for the production of their lower range lines. Interestingly, the philosopher Zecchi has labelled this phenomenon as the 'fashion-ification' of luxury.[25] In order to ensure the commercial profitability of their luxury brands, the calendar of their prêt-à-porter collections has been gradually populated with inter-seasonal collections, resort and cruise collections, capsule collections. This, in turn, has resulted in an increased turnover of worn-out fashion design-ers – Raf Simons, Donna Karan, Jil Sander, Nicolas Ghesquière, Alber Elbaz, Ann Demeulemeester, whose incubation process struggles to keep up with the corpo-rate tight schedule. As Raf Simons points out, '[w]hen you do six shows a year, there's not enough time for the whole process. Technically, yes ... But you have

22   B. Adam, *Timewatch: The Social Analysis of Time*, Polity Press, Cambridge, 1995, p. 87.

23   Hassan, *Empires of Speed*; Adam, *Time*.

24   L. Lenihan, 'How Small Will Beat Big and Save the Fashion Industry', *The Business of Fashion*, 19 June 2017 <https://www.businessoffashion.com/articles/opinion/lawrence-lenihan-resonance-how-small-will-beat-big-and-save-the-fashion-industry> (Accessed 20 June 2017).

25   S. Zecchi, *Il lusso: eterno desiderio di voluttà e bellezza*, Mondadori, Milano, 2015.

no incubation time for ideas, and incubation time is very important'.[26] Alber El-baz, dismissed by Lanvin in 2015 for 'lack of creative designs',[27] well described the feeling of 'finishing a collection and being half-dead, and knowing that you're late with the next collection'.[28]

This is not just about the clash between the creative and the business cycles. For Elbaz, the matter has a wider reach, and leads to question the same role of fashion designers. By synchronising with the industry's rhythm, designers are de-prived of any 'demiurgic agency' over setting the tempo of novelty, and they find themselves merely 'executing novelty' *as and when* required by the industry:

> [i]s this industry only about numbers and shows? That's a question. And we, the designers, did we change? Our title first was designer and then chief creative director, because we have to be creative, we have to direct. Now we have a title, it's image-maker. Image became a huge part of our job. [29]

With image making and branding at the core of their business, high-end fash-ion companies now seem to bypass the issue by diverting their focus from time-consuming clothing design to time-effective extensions in accessories or perfumes.[30]

As such, the frantic spiralling-up of the fashion rhythm seems to annihilate the essence of fashion, that of novelty: the increasingly faster replacement of the 'new' with a 'newer new' is eventually forcing both 'news' into a flattened co-existence.[31] In this scenario, 'neophilia' itself seems to be heading for implosion.

---

26   C. Horyn, 'Why Raf Simons is Leaving Christian Dior', *The Cut*, 22 October 2015 <https://www.thecut.com/2015/10/raf-simons-leaving-christian-dior.html> (Accessed 3 Janu-ary 2018).

27   S. Conlon, 'Elbaz Hits Back at Poor-Quality Claims', *Vogue*, 10 November 2015 <http://www.vogue.co.uk/article/alber-elbaz-lanvin-disagreement-over-departure> (Accessed 3 January 2018).

28   A. Jones, 'The Creative Brain, Unravelled: How the Highly Pressured Fashion Industry is Tackling Mental Health', *Stylist*, February 2017<https://www.stylist.co.uk/fashion/creative-brain-unravelled-mental-health-fashion-industry-alexander-mcqueen-isabella-blow-depression/122121> (Accessed 3 January 2018).

29   WWD Staff, 'Overheated! Is Fashion Heading for a Burnout?', *WWD*, 27 October 2015 <http://wwd.com/fashion-news/fashion-features/fashion-designers-karl-lagerfeld-marc-jacobs-10269092/> (Accessed 26 September 2016).

30   Ibid.; I. Amed, 'Demna Gvasalia Reveals Vetements' Plan to Disrupt the Fashion System', *The Business of Fashion*, 5 February 2016 <https://www.businessoffashion.com/articles/intelligence/demna-gvasalia-reveals-vetements-plan-to-disrupt-the-fashion-system> (Accessed 26 September 2016).

31   Svendsen, *Fashion.*

4   The Temporalities of Contemporary Fashion

Time acceleration, however, is just one of the many features characterising the current fashion 'timescape'. Below, the chapter proposes an outline of the most recent temporalities.

4.1   'Slowphilia'

If we are virtually able to produce faster, what does it mean to willingly opt out the system? First of all, it means to adopt a very different approach towards time.

As mentioned above, for the fashion industry the passing of time is a 'necessary evil'. In corroding the veneer of novelty of the 'current new', time passing frees the space for a 'newer new' to advance. This both destroys *and* regenerates the business of fashion.

In a slow production of fashion, 'being slow' entails synchronizing with a different temporality, that regulating the organic world.

The organic temporality is an entropic one, in which all the macro- and micro-elements of the ecosystem are interconnected, and the depletion of some favour the replenishment of others. Industrial products, on the other hand, are designed within the one-dimensional timeframe of their utility existence, with no consideration for their long-term or wider impact.[32] By implementing the organic cycle approach in the fashion production cycle, companies take into account the replenishment cycle of their resources – human, natural, and economic.

Thus, in sourcing the yak *khullu* for its scarves, Nohrla respects the numerical and temporal constraints of the local herding practices;[33] Kowtow manufactures its items in Indian SA8000 °-certified organisations, that favours their staff 'time-off' through paid holiday leaves and sick pay schemes.[34]

With a conscious deceleration of time, in addition, we acknowledge and allow the action of time to unfold as an ennobling agent. In his work on craftsmanship, the sociologist Sennett reminds us that excellence emerges only through time. Acquisition of mastery as 'getting something right' is in fact a purposeful training activity that can be qualitatively incremented *because of* time passing. This is quite different from the capitalistic idea of 'getting something

---

32   B. Adam, *Time and Social Theory*, Polity Press, Cambridge, 1994.

33   'A Yak Wool Factory on the Tibetan Plateau' [video], *Norlha*, 2012 <https://www.norlha-textiles.com/pages/about-us-another-kind-of-luxury-tibetan-plateau?ref=menu#oursto-ry> (Accessed 8 February 2018).

34   'Ethical & Sustainable', *Kow Tow* [corporate website] <https://nz.kowtowclothing.com/pages/ethical-sustainable> (Accessed 8 February 2018).

done',[35] which is usually benchmarked through chronometric parameters such as completion speed or quantity produced within a certain interval.

The appreciation of deceleration, or 'slowphilia', has also specific implications for the consumption of fashion. In the purchase of a new item of clothing, the consumer seeks the fashion experience, i.e., to experience the rejuvenation of the dressed self.[36] In contrast to this, the choice of an item in accordance to one's own personal preference puts the item in sync with a different temporal agenda. As Kopytoff argues, the item is removed from the whimsical and wasteful tempo of 'fashion-ability', and it is placed within the time frame of familiarity.[37] There, clothes are likely to be 'singularized' and 'decommoditized', i.e. they can be worn across seasons until they are 'fit to be used' or anyway enjoyed by the wearer. This is, ultimately, about the wearer re-discovering through his/her daily dressing practice: '[y] eah. I still want to wear this'.[38]

The positive transformative action of time passing of time emerges also in the waiting. As considered by Adam, '[i]n waiting [...] usable time is transformed into a resource that expresses the value of service'.[39] Luxury companies have been strategically taking advantage of the waiting time to increase their clients' desire and to endow their products with the patina of exclusivity – as the Hermès waiting list for the Birkin bag. In an era where the Internet has made the items' purchase 'only a click away' and where the fashion clientele has consequently developed a *IWWIWWIWI* ('I want what I want when I want it') mind-set, waiting has become even more meaningful. In a recent interview about the digital exposure of luxury and the events' multiplication in the fashion calendar, Nicolas Ghesquière reflects on the importance of re-discovering 'the temporality of luxury'. While stressing the necessity of 'giving time' to luxury creation and production, Ghesquière considers the matter also from a consumption perspective, by stating how being able to wait for a product 'is some [thing] of a luxury now'.[40] In other words, the skill of managing the time of expectation is to become the main attribute of the ultimate luxury *connoisseur*.

35   R. Sennett, *The Craftsman*, Penguin Books, London, 2009, p. 46.

36   L. Medine, 'In Defense of Slow Fashion', *Man Repeller* [blog], 7 July 2015 <http://www.manrepeller.com/2015/07/fast-fashion-shopping.html> (Accessed 26 September 2016).

37   I. Kopytoff, 'The Cultural Biography of Things: Commoditization as Process', in A. Appadurai (ed.), *The Social Life of Things: Commodities in Cultural Perspective*, Cambridge University Press, Cambridge, 1986, pp. 64–91.

38   Medine, 'In Defense of Slow Fashion'.

39   Adam, *Time and Social Theory*, p. 124.

40   N. Vogelson, 'Louis Vuitton's Creative Director Nicolas Ghesquière Looks to the Past to See the Future', *Document*, 3 October 2017 <http://www.documentjournal.com/article/louis-vuittons-creative-director-nicolas-ghesquiere-looks-to-the-past-to-se> (Accessed 12 October 2017).

However, this requires companies and brands to educate their consumers in the appreciation of the 'hedonic elevation'[41] behind waiting. Since last year, the attention of the press has been drawn by the hype streetwear brand Supreme, whose customers are willing to queue for hours and even camp outside their stores, from London to Singapore. [42]

According to the marketing scholar Richins, pre-purchase waiting – especially for high-end products – provides consumers with a greater sense of excitement than the actual act of purchase.[43] In the case of Supreme, the act of waiting generates a temporal space where the consumers live in the pleasant anticipation of the purchase. In addition, the fact that the waiting happens 'in a queue' somehow elongates the process of purchasing itself, creating also a bond between the waiters. They convert the potential 'waste of time' of waiting into a unique social event, to be remembered after the act of purchase. In its ability to generate the time for waiting and to charge it with meaning, Supreme can be thus considered as a luxury brand *à-la-Ghesquière*, besides the recent collaboration with Louis Vuitton.

4.2   'Momentization'

As mentioned above, the Internet has profoundly impacted on the modern timeframe, both in terms of compression ('one click away') and expansion ('accessibility at any time'). As a new dimension of the human existence, however, the Internet has also developed its own specific temporality.

The digital temporality is tightly linked to a networked socialization pattern. Connected individuals find themselves immersed in 'an ego-centric network of relationships centred around oneself and one's interests'.[44] Digital sociability is therefore emerging from the ritual and instantaneous sharing of information, comments, likes, tweets *etc.* between the individual and the groups/individuals he/she is connected with, follower of/followed from, or friends of.[45]

41   M. Richins, 'When Wanting is Better than Having: Materialism, Transformation Expectations, and Product-Evoked Emotions in the Purchase Process', *Journal of Consumer Research*, vol. 40, 2013, pp. 1–18.

42   A. Woodhall, 'Meet the People who Queue Outside Supreme Every Week', *Shift*, 17 March 2016 <http://shiftlondon.org/fashion/meet-people-queue-outside-supreme-every-week/> (Accessed 26 September 2016); A. Woo, 'Excited Fans Queue Overnight Outside Ion Orchard for Louis Vuitton and Supreme Collaboration', *The Straits Times*, 14 July 2017 <http://www.straitstimes.com/lifestyle/fashion/excited-fans-queue-up-outside-ion-orchard-for-louis-vuitton-and-supreme> (Accessed 19 October 2017).

43   Richins, 'When Wanting is Better than Having'.

44   V. Miller, *Understanding Digital Culture*, Sage Publications, London, 2013, p. 196.

45   C. Hine, *Virtual Ethnography*, Sage Publications, London, 2003; S.G. Jones, *Cybersociety: Computer-mediated Communication and Community*, Sage Publications, London, 1995.

The time feature characterizing this networked socialization is somehow close to the idea of quantum, defined as 'a unit of action which contains energy and time'.[46] Online, the unit of action is represented by the sharing of a post, which contains in itself social inputs and the dimension of the 'hyper-now',[47] an eternal present with no past on which to reflect upon and no future to imagine or create. The quantic temporality of the Internet, therefore, does not entirely spoil time of its value. Rather, the 'hyper-now' creates a gulf around a specific time point: the moment.

As a way to capitalize on the moment as the currency unit of the 'hyper-now', fashion houses are now providing relevant meanings to their digital audience. After all, 'whatever space and time mean, place and occasion mean more'.[48]

In order to turn moments into occasions, brands operate on a double temporal frequency. They disseminate moments on a constant basis on social media such as Facebook and Instagram, thus trying to capture the span of attention of the digital individuals, which is timed along the speed of a like, a post, a tweet. Quite similarly, 'momentization' is also the time pattern followed by Supreme in its retail operations. By 'dropping' a few new items on the retail circuit on a weekly basis, Supreme actually takes the distance from the 'neophilia' of the fast-fashion. Rather, this strategy shares more with the purpose of a digital feed: to create a sense of consistency, day by day.[49]

Companies – including the luxury segment represented by Stella McCartney, Michael Kors, Valentino – also create one-off moments, as in the recent introduction of Snapchat. Among the digital social platforms, Snapchat, and more recently Instagram Stories, are the very places for 'momentization'.[50] The instantaneous, perishable, and amateur photographs and video snippets appear in stark semiotic opposition to the polished fashion statements of the conventional ad campaigns. The subjects portrayed are also very different: here, it is the backstage rather than the catwalk; it is the interaction

---

46   Adam, *Time*, p. 63.

47   Hassan, *Empires of Speed*, p. 103.

48   Van Eyck, quot. in Sennett, *The Craftsman*, p. 235.

49   J. Deleon, 'What the Fashion System Can Learn from Supreme-Style Product Drops', *The Business of Fashion*, 31 August 2016 <https://www.businessoffashion.com/articles/intelligence/high-fashion-lessons-from-streetwear-drops-supreme-palace-gosha?utm_source=Subscribers&utm_campaign=ddc15f7676-&utm_medium=email&utm_term=0_d2191372b3-ddc15f7676-418057225> (Accessed 26 September 2016).

50   J. Frank, 'Could Snapchat be the Fashion Industry's Next Instagram?', *Vogue Australia*, 20 May 2014 <http://www.vogue.com.au/fashion/news/could+snapchat+be+the+fashion+industrys+next+instagramr+,30843> (Accessed 26 September 2016).

between designers and models with their family and VIP friends than the red carpet. In other words, in the quantic digital space it is all about the moment in action, rather than a moment that is staged – and therefore already gone.[51]

4.3   'Past-iche'

As scholars point out, in its obsession with 'present-ness' fashion has developed a very ambivalent relationship with the past.[52] On the one hand, the fashion system needs to reject the past for the sake of novelty; on the other hand, fashion companies often build up on their own past in order to ensure continuity in the future. This is especially the case of those luxury brands with a strong and distinctive historical heritage – let us think about John Galliano and Raf Simons' research in Dior's archives when they took over the haute couture collections for the *maison*.[53]

However, the past of the luxury brands is not past, i.e., devalued *because* it is different from the present. Rather, it is timeless, i.e. sanctified *in that* it is different from the present.[54]

History and tradition are human manipulations of the past that marketers use as repositories to shape their brands' storytelling. Cultural sociologist Appadurai has underlined that the past retrieved by the fashion marketers does not adhere to the chronological rigour of the historian or the archaeologist. It is rather a 'commoditized past', an artificial construct crafted to trigger consumers' desire. As a matter of fact, consumers are prompted to feel nostalgia for a past reality they might have not had any direct experience of.[55] The free exhibitions organised by Louis Vuitton and Chanel in London in 2015 offer a revealing insight into the use of the past as a marketing tool. In both the exhibitions, the complexity of history was flattened and fragmented: logos, symbols, iconic elements were extrapolated from their original context, re-packaged, and displayed as attractions in a 'branded thematic park'. Past, in other words, was there commoditized as 'past-tainment'.

---

51   E. Holmes, 'Snapchat Captures Fashion Week', *Wall Street Journal*, 11 March 2015 <https:// www.wsj.com/articles/snapchat-captures-fashion-week-1426098132> (Accessed 3 January 2018); S. Jones, 'Snapchat Enables Intimate Storytelling During Fashion Month', *Luxury Daily*, 13 March 2015 <https://www.luxurydaily.com/snapchat-enables-intimate-storytelling-during-fashion-month/> (Accessed 26 September 2016).

52   Van de Peer, 'So Last Season'.

53   D. Thomas, *Gods and Kings: The Rise and Fall of Alexander McQueen and John Galliano*, Penguin Books, London, 2015; F. Tcheng (dir.), *Dior and I* [DVD], France, 2014.

54   Zecchi, *Il lusso*.

55   A. Appadurai, *Modernity at Large: Cultural Dimensions in Globalization*, University of Minnesota Press, Minneapolis, MN, 1996.

More recently, the Versace Spring 2018 ready-to-wear fashion show provides another interesting junction of past and present.

The fashion show is usually considered the point in time where fashion creation becomes temporally and spatially present. For the show, which marked 20 years from the murder of her brother Gianni, Donatella Versace recalled Gianni's creative years through a 'tribute collection', that was inserted in the 'so 80s' frame of the very top models (Naomi Campbell, Carla Bruni, Claudia Schiffer, Cindy Crawford, Helena Christensen) walking on the notes of *Freedom!* by the late George Michael. Through the patina of nostalgia, Versace was thus able to bring together both older and younger generations of consumers.[56]

Another instance of past manipulation involves vintage fashion. Until a few decades ago, vintage fashion used to be a niche preference for the wardrobe of a few *connoisseurs*. In the early 2000s, Hollywood stars like Winona Rider and Julia Roberts chose for the Oscars vintage gowns of Pauline Trigére and Valentino, respectively.[57] Since then, vintage fashion has been attracting wider attention.

Certainly, behind the vintage-mania lies the reaction to the frantic 'neophilia' of the fashion system. As mentioned above, 'neophilia', coupled with the instantaneous availability of trends and collections through social media, has generated a 'fashion temporal fatigue', by which the new is perceived as somehow already seen. The vintage piece, on the contrary, is completely asynchronous from the impatient and accelerated clock of the fashion industry.[58] To be precise, vintage doesn't run at any specific rhythm, but resides on the solemn stillness of its being 'beyond time'.

And yet, past can also be 'dragged back into fashion', as in the so-called 'new vintage look' that characterised the fashion collections in 2016 and that had been already anticipated by Gucci's latest collections.[59] This revival often

---

56   T. Blanks, 'Donatella Versace, Her Brother's Keeper', *The Business of Fashion*, 23 September 2017 <https://www.businessoffashion.com/articles/fashion-show-review/donatella-versace-her-brothers-keeper> (Accessed 12 October 2017).

57   M. Ferrier, 'Vintagewear Takes Over the Catwalk … with Help from Amal Clooney and Alexa Chung', *The Guardian*, 19 June 2016 <https://www.theguardian.com/fashion/2016/jun/18/vintagewear-takes-over-the-catwalk-with-help-from-amal-clooney-and-alexa-chung> (Accessed 26 September 2016).

58   Bloomberg, 'Inside the Booming Vintage Luxury Fashion Market', *The Business of Fashion*, 8 March 2016 <https://www.businessoffashion.com/articles/news-analysis/inside-the-booming-vintage-luxury-fashion-market> (Accessed 26 September 2016).

59   S. Oliva, '2016 Summer Fashion Trends: The New Vintage', *Vogue*, 26 January 2016 <http://www.vogue.it/en/trends/trend-of-the-day/2016/01/fashion-trend-summer-2016-neo-vintage#ad-image> (Accessed 26 September 2016).

stimulates 'purist consumers' to actually go back to the vintage originals, i.e. to 'archetypical' styles.[60]

In between archaeological rigour and contemporary trendification, vintage pieces can coexist with pieces from the present, as in Elizabeth and James, the concept store of Mary-Kate and Ashley Olsen.[61]

Or vintage can be reproduced, as in the collaboration of Alexa Chung with Marks & Spencer, which took off in 2016. Chung is one of the most popular advocates of the vintage a-temporal *allure*.[62] Like Raf Simons and John Galliano, she has been digging into archives in search for the past. Differently from Simons and Galliano, though, Chung has retrieved some pieces with 'past-ness' character and fashion-ability potential, and she revived them with minor adjustments. In the video documenting her work, she proudly describes her fluid relationship with time: 'I've just found the future of Marks & Spencer in the past'.[63] Hence, if from a material point of view, fashion has thus become an 'aesthetic blender' or a 'supermarket of style',[64] from a temporal perspective, the present use of past as fashion novelty can be considered a 'past-iche'.

Above in this chapter we talked about the implosion of 'neophilia', which leads to the coexistence of different 'news'. Here, it is the sequence between past present and future that seems to lose its linear logic.

5   Conclusion

If fashion is the celebration of the social present, the social present of fashion presents us with a very interesting scenario to interpret.

---

60   Ferrier, 'Vintagewear Takes Over the Catwalk'.

61   S. Reed, 'Inside Mary-Kate and Ashley Olsen's First Elizabeth and James Store', *Pret-a-Reporter*, 22 July 2016 <http://www.hollywoodreporter.com/news/elizabeth-james-at-grove-inside-913660> (Accessed 12 October 2017).

62   Ferrier, 'Vintagewear Takes Over the Catwalk'.

63   Harper's Bazaar UK, 'The Making of: Archive by Alexa Chung for Marks & Spencer' [video], *YouTube*, 13 April 2016 <https://www.youtube.com/watch?v=Wnrf-LWH4T8> (Accessed 3 October 2016).

64   O. Ahmed, 'In the Aesthetic Blender', *The Business of Fashion*, 30 September 2017 < https://www.businessoffashion.com/articles/opinion/in-the-aesthetic-blender?utm_source=-Subscribers&utm_campaign=ded9f69518-saving-the-mall-changes-at-alexander-wang-si-newho&utm_medium=email&utm_term=0_d2191372b3-ded9f69518-418057225> (Accessed 12 October 2017); T. Polhemus, 'In the Supermarket of Style', *Ted Polhemus in The 21st Century* [personal website] <http://www.tedpolhemus.com/index.html> (Accessed 8 February 2018).

As the overview on the relationship between fashion and time has shown, the phenomenon of fashion originated from a specific cultural meaning attached to time, which in turn articulated around 'present-ness' and change. The post-Fordist fashion industry has instead been focussing on the speed as the tempo regulating production. The 'see-now-buy-now' scheme adopted in 2016 was indeed saluted as time-changing and revolutionary. After a few seasons, however, the introduction of the 'see-now-buy-now' got somehow stuck: Tom Ford and others have abandoned it, Ralph Lauren and Tommy Hilfiger are sticking to it, but the industry in general is still holding on.[65]

As a matter of fact, the concept of 'timescape' as described by Adam shows that the time of fashion emerge from the interaction of different temporal features, each one with a different weight depending on the circumstances. From this perspective, rather than being an encompassing temporality dominating the contemporary fashion 'timescape', the 'see-now-buy-now' model appears more as one of many other temporalities, such as 'slowphilia', 'momentization', 'past-iche'.

As analysed here, all of these represent the on-going and contradictory agency of human beings and social forces in accelerating, decelerating, fragmenting or extending the time of fashion.

Bibliography

'A Yak Wool Factory on the Tibetan Plateau' [video], *Norlha*, 2012 <https://www.norlhatextiles.com/pages/about-us-another-kind-of-luxury-tibetan-plateau?ref=menu#our-story> (Accessed 8 February 2018).

Adam, B., *Time and Social Theory*. Polity Press, Cambridge, 1994.

Adam, B., *Timewatch: The Social Analysis of Time*. Polity Press, Cambridge, 1995.

Adam, B., *Time*. Polity Press, Cambridge, 2004.

Ahmed, O., 'In the Aesthetic Blender', *The Business of Fashion*, 30 September 2017 <https://www.businessoffashion.com/articles/opinion/in-the-aesthetic-blender?utm_source=Subscribers&utm_campaign=ded9f69518-saving-the-mall-changes-at-alexander-wang-si-newho&utm_medium=email&utm_term=0_d2191372b3-ded9f69518-418057225> (Accessed 12 October 2017).

---

65   H. Milnes, 'Three Seasons in, See-Now-Buy-Now Is Going Anywhere', *Digiday UK*, 18 September 2017 <https://digiday.com/marketing/three-seasons-see-now-buy-now-going-nowhere/> (Accessed 12 October 2017).

Amed, I., 'Demna Gvasalia Reveals Vetements' Plan to Disrupt the Fashion System', *The Business of Fashion*, 5 February 2016 <https://www.businessoffashion.com/articles/intelligence/demna-gvasalia-reveals-vetements-plan-to-disrupt-the-fashion-system> (Accessed 26 September 2016).

Appadurai, A., *Modernity at Large: Cultural Dimensions in Globalization*. University of Minnesota Press, Minneapolis, MN, 1996.

Belfanti, C. M., *Civiltà della moda*. Il Mulino, Bologna, 2008.

Berry, C.J., *The Idea of Luxury: A Conceptual and Historical Investigation*. Cambridge University Press, Cambridge, 1994.

Blanks, T., 'Donatella Versace, Her Brother's Keeper', *The Business of Fashion*, 23 September 2017 <https://www.businessoffashion.com/articles/fashion-show-review/donatella-versace-her-brothers-keeper> (Accessed 12 October 2017).

Bloomberg, 'Inside the Booming Vintage Luxury Fashion Market', *The Business of Fashion*, 8 March 2016 <https://www.businessoffashion.com/articles/news-analysis/inside-the-booming-vintage-luxury-fashion-market> (Accessed 26 September 2016).

Chrisman-Campbell, K., *Fashion Victims: Dress at the Court of Louis XVI and Marie-Antoinette*. Yale University Press, New Haven (CT) and London, 2015.

Conlon, S., 'Elbaz Hits Back at Poor-Quality Claims', *Vogue*, 10 November 2015 <http://www.vogue.co.uk/article/alber-elbaz-lanvin-disagreement-over-departure> (Accessed 3 January 2018).

Danziger, P.N., 'Why Instant Gratification Isn't so Gratifying', *Forbes*, 19 September 2017 <https://www.forbes.com/sites/pamdanziger/2017/09/19/why-instant-gratification-isnt-so-gratifying/2/#27acb2f77135https://www.forbes.com/sites/pamdanziger/2017/09/19/why-instant-gratification-isnt-so-gratifying/2/#27acb2f77135> (Accessed 12 October 2017).

Deleon, J., 'What the Fashion System Can Learn from Supreme-Style Product Drops', *The Business of Fashion*, 31 August 2016 <https://www.businessoffashion.com/articles/intelligence/high-fashion-lessons-from-streetwear-drops-supreme-palace-gosha?utm_source=Subscribers&utm_campaign=ddc15f7676-&utm_medium=email&utm_term=0_d2191372b3-ddc15f7676-418057225> (Accessed 26 September 2016).

'Ethical & Sustainable', *Kow Tow* [corporate website] <https://nz.kowtowclothing.com/pages/ethical-sustainable> (Accessed 8 February 2018).

Fernandez, C., 'French Fashion Excess Vote Against "See Now, Buy Now" Schedule', *Fashionista*, 23 February 2016 <http://fashionista.com/2016/02/see-now-buy-now-paris> (Accessed 26 September 2016).

Ferrier, M., 'Vintagewear Takes Over the Catwalk ... with Help from Amal Clooney and Alexa Chung', *The Guardian*, 19 June 2016 <https://www.theguardian.com/fashion/2016/jun/18/vintagewear-takes-over-the-catwalk-with-help-from-amal-clooney-and-alexa-chung> (Accessed 26 September 2016).

Frank, J., 'Could Snapchat be the Fashion Industry's Next Instagram?', *Vogue Australia*, 20 May 2014 <http://www.vogue.com.au/fashion/news/could+snapchat+be+the+-fashion+industrys+next+instagramr+,30843> (Accessed 26 September 2016).

Hall, L., 'Gucci's Owner Kering Rejects See Now Buy Now ... but for How Long?', *WGSN*, 22 February 2016 <https://www.wgsn.com/blogs/guccis-owner-kering-rejects-see-now-buy-now-but-for-how-long/> (Accessed 26 September 2016).

Harper's Bazaar UK, 'The Making of: Archive by Alexa Chung for Marks & Spencer'[video], *YouTube*, 13 April 2016 <https://www.youtube.com/watch?v=Wnrf-LWH4T8> (Accessed 3 October 2016).

Hassan, R., *Empires of Speed: Time and the Acceleration of Politics and Society*. Brill, Leiden, 2009.

Hine, C., *Virtual Ethnography*. Sage Publications, London, 2003.

Holmes, E., 'Snapchat Captures Fashion Week', *Wall Street Journal*, 11 March 2015 <https://www.wsj.com/articles/snapchat-captures-fashion-week-1426098132> (Accessed 3 January 2018).

Horyn, C., 'Why Raf Simons is Leaving Christian Dior', *The Cut*, 22 October 2015 <https://www.thecut.com/2015/10/raf-simons-leaving-christian-dior.html> (Accessed 3 January 2018).

Indvik, L., 'Fashion Week Transformation is Already Underway', *Fashionista*, 8 February 2016 <http://fashionista.com/2016/02/fashion-week-overhaul-burberry-tom-ford-vetements> (Accessed 26 September 2016).

Jones, A., 'The Creative Brain, Unravelled: How the Highly Pressured Fashion Industry is Tackling Mental Health', *Stylist*, February 2017 <https://www.stylist.co.uk/fashion/creative-brain-unravelled-mental-health-fashion-industry-alexander-mcqueen-isabella-blow-depression/122121> (Accessed 3 January 2018).

Jones, S., 'Snapchat Enables Intimate Storytelling During Fashion Month', *Luxury Daily*, 13 March 2015 <https://www.luxurydaily.com/snapchat-enables-intimate-storytelling-during-fashion-month/> (Accessed 26 September 2016).

Jones, S.G., *Cybersociety: Computer-mediated Communication and Community*. Sage Publications, London, 1995.

Kaiser, S.B., 'Place, Time and Identity: New Directions in Critical Fashion Studies', *Critical Studies in Fashion & Beauty*, vol. 4, no. 1&2, 2013, pp. 3–16.

König, R., *The Restless Image: A Sociology of Fashion*. Trans. F. Bradley. Allen & Unwin, London, 1973.

Kopytoff, I., 'The Cultural Biography of Things: Commoditization as Process', in A. Appadurai (ed.), *The Social Life of Things: Commodities in Cultural Perspective*. Cambridge University Press, Cambridge, 1986, pp. 64–91.

Lenihan, L., 'How Small Will Beat Big and Save the Fashion Industry', *The Business of Fashion*, 19 June 2017 <https://www.businessoffashion.com/articles/opinion/lawrence-lenihan-resonance-how-small-will-beat-big-and-save-the-fashion-industry > (Accessed 20 June 2017).

Lipovetsky, G., *The Empire of Fashion: Dressing Modern Democracy*. Trans. C. Porter. Princeton University Press, Princeton, NJ, 1994.

Martineau, J., *Time, Capitalism and Alienation: A Socio-Historical Inquiry into the Making of Modern Time*. Haymarket Books, Chicago, IL, 2015.

Medine, L., 'In Defense of Slow Fashion', *Man Repeller* [blog], 7 July 2015 <http://www.manrepeller.com/2015/07/fast-fashion-shopping.html> (Accessed 26 September 2016).

Milnes, H., 'Three Seasons in, See-Now-Buy-Now is Going Anywhere', *Digiday UK*, 18 September 2017 <https://digiday.com/marketing/three-seasons-see-now-buy-now-going-nowhere/> (Accessed 12 October 2017).

Miller, V., *Understanding Digital Culture*. Sage Publications, London, 2013.

Oliva, S., '2016 Summer Fashion Trends: The New Vintage', *Vogue*, 26 January 2016 <http://www.vogue.it/en/trends/trend-of-the-day/2016/01/fashion-trend-summer-2016-neo-vintage#ad-image> (Accessed 26 September 2016).

Osborne, P., *The Politics of Time: Modernity and Avant-Garde*. Verso, London, 1995.

Pike, H., 'Tom Ford Shifts Fashion Show to Match Retail Cycle', *The Business of Fashion*, 5 February 2016 <https://www.businessoffashion.com/articles/news-analysis/tom-ford-shifts-show-to-match-retail-cycle> (Accessed 26 September 2016).

Polhemus, T., 'In the Supermarket of Style', *Ted Polhemus in the 21st Century* [personal website] <http://www.tedpolhemus.com/index.html> (Accessed 8 February 2018).

Reed, S., 'Inside Mary-Kate and Ashley Olsen's First Elizabeth and James Store', *Pret-a-Reporter*, 22 July 2016 <http://www.hollywoodreporter.com/news/elizabeth-james-at-grove-inside-913660> (Accessed 12 October 2017).

Richins, M., 'When Wanting is Better than Having: Materialism, Transformation Expectations, and Product-Evoked Emotions in the Purchase Process', *Journal of Consumer Research*, vol. 40, 2013, pp. 1–18.

Sennett, R., *The Craftsman*. Penguin Books, London, 2009.

Sherman, L., and K. Abnett, 'Hugo Boss Unveils First See Now, Buy Now Product', *The Business of Fashion*, 14 September 2016 <https://www.businessoffashion.com/articles/news-analysis/a-guide-to-fashion-immediacy?utm_source=Subscribers&utm_campaign=ab82523603-&utm_medium=email&utm_term=0_d2191372b3-ab82523603-418057225> (Accessed 26 September 2016).

Simmel, G., 'Fashion', *The American Journal of Sociology*, vol. 62, no. 6, 1957 [1904], pp. 541-558.

Sombart, W., *Luxury and Capitalism*. Trans. W.R. Dittmar. The University of Michigan Press, Ann Arbor, MI, 1967.

Svendsen, L.Fr.H., *Fashion: A Philosophy*. Trans. J. Irons. Reaktion Books, London, 2006.

Tcheng, F. (dir.), *Dior and I* [DVD]. France, 2014.

Thomas, D., *Gods and Kings: The Rise and Fall of Alexander McQueen and John Galliano*. Penguin Books, London, 2015.

Van de Peer, A., 'So Last Season: The Production of the Fashion Present in the Politics of Time', *Fashion Theory*, vol. 18, no. 3, 2014, pp. 317–340.

Vogelson, N., 'Louis Vuitton's Creative Director Nicolas Ghesquière Looks to the Past to See the Future', *Document*, 3 October 2017 <http://www.documentjournal.com/article/louis-vuittons-creative-director-nicolas-ghesquiere-looks-to-the-past-to-se> (Accessed 12 October 2017).

Woo, A., 'Excited Fans Queue Overnight Outside Ion Orchard for Louis Vuitton and Supreme Collaboration', *The Straits Times*, 14 July 2017 <http://www.straitstimes.com/lifestyle/fashion/excited-fans-queue-up-outside-ion-orchard-for-louis-vuitton-and-supreme> (Accessed 19 October 2017).

Woodhall, A., 'Meet the People who Queue Outside Supreme Every Week', *Shift*, 17 March 2016 <http://shiftlondon.org/fashion/meet-people-queue-outside-supreme-every-week/> (Accessed 26 September 2016).

WWD Staff, 'Overheated! Is Fashion Heading for a Burnout?', *WWD*, 27 October 2105 <http://wwd.com/fashion-news/fashion-features/fashion-designers-karl-lagerfeld-marc-jacobs-10269092/> (Accessed 26 September 2016).

Zecchi, S., *Il lusso: eterno desiderio di voluttà e bellezza*. Mondadori, Milano, 2015.

CHAPTER 3

The Art Foundations of Luxury Fashion Brands: An Exploratory Investigation

Alessia Grassi, Steve Swindells, and Stephen Wigley

Abstract

During the past 30 years, several Western European luxury fashion brands have invested resources in cultural initiatives distinctive from their core commercial activities. In particular, this has involved the brands establishing organisations (typically identified as 'foundations') dedicated to collecting and commissioning contemporary art by established and emerging artists. The suggested motives for these activities range from indulging the personal interest of the brands' owners and managers, to a desire to invest their brands with cultural capital or creative heritage. This chapter is the first to explicitly investigate the phenomenon of luxury fashion brands' ownership of contemporary art foundations, with the aim of understanding its nature, scope, and purpose. These will be considered in the context of the contradiction between the apparent desire for public engagement with the art foundations and the perceived exclusivity of the patron brands' products and retail venues. The chapter investigates the phenomenon in two phases. First, an insight into specific cases of art foundations owned by luxury fashion brands is offered. This explores the internal structures of the relevant foundations and examines their programmes, communications, initiatives and connections with the patron brands. Secondly, expert interviews with relevant professionals will contextualise the role of the art foundations as a presumed meeting point between the inclusivity of public engagement and the exclusivity of fashion branding. This is an exploratory study representing the first stage of an on going project. It is informed by secondary research and primary qualitative research aimed at establishing a clearer understanding of the phenomenon under investigation. The chapter will provide insight into the contemporary nature of both luxury fashion branding and public engagement in an art exhibition.

Keywords

luxury fashion brands – public engagement – private art foundations – contemporary art – co-production

1   Introduction

There has always been interest in understanding the relationship between fashion and art.[1] This relationship has been the subject of many studies: from the use of art images[2] and contemporary art visual installations[3] in fashion brands marketing strategies, to the constant inspiration that designers find in art;[4] from artists belief, at the beginning of the 20th century, to be the best in designing garments,[5] to the growing trend of exhibiting fashion items as pieces of art in museums and galleries.[6]

However, previous studies of this relationship have not dealt with a growing trend towards fashion brands' investments in art.[7] Often, art has been used by the fashion industry as a marketing means.[8] Arguably for the same reason, in the last three decades Western European fashion brands are establishing a consistently increasing number of private art foundations. This hypothesis derives both from an analysis of how customers' consumption attitudes have changed over the past few years and from an overview of luxury fashion brands strategies.[9] More specifically, it is possible to notice that today very wealthy people, or 'old rich' are no longer buying luxury products.[10] The majority of

1   S. Mendes and N. Rees-Roberts, 'New French Luxury: Art, Fashion and the Re-Invention of a National Brand', *Luxury*, vol. 2, no. 2, 2015, pp. 53–69; L. Crewe, 'Placing Fashion: Art, Space, Display and the Building of Luxury Fashion Markets Through Retail Design', *Progress in Human Geography*, vol. 40, no. 4, 2016, pp. 511–529; U. Lehmann, 'Art and Fashion', *Love to Know*, 15 March 2010 <http://fashion-history.lovetoknow.com/fashion-history-eras/art-fashion> (Accessed 3 February 2016).

2   H. Hagtvedt and V.M. Patrick, 'Art and the Brand: The Role of Visual Art in Enhancing Brand Extendibility', *Journal of Consumer Psychology*, vol. 18, no. 3, 2008, pp. 212–222.

3   Y. Lee, *A Study on the Application of Contemporary Visual Art into Flagship Stores of Luxury Fashion Brands* [Ph.D. dissertation], Brunel University School of Engineering and Design, 2014.

4   M. Oakley Smith and A. Kubler, *Art/Fashion in the 21st Century*, Thames & Hudson, London, 2013.

5   R. Stern, *Against Fashion: Clothing as Art, 1850–1930*, MIT, Cambridge, MA, 2004.

6   V. Steele, 'Museum Quality: The Rise of the Fashion Exhibition', *Fashion Theory: The Journal of Dress, Body & Culture*, vol. 12, no.1, 2008, pp. 7–30.

7   Mendes and Rees-Roberts, 'New French Luxury'.

8   Hagtvedt and Patrick, 'Art and the Brand'; Lee, *A Study on the Application of Contemporary Visual Art*.

9   C. D'Arpizio, F. Levato, D. Zito, and J. de Montgolfier, 'Luxury Goods Worldwide Market Study Fall-Winter 2014 – The Rise of the Borderless Consumer' [report], *Bain & Company* <http://www.bain.com/bainweb/PDFs/Bain_Worldwide_Luxury_Goods_Report_2014.pdf> (Accessed 7 January 2015); L. Solca, 'The Rich Don't Drive the Luxury Sector', *The Business of Fashion*, 26 January 2016 <https://www.businessoffashion.com/articles/opinion/the-rich-dont-drive-the-luxury-sector> (Accessed 25 May 2016).

10   Solca, 'The Rich Don't Drive the Luxury Sector'.

these products are bought by millennials, by the middle class, or by 'new rich' showing their new acquired capability in buying luxury.[11]

Diversification of a brand through products such as cosmetics, perfumes, underwear, and accessories is what generates the most of the profits.[12] Because of all these diversified products, brands are losing that characteristic of exclusivity that is considered particular of luxury brands.[13] On the contrary, previous studies have reported that fashion brands proximity with the arts enables the brands to be perceived as more luxurious.[14] In this scenario, this study hypothesis is that brands ownership of private art foundations is a mean for reconnecting with top customers, using public engagement strategies instead of more common marketing strategies. Indeed, needs and techniques might be slightly different, but the importance of communication and the attempt in involving people in a process and/or relationship can be considered as a shared characteristic between marketing and public engagement. This chapter is the first stage of a project that attempts to validate or confute the hypothesis that fashion private foundations are a marketing means only.

The main literature analysis can be divided into two stages: (i) the first is an exploration of fashion cultural initiatives' characteristics, locations, and programs; (ii) the second stage investigates the notions of luxury fashion brand and public engagement, looking at fashion private foundations as a point of conjunction between these two opposite concepts. Finally, interviews with experts in fashion and public engagement helped in defining these two concepts for the purpose of this study.

2   Private Art Foundations Related to Fashion

In the last 30 years, Western European luxury fashion brands have increased their investment in artistic initiatives. Table 3.1 shows a list of projects in which fashion brands are involved today.

---

11   Ibid.
12   D'Arpizio *et al.*, 'Luxury Goods Worldwide'.
13   I. Phau and G. Prendergast, 'Consuming Luxury Brands: The Relevance of the "Rarity Principle" ', *Journal of Brand Management*, vol. 8, no. 2, 2000, pp. 122–138; H. Pike, 'The Luxury Brand Balancing Act', *The Business of Fashion*, 18 January 2016 <https://www.businessoffashion.com/articles/intelligence/the-luxury-brand-balancing-act> (Accessed 20 January 2016).
14   Hagtvedt and Patrick, 'Art and the Brand'; Lee, *A Study on the Application of Contemporary Visual Art.*

TABLE 3.1   Fashion brands' cultural initiatives

Private art foundations (*long-term artistic programs*)	Art and cultural projects (*single project's sponsorship*)
Fondazione Alda Fendi	Bulgari for Trinità dei Monti
Fondazione Carla Fendi	Fendi for Fountains
Fondation Cartier pour l'Art Contemporain	Fendi for EUR
Fondation d'Enterprise Hermès	Gucci Museo
Fondazione Ferragamo	Museo Ferragamo
Fundación Loewe	Tod's for Colosseo
Fondation Louis Vuitton	
Fondazione Prada	
Fondazione Nicola Trussardi	
Fondazione Zegna	

Most of brands are claiming that their projects are 'dedicated to promoting and raising awareness of Contemporary Art',[15] or are 'contributing to the preservation of cultural heritage and values from the past, and to guarantee their continuity and future growth, primarily in the art',[16] and brands are claiming to be 'supporting contemporary artistic creation and making it accessible to as many people as possible'.[17] Interestingly, these projects have differences and similarities in their artistic programs, venues, and goals.

2.1   Artistic Programs

Most of the fashion private foundations are promoting contemporary art in three different ways: (i) owning a private collection, (ii) commissioning artistic works, and (iii) organising special exhibitions in collaboration with institutions, such as

---

15   'Introduction: An Original Approach to Corporate Patronage', *Fondation Cartier pour l'art contemporain* [official website] <https://www.fondationcartier.com/en/history-and-mission/philanthropy> (Accessed 27 May 2015).

16   'The Foundation: Mission', *Fondazione Carla Fendi* [official website] <http://fondazione-carlafendi.it/en/la-fondazione/mission/> (Accessed 15 October 2015).

17   'The Fondation Louis Vuitton: Art & Culture', *LVMH* [corporate website] <http://www.lvmh.com/group/lvmh-commitments/art-culture/fondation-louis-vuitton/> (Accessed 3 November 2014).

the Museum of Modern art in New York and the London National Gallery.[18] A different example of collaboration is brand's artist sponsorship, such as Yayoi Kusama's exhibition in 2012 at London Tate Modern, which was completely sponsored by the Louis Vuitton foundation.[19]

Finally, there are brands that are investing in artistic expressions different from fine art. Gucci, Prada, Carla Fendi and Alda Fendi are investing in cinema; Louis Vuitton and Cartier in music; Carla Fendi, Alda Fendi and Louis Vuitton are investing also in theatre; Loewe foundation invests in poetry, photography and design; finally, Ferragamo foundation invests in 'made in Italy' and craftsmanship.

2.2   *Exhibition Spaces*

Four fashion brands decided to create a new space for their art exhibitions: Louis Vuitton, Prada, Cartier and Gucci.[20] However, most of the analysed cultural initiatives have shown a strong relationship within the partner brands' hometowns, such as Paris, Milan, Rome, and Florence. A famous example is Maurizio Cattelan's exhibition *Psychological Lab in Real Life*, hosted in a Milan's square and sponsored by Trussardi: it was a shocking installation of three children hanging by their necks from an ancient oak tree.

Other examples of an existing relationship between brands and cities are: Fendi project of Fontana di Trevi refurbishment,[21] EUR building renewal in 2015 to host Fendi headquarters,[22] and Tod's investment in refurbishing

---

18   'List of exposed artworks', *Fondation Louis Vuitton* [official website] <http://www.fon-dationlouisvuitton.fr/en/expositions/listes-des-oeuvres-exposees.html> (Accessed 12 March 2015); H.U. Obrist, 'Avere Fame di Vento', *Fondazione Nicola Trussardi* [official website], February 2010 <http://www.fondazionenicolatrussardi.com/the_foundation/creation_of_temporary_events.html> (Accessed 10 April 2015); 'Tobias Rehberger: On Otto', *Fondazione Prada* [official website] <http://www.fondazioneprada.org/project/tobias-rehberger-on-otto/> (Accessed 15 May 2015).

19   'Louis Vuitton at Selfridges', *Akt II* [corporate website] <http://akt-uk.com/projects/louis%20vuitton%20at%20selfridges> (Accessed 2 February 2015).

20   'The Building', *Fondation Louis Vuitton* [official website] <http://www.fondationlouisvuitton.fr/en/l-edifice.html> (Accessed 3 November 2014); 'Milano', *Fondazione Prada* [official website] <http://www.fondazioneprada.org/visit/visit-milano/> (Accessed 25 May 2015); J. Cartner-Morley, 'The Museo Gucci Left Me Wanting More', *The Guardian*, 29 September 2011 <http://www.theguardian.com/fashion/fashion-blog/2011/sep/29/gucci-90-birthday-museum> (Accessed 12 November 2015).

21   'Fendi for Fountains', *Fendi* [corporate website] <http://www.fendi.com/it-en/the-magic-of-fendi/fountains> (Accessed 30 April 2015).

22   I. Amed, 'Fendi Opens New Headquarters, as Industry Mulls Simons' Exit from Dior', *The Business of Fashion*, 23 October 2015 <https://www.businessoffashion.com/articles/week-in-review/fendi-opens-new-headquarters-as-industry-mulls-simons-exit-from-dior> (Accessed 24 October 2015).

the Colosseo. Without doubt, brands have developed undeniable relationships with all these cities and municipalities to be able to organise such events. It is also true that investing a significant amount of money in such places give these brands privileged access to important historical sites: see Fendi's 90-year-anniversary fashion show at Fontana di Trevi.[23]

2.3   Secondary Educational Programmes

In the end, it is noteworthy that some of these artistic projects, such as Gucci, Vuitton, Prada, Hermès, and Cartier have set a detailed program for children and families. Examples are Fondazione Prada and Fondation d'Entreprise Hermès that aim to create 'multidisciplinary activities, not strictly connected with art exhibitions, but also cultural issues to be experienced through gameplay, creativity, learning and exchange'[24] and help children 'to flourish and acquire valuable skills in preparation for adult life'.[25] These ambitious statements are clearly indicating brands attempt to show a kind of cultural leadership and to be culturally inspiring. In summary, all these projects are arguably attempting to give a new *allure* to brands, but they are also bringing investments for cities, new jobs, a new attraction for tourists, and re-evaluating areas or buildings.

These paragraphs examined fashion cultural and artistic initiatives with the scope of understanding shared characteristics and differences between them. It is possible to define Prada, Cartier, and Louis Vuitton initiatives as similarly structured: they own a private collection and give the public access to it; they are commissioning artworks by established and emerging artists; and they are organising special exhibitions in collaboration with important institutions or private collectors. Moreover, these foundations are also dedicating specific venues to make their foundations accessible. Arguably, this makes these foundations even more similar to museums and for this reason an interesting intersection between a luxury fashion brand and public engagement, between exclusivity and inclusivity.

The next sections provide an overview of the existing literature on the meaning of luxury fashion brand and public engagement, with regards to aspects that are relevant for the purpose of this chapter.

---

23   F. Sinclair Scott, 'Kendall Walked on Water in Karl Lagerfeld and Fendi's Celebration of 90 Years in Rome', *CNN*, 15 August 2016 <http://edition.cnn.com/2016/07/20/fashion/fendi-historical-couture-show-trevi-fountain/index.html> (Accessed 23 August 2016).

24   'Accademia dei Bambini', *Fondazione Prada* [official website] <http://www.fondazione-prada.org/accademia-dei-bambini-en/?lang=en> (Accessed 2 June 2015).

25   'Fondation d' Entreprise Hermès Activity Report April 2008–April 2013' [report], *Fondation d'Entreprise Hermès* [official website] <https://slidex.tips/download/fondation-d-entreprise-hermes-activity-report-april-april-2013> (Accessed 12 February 2018), p.135.

3   Definition of Luxury Fashion Brand

To date, there is no overarching consensus in defining what a luxury fashion brand is.[26] First, it is apparently difficult to identify characteristic aspects belonging to fashion brands only.[27] Second, many fast changes are continually occurring in the fashion industry making it hard to understand what is considered as luxury and why.[28] Third, the large range of goods produced, such as accessories, cosmetics, clothes *etc.*, generates confusion with regards to what are defined as fashion products.[29] Lastly, there is a persistent difficulty in understanding what luxury means.[30] Nevertheless, luxury fashion scholars agree that identifying distinctive key factors might help in finding a unanimously agreed definition.[31]

Some of the most cited key factors are: clear brand identity, marketing communication, icon items, high quality of product and craftsmanship,[32] global reputation, premium price, high visibility, innovative and unique products,[33] exclusivity.[34] Yet, there are two main issues related to these factors. First, they are not exclusively characteristics of fashion, but they are factors generally identifiable in all luxury goods. Second, these key aspects are mostly subjective perceptions in customers' mind than a physical aspect,[35] as well as the very concept of luxury is considerable as merely subjective.[36]

Of all the aforementioned factors, arguably the most susceptible of subjectivity is the concept of exclusivity. Indeed, luxury brands aim to sell every year a broader portfolio of products,[37] in order to earn the highest

---

26   A.M. Fionda and C.M. Moore, 'The Anatomy of the Luxury Fashion Brand', *Journal of Brand Management*, vol. 16, no. 5–6, 2009, pp. 347–363; J. Kapferer, 'Why Are We Seduced by Luxury Brands?', *Journal of Brand Management*, vol. 6, no.1, 1998, pp. 44–49.

27   K.W. Miller and M.K. Mills, 'Contributing Clarity by Examining Brand Luxury in the Fashion Market', *Journal of Business Research*, vol. 65, no. 10, 2012, pp. 1471–1479.

28   Kapferer, 'Why Are We Seduced by Luxury Brands?'.

29   D'Arpizio *et al.*, 'Luxury Goods Worldwide'.

30   C. Kovesi, 'What Is Luxury? – The Rebirth of a Concept in the Early Modern World', *Luxury*, vol. 2, no. 1, 2015, pp. 25–40.

31   U. Okonkwo, *Luxury Fashion Branding: Trends, Tactics, Techniques*, Palgrave Macmillan Ltd., Basingstoke, 2007; Fionda and Moore, 'The Anatomy of the Luxury Fashion Brand'.

32   Fionda and Moore, 'The Anatomy of the Luxury Fashion Brand'.

33   Okonkwo, *Luxury Fashion Branding*.

34   Phau and Prendergast, 'Consuming Luxury Brands'.

35   J.L. Nueno and J.A. Quelch, *The Mass Marketing of Luxury*, Elsevier Inc., Greenwich, 1998.

36   F. Vigneron and L.W. Johnson, 'Measuring Perceptions of Brand Luxury', *Journal of Brand Management*, vol. 11, no. 6, 2004, pp. 484–506.

37   D'Arpizio *et al.*, 'Luxury Goods Worldwide'.

revenue. However, at the same time, they also want to maintain the idea of scarcity and exclusivity of their products.[38] Therefore, to maintain this illusion of exclusivity, brands apply a peculiar strategy.[39] They exploit the most sophisticated marketing techniques to increase awareness of their brand in potential customers.[40] Simultaneously, they keep tightly controlled the distribution of their product through, for example, limited editions.[41] This generates a high desire for the product, and the idea that it is just for an elite. Exclusivity is just an example of subjective perceptions generated in people's minds that lead luxury fashion brands to be considered as luxurious.

After literature analysis and interviews with experts in fashion and luxury fields, a definition of 'luxury fashion brand' was generated for the purpose of this chapter and it is provided in the findings section.

4 Definition of Public Engagement in Contemporary Art

The main aim of public engagement should be to facilitate conversations regarding an understanding of the arts, avoiding any sort of power structure that could complicate any sharing of knowledge. Therefore, defining people involved in the process 'professional' (or 'specialist') and 'non-professional' (or 'not specialist')[42] can be arguably wrong. Indeed, not only 'professionals' produce art, and not only 'non-professionals' are part of the audience in exhibitions. For the purpose of this chapter a 'producer' of art is defined as any figure, such as artist, curator, museum or art gallery director, that is delivering artwork to a 'receiver', that is considered as any kind of audience for this artwork. Referring to people involved in public engagement process as 'receiver' and 'producer' of art is important for three reasons.

---

38   Phau and Prendergast, 'Consuming Luxury Brands'.

39   A. Radon, 'Luxury Brand Exclusivity Strategies – An Illustration of a Cultural Collaboration', *Journal of Business Administration Research*, vol. 1, no. 1, 2012, pp. 106–110.

40   R. Huang and E. Sarigollu, 'How Brand Awareness Relates to Market Outcome, Brand Equity, and the Marketing Mix', *Journal of Business Research*, vol. 65, no. 1, 2012, pp. 92–99.

41   K. Heine, 'The Personality of Luxury Fashion Brands', *Journal of Global Fashion Marketing*, vol. 1, no. 3, 2010, pp. 154–163; Radon, 'Luxury Brand Exclusivity Strategies'.

42   'What is Public Engagement?', *National Co-ordinating Centre for Public Engagement* <https://www.publicengagement.ac.uk/explore-it/what-public-engagement> (Accessed 15 February 2016).

First, scholars in defining public engagement often used terms as 'specialist' (or 'professional') and 'not specialist' (or 'not professional').[43] Yet, an artist, a curator or a museum director can be part of the audience; the fact that his/her work is related to the arts is not a reason to not engage with him/her. Second, using terms such as 'receiver' and 'producer' helps in investigating literature examples of public engagement, and allows to notice that in most of the studies it is not clear who is involved in the process,[44] who receives benefits[45] and what kind of benefits they receive.[46] As a consequence, 'receiver' and 'producer' were chosen as terms for this chapter definition in the attempt to avoid generation and/or recognition of power structures.

Indeed, to ensure that the aforementioned conversation occurs between equals, it is important to avoid any conscious or unconscious generation of hierarchies, and this also using appropriate terms. In the spirit of creating this peer-to-peer sharing of knowledge, there are three factors that need to be present together: (i) two-way conversation; (ii) the aim of co-producing benefits and/or improving existing situations; (iii) active participation of both 'receiver' and 'producer'.

Examples of literature show that there is no public engagement when one of the aforementioned factors is missing. There are projects generating improvement in older adults' health,[47] or feeling of social inclusion, or acquisition of new work skills.[48] However, all these benefits refer to 'receivers' and not to the 'producer'. It is clear that the lack of two-way conversation questioned the existence of co-production, and also the active participation of producer. In the above examples, there is both audience interaction and people involvement, but they do not represent public engagement. Instead, an example of public engagement can be considered in the 'studio as laboratory'

43   The Carnegie Foundation for the Advancement of Teaching, 'Definition of Engagement and Partnership', *Northern Illinois University* [official website] <http://www.niu.edu/outreach/documents/Definitions%20of%20Engagement/Carnegie%20-%20Definitions%20of%20Engagement%20and%20Partneships.pdf. > (Accessed 15 February 2016).

44   S.S. Lowe, 'Creating Community: Art for Community Development', *Journal of Contemporary Ethnography*, vol. 29, no. 3, 2000, pp. 357–386.

45   A. Kay, 'Art and Community Development: The Role the Arts Have in Regenerating Communities', *Community Development Journal*, vol. 35, no. 4, 2000, pp. 414–424.

46   S. Warren, 'Audiencing James Turrell's Skyspace: Encounters between Art and Audience at Yorkshire Sculpture Park', *Cultural Geographies*, vol. 20, no. 1, 2013, pp. 83–102.

47   A. Phinney, E.M. Moody, and J. A. Small, 'The Effect of a Community-Engaged Arts Program on Older Adults' Well-Being', *Canadian Journal on Aging*, vol. 33, no. 3, 2014, pp. 336–345.

48   E. Belfiore, 'Art as a Means of Alleviating Social Exclusion: Does it Really Work? A Critique of Instrumental Cultural Policies and Social Impact Studies in the UK', *International Journal of Cultural Policy*, vol. 8, no. 1, 2002, pp. 91–106.

project[49] that generates communication and benefits for the audience, the artist and the curator. Another example of public engagement might also be a well-thought use of social media.

After literature analysis and interviews with experts in museums and public engagement, a definition of public engagement was generated for the purpose of this chapter and it is provided in the findings section.

5 Methodology

To better understand what public engagement and luxury fashion brand are, a series of unstructured interviews were conducted. A list of contacts was built by scoping the Internet and via other professional networks. This list included: experts in fashion, such as magazine editors, brand employees, academic journal editors and British Fashion Council employees; experts in public engagement, such as museums and galleries employees, fashion brands private foundations employees, and members of the National Co-ordinating Centre for Public Engagement. Of all the contacted people, four were interviewed and one via email. Some of these contacts might be considered as experts in both fields. A compare and contrast approach was adopted considering it the most suitable for interview analysis because of content's similarities.

6 Findings

The main findings of this chapter are two definitions: (i) what a luxury fashion brand is, and (ii) what public engagement is. As explained in the review of the literature, these two concepts have been defined differently by several researchers, and none of the existing definitions suited this chapter. For this reason, it was considered fundamental elaborating new definitions. They were discussed with experts in a sort of co-productive environment. These definitions are a starting point for further study development in understanding how exclusivity of luxury and inclusivity of public engagement might coexist in fashion brands' private foundations.

With regards to defining what a luxury brand is, there were some key points highlighted in all of the interviews. First is that a luxury brand is to be associated with high status. Second, the idea that the product, the packaging, the

---

49   E. Edmonds, L. Muller, and M. Connell, 'On Creative Engagement', *Visual Communication*, vol. 5, no. 3, 2006, pp. 307–322.

training of the staff, everything is traditional and coherent with the characteristic of the brand, and this makes everything to be perceived as exclusive and luxurious. The brand can innovate, sell online, advertise digitally, but then what a brick-and-mortar store can give to the consumer is irreplaceable. The experience that it is possible to enjoy walking into a flagship store is different. The brand is sending specific messages to the consumer, even through the appearance of its trained staff. Moreover, a luxury product is to be considered as an investment not only for money, but also for the people to be perceived as being someone else, or someone who can afford that statement piece.

A respondent interestingly said: 'the luxury product is not just the product. People buy luxury because of what the brand represents or because it makes them feel more confident and secure'. A second interviewee stated:

> I did an event once for Dolce and Gabbana [...] they spend a lot of time doing research and efforts to get the 'click', it was like a little powder thing. [...] it was a very specific click. The reference that was used was: when you shut the car door on a Mercedes, BMW or an Audi, it's a certain type of noise; a certain type of click. And that's what they really invested in.

As the result of the described co-productive and stimulating conversations, hereafter is the luxury fashion brand definition for this chapter. A luxury fashion brand is a brand that, using marketing and communication strategies based on storytelling and brand heritage, is able to evoke the idea of exclusivity, high quality, craftsmanship and a distinctive brand image in customers' minds, even when these elements are subjective.

With regards to public engagement, when asked what public engagement is, most of the respondents gave similar answers based on a few key themes. Public engagement should be a medium to involve as many people as possible in a conversation, an interaction with something that has always been considered for an elite, the art. Another common answer was that engagement should involve education activities. Finally, the main aspect of public engagement should be that it aims at generating personal development and in creating well-being. As interestingly highlighted by an interviewee: 'at the heart of engagement we're looking at social, so looking for new connections, finding new ways to interact with new people, developing yourself'.

Hereafter the definition of public engagement derived by the aforementioned conversations. Public engagement is the involvement, participation and interaction between one 'producer' of art and one (or a group of) 'receiver/s' of art in a two-way conversation for co-producing benefits and/or improving a situation.

7   Conclusion

In conclusion, some luxury fashion brands are shifting their effort from fashion production to art investments, and the reason behind these investments is still to be determined. However, fashion brands proximity with the arts enables the brands to be perceived as more luxurious.[50] From this perspective, at a very first stage of this study, the main assumption is that opening of private art foundations by luxury fashion brands is a new way to generate a higher level of associated luxury, by associating seminal works of art with a fashion brand image and identity. It is in this context that brands are also enhancing their marketing strategies with public engagement strategies in contemporary art. Indeed, both marketing strategies in fashion and strategies in public engagement with art aim to generate relationships with the audience/customers and make inclusive something that by nature is considered exclusive.

Arguably, public engagement is the name these brands are giving to their new marketing plans and private art foundations are their new means to generate a new level of luxury for their top customers. Further developments will require a deeper analysis of fashion brands' foundations, how being a luxury fashion brand is influencing their public, what brands' customers think of brands' investments in art, and how this is influencing their consumption attitudes.

Bibliography

'Accademia dei Bambini', *Fondazione Prada* [official website] <http://www.fondazioneprada.org/accademia-dei-bambini-en/?lang=en> (Accessed 2 June 2015).

Amed, I., 'Fendi Opens New Headquarters, as Industry Mulls Simons' Exit from Dior', *The Business of Fashion*, 23 October 2015 <https://www.businessoffashion.com/articles/week-in-review/fendi-opens-new-headquarters-as-industry-mulls-simons-exit-from-dior> (Accessed 24 October 2015).

Belfiore, E., 'Art as a Means of Alleviating Social Exclusion: Does it Really Work? A Critique of Instrumental Cultural Policies and Social Impact Studies in the UK', *International Journal of Cultural Policy*, vol. 8, no. 1, 2002, pp. 91–106.

Cartner-Morley, J., 'The Museo Gucci Left Me Wanting More', *The Guardian*, 29 September 2011 <http://www.theguardian.com/fashion/fashion-blog/2011/sep/29/gucci-90-birthday-museum> (Accessed 12 November 2015).

---

50   Hagtvedt and Patrick, 'Art and the Brand'; Lee, *A Study on the Application of Contemporary Visual Art.*

Crewe, L., 'Placing Fashion: Art, Space, Display and the Building of Luxury Fashion Markets Through Retail Design', *Progress in Human Geography*, vol. 40, no. 4, 2016, pp. 511–529.

D'Arpizio, C., F. Levato, D. Zito, and J. de Montgolfier, 'Luxury Goods Worldwide Market Study Fall-Winter 2014 – The Rise of the Borderless Consumer' [report], *Bain & Company* <http://www.bain.com/bainweb/PDFs/Bain_Worldwide_Luxury_Goods_Report_2014.pdf> (Accessed 7 January 2015).

Edmonds, E., L. Muller, and M. Connell, 'On Creative Engagement', *Visual Communication*, vol. 5, no. 3, 2006, pp. 307–322.

'Fendi for Fountains', *Fendi* [corporate website] <http://www.fendi.com/it-en/the-magic-of-fendi/fountains> (Accessed 30 April 2015).

Fionda, A.M., and C.M. Moore, 'The Anatomy of the Luxury Fashion Brand', *Journal of Brand Management*, vol. 16, no. 5–6, 2009, pp. 347–363.

'Fondation d'Entreprise Hermès Activity Report April 2008–April 2013' [report], *Fondation d'Entreprise Hermès* [official website] <https://slidex.tips/download/fondation-d-entreprise-hermes-activity-report-april-april-2013> (Accessed 12 February 2018).

Hagtvedt, H., and V.M. Patrick, 'Art and the Brand: The Role of Visual Art in Enhancing Brand Extendibility', *Journal of Consumer Psychology*, vol. 18, no. 3, 2008, pp. 212–222.

Heine, K., 'The Personality of Luxury Fashion Brands', *Journal of Global Fashion Marketing*, vol. 1, no. 3, 2010, pp. 154–163.

Huang, R., and E. Sarigollu, 'How Brand Awareness Relates to Market Outcome, Brand Equity, and the Marketing Mix', *Journal of Business Research*, vol. 65, no. 1, 2012, pp. 92–99.

'Introduction: An Original Approach to Corporate Patronage', *Fondation Cartier pour l'art contemporain* [official website] <https://www.fondationcartier.com/en/history-and-mission/philanthropy> (Accessed 27 May 2015).

Kapferer, J., 'Why Are We Seduced by Luxury Brands?', *Journal of Brand Management*, vol. 6, no.1, 1998, pp. 44–49.

Kay, A., 'Art and Community Development: The Role the Arts Have in Regenerating Communities', *Community Development Journal*, vol. 35, no. 4, 2000, pp. 414–424.

Kovesi, C., 'What Is Luxury? – The Rebirth of a Concept in the Early Modern World', *Luxury*, vol. 2, no. 1, 2015, pp. 25–40.

Lee, Y., *A Study on the Application of Contemporary Visual Art into Flagship Stores of Luxury Fashion Brands* [Ph.D. dissertation], Brunel University School of Engineering and Design, 2014.

Lehmann, U., 'Art and Fashion', *Love to Know*, 15 March 2010 <http://fashion-history.lovetoknow.com/fashion-history-eras/art-fashion> (Accessed 3 February 2016).

'List of exposed artworks', *Fondation Louis Vuitton* [official website] <http://www.fondationlouisvuitton.fr/en/expositions/listes-des-oeuvres-exposees.html> (Accessed 12 March 2015).

'Louis Vuitton at Selfridges', *Akt II* [corporate website] <http://akt-uk.com/projects/louis%20vuitton%20at%20selfridges> (Accessed 2 February 2015).

Lowe, S.S., 'Creating Community: Art for Community Development', *Journal of Contemporary Ethnography*, vol. 29, no. 3, 2000, pp. 357–386.

Mendes, S., and N. Rees-Roberts, 'New French Luxury: Art, Fashion and the Re-Invention of a National Brand', *Luxury*, vol. 2, no. 2, 2015, pp. 53–69.

'Milano', *Fondazione Prada* [official website] <http://www.fondazioneprada.org/visit/visit-milano/> (Accessed 25 May 2015).

Miller, K.W., and M.K. Mills, 'Contributing Clarity by Examining Brand Luxury in the Fashion Market', *Journal of Business Research*, vol. 65, no. 10, 2012, pp.1471–1479.

Nueno, J.L., and J.A. Quelch, *The Mass Marketing of Luxury*. Elsevier Inc., Greenwich, 1998.

Oakley Smith, M., and A. Kubler, *Art/Fashion in the 21st Century*. Thames & Hudson, London, 2013.

Obrist, H.U., 'Avere Fame di Vento', *Fondazione Nicola Trussardi* [official website], February 2010 <http://www.fondazionenicolatrussardi.com/the_foundation/creation_of_temporary_events.html> (Accessed 10 April 2015).

Okonkwo, U., *Luxury Fashion Branding: Trends, Tactics, Techniques*. Palgrave Macmillan Ltd., Basingstoke, 2007.

Phau, I., and G. Prendergast, 'Consuming Luxury Brands: The Relevance of the "Rarity Principle"', *Journal of Brand Management*, vol. 8, no. 2, 2000, pp.122–138.

Phinney, A., E.M. Moody, and J.A. Small, 'The Effect of a Community-Engaged Arts Program on Older Adults' Well-Being', *Canadian Journal on Aging*, vol. 33, no. 3, 2014, pp. 336–345.

Pike, H., 'The Luxury Brand Balancing Act', *The Business of Fashion*, 18 January 2016 <https://www.businessoffashion.com/articles/intelligence/the-luxury-brand-balancing-act> (Accessed 20 January 2016).

Radon, A., 'Luxury Brand Exclusivity Strategies – An Illustration of a Cultural Collaboration', *Journal of Business Administration Research*, vol. 1, no. 1, 2012, pp.106–110.

Sinclair S. F., 'Kendall Walked on Water in Karl Lagerfeld and Fendi's Celebration of 90 Years in Rome', *CNN*, 15 August 2016 <http://edition.cnn.com/2016/07/20/fashion/fendi-historical-couture-show-trevi-fountain/index.html> (Accessed 23 August 2016).

Solca, L., 'The Rich Don't Drive the Luxury Sector', *The Business of Fashion*, 26 January 2016 <https://www.businessoffashion.com/articles/opinion/the-rich-dont-drive-the-luxury-sector> (Accessed 25 May 2016).

Steele, V., 'Museum Quality: The Rise of the Fashion Exhibition', *Fashion Theory: The Journal of Dress, Body & Culture*, vol. 12, no. 1, 2008, pp. 7–30.

Stern, R., *Against Fashion: Clothing as Art, 1850–1930*. MIT, Cambridge, MA, 2004.

'The Building', *Fondation Louis Vuitton* [official website] <http://www.fondationlouis-vuitton.fr/en/l-edifice.html> (Accessed 3 November 2014).

The Carnegie Foundation for the Advancement of Teaching, 'Definition of Engagement and Partnership', *Northern Illinois University* [official website] <http://www.niu.edu/outreach/documents/Definitions%20of%20Engagement/Carnegie%20-%20Definitions%20of%20Engagement%20and%20Partneships.pdf.> (Accessed 15 February 2016).

'The Foundation: Mission', *Fondazione Carla Fendi* [official website] <http://fondazionecarlafendi.it/en/la-fondazione/mission/> (Accessed 15 October 2015).

'The Fondation Louis Vuitton: Art & Culture', *LVMH* [corporate website] <http://www.lvmh.com/group/lvmh-commitments/art-culture/fondation-louis-vuitton/> (Accessed 3 November 2014).

'Tobias Rehberger: On Otto', *Fondazione Prada* [official website] <http://www.fondazioneprada.org/project/tobias-rehberger-on-otto/> (Accessed 15 May 2015).

Vigneron, F., and L.W. Johnson, 'Measuring Perceptions of Brand Luxury', *Journal of Brand Management*, vol. 11, no. 6, 2004, pp. 484–506.

Warren, S., 'Audiencing James Turrell's Skyspace: Encounters between Art and Audience at Yorkshire Sculpture Park', *Cultural Geographies*, vol. 20, no. 1, 2013, pp. 83–102.

'What is Public Engagement?', *National Co-ordinating Centre for Public Engagement* <https://www.publicengagement.ac.uk/explore-it/what-public-engagement> (Accessed 15 February 2016).

PART 2

Consuming

∴

CHAPTER 4

Ethical and Sustainable Luxury: The Paradox of Consumerism and Caring

Deidra W. Arrington

Abstract

The exposure of the dark underbelly of fashion sheds light on the ethical dilemma of manufacturing and consuming apparel. Tragedy caused by deplorable working conditions and human exploitation is as much a part of the fashion landscape as textiles and garments. What lessons were learned after the 1911 Triangle Shirtwaist fire killed 145 workers in New York City?[1] Not many, based on the 2013 Rana Plaza collapse where 1,134 factory workers died.[2] Over 100 years after the Triangle fire and the fashion industry's failure to provide measures ensuring safety and the ethical treatment of workers continues. The environment also suffers from the absence of sustainable and renewable resources in the production of fashion. Twenty per cent of global industrial water pollution comes from the treatment and dyeing of textiles.[3] Water usage, the destruction of the rain forests, bulging landfills, and toxic chemicals are incalculably detrimental to the environment, yet the fashion industry lags woefully behind in creating sustainable solutions. The root of the fashion industry's ethical problems is consumer demand for more goods at every price point, including the luxury sector. Yet, many consumers believe they purchase fashion responsibly. In *The Ethical Consumer Report* (*2015*), 70 per cent of consumers said their purchasing decisions are influenced by ethics. However, a mere 23 per cent are 'often or always' influenced by ethics.[4] 'It is well known consumers saying they want ethical products does not necessarily translate

1   H. Kosak, 'Triangle Shirtwaist Fire', *Jewish Women's Archive*, 20 March 2009 <http://jwa.org/encyclopedia/article/triangle-shirtwaist-fire> (Accessed 1 August 2016).

2   K. Abnett, 'Three Years After Rana Plaza, Has Anything Changed?', *The Business of Fashion*, 19 April 2016 <https://www.businessoffashion.com/articles/intelligence/three-years-... rana-plaza-has-anything-changed-sustainability-safety-workers-welfare> (Accessed 5 August 2016).

3   D. Maxwell, L. McAndrew, and J. Ryan, 'The State of the Apparel Sector Report – Water' [report], *Glasaaward.com*, 2015 <https://glasaaward.org/wp-content/uploads/2015/05/GLASA_2015_StateofApparelSector_SpecialReport_Water_150624.pdf> (Accessed 3 March 2016).

4   L. Bonetto, 'The Ethical Consumer' [report], *Mintel Group*, July 2015 <http://academic.mintel.com.proxy.library.vcu.edu/display/716584/> (Accessed 4 April 2016).

into greater sales'.[5] Therein lies the rub, consumers say they care, but they do not purchase like they care. The paradox of consumerism and caring is real.

Keywords

ethics – consumerism – corporate responsibility – sustainability – human rights

1   Introduction

> The clothing we choose to wear everyday has an enormous impact on the planet and its people. Our clothing can either continue to be a major part of the problem, or it can be an enormous part of getting our planet on track. The choice is ultimately ours.[6]
>
>   MAXINE BEDAT, CEO, ZADY

The exposure of the dark underbelly of fashion sheds light on the social responsibility dilemma of manufacturing and consuming apparel. Social responsibility means a company is ethical to all its constituents, philanthropic and charitable and environmentally friendly. Deplorable working conditions and worker exploitation remains as much a part of the fashion landscape as the garments and accessories produced. The environment continues to suffer from the lack of sustainable and renewable resources in the production of fashion. From the amount of water used to the chemicals needed to the destruction of natural resources, fashion is woefully slow to make changes to improve its impact on the environment.

Why, after so many years, are human and environmental issues still part of the fashion production conversation? The answer lies in consumer demand. Consumers want a lot of choices at cheap prices and manufacturers cut corners and make decisions, which provide what the consumer demands. After all, manufacturers are in business to make a profit, often regardless of what is best for the worker and the environment. Are consumers bad people? No, in fact 70 per cent of consumers perceive themselves to be ethical decision

---

5   Ibid.
6   J. Conca, 'Making Climate Change Fashionable – The Garment Industry Takes on Global Warming', *Forbes*, 3 December 2015 <http://www.forbes.com/sites/jamesconca/2015/12/03/making-climate-change-fashionable-the-garment-industry-takes-on-global-warming/#389f6849778a> (Accessed 5 August 2016).

makers. If this is the case, why are conversations about sustainability and ethics still needed in fashion? Because consumers say they care, but they do not purchase like they care. The paradox of consumerism and caring is real.

2 The Triangle Shirtwaist Factory and Rana Plaza

One of the worst industrial disasters in New York City history was the 1911 Triangle Shirtwaist Fire that killed 146 workers, most of whom were immigrant Jewish and Italian, non-English speaking women aged between 16–23 years. The factory workers were subjected to appalling working conditions and were often locked in the factory without breaks, food, or fresh air. The fire started when someone dropped a cigarette into a bin of scrap fabric. With emergency exits locked, many workers were trapped while others jumped from the building or down the elevator shaft seeking safety. The owners of the Triangle Shirtwaist Factory were tried for first and second-degree manslaughter and acquitted. They later collected insurance money and reopened the factory.[7] The fire shed light on the garment worker and factory conditions, which started regulation of the garment industry.

In 2013, Rana Plaza (Bangladesh) housed five garment factories. Additional floors added to the building, intended for office and retail space, were used for factories. The building collapsed from the illegally built floors, killing 1,134 workers. The disaster was another vivid demonstration of the grim working conditions garment workers all over the world are subjected to and a harrowing reminder the regulations and reforms of the past are inadequate. Rana Plaza was the worst industrial disaster in Bangladesh's history. Murder charges were filed against 41 people, including the factory owners, for their roles in the building's collapse.[8]

The Rana Plaza disaster is one of several in Bangladesh in recent years. In 2012, less than a year prior to the Rana Plaza collapse, a fire at the Tazreen Fashion factory killed 117 people.[9] As recently as February 2016, a fire in a Bangladeshi sweater factory injured four.[10] Significant casualties were

---

7   Kosak, 'Triangle Shirtwaist Fire'.

8   Associated Press in Dhaka, 'Rana Plaza Collapse: Dozens Charged with Murder', *The Guardian*, 1 June 2015 <http://www.theguardian.com/world/2015/jun/01/rana-plaza-collapse-dozens-charged-with-murder-bangladesh> (Accessed 4 April 2016).

9   C. Stangler, 'Major Fire at Bangladesh Sweater Factory Raises Questions About Continuing Safety Improvements', *International Business Times*, 2 February 2016 <http://www.ibtimes.com/major-fire-bangladesh-sweater-factory-raises-questions-about-continuing-safety-2290608> (Accessed 8 August 2016).

10   Ibid.

avoided due to the time the fire started. The death, injury and destruction occurring in Bangladeshi factories is not enough for factory owners to complete safety renovations and eliminate fire hazards, in some cases years after inspections.[11]

The garment industry contributes $26 billion to Bangladesh's economy, which equates to 80 per cent of its exports and four million jobs in 5,400 garment factories. Bangladesh is second to China as a supplier of apparel to Western countries. Furthermore, foreign direct investment rose to $42.5 billion in 2014 from $448 million 10 years prior. The recent tragedies are cause for concern foreign investment will be reduced and further aggravate and complicate the problems in Bangladesh's garment industry.[12]

3   Sustainability

Fashion is responsible for massive pollution, second only to oil, and accounts for ten per cent of global carbon emissions.[13] Historic levels of shopping feed the endless production. Americans buy five times more apparel today than they did in 1980,[14] contributing almost a third of the global total.[15] It takes 2,700 litres of water to grow the cotton to produce one t-shirt[16] and 70 billion barrels of oil to produce the world's polyester fibres, the most commonly used fibre in apparel, which takes 200 years to decompose.[17] Twenty-five per cent of chemicals produced worldwide are used for textiles then dumped into the environment; garment production is packing quite the environmental impact. But it does not end there, clothing is produced and purchased and thrown away amounting to 10.5 million tons of clothing tossed in landfills each year.[18]

Complete transparency in the supply chain is the foundation for a sustainable and ethical fashion industry. Zady, an e-commerce store specializing in sustainable goods, provides 'traceability', or details about the production of

11   Ibid.
12   R. Chandran, 'Dhaka Attack Deals Blow to Improvements in Post Rana Plaza Garment Industry', *Thomas Reuters Foundation News*, 5 July 2016 <http://news.trust.org/item/20160705124925-lauux/> (Accessed 5 August 2016).
13   Conca, 'Making Climate Change Fashionable'.
14   Abnett, 'Three Years After Rana Plaza, Has Anything Changed?'.
15   Conca, 'Making Climate Change Fashionable'.
16   Abnett, 'Three Years After Rana Plaza, Has Anything Changed?'.
17   Conca, 'Making Climate Change Fashionable'.
18   Abnett, 'Three Years After Rana Plaza, Has Anything Changed?'.

every item it sells.[19] Nike's revolutionary Flyknit changed the way athletic shoes are produced. The shoe's uppers are knitted from individual strands of yarn, which produces 60 per cent less waste than the traditional cut-and-sew process of shoe production. Since 2012, the knitting of shoe uppers has saved 3.5 million pounds of waste and in the process created a billion dollar business, proving it is possible to be sustainable and profitable simultaneously.[20]

Few companies view meeting environmental impact standards as a metric for performance and until they do so, nothing much will change.[21] However, there are companies such as Renewcell, Lenzing, and Evrnu making great strides in recycled fibre.[22] Likewise, Zady is leading the charge for 'slow fashion' by providing resources for consumers to learn how what they buy impacts the environment.[23] Hannah Jones of Nike, Inc. suggests rapid change will occur only with 'a single code of conduct, common monitoring protocols and auditing standards for the industry'.[24] The luxury industry saw improvements in 2015, when investors began to demand financial performance combined with a company's environmental and social performance. Additionally, in 2015 world leaders and governments launched 'Sustainability Development Goals' and the 'Modern Slavery Act', which legally obligates companies to be responsible global citizens.[25] Move over bottom line, there is a new metric in town!

4 Ethical Issues – Making a Difference

Fashion is a three trillion dollar industry annually driven in large part by low prices and availability. Behind the veil of low prices and plentiful selection lies the ugly truth about filling closets with more clothes, accessories, and shoes. The plethora of stores offering cheap apparel has changed the way consumers perceive value. As retail prices tumble, materials prices rise and the only way

19   E. Farra, '3 Designers Who Are Making It Easy (and Chic!) to Shop Sustainable', *Vogue*, 8 April 2016 <http://www.vogue.com/13424418/best-sustainable-fashion-designers-zady-datura-plyknits/> (Accessed 5 August 2016).

20   L. Guilbault, 'Future of Sustainablility Shapes Up at Copenhagen Fashion Summit', *WWD*, 14 May 2016 <http://wwd.com/fashion-news/fashion-features/sustainability-copenhagen-fashion-summit-10429848/> (Accessed 30 May 16).

21   Abnett, 'Three Years After Rana Plaza, Has Anything Changed?'.

22   Ibid.

23   Conca, 'Making Climate Change Fashionable'.

24   Guilbault, 'Future of Sustainablility Shapes Up'.

25   J. Tutty, '2016 Predictions for the Luxury Industry: Sustainability and Innovation' [executive summary], *The Positive Guide*, 20 January 2016 <http://blog.positiveluxury.com/2016/01/2016-predictions-luxury-world-sustainability-innovation/> (Accessed 7 April 2016).

to achieve the unachievable is by paying the garment worker less, especially in Bangladesh where workers earn roughly half of Chinese workers, about 58 cents for sewing a garment, which retails for $14.[26] 'Only 2 percent of apparel companies source from companies that pay their workers a fair and living wage', Shannon Whitehead, *The Huffington Post*.[27] Workers are vulnerable and factory owners take advantage of the power they have over wages and therefore the workers.[28] The entire industry is challenged with fair wages, working hours, forced confinement, child labour, and safety for over 10 million people working in the industry. The social implication of these issues is immeasurable. There are companies within the industry working to make a difference; however, the solution begins with consumers.

Social issues and awareness has been part of the retailing landscape for years. Recently, the term 'Lux-Anthropy', meaning when one purchases an expensive item with a positive impact on mankind, was coined.[29] Who better than the rich to buy products making a difference in the world? Not so fast, only 39 per cent of consumers earning more than $150,000 are willing to spend more for ethical products. The paradox is about 45 per cent of wealthy consumers report seeking out ethical brands.[30] The luxury consumer is very vocal about social and environmental issues and they are willing and able to make their concerns a priority with the way they purchase.

Likewise, investors in luxury companies are interested in a how a brand approaches sustainability and social issues. PETA U.S. purchased shares in Hermès and Prada to exert influence over the brand's use of exotic animal skins.[31] It is a clever approach, which gives PETA the right to speak out at shareholder meetings. However, PETA will have to continue to buy shares to exert any real power.[32]

---

26   R. Dalton, 'A T-Shirt Should Never Cost $10, Time to End the Fast Fashion Mentality', *Catalogue*, 2016 <https://www.cataloguemagazine.com.au/feature/a-t-shirt-should-never-cost-10-time-to-end-the-fast-fashion-mentality> (Accessed 5 August 2016).

27   V. Vij, 'Luxury Brands Putting More Weight Into Sustainability', *Justmeans*, 18 February 2016 <http://www.justmeans.com/blogs/luxury-brands-putting-more-weight-into-sustainability> (Accessed 7 April 2016).

28   Dalton, 'A T-Shirt Should Never Cost $10'.

29   R. Frank, 'Wealthy Shoppers Don't Buy into Lux-Anthropy', *CNBC*, 27 June 2012 <http://www.cnbc.com/id/47979078> (Accessed 7 April 2016).

30   Ibid.

31   J. Diderich, 'PETA Confronts Hermes CEO Over Exotic Skins', *WWD*, 31 May 2016 <http://wwd.com/fashion-news/designer-luxury/peta-confronts-hermes-ceo-exotic-skins-10439851/> (Accessed 27 July 2016).

32   L. Zargani, 'PETA Invests in Prada to Protest Ostrich-Skin Products', *WWD*, 29 April 2016 <wwd.com/fashion-news/fashion-scoops/prada-peta-shareholder-protect-ostrich-skin-10421026/> (Accessed 31 January 2018).

Additionally, luxury conglomerates publicize their sustainability practices and polices. For example, LVMH makes their sustainability practices and policies known at conferences, summits and through social media. Likewise, Kering, uses an interactive environmental profit and loss statement, which is available on their website.[33] In January 2018, for the third time, Kering was 'named the top sustainable textile, apparel, and luxury goods corporation' by the Corporate Knights Global 100 index published at the World Economic Forum in Davos, Switzerland. The company was first place in its category and was ranked 47th overall. Marie-Claire Daveu, chief sustainability officer stated: '[w]e consider sustainability to be the Kering seal of savoir-faire, a criterion in all business decisions, traversing all departments and areas of our supply chain'.[34] Kering's actions confirm the company's statements. In 2017, the company introduced a program with a goal of reducing its environmental footprint by 40 percent by 2025.[35]

Murky supply chains, which lack transparency, create an almost impossible situation in determining if a company's operational policies are ethical and sustainable. Companies may publish their suppliers, but rarely do they know who supplies their suppliers. To find truly ethical products, one has to look beyond the factory to where the raw materials originate.[36] Brands are becoming more aware of the supply chain and a few, like Prada and Chanel, are purchasing companies within the supply chain to protect the craft and the workers.[37]

In the United Kingdom, luxury department store Selfridges began a 'Buying Better Initiative', which requires brands to meet ethical trade standards and focuses on brands with an emphasis on sustainability.[38] H&M published its supplier list, which now includes fabric and yarn mills for about 50 per cent of the garments sold in its stores. While publishing suppliers may not sound like great strides are being made, it is important to note supplier lists were once kept in a safe.[39]

33   Vij, 'Luxury Brands Putting More Weight Into Sustainability'.

34   L. Marfil, 'Kering Named Most Sustainable Global Corporation', *WWD*, 23 January 2018 <wwd. com/fashion-news/fashion-scoops/kering-most-sustainable-global-corporation-11122255/ > (Accessed 30 January 2018).

35   Ibid.

36   T. Hoskins, 'Luxury Brands: Higher Standards or Just a Higher Mark-up?', *The Guardian*, 10 December 2014 <http://www.theguardian.com/sustainable-business/2014/dec/10/luxury-brands-behind-gloss-same-dirt-ethics-production> (Accessed 7 April 2016).

37   J. King, 'Sustainability Efforts to Boost Investor Interest in Luxury Houses', *Luxury Institute*, 26 January 2016 <http://luxuryinstitute.com/blog/?p=3312> (Accessed 7 April 2016).

38   Abnett, 'Three Years After Rana Plaza, Has Anything Changed?'.

39   Guilbault, 'Future of Sustainability Shapes Up'.

Reformation, a U.S. based apparel manufacturer, reduces waste with sustainable practices throughout the supply chain. Reformation produces the majority of their garments in Los Angeles (California) using sustainable methods and materials, including reusing vintage garments.[40] Their motto is '[w]e make killer clothes that don't kill the environment'. The company is insistent fashion and sustainability must coexist. Reformation focuses on items made in limited quantities that are well constructed and seasonless. There is a curatorial approach with garments released one at a time throughout a year.[41] Driving business at Reformation and similar brands is a growing contingent of consumers interested in buying less, but buying better.

Similarly, Brunello Cucinelli is an ethical success story. The company based in Solomeo (Italy), produces luxurious cashmere clothes, which retail in the thousands of dollars. Brunello Cucinelli's humble beginnings influence how he operates his business. His father, a farmer turned factory worker, suffered great humiliation working in the factories. His father's experience inspired Cucinelli to 'work for the moral and economic dignity of the human being'.[42] Cucinelli revolutionized the cashmere business by dying the usual natural coloured fibres bright colours. This was the turning point in his business, which now employs thousands of workers. The company takes care of its workers by paying them more than the industry average and limiting the employee's working hours. Cucinelli believes in the 'ethicalisation of mankind'.[43] The company reported nine per cent growth the first quarter of 2016 and is tracking towards double-digit growth for the year.[44] Evidence a company, which cares for its workers, craft and the world can coexist with the bottom line.

Lafayette 148, like Brunello Cucinelli, believes in a moral and honourable business model. Lafayette 148 is a contemporary luxury brand founded in 1996. The completely vertical brand is based in New York City (New York) and Shantou (China). In Shantou, the company built the 'School of Dreams' for the children of its factory workers, which has grown and currently serves the entire

---

40   'Who We Are', *Reformation* [corporate website] <https://www.thereformation.com/whoweare> (Accessed 27 August 2016).

41   A. Andjelic, 'Fashion Brands, Long Focused on Excess, Are Finally Waking Up to Sustainability', *Adweek*, 20 May 2016 <http://www.adweek.com/news/advertising-branding/fashion-brands-long-focused-excess-are-finally-waking-sustainability-171609> (Accessed 30 May 2016).

42   N. Koenig, 'Can Ethics Help Your Luxury Business Live Forever?', *BBC*, 23 February 2016 <http://www.bbc.com/news/business-35629880> (Accessed 25 February 2016).

43   Ibid.

44   Reuters Staff, 'Cucinelli Sees Double-digit Sales and Profits Growth in 2016', *Reuters*, 11 May 2016 <http://www.reuters.com/article/idUSL5N1885DN> (Accessed 30 May 2016).

community. Lafayette 148 is also a partner with Columbia University Medical Centre in the Promise Project to develop low-cost prevention and intervention programs for underprivileged children. By providing diagnoses of learning disabilities in underprivileged children, the Promise Project ensures all children have an equal opportunity to learn.

Stella McCartney is arguably the standard for sustainable and ethical fashion companies. She runs her business from her heart, so much so she considers her company the 'most ethical and loving company in the fashion industry'.[45] As a life-long vegetarian, animal materials are not used, which creates a design conundrum, especially in categories traditionally made of leather. McCartney saw confirmation of her convictions in a 2007 report published by Dr. Rajendrar Pachauri, which found the livestock industry accounted for 18 per cent of the world's greenhouse emissions. McCartney 'connected the dots between animal rights and sustainability'. Sustainability is the core of the company's values, which is aligned with the business model and brand mission. The company is thriving seeing annual global sales between $150 and $200 million with profits of about $5 million.[46]

5   Consumer Demand

The real issue is consumer demand; it is the elephant in the room. Consumers expect companies to behave ethically; however, a mere 23 per cent report a company's ethics as influential in purchasing decisions. Other purchasing factors, such as price and availability, usually bear more influence on why consumers purchase. Problematic is the definition of ethical, what is ethical to one person may be unethical to another. But the winds are shifting and as more consumers become influenced by ethics, 63 per cent report ethical issues becoming more important.[47] Livia Firth, founder of Eco Age states: '[t]he problem is not sustainability – the problem is the ever-increasing demand for fast fashion'.[48] Massive amounts of apparel is produced fast and cheap, consumed and quickly disposed of. Fast fashion is worn fewer than five times and kept on average 35 days producing 400 per cent more carbon emissions per item

---

45   I. Amed, 'Stella McCartney: Change Agent', *The Business of Fashion*, 29 March 2015 <http:// www.businessoffashion.com/community/voices/discussions/can-fashion-industry-become-sustainable/stella-mccartney-change-agent> (Accessed 3 October 2016).

46   Ibid.

47   Bonetto, 'The Ethical Consumer'.

48   Abnett, 'Three Years After Rana Plaza, Has Anything Changed?'.

than garments worn 50 times and kept for a year.[49] The more accurate name for fast fashion is 'disposable fashion' as it disposes of clothing and the people who make it.

Consumers hold all the power and retailers know the way to success is to give consumers what they want. As consumers demand companies to produce ethically and sustainable products, change will happen. Ethical efforts are more effective when they relate to the brand. Also, helping consumers understand the impact of their purchases is important to consumers wishing to make a difference.[50] Producers of goods failing to take notice and adapt their business models to socially accepted business practices may find consumers spending their money elsewhere.

6   Conclusion

Why are consumers complacent about ethical and sustainable fashion? Because they are detached and disengaged from the people across the globe who struggle to survive while employed by factories supplying clothing at low prices. The Rana Plaza disaster brought the dirtiness of the garment industry into living rooms and people saw the horrifying truth about fashion. The challenge is to change consumer behaviour so they seek brands committed to ethical and sustainable fashion. While consumers are more aware and demand more ethical and sustainable products, they remain more concerned about price.

The importance and focus of ethical behaviour by companies in the last 20 years, moving from a minor concern to a cost of doing business, is encouraging. Plus, some progress has been made in governance mechanisms, transparency, and installing systems, which allow for auditing the issues faced by the garment industry. Elisa Niemtzow states,

> [o]ur current mainstream fashion business model hinges on selling customers many clothes, accessories, and other products at the highest possible margin. As an industry, we need to re-invent this business model, including innovating for more sustainable and recyclable materials and extending the lifespan of garments through better design, manufacturing, and re-use.[51]

---

49   Conca, 'Making Climate Change Fashionable'.
50   Bonetto, 'The Ethical Consumer'.
51   Conca, 'Making Climate Change Fashionable'.

With more acute consumer awareness and manufacturers responding to consumer and shareholder demands, change is happening. Sadly, change comes slowly. As Diana Verde Nieto, CEO of Positive Luxury states, 'I feel strongly that if retailers care brands will have no choice than to address the issues much faster – most brands are doing something, the problem is the pace'.[52]

I am part of the problem ... and so are you! We have gone down the shopping rabbit hole with seemingly no way out, because we cannot stop shopping. Too many people in too many developing countries depend on us to shop. As part of the problem, we can also be part of the solution. We can buy smarter. Stop looking for the cheapest price, but instead look for the best quality. Know brands and their position on ethics and sustainability. We can be more curatorial in our approach to our wardrobes. We can work at being less awful. We need less talk of caring and more action proving we care.

Bibliography

Abnett, K., 'Three Years After Rana Plaza, Has Anything Changed?', *The Business of Fashion*, 19 April 2016 <https://www.businessoffashion.com/articles/intelligence/three-years-...rana-plaza-has-anything-changed-sustainability-safety-workers-welfare> (Accessed 5 August 2016).

Amed, I., 'Stella McCartney: Change Agent', *The Business of Fashion*, 29 March 2015 <http://www.businessoffashion.com/community/voices/discussions/can-fashion-industry-become-sustainable/stella-mccartney-change-agent> (Accessed 3 October 2016).

Andjelic, A., 'Fashion Brands, Long Focused on Excess, Are Finally Waking Up to Sustainability', *Adweek*, 20 May 2016 <http://www.adweek.com/news/advertising-branding/fashion-brands-long-focused-excess-are-finally-waking-sustainability-171609> (Accessed 30 May 2016).

Associated Press in Dhaka, 'Rana Plaza Collapse: Dozens Charged with Murder', *The Guardian*, 1 June 2015 <http://www.theguardian.com/world/2015/jun/01/rana-plaza-collapse-dozens-charged-with-murder-bangladesh> (Accessed 4 April 2016).

Bonetto, L., 'The Ethical Consumer' [report], *Mintel Group*, July 2015 <http://academic.mintel.com.proxy.library.vcu.edu/display/716584/> (Accessed 4 April 2016).

Chandran, R., 'Dhaka Attack Deals Blow to Improvements in Post Rana Plaza Garment Industry', *Thomas Reuters Foundation News*, 5 July 2016 <http://news.trust.org/item/20160705124925-lauux/> (Accessed 5 August 2016).

---

52   Abnett, 'Three Years After Rana Plaza, Has Anything Changed?'.

Conca, J., 'Making Climate Change Fashionable – The Garment Industry Takes on Global Warming', *Forbes*, 3 December 2015 <http://www.forbes.com/sites/jamesconca/2015/12/03/making-climate-change-fashionable-the-garment-industry-takes-on-global-warming/#389f6849778a> (Accessed 5 August 2016).

Dalton, R., 'A T-Shirt Should Never Cost $10, Time to End the Fast Fashion Mentality', *Catalogue*, 2016 <https://www.cataloguemagazine.com.au/feature/a-t-shirt-should-never-cost-10-time-to-end-the-fast-fashion-mentality> (Accessed 5 August 2016).

Diderich, J., 'PETA Confronts Hermes CEO Over Exotic Skins', *WWD*, 31 May 2016 <http://wwd.com/fashion-news/designer-luxury/peta-confronts-hermes-ceo-exotic-skins-10439851/> (Accessed 27 July 2016).

Farra, E., '3 Designers Who Are Making It Easy (and Chic!) to Shop Sustainable', *Vogue*, 8 April 2016 <http://www.vogue.com/13424418/best-sustainable-fashion-designers-zady-datura-plyknits/> (Accessed 5 August 2016).

Frank, R., 'Wealthy Shoppers Don't Buy into Lux-Anthropy', *CNBC*, 27 June 2012 <http://www.cnbc.com/id/47979078> (Accessed 7 April 2016).

Guilbault, L., 'Future of Sustainablility Shapes Up at Copenhagen Fashion Summit', *WWD*, 14 May 2016 <http://wwd.com/fashion-news/fashion-features/sustainability-copenhagen-fashion-summit-10429848/> (Accessed 30 May 16).

Hoskins, T., 'Luxury Brands: Higher Standards or Just a Higher Mark-up?', *The Guardian*, 10 December 2014 <http://www.theguardian.com/sustainable-business/2014/dec/10/luxury-brands-behind-gloss-same-dirt-ethics-production> (Accessed 7 April 2016).

King, J., 'Sustainability Efforts to Boost Investor Interest in Luxury Houses', *Luxury Institute*, 26 January 2016 <http://luxuryinstitute.com/blog/?p=3312> (Accessed 7 April 2016).

Koenig, N., 'Can Ethics Help Your Luxury Business Live Forever?', *BBC*, 23 February 2016 <http://www.bbc.com/news/business-35629880> (Accessed 25 February 2016).

Kosak, H., 'Triangle Shirtwaist Fire', *Jewish Women's Archive*, 20 March 2009 <http://jwa.org/encyclopedia/article/triangle-shirtwaist-fire> (Accessed 1 August 2016).

Marfil, L., 'Kering Named Most Sustainable Global Corporation', *WWD*, 23 January 2018 <wwd.com/fashion-news/fashion-scoops/kering-most-sustainable-global-corporation-11122255/> (Accessed 30 January 2018).

Maxwell, D., L. McAndrew, and J. Ryan, 'The State of the Apparel Sector Report – Water' [report], *Glasaaward.com*, 2015 <https://glasaaward.org/wp-content/uploads/2015/05/GLASA_2015_StateofApparelSector_SpecialReport_Water_150624.pdf> (Accessed 3 March 2016).

Reuters Staff, 'Cucinelli Sees Double-digit Sales and Profits Growth in 2016', *Reuters*, 11 May 2016 <http://www.reuters.com/article/idUSL5N1885DN> (Accessed 30 May 2016).

Stangler, C., 'Major Fire at Bangladesh Sweater Factory Raises Questions About Continuing Safety Improvements', *International Business Times*, 2 February 2016 <http://www.ibtimes.com/major-fire-bangladesh-sweater-factory-raises-questions-about-continuing-safety-2290608> (Accessed 8 August 2016).

Tutty, J., '2016 Predictions for the Luxury Industry: Sustainability and Innovation' [executive summary], *The Positive Guide*, 20 January 2016 <http://blog.positiveluxury.com/2016/01/2016-predictions-luxury-world-sustainability-innovation/> (Accessed 7 April 2016).

Vij, V., 'Luxury Brands Putting More Weight Into Sustainability', *Justmeans*, 18 February 2016 <http://www.justmeans.com/blogs/luxury-brands-putting-more-weight-into-sustainability> (Accessed 7 April 2016).

'Who We Are', *Reformation* [corporate website] <https://www.thereformation.com/whoweare> (Accessed 27 August 2016).

Zargani, L., 'PETA Invests in Prada to Protest Ostrich-Skin Products', *WWD*, 29 April 2016 <wwd.com/fashion-news/fashion-scoops/prada-peta-shareholder-protect-ostrich-skin-10421026/> (Accessed 31 January 2018).

CHAPTER 5

Martin House Makers: Exploring Modes of Upcycling and Make within the Charity Retail Sector

Karen Dennis

Abstract

The current global fashion system is neither thrifty nor sustainable. With its reliance on inbuilt obsolescence it maintains itself by rendering products psychologically out of date before their physical degradation. As a result 14 million tonnes of discarded clothes and textiles are estimated to leave American wardrobes every year with 350,000 tonnes leaving UK households annually.[1] The charity retail sector absorbs a vast amount of discarded products and as a product of material culture, second-hand clothing/clothes (SHC) represent an interesting context from which to analyse practices of sustainable consumption. Their existence within present fashion systems highlight how such practices can contribute to responsible consumption and produce gains for the charitable sector. This paper discusses practice-led research that has sought to investigate the re-appropriation of waste materials into the charity retail sector and in particular the initiative Martin House Makers that was established to engage the community in modes of make. It frames its discussion and conclusions upon experiences gained as a result of immersion in a pop-up retail project and the development of a range of upcycled clothes and products to be sold at Martin House Charity shops throughout Yorkshire, North of England (UK).

Keywords

upcycling – sustainable manufacture – second-hand clothes – charity retail

---

1 'Valuing Our Clothes: The Cost of UK Fashion' [report], *Wrap*, July 2017 <http://www.wrap.org.uk/sites/files/wrap/valuing-our-clothes-the-cost-of-uk-fashion_WRAP.pdf> (Accessed 23 August 2017).

1   Introduction

Waste, garbage, rubbish, trash exists as both material manifestation and meta-physical construct fostering our connection between nature and culture, be-tween things and value.[2] When something is thrown away, discarded and seen as no longer valuable it has been argued how this says a lot about both society and the individual.[3] Scanlan argued how the 'core of all we value results from garbage' and that the 'spectres of garbage serve as a stark reminder of what we really are'.[4] Upcycling and transforming this 'garbage' as a practice can thus be viewed as both philosophical and activist endeavor.[5] Setting the context for related design activities, reflection on studies such as Scanlan's have been used as a way of analysing approaches to the study of unwanted items and methods for their appropriation into meaningful retail and manufacturing systems. This chapter takes textiles and clothing discarded as considered no longer valuable to the original owner and shows their conversion into viable mainstream designs.

The consumption of second-hand clothing (SHC) and active participation in recycling provides an alternative to the current fashion industry which is marked by an over productive and over consumptive system. By recycling and reusing resources two aspects of austerity come into play: that of eco-austerity (saving the planet), and thrift (making do with the resources we have at hand).

Martin House Makers was established in 2017 as an initiative to work with donated, unwanted materials and to develop a range of upcycled products that could be sold within Martin House Charity Shops and at Pop-up events throughout Yorkshire. As such it seeks to address issues to do with waste not just within its internal structure but also externally as a way of demonstrating upcycling practices.

This chapter provides exploration of the conception of the idea together with the material manifestations in the form of a clothing range targeted at Martin House customers. It goes further to analyse the marketing implications of the initiative and methods for engaging both consumers and makers with the project.

2 S. Foote and E. Mazzolini, *Histories of the Dustheap: Waste, Material Cultures, Social Justice*, The MIT Press, Cambridge, MA, 2012.

3 R. Oldenziel and H. Weber, 'Introduction: Reconsidering Recycling', *Contemporary European History*, vol. 22 no. 3, 2013, pp. 347–370.

4 J. Scanlan, *On Garbage*, Reaktion Books, London, 2005, p. 5.

5 O. von Busch, *Fashion-able: Hacktivism and Engaged Fashion Design*, Art Monitor, Gothen-burg, 2008; G. Julier, 'From Design Culture to Design Activism', *Design and Culture*, vol. 5, no. 2, 2013, pp. 215–236.

2   Practice-Led Methodology

There are several methods of research that have resonance to us as design practitioners operating within academic and commercial contexts, the most relevant being practice-led research, reflective practice, action research and grounded theory. These have gradually become subsumed within the academic research canon and have led to interesting outputs and a reframing of what may constitute research particularly within a design-based context.[6] It is generally recognised that these creative outputs can only become academic research when they are embedded within a suitable accompanying text leading some to reflect upon both the validity and rigour of this approach to research.[7]

In the case of recycled fashion outputs, there is no substitute for the analysis of actual garments and processes and thus research in the context of this paper has been centred on the development of processes, context and artefacts. This is supported by the thoughts of Till *et. al.* and the way in which practice-led research can concentrate on how issues, concerns and interests can be examined and brought about by the production of an artefact.[8] Similarly, the study by Smith and Dean into practice-led research also provided inspiration in terms of their identified types of practice namely: conceptual practice, dialectical practice and contextual practice.[9] This classification of practice is useful to academic practitioners since it allows those engaged in this work to give form to thought (conceptual), to explore the unique human process of making that is felt, lived, reconstructed and reinterpreted (dialectical) and scope for thinking in a setting (contextual).

The following case study outlines the journey of a design practice as a way of showing how this may be conceived as research and the value of design and manufacturing processes to the attainment of new knowledge, particularly as it relates to the practice of upcycling, retail, marketing and consumption. Practice together with theory has informed this enquiry and was carried out in order to make use of visual texts, issues, debates, materials and desires that were local in focus but global in reach.[10] A key aim of the research was to ensure that full

---

6   H. Smith, and R.T. Dean, *Practice-led Research, Research-led Practice in the Creative Arts*, Edinburgh University Press, Edinburgh, 2009.

7   J. Till, J. Mottram, and C. Rust, 'Adapting Research Activity AHRC Review of Practice-led Research', *Architectural Research Quarterly*, vol. 9, no. 2, 2005, pp. 103–104.

8   Ibid.

9   Smith and Dean, *Practice-led Research, Research-led Practice in the Creative Arts*.

10   Ibid.

immersion in both the design and manufacture of garments made from recycled materials was achieved and that there should be tangible outputs in terms of products, sales and dissemination of practices as a result of the research. This has been done in order to test the validity of the remanufacturing processes. Research methodology was centred on the conceptual ways in which theory relating to waste, manufacture and consumption could be put into practice: dialectical – sourcing and handling waste in order to inform resultant design, and contextual – embedding the practice within certain loci in order to experience the problem of waste and ways in which modes of make could have an impact upon how products were viewed both by maker and consumer.

The artifacts and practices explored within this chapter are all drawn from aspects of theoretical practice and in particular the dilemmas we face as creative practitioners to make work of meaning and within a meaningful setting. They have been crafted from items discarded as unwanted and thus provide interesting reflection on the trajectory of objects and how fashion details may be re-appropriated. Setting the context within the charity retail sector also provides insight into the trade in second-hand clothes (SHC) and how they are distributed, sorted and ultimately passed on to the consumer. Crafting pieces that were relevant to these contexts was thus important as were the visual signs and symbols needed to reach the consumer and convey current and future trends, particularly relating to sustainability. The aim of the pieces is to point the way to revised schemes of making and creating and to test out theory as we go along. It is about reflection into past, present and futures roles of the 'maker' and ways in which autonomy waxes and wanes in the design industry. It is also about how this practice can feed into discussions on sustainability and the role that manufacture and consumption can play in this.

3   Contextualising Recycling

Recycling is nothing new. Past civilisations were based upon making use of what was at hand, of utilizing any available resource whatever its state. It would have seemed logical and natural. In a predominantly pre-industrial state much of what we may have construed as waste would have derived from a natural source. We don't necessarily consider the falling of leaves as recycling but that is what the tree is doing. Discarding spent leaves at its roots to provide valuable nutrients for its life to come. Thus the earth becomes the grand recycler converting leaves into fertiliser. However, we have long lost our natural selves and now live in a very changed world. Industrial waste is a different beast. It contains toxins and a vast amount of 'unnatural' waste that the earth just cannot absorb. In this state it becomes a problem and an environmental time bomb. In reflecting on eco-austerity in relation to the car automobile industry, Wells stated how

> [i]t is an entire package of disasters that threatens our very social existence that scientists are seriously discussing now. Be it water shortages or the decline in petroleum production, encroaching deserts or the loss of forests, species extinction or the collapse of fish stocks – everywhere the pressure of humanity on the planet is reaching critical levels. Until recently, we believed that we could face these challenges and had the economic power to overcome them, because we could afford to be green. Well, we don't have the money any more, but we cannot afford not to be green.[11]

Arguing how sustainable technology existed (or nearly existed), this was not the problem, rather it was the economic incentives and business models that were hindering the uptake of this technology. He went further to state how 'sustainability entails accommodating temporal heterogeneity'[12] and proposed economic gardening rather than economic hunting.[13] Thus we can see how recycling and its links to austerity are nothing new, but they are beginning to have relevance again as cited by Hall and Jayne:

> [m]ore specifically these forms of crafting, cultivation and cooking have become representative of a successful historic response to economic crisis and austerity during and between the First World War and the Second World War, with particular reference to the 'Make-do-and-mend' national campaign facilitated by the British Government during a period of wartime and post-war rationing of clothes. In their present guise, they have come to symbolise 'ideal responses to austerity'... This moment of hope in the face of widespread devastation and loss is also valued as signifying certain production techniques and consumption cultures, particularly those of handicraft, which existed prior to the intensification of consumer capitalism and emergence of mass consumerism.[14]

---

11   P.E. Wells, *The Automotive Industry in an Era of Eco-austerity: Creating an Industry as if the Planet Mattered*, Edward Elgar Publishing, Cheltenham, 2010, preface.

12   Ibid., p.159.

13   Ibid.

14   S.M. Hall and M. Jayne, 'Make, Mend and Befriend: Geographies of Austerity, Crafting and Friendship in Contemporary Cultures of Dressmaking in the UK', *Gender, Place and Culture*, vol. 23, no. 2, 2015, pp. 216–219, p. 216.

In the past 'make-do-and-mend' practices played a key role in saving our pockets, now it appears to be more about saving our planet. Recycling has come to mean both a sense of using and viewing old items as they were and also of transforming them beyond their former self into something significantly different. This shift has been attributed to the predominance of Western attitudes particularly as they relate to the growth of a consumer society and the nature of inbuilt obsolescence.[15] As argued by Oldenziel and Weber, the growth of recycling has come about due to an increase in the amount of consumables that are being discarded:

> [t]he Western world's post-war shift to a society based on discarding things after their first use is – in the history of humankind – the exception rather than the rule ... recycling is neither an invention of the affluent post-modern environmental era nor driven exclusively by ecological concerns.[16]

In this context recycling becomes a reaction to overconsumption and our relationship to waste. In a modern industrial and capitalist context, recycling is intrinsically linked to rubbish and seen as an exchange between 'material incarnations and symbolic iterations'.[17] To fully understand its place within society reflection on how rubbish comes about is thus necessary. Scanlan in his study on garbage defined it as 'things, people or activities that are separated, removed and devalued'.[18] Thus, in analysing rubbish we are looking for connection in the 'hidden, forgotten, thrown away and residual phenomena'.[19] Foote and Mazzolini argued how 'garbage is ... quite ordinary ... a by-product of merely being alive'[20] and that garbage and waste bring into sharp focus the complicated relationship between nature and culture.

This relationship to both our natural and cultural self is of particular relevance to clothes and the nature of fashion. As argued by Bauman, fashion, as a

---

15   V. Papanek, *Design For The Real World: Human Ecology and Social Change*, Pantheon Press, New York, NY, 1971; G. Ritzer, *The McDonaldization of Society*, Pine Forge Press, Thousand Oaks, CA, 2000; M. Braungart and W. McDonough, *Cradle to Cradle: Re-Making The Way We Make Things*, Vintage Books, London, 2008; K. Fletcher, *Sustainable Fashion and Textiles: Design Journeys*, Earthscan Publications, Oxford 2008; P. Boradkar, *Designing Things: a Critical Introduction to the Culture of Things*, Berg Publishers, Oxford, 2010.

16   Oldenziel and Weber, 'Introduction: Reconsidering Recycling', p. 2.

17   Foote and Mazzolini, *Histories of the Dustheap*, p. 3.

18   Scanlan, *On Garbage*, p.5.

19   Ibid., p. 45.

20   Foote and Mazzolini, *Histories of the Dustheap*, p. 3.

result of postmodern states, produces conflicting notions of self and identity. Identities becoming hostage to change as new versions of self, appearance and behaviours come into being.[21] Citing inbuilt obsolescence and a craving for the new as reasons behind this wasteful approach to consumption, Bauman also introduced interesting new contexts and analysis for the critiquing of waste in a modern, consumer and consumption driven society. Posing questions such as 'are things thrown away because of their ugliness, or are they ugly because they have been earmarked for the tip?'[22] he extended the context for waste to include human beings and the effects of modernity on the production of a transient and disposable work force separated from the benefits of development.

This link between fashion and waste becomes all the more relevant when we consider the role concepts such as fast fashion and being 'in fashion' play in a modern world. The ability to purchase cheap clothing has contributed to a devaluing of clothes to the point that single use wear and an abundance of unused clothes languishing in wardrobes is common place.[23] Recycling has thus provided a basis on which an ever increasing number of artists and designers are focusing their practice upon and this is borne of social, political and environmental concerns.[24] In the main this has been attributed to the fact that practitioners are keen to explore more sustainable and environmentally sensitive approaches to the manufacture and consumption of artefacts, and in the process comment upon the wastefulness of our current societal attitudes and action.[25] They also share an intimate relationship with waste, garbage, rubbish and trash. Viewing the world around them they have responded with both artistic and designerly tendencies and produced a number of very interesting prototypes. Providing a comprehensive study of 'Junk Art', Whiteley highlighted a context for the production of this work when she stated that

> [s]ustainability and thinking green are increasingly fashionable in the economically rich West but working with trash, creatively or in any other way, has historical, cultural and social connotations which relate to hierarchies of materials at particular times and particular places. Detritus has

21 Z. Bauman, *Liquid Life*, Polity Press, Cambridge, 2005.

22 Ibid., p. 3.

23 V.L. Isla, 'Investigating Second-hand Fashion Trade and Consumption in the Philippines: Expanding Existing Discourses', *Journal of Consumer Culture*, vol.13, no. 3, 2013, pp. 221–240.

24 G. Whiteley, *Junk: Art and the Politics of Trash*, I.B.Tauris, London and New York, NY, 2011; S. Brown, *Eco Fashion*, Laurence King Publishing Ltd., London, 2011.

25 S. Brown, *Refashioned – Cutting Edge Clothes from Up-cycled Materials*, Laurence King Publishing Ltd., London, 2014.

ideological, social, political contexts and associations. Anyone forced to work with other people's garbage – from office cleaners to sewage workers – recognises this. Everyone contributes to the domestic rubbish tip and landfill sites but the processing of waste is generally left to those on the social and economic margins.[26]

It is interesting to note that within the context of waste, within contemporary innovative fashion design, many of the practices of recycling have been applied to the couture/high end of the market. In her comprehensive book *Refashioned*, Brown outlined the practices of a number of fashion designers and showed how textile and clothing waste had been used in the development of clothing ranges.[27] Citing companies such as the Mayer Peace Collection, Denham, Schmidt Takahashi, Reet Aus, Paulina Plizga as innovators, it is difficult to imagine how they may be considered to be on the social and economic margins. The purchase and use of SHC has long been seen as a lifestyle choice in the Western world and a signifier of beliefs centred upon thrift, 'make-do-and-mend' and a desire not to waste.[28] The sense of projecting a retro look is also of importance. Thus SHC have provided the focus for a number of research projects and analysis has been made concerning their environmental benefits,[29] their appropriation amongst younger consumers,[30] and the impact of their export on economies such as Africa.[31] As stated by Song and van Dyke,

> [i]t was estimated that the purchase of 100 second-hand clothes would save between 60 and 85 new garments dependent of the place of reuse, The LCA showed that the collection, processing and transport of second hand clothing have significant impacts on the environment in comparison to the savings that are achieved by replacing virgin clothing. The reduction of impacts resulting from the collection of 100 used garments ranges from 14% decrease in global warming for the cotton T-shirt to 45% reduction of human toxicity for the polyester/cotton trousers. The results

---

26   Ibid., p. 5.

27   Ibid.

28   K. Reiley and M. DeLong, 'A Consumer Vision for Sustainable Fashion Practice', *Fashion Practice*, vol. 3, no. 1, 2011, pp. 63–84.

29   L. Farrant, S.I. Olsen, and A. Wangel, 'Environmental Benefits from Reusing Clothes', *The International Journal of Life Cycle Assessment*, vol. 15, no. 7, 2010, pp. 726–736.

30   Reiley and DeLong, 'A Consumer Vision for Sustainable Fashion Practice'.

31   G. Dissanayake and P. Sinha, 'An Examination of the Product Development Process for Fashion Remanufacturing', *Resources, Conservation and Recycling*, vol.104, part A, 2015, pp. 94–102.

of the study thus show that clothes reuse can significantly contribute to reducing the environmental burden of clothing.[32]

Studies similarly concerned with the environmental impact of using SHC in turn have highlighted ways in which they have been used, in the process proposing models for the incorporation of SHC into existing global fashion systems.[33] In the main these have led to the conclusion that current rates of overconsumption are unsustainable, and to seriously reincorporate waste materials back into the fashion system requires a restructuring of present manufacture and consumption practices. This is particularly true when we consider the impact of the export of SHC, especially to countries in Africa. In his study into clothing poverty and the hidden world of fast fashion, Brooks stated how

> [u]sed clothing has outcompeted and displaced African clothing manufacturing in Kenya, Malawi, Mozambique, Tanzania, Zambia and other countries which permitted imports of SHC. In Uganda second-hand garments account for 81% of all clothing purchases.[34]

Visits to second-hand markets by the author in Dar Es Salaam (Tanzania) in 2016 revealed a bustling market space. Workspaces had been set up to repair and transform clothes, shoes *etc.* and vendors stated that business was good and profitable. Seen in this light, the problem becomes a solution for a related activity – that of clothing our backs to satisfy both basic and complex social, environmental and cultural demands. As positioned by Isla in relation to the various discourses we can use to investigate the second-hand fashion trade and consumption, she argued that 'at one end is a noticeably modern and functional outlook and on the other is a distinctly postmodern and consumerist perspective'.[35] This was seen to give rise to the coexistence of both positive and negative orientations and connotations and she posited that

> [w]hile the United States and western Europe tend to frame second-hand fashion consumption almost entirely with the notion of constructed identity and other 'postmodern' notions, African feelings could very well be

---

32   H.K. Song and L. Van Dyke, 'Development of a System for Sustainable Fashion from Recycled Clothes Based on U.S. Fashion Brands', *Research Journal of Costume Culture*, vol. 21, no.1, 2013, pp. 139–150, p. 142.

33   Ibid.

34   A. Brooks, *Clothing Poverty: The Hidden World of Fast Fashion and Second-hand Clothes*, Zed Books, London, 2015, p. 145.

35   Isla, 'Investigating Second-hand Fashion Trade and Consumption in the Philippines', p. 222.

located towards the middle of the continuum with their recognition of functional and rational socio-economic motivations in used clothing consumption, as well as consumption practices that are informed by local cultural norms and through which identities are constructed and contested.[36]

In this context SHC serve a function and provide a much needed resource. They satisfy the need for affordable, available and quality clothing and the sorting, distribution and sale of second-hand clothes provide valuable income-generating opportunities for tailors, fixers and entrepreneurs. As stated by Brooks,

> [p]oor people may have little agency in shaping used clothing systems of provision, but they can and do respond in creative and unanticipated ways to imports of used garments. Imports have diverse affects within different societies. Norms of dress are transmitted by the prevalence of Western clothing. Yet rather than everyone being passive receivers of clothing culture evidence shows how individuals give textiles a new lease of life and create their own creolized trends.[37]

This represents the potential for SHC and the positive manner in which it is adopted within a developmental context, however, changing opinions are beginning to emerge in relation to this export of clothing from one context to another. The Tanzanian government is one such body that is seeking to ban the import of SHC, framing their justification around the premise that their processing represents major health hazards and their presence work at the detriment of the growth and development of local manufacturing capacity. This will have an impact upon the ability of Western nations to export SHC and the need to find internal systems for its disposal, conversion and resale. Initiatives such as the Martin House Makers project could help to find solutions within the charity retail sector and in the process reinvigorate making communities and practices.

4   Martin House Makers: The Journey So Far

Twenty-five years ago a project 'NoLoGo' was established in London by Oxfam, led by a designer Janette Swift. Based in Tottenham Court Road with a shop in Soho, this project tapped into the prevailing zeitgeist by offering upcycled garments to a young trendy consumer. It attracted several volunteers keen to

---

36   Ibid., p. 223.
37   Ibid., p. 145.

develop their skills in remanufacture (including the author of this chapter, Karen Dennis). When a place at Leeds University in Textile Design necessitated a move northwards, contact was made with a local Oxfam store to investigate whether the project could be replicated in the North. Vicki Burnett, then a manager of a local store, took hold of the project and within a few months a retail space was found within one of Oxfam's city centre stores in Leeds. Housing a fully stocked workroom with industrial machines and cutting table above the retail space, it was soon a hive of activity as both volunteers and consumers came to make, buy and generally promote the initiative. It was deemed a success and in its time managed to change the demographic of the Oxfam consumer, alter recycling practices internally within the organisation and provide an alternative to conventional fashion stores, particularly in terms of providing relatively low cost, high fashion individual clothing and related items. After three years, the project ran its course as both parties moved onto other roles, Dennis into academia and Burnett into charity retail management.

In 2017 the paths of the two individuals met again when, with Burnett now as Head of Retail at Martin House Children's Hospice, proposed a pop-up retail manager and makers role to the author. The underlying premise to the position was that the charity wished to increase its presence within the community by engaging in pop-up events at festivals and specialist markets. This was felt necessary as a way of raising awareness of the charity's work in areas where there wasn't currently a retail presence and as a fundraising exercise through the sale of donated and upcycled stock. The charity was already engaged in upcycling furniture through an initiative with a local prison that took tired pieces of stock, revamped them and sold them on for a higher price. This was extended into clothing with the appointment of the author, who had already, through her initiative Ketchup Clothes and 15 years' experience in higher education, developed many upcycling techniques and products and embedded these within an academic context.[38] Throwing herself back into the charity retail world afforded the opportunity to access donated materials, test out ideas and begin to contextualise these within a commercial, practical context.

Still in its relative infancy, the project so far has proved a success in terms of bringing in higher financial rewards from the sale of donated vintage

---

38   K. Shah, 'Dilemmas of Development and the Reconstruction of Fashion', in S.S. Muthu (ed.), *Environmental Implications of Recycling and Recycled Products*, Springer, London, 2015, pp.101–134; K. Shah, *Ketchup Clothes: a Catalogue of Ideas* [teaching resource], 2015 <https://designforinteractivity.files.wordpress.com/2015/05/part-1.pdf>; K. Shah, 'Revolutions Come in Cycles: Mapping New Paradigms in Fashion Research and Practice To Social Change' [conference paper], *Fashion: Exploring Critical Issues, 8th Global Meeting*, Mansfield College, Oxford University, Oxford, 5–7 September 2016.

pieces and of engaging the community through the presentation of items made from recycled materials. Appearing at pop up specialist markets has enabled the charity to access a wider audience and, outside the confines of a traditional charity shop setting, has been able to sell the pieces at higher prices that are more consistent with their intrinsic and extrinsic value. Developing the full potential of the Martin House Makers brand will take time, but workshops and discussions with various individuals and groups have demonstrated an enthusiasm for engagement in craft based activities and it is expected that this will grow over time. The images (Figures 5.1–5.4) document a recent fashion shoot conducted to capture the essence of the collection so far and highlight the diversity of materials and garments used in its creation.

FIGURE 5.1 Sheepskin trimmed wool jacket with sequin leggings. Jacket made from sheepskin
rug rescued from a bin and sample woollen fabric from local factory, donated
leggings.
PHOTOGRAPHER: CLARK, 2017.

FIGURE 5.2   Jersey and lace dress with leather jeans style trousers dress made from
                    repurposed Martin House 'Centre Stage' T- shirt and donated lace tablecloth.
                    Trousers made from long leather coat.
                    PHOTOGRAPHER: CLARK, 2017.

Reflecting upon the practice thus far has highlighted how the theory of upcycling and in particular the link it has to sustainable design and consumption
can be expanded and disseminated to a wider audience. Theory would suggest
that in order to address the mountains of clothes that get discarded, finding
their way into charity shops, landfill or languishing in developing countries,
more is needed to be done to convert this waste into saleable, reusable items.
Upcycling is the active process of taking an item from its current state into a
more highly valued, relevant and often structurally altered piece.

In the case of the Martin House Makers project, some items have been converted from one context into another, such as in the case of the items made
from upholstery fabric – i.e. curtains *etc.*, others have been a case of bringing
together materials from several items of clothing into one. Raw materials were

FIGURE 5.3   Contextualising Collection within the Studio Environment.
PHOTOGRAPHER: CLARK, 2017.

drawn from 'waste' bags (i.e. discarded at the sorting point due to faults, stains *etc.*), or culled from the shop floors after they had been out for some time and not sold. Methods of construction and pattern cutting used have been consistent with industrial standards and it is hoped, that as prototypes, they can be up-scaled into larger manufacturing systems and through the network of 'maker' groups being developed under the initiative.

5   Conclusion

To be involved in the active process of recycling materials requires time, patience and skill. The charity retails sector is marked by an abundance of discarded items all of which require careful sorting and organizing. Whilst they do bring in much needed revenue for the sector, there is still a significant proportion of items that never make it onto the shop floor and for this avenues of ragging are utilized. Some of these items can be saved from ragging and form the basis for reimagined and remanufactured garments and products. Other items such as donated vintage pieces can be incorporated into a modern day collection that has appeal for its aesthetic and activist tendencies. The active process of remanufacture can engage makers who wish to develop and

FIGURE 5.4 'Two shirt' bell sleeved top and donated mini skirt.
PHOTOGRAPHER: CLARK, 2017.

dedicate their skills to charitable causes and feel that they are contributing
to a greater good, something that may not be all together possible within the
traditional commercial sector.

The extent to which these practices can be viewed as academic research
occurs under the guise within which they operate. Practice highlights the barrier and opportunities that present themselves as materials are handled and
contextualized. The photo shoot for the garments presented in this chapter
was deliberately situated in the author's studio since it was from here that
the garments were originally conceived and remanufactured. Set in the urban
landscape the outdoor scenes further make links between urban industrial
decay and the encroachment of nature, highlighting the incongruous nature
of industrial waste and its impact on the environment. It is estimated that
we are reaching a tipping point in the amount of waste that litters our planet

and the lasting impact this will have on ecosystems and quality of life. Efforts to stem the flow of goods finding their way into landfill are needed and up-cycling provides an alternative to traditional modes of manufacture and consumption.

Bibliography

Bauman, Z., *Liquid Life*. Polity Press, Cambridge, 2005.

Boradkar, P., *Designing Things: a Critical Introduction to the Culture of Things*. Berg Publishers, Oxford, 2010.

Braungart, M., and W. McDonough, *Cradle to Cradle: Re-Making The Way We Make Things*. Vintage Books, London, 2008.

Brooks, A., *Clothing Poverty: The Hidden World of Fast Fashion and Second-hand Clothes*. Zed Books, London, 2015.

Brown, S., *Eco Fashion*. Laurence King Publishing Ltd., London, 2011.

Brown, S., *Refashioned – Cutting Edge Clothes from Up-cycled Materials*. Laurence King Publishing Ltd., London, 2014.

Dissanayake, G., and P. Sinha, 'An Examination of the Product Development Process for Fashion Remanufacturing', *Resources, Conservation and Recycling*, vol. 104, part A, 2015, pp. 94–102.

Farrant, L., S.I. Olsen, and A. Wangel, 'Environmental Benefits from Reusing Clothes', *The International Journal of Life Cycle Assessment*, vol. 15, no. 7, 2010, pp. 726–736.

Fletcher, K., *Sustainable Fashion and Textiles: Design Journeys*. Earthscan Publications, Oxford, 2008.

Foote, S., and E. Mazzolini, *Histories of the Dustheap: Waste, Material Cultures, Social Justice*. The MIT Press, Cambridge, MA, 2012.

Hall, S. M., and M. Jayne, 'Make, Mend and Befriend: Geographies of Austerity, Crafting and Friendship in Contemporary Cultures of Dressmaking in the UK', *Gender, Place and Culture*, vol. 23, no. 2, 2015, pp. 216–219.

Isla, V. L., 'Investigating Second-hand Fashion Trade and Consumption in the Philippines: Expanding Existing Discourses', *Journal of Consumer Culture*, vol. 13, no. 3, 2013, pp. 221–240.

Julier, G., 'From Design Culture to Design Activism', *Design and Culture*, vol. 5, no. 2, 2013, pp. 215–236.

Monbiot, G., *Captive State: The Corporate Takeover of Britain*. Macmillan, London, 2000.

Oldenziel, R., and H. Weber, 'Introduction: Reconsidering Recycling', *Contemporary European History*, vol. 22 no. 3, 2013, pp. 347–370.

Papanek, V., *Design For The Real World: Human Ecology and Social Change*. Pantheon Press, New York, NY, 1971.

Reiley, K., and M. DeLong, 'A Consumer Vision for Sustainable Fashion Practice', *Fashion Practice*, vol. 3, no. 1, 2011, pp. 63–84.

Ritzer, G., *The McDonaldization of Society*. Pine Forge Press, Thousand Oaks, CA, 2000.

Ritzer, G., *The Globalization of Nothing*. Pine Forge Press, Thousand Oaks, CA, 2004.

Ritzer, G., 'Rethinking Globalization: Glocalization/Grobalization and Something/Nothing', *Sociological Theory*, vol. 21, no. 3, 2003, pp. 193–209.

Scanlan, J., *On Garbage*. Reaktion Books, London, 2005.

Schumacher, E.F., *Small Is Beautiful: A Study of Economics as if People Mattered*. Abacus, London, 1978.

Shah, K., 'Dilemmas of Development and the Reconstruction of Fashion', in S.S. Muthu (ed.), *Environmental Implications of Recycling and Recycled Products*. Springer, London, 2015, pp. 101–134.

Shah, K., *Ketchup Clothes: a Catalogue of Ideas* [teaching resource], 2015 <https://designforinteractivity.files.wordpress.com/2015/05/part-1.pdf>.

Shah, K., 'Revolutions Come in Cycles: Mapping New Paradigms in Fashion Research and Practice To Social Change' [conference paper], *Fashion: Exploring Critical Issues, 8th Global Meeting*, Mansfield College, Oxford University, Oxford, 5–7 September 2016.

Smith, H., and R. T. Dean, *Practice-led Research, Research-led Practice in the Creative Arts*. Edinburgh University Press, Edinburgh, 2009.

Song, H. K., and L. Van Dyke, 'Development of a System for Sustainable Fashion from Recycled Clothes Based on U.S. Fashion Brands', *Research Journal of Costume Culture*, vol. 21, no.1, 2013, pp. 139–150.

Till, J., J. Mottram, and C. Rust, 'Adapting Research Activity AHRC Review of Practice-led Research', *Architectural Research Quarterly*, vol. 9, no. 2, 2005, pp. 103–104.

'Valuing Our Clothes: The Cost of UK Fashion' [report], *Wrap*, July 2017 <http://www.wrap.org.uk/sites/files/wrap/valuing-our-clothes-the-cost-of-uk-fashion_WRAP.pdf> (Accessed 23 August 2017).

von Busch, O., *Fashion-able: Hacktivism and Engaged Fashion Design*. Art Monitor, Gothenburg, 2008.

Wells, P. E., *The Automotive Industry in an Era of Eco-austerity: Creating an Industry as if the Planet Mattered*. Edward Elgar Publishing, Cheltenham, 2010.

Wheeler, A., 'Clothing Industry Wakes up to Sustainability', *Recycling and Waste World*, 29 January 2016 <http://www.recyclingwasteworld.co.uk/in-depth-article/clothing-industry-wakes-up-to-sustainability/114555/> (Accessed 23 July 2016).

Whiteley, G., *Junk: Art and the Politics of Trash*. I.B. Tauris, London and New York, NY, 2011.

CHAPTER 6

The Borrowing of Emotive Connotation between Fashion and Music

Claire Allen

Abstract

The relationship between fashion and music is an accepted product of our culture in both their expressive nature and performative requirements. 'Both the fashion and music industries ... are image-making industries'.[1] Fashion and music co-exist in cultural institutions and are active in the production and expression of new and revised symbolism. Fashion is embedded in a social context providing a visual narrative, expressive of the culture. Likewise popular music exists in the same social context where the expressive narrative is audio. In a world obsessed with consuming increasingly more information content, the need to break out from this with cultural rhetoric increases ten-fold.

This chapter explores the fluid relationship of fashion and music, discussing the legitimisation of a specific moment through the mutual engagement of visual and aural expressions. Kawamura argues that 'culture is not simply a product that is created, disseminated and consumed, but it is a product that is processed by organisational and macro-institutional factors'.[2]

The obsession of image construction for both industries (fashion and music) creates strong bonds, but all too often neglects the art form in favour of the commercially safe and proven formula informed by current consumer trends. Innovation remains on the fringes of both industries neither considering the other until commercialisation insists on a mutual collaboration in order to sell the product to consumers – each industry with the goal that the other will add legitimisation to their own art form.

There are four key areas considered in this paper: (i) the partnership of both art forms (fashion and music) and how they engage (ii) fulfilling emotional needs, (iii) the purpose of the bond and interdependency, and (iv) the cultural narrative, that is greater than the sum of its parts. The discussion draws together research from the two disciplines to explore their interdependency in the cultural legitimation process.

---

1 Y. Kawamura, *Fashionology: An Introduction to Fashion Studies*, Bloomsbury, London, 2005, p. 35.
2 Ibid.

Keywords

fashion – music – fashion narrative – emotive – connotation

1   Introduction

Fashion and music play a central role in the cultural narrative of a time period, and the art forms are often expressive of the zeitgeist of that period. The performances and visualisations of the art forms continue to create memory reminiscent triggers to our former selves and have the potential to be triggers to other memories and experiences in association.

This chapter explores how the interdependency of both art forms can create powerful reminiscent retrieval triggers by asking the question: how does this interdependent bond become meaningful? Does the collaboration trigger a continuing narrative within our minds; each a trigger to connect with the other creating a powerful image within ourselves? The performative self interlocks the emotive expressions with both phonological coding and visual coding, each triggering the other to fire in our reminiscence, each firing further reinforces the mutual dependency embedded in our memories. Reminiscent workshops are increasingly used as therapy for engaging people living with dementia, music has been used to stimulate reminiscence of a past decade and support the recall and conversation of past times. Simmons-Stern *et al.*[3] demonstrated through their research of 'song lyrics recognition memory test' that musical mnemonics did improve memory and recall of general information for healthy adults and people living with dementia.

2   The Partnership

In today's branded world a music artist's 'stylistic look' becomes synonymous with the artist and often the wider music genre – creating a branded look. Adopted by their music fans as a visual badge of recognition and creating a bond of belonging. Baudrillard [4] states 'the brand's primary function is to designate a product: its secondary function is to mobilize emotional connotations' thus

---

3   N.J. Simmons-Stern, R. G. Deason, B. J. Brandler, B. S. Frustace, M. K. O'Connor, B. A. Ally, and A. E. Budson, 'Music-based Memory Enhancement in Alzheimer's Disease: Promise and Limitations', *Neuropsychologia*, vol. 50, 2012, pp. 3295–3303.
4   J. Baudrillard, *The System of Objects*, trans. J. Benedict, Verso, London, 2005 [1968], p. 209.

the bonds of fashion and music borrow emotive connotation from the other as part of the process of defining the branded look. Music gives meaning to fashion as fashion gives meaning to music. It is the media based dissemination channels that draw the two together, each seeking to borrow an icon of the other to enhance the absorption of meaning. This can be illustrated in the creative partnership of David Bowie and Kansai Yamamoto established on the runway in 1971, uniting their shared obsession for performance, theatre and identity.

Kawamura argues that 'culture is not simply a product that is created, disseminated and consumed, but it is a product that is processed by organisational and macro-institutional factors'.[5] The social and cultural phenomenon is an increasingly 'manufactured' institution that is risk adverse and formulaic in its construction. The authenticity of the art can be lost in the branding process, to facilitate greater impact in dissemination and engagement of time poor consumers who also want to be assured of belonging to the momentary 'cool' or 'popular'. This has become prevalent in recent years through TV 'star-making' shows such as the *X Factor* and *The Voice*, both seeking to identify musical talent but working to a predetermined strategic formula that both provides popular entertainment, audience engagement and prime time exposure of a hitherto unknown artist.

Fashion and music require consuming by a public to commercially exist and sustain themselves in continued production engagement. Considering the co-dependency as an increasing bond that allows for greater impact and facilitates increased legitimation and sub-narratives.

Fashion and music have been long time 'bedfellows', each accepting the presence of the other and in turn believing their own art to be the most prominent and authentic. The togetherness of both creative expressions and their interdependency and mutual understanding are discussed and portrayed as equal partners in cultural expressionism by commentators of subculture and more precise youth subculture. Because it is an established partnership, there has been limited focus on how that partnership works and the benefits for each. Exploring this issue develops an understanding of the partnership in its own right but suggests how consumers use this connectivity in forming their own understanding of the cultural narrative and how each act as a stylistic prompt to the consumer.

What are the bonds in this relationship that each feels the dependency is necessary? Fashion and music are products that have been created artificially,

---

5   Kawamura, *Fashionology*, p. 35.

a physical manifestation of our own cognitive responses to the underlying so-cio-cultural drivers. To borrow a term from trend forecaster Faith Popcorn, the arts apply 'cultural brailing'[6] the process of constantly scanning our environment with great sensitivity for the 'new' ideas and concepts for the 'big' issues of our society such as that of the invisible threat of terrorism or the challenges of sustaining our planet for generations to come. The arts develop narratives around societies questions, problems and challenges and presents conceptualised thoughts manifested in art-forms. So, in its purest art-form there is a drive for authenticity to the socio-cultural or existential narratives, however this applies to the most creative outputs of the art forms and their creators who are often ridiculed for their eccentricity as they challenge the realm of acceptability.

3   Fulfilling Emotional Needs

The underlying narratives of the art-forms are what bring fashion and music together, they are both seeking to express this narrative through their own creative medium and the process of dissemination is the 'performance'.

North, Hargreaves and O'Neill's[7] research of the importance of music to adolescents found the reasons for listening to music were 'creating an image' and being 'cool and trendy', 'fulfilment of emotional needs' thereby 'expressing emotions', 'getting through difficult times and reducing tension and stress'. Finally, 'enjoyment', 'enjoyment of the music and relief from boredom'. There are some contradictory factors here – how can creating an image come from consuming music? An image assumes a visual dominance, the art form is aural. Fulfillment of emotional needs is about feelings and how we manage those feelings, it is very much an internal cognitive process neither visual nor aural, it is 'our thinking'. Perhaps the most authentic reason for listening to music, as North *et al.* state, is the enjoyment and to relieve periods of nothingness.[8] Fashion too addresses the issue of enjoyment and relief of boredom as illustrated by the most carefully created styled looks often emanating from the youth and 'street-style'. Fashion too fits all those reasons as Polhemus explains the meaning of 'hanging out':

6   M. Raymond, *The Trend Forecaster's Handbook*, Laurence King Publishing Ltd., London, 2010, p. 36.

7   A.C. North, D.J Hargreaves, and S.A O'Neil, 'The Importance of Music to Adolescents', *British Journal of Educational Psychology*, vol. 70, 2000, pp. 255–272.

8   Ibid.

[t]he art of being at the right place at the right time. Just hanging around. Looking sharp. All dressed up and nowhere to go. Doing nothing in particular. Making history.[9]

Frith noted that 'adolescents use music as a badge'.[10] This idea has also been supported in the research findings of North *et al.*,[11] who found adolescent males were more concerned with the external expression created by their music listening preferences. They communicate these preferences to others in everyday situations through their dress style choices, as McCracken explains: 'clothing opens up the possibility of examining culture as it is enacted by individuals in their negotiation of daily life'.[12] The anthropologist Daniel Miller explains this further: '[c]lothes are among our most personal possessions. They are the main medium between our sense of our bodies and our sense of the external world'.[13]

4   The Purpose of the Bond and Interdependency

The music preference is outwardly exhibited by imitating visual dress style of the music artists or bands they relate to. They imitate the performance costumes of their stylistic heroes. This was particularly evident with the fans of David Bowie in the 1970s with the adoption of the 'Ziggy Stardust flash' painted on the face, and the New Romantics that followed on with their glamourous and slick look of the early 1980s. Others choose to wear a more traditional badge denoting belonging such as a T-shirt with the music band or artist's performance name on or an image of the artist/s or the album art such as the fans of heavy metal with much more understated style. McCracken argues that consumption is cultural in character therefore clothing affords us the basic co-ordinates for a world divided by culture and symbolic integrations.[14] Mead defines the self as an ongoing active being.[15] The individual identity is

9   T. Polhemus, *Street Style*, PYMCA, London, 2010, p. 6.
10   S. Frith, *Sound Effects: Youth, Leisure and the Politics of Rock 'n' Roll*, Pantheon, New York, NY, 1981, p. 217.
11   North, Hargreaves and O'Neil, 'The Importance of music to adolescents'.
12   G. McCracken, *Culture & Consumption*, Midland Book Edition, Indiana University Press, Bloomington and Indianapolis, IN, 1990, p. 61.
13   D. Miller, *Stuff*, Polity Press, Cambridge, 2009, p. 23
14   McCracken, *Culture & Consumption*.
15   G. Mead, *Mind, Self and Society From the Standpoint of a Social Behaviorist*, University of Chicago Press, Chicago, IL, 1967 [1934].

drawn from feedback from symbolic resources that are present and active in our lived environment. Goffman defines the knowledgeable self as related to the performance and interaction of personal engagements that are monitored and manipulated as a process of feedback evaluation and re-evaluation for the continued production of our self-identity.[16]

Music anthropologist Merriam identified a functional framework that enables us to understand the bonds of the partnership.[17] The ten functions of music when also applied to fashion help to breakdown our understanding of the interdependency. The functions are: (i) emotional expression; (ii) aesthetic enjoyment; (iii) entertainment; (iv) communication; (v) symbolic representation; (vi) physical response; (vii) enforcing conformity to social norms; (viii) validating social institutions; (ix) continuity and stability of culture; (x) integration of society.

Firstly, 'emotional expression': North *et al.* identified adolescent females engaged with music to fulfill their emotional needs.[18] Clothing can be used to conceal or reveal emotional states this is clearly evident with the sub-cultural dress style of 'Goths' and 'Emos' of the 1980s and 1990s.

Secondly, 'aesthetic enjoyment' seems to be more ambiguous when applied to youth culture. The rebellious nature of youth culture has redefined what is aesthetically pleasing from that of the previous generation, reinventing what is 'cool'. René König talks of the social structural change that was taking place towards the end of the industrial period that repositioned youth in modern society as exponents of new ideas in fashion rather than the elite classes.[19] The influence of youth fashion, König explains, goes beyond their own discrete group and influenced a new attitude to fashion that not only was disseminated widely but remained with this group as they have aged. Industrialisation increased leisure time and it was the youth that sought to fill the void by engaging in activities to relieve boredom and entertain themselves, thus increasing engagement in fashion and music.

Thirdly, 'entertainment': the act of entertaining is the performance which naturally brings together fashion and music. Fashion provides a visual expression that contributes to a performance that presents the music for experiencing by listening. The need for visualisation of the performance of

---

16   E. Goffman, *The Presentation of Self in Everyday Life*, Penguin Books, London, 1990 [1959].

17   A. P. Merriam, *The Anthropology of Music*, Northwestern University Press, Evanston, IL, 1964.

18   North., Hargreaves, and O'Neil, 'The Importance of Music to Adolescents'.

19   R. König, *The Restless Image: A Sociology of Fashion*, trans. F. Bradley, Allen & Unwin Ltd., London, 1973.

music has grown significantly with the advances in communication technology so much so that the costume is an integral part of presenting music to an audience today. The growth of music videos in the 1980s brought
about an increased focus on performance narrative and costume that has
continued with the exponential growth of digital media advances. Goffman
explains that a performance is often perceived to be for the benefit of the
audience, but that feedback can contribute to the performer being taken
in by their own act altering their own perceptions of reality.[20] Appearances
are an integral part of the performance, Baudrillard's perspective focuses
on the postmodern effect of hyper-reality – we live in a world where images are more real than physical experiences, and have a greater impact on
our self-identity as we seek feedback via our screens.[21] This is consumption
motivated by the need to define and express our self-identity engendering
narcissistic tendencies.

'Communication' and 'symbolic representations' are the fourth and fifth
functions identified by Merriam. Both fashion and music are often considered
to be a language with various attempts by academics such as Barthes,[22] whose
semiological approach presented in *The Fashion System* was first published
in 1967 as an attempt to decode the garment. Miller reinforces this idea arguing: '[t]he relationship between fashion and music is embedded in and emphasized by sharing of language'.[23] A quote from the pop star Kylie Minogue,
referring to her collaboration with William Blake creative director, captures
the importance of the interplaying narrative:

> [o]ver the years, we have built a language, which I feel is our own. Music
> and fashion, music as fashion, fashion as expression – it's so important
> because it's able to pinpoint a moment in time without any dialogue.[24]

Fashion and music are expressive communications of a connective cultural
narrative and responsible for expressing the zeitgeist of the moment. Stylist
Johnny Wujek talks of his collaboration as stylist with pop music artist Katy
Perry: '[a]nything but subtle. We do tend to push things, any ideas, to their limits and would probably be fair to say that I do get off on chaos'.[25] But he goes

20   Goffman. *The presentation of Self in Everyday Life.*

21   Baudrillard, *The System of Objects*, p. 209.

22   R. Barthes, *The Fashion System*, trans. M. Ward and R. Howard, Vintage, London, 2010
     [1967].

23   J. Miller, *Fashion and Music*, Berg Publishers, Oxford, 2011, p. 1.

24   K. Baron, *Fashion + Music*, Laurence King Publishing Ltd., London, p. 29.

25   Ibid., p. 185.

on to say: 'it's about making an outrageous costume for a performance that will really resonate'.[26]

The sixth function is 'physical response'. There is growing research in the physical responses to music however the most obvious is the elicited movement to music in the form of choreographed/un-choreographed dance that is often very specific to the genre, such as 'pogoing' of punks or 'moshing' to heavy rock or highly choreographed pop dances. Fashion is created to encourage the onlookers gaze either in admiration or bemusement particularly for youth subcultures where often fashion is about making a physical visual expression of the cultural narrative often designed to shock. Fashion expression becomes increasingly important in the spaces that allow physical responses to the music such as dance venues, festivals and concerts.

The four final functions of 'enforcing conformity to social norms', 'validating social institutions', 'continuity and stability of culture', and 'integration of society'. In the adoption of the genre comes with it a social acceptance for both fashion and music. Even the most rebellious of genres such as punk have now become accepted and normalised as a defined style of music and dress be it all arguably very stylised and lacking in the original narrative of political activism and youth angst. It is only when the narrative of the genre is widely accepted can it act as a cultural stabiliser and validates social institutions. Fashion validates music as music validates fashion; each seeks out a 'star muse' that has the creativity to bond them together creating a visual spectacle. None more so than David Bowie and Kansai Yamamoto's creative partnership that was struck following Yamamoto's iconic first runway show in London in 1971. Bowie and Yamamoto shared the same obsession for performance theatre and identity as explored further by Baron.[27] Both fashion and music need those stars to shoot through the media stratosphere creating a spectacle that makes audiences stop and stare in awe, freeze framing that seminal moment forever.

In a recent exhibition at Somerset House (London), called *North, Fashioning Identity*, Charlie Porter talks of the North of England's impact on the catwalk and the inspiration drawn from music and music associated graphics. Porter notes Raf Simon's use of Peter Saville's graphic imagery '... in his Autumn/Winter 2003 collection. It was the one with Joy Division and New Order graphics on the back of cotton parkas'.[28] Raf Simons revisited the same graphics in different way for his spring summer 2018 collection. Porter also notes how Japanese

---

26   Ibid.

27   Ibid.

28   C. Porter, 'The North on the Catwalk', in L. Stoppard and A. Murray (eds.), *North: Fashioning Identity*, Somerset House, London, 2017, pp. 99–102, p. 99.

designer Jun Takahashi used Saville's graphics from Joy Division's album *Unknown Pleasures* as he realized 'their adolescent interest in youth subcultures could be extended into adulthood, in his case through the media of fashion'.[29] The bonds of fashion and music established in youth often stay with us not necessarily as a visual freeze frame, a style that never changes but as a powerful trigger to our younger self.

5   The Cultural Narrative

As posited by Baudrillard,[30] image indicates an absence which in turn is evocative and provokes a cathexis. The spectacle itself presents an evolved narrative that needs responding to, as although evocative it has created a void in the mind of the consumer. This mediates a motivation to fulfill by consuming the tangible aspects of the image created; that of the ownership of the recorded music or the clothing that creates an imitated look. As fashion dictates, the image is transient, ephemeral as the creators move the narrative on and even subvert the connotation as Bowie so often did by using bold visual statements that appear to contradict the musical content narrative of the song. His most famous stylistic persona was Ziggy Stardust, appearing first in 1972 representing not just an alien from Mars in a dress, but challenging the popular visual concept of an alien at that time which was not man or woman but more insect and bug like. In a *BBC2* documentary on the 1970s, Dominic Sandbrook explains the Ziggy Stardust persona of Bowie and its visual stylistic manipulation of stereotyped gender representation as 'a kind of performance as well as a remarkably successful marketing exercise'.[31] Bowie himself explains on the Russell Harty show in 1973:

> I am a person who can take on the guises of the different people I meet. I can switch accents in seconds of meeting somebody and I can adopt their accent. I have always found I collect, I am a collector.[32]

This creates the methodology that surrounds the creative performative star and in turn legitimizes the cultural narrative disseminated through the diverse media channels repeatedly engaging and re-engaging the consumer in the narrative reducing the cognitive dissonance and promoting collective warmth of

---

29   Ibid.
30   Baudrillard, *The System of Objects*.
31   D. Sandbrook, 'The 70's Documentary' [programme], *BBC2*, 16 April 2012.
32   R. Juzwiak (comp.), 'David Bowie Was Too Weird For 70s TV', *Gawker Media*, 2016.

belonging and togetherness. As consumers of cultural narrative, we place ourselves in connection to the seminal moment as it is located in time and space.
As König discusses, this is not an extinction of fashion but the tangible expression of the spirit of youth to react to creative forces and respond positively to
the evolving narrative.[33]

The cultural narratives of fashion and music that create lasting images and
stimulate our thinking, self-reflection and narcissistic tendencies contribute to
the voices within our own internalised narrative of self-identity. Fernyhough
coins the phrase 'dialogic thinking'[34] to describe the multi-voice quality of
experience that represents a particular perspective on the world; our understanding and experience of cultural narrative along with emotions and values.
Research into the role of inner speech is now suggesting that it is a process by
which we seek to regulate behaviour and conscious expressions of self. Memories are notoriously fallible and our memories of cultural experiences are often
collective memories of images, a series of memories we continually update, our
knowledge modifying the original memory with subsequent thoughts, ideas
and images. This concept of constant reforming the self in response to external information is central to the work of Giddens ideas of the 'reflexive self',[35]
although his concept does not fully acknowledge the internalization process
that impacts that of emotions and memory. Your memory of your youth is not
a true record as you will have quite a unique viewpoint that you continue to
update and modify through life and even manufacture to fill in the gaps and
respond to digital media channeled feedback via multiple screens. The neuroscientist Eagleman states that 'cells that fire together, wire together',[36]giving a
scientific rationale to the interdependency of music and fashion they not only
express the popular cultural narrative of the time but by working in sync they
increase the impact on the internalisation and cognition of the experience creating complex memory retrieval pathways.

6   Conclusion

It is the functions of the bond between fashion and music that provides the
clues for exploring the emotive connotation between the two, validating

---

33   König, *The Restless Image*.
34   C. Fernyhough, *The Voices Within: The History and Science of How We Talk to Ourselves*,
      Profile Books Ltd., London, 2016.
35   A. Elliot, *Concepts of the Self*, Polity Press, Cambridge, 2008.
36   D. Eagleman, *The Brain: The Story of You*, Canongate Books Ltd., London, 2015, p. 23.

authenticity of the stimuli meaning in a visually sensitized world. The bonds have become stronger and the connotations added over time with exposure to one or other of the related stimuli of fashion and music. Each industry seeks to validate its existence by borrowing reference cues reinforcing the emotive connotation and expanding the reminiscent triggers within the memories of consumers of the art form.

The partnership has clear external commercial drivers for marketing but consumers also drive consumption by demanding visual expressions of the zeitgeist of the time and external expressions of their emotions through the channels of the two art forms. The ten functions of music identified by Merriam considered along with the application of fashion gives us a useful framework to discuss the bond and interdependency with clear parallels for both art forms. The cultural narrative of fashion and music particularly in youth, creates lasting images in the minds of consumers so powerful they continue to modify and develop this overtime. The powerful bond and imagery contained within our memories give complex retrieval triggers to memories, experiences and emotions. This allows reminiscence and reflection on our former selves and contributes to ongoing development of our reflexive self-identity.

Bibliography

Baron, K., *Fashion + Music.* Laurence King Publishing Ltd., London, 2016.

Barthes, R., *The Fashion System.* Trans. M. Ward and R. Howard. Vintage, London, 2010 [1967].

Baudrillard, J., *The System of Objects.* Trans. J. Benedict. Verso, London, 2005 [1968].

Eagleman, D., *The Brain: The Story of You.* Canongate Books Ltd., London, 2015.

Elliot, A., *Concepts of the Self.* Polity Press, Cambridge, 2008.

Fernyhough, C., *The Voices Within: The History and Science of How We Talk to Ourselves.* Profile Books Ltd., London, 2016.

Frith, S., *Sound Effects: Youth, Leisure and the Politics of Rock 'n' Roll.* Pantheon, New York, NY, 1981.

Goffman, E., *The Presentation of Self in Everyday Life.* Penguin Books, London, 1990 [1959].

Juzwiak, R. (comp.), 'David Bowie Was Too Weird For '70s TV', *Gawker Media*, 2016.

König, R., *The Restless Image: A Sociology of Fashion.* Trans. F. Bradley. George Allen & Unwin Ltd., London, 1973.

Kawamura, Y., *Fashionology: An Introduction to Fashion Studies.* Bloomsbury, London, 2005.

McCracken, G., *Culture & Consumption.* Midland Book Edition, Indiana University Press, Bloomington and Indianapolis, IN, 1990.

Mead, G., *Mind, Self and Society From the Standpoint of a Social Behaviorist.* University of Chicago Press, Chicago, IL, 1967 [1934].

Merriam, A., *The Anthropology of Music.* Northwestern University Press, Evanston, IL, 1964.

Miller, D., *Stuff.* Polity Press, Cambridge, 2009.

Miller, J., *Fashion and Music.* Berg Publishers, Oxford, 2011.

North, A.C, D.J Hargreaves, and S.A O'Neil. 'The Importance of Music to Adolescents', *British Journal of Educational Psychology*, vol. 70, 2000, pp. 255–272.

Polhemus, T., *Street Style.* PYMCA, London, 2010.

Porter, C., 'The North on the Catwalk', in L. Stoppard and A. Murray (eds.), *North: Fashioning Identity.* Somerset House, London, 2017, pp. 99–102.

Raymond, M., *The Trend Forecaster's Handbook.* Laurence King Publishing Ltd., London, 2010.

Sandbrook, D., 'The 70's Documentary' [programme], *BBC2*, 16 April 2012.

Simmons-Stern, N.J., R. G. Deason, B. J. Brandler, B. S. Frustace, M. K. O'Connor, B. A. Ally, and A. E. Budson, 'Music-based Memory Enhancement in Alzheimer's Disease: Promise and Limitations', *Neuropsychologia*, no. 50, 2012, pp. 3295–3303.

CHAPTER 7

Recent Gastro-Trends: Food Surfing on the Streets

Cecilia Winterhalter

Abstract

Fashion is not only important in the apparel sector, but in many other fields. Everything that is subject to fashions must be ruled by comparable laws. This text, which studies the 'fashionalization' of cooking styles and eating practices, is based on the hypothesis that the theories by the anthropologist Ted Polhemus about the recent evolution in fashion and streetstyle, are applicable to gastro-trends or the 'new eating'. In the new ways of eating one can identify a 'streetstyle', a 'style surfing', a 'supermarket of style' and a 'sampling & mixing' which are comparable with fashion. To illustrate a free and creative mode of eating, this paper observes the recent gastro-trends of street foods, street food collectives, street food TV programs, 'food trucks', the Italian Ape Piaggio mini-truck invasion and the new eating opportunities at gastro-markets or clandestine supper clubs. It also deals with the free composition of surprising and innovative food preparations presented at culinary conferences by avant-garde chefs. Peoples' eating, on the street, with their hands, their consumption of 'gastronomic extravaganzas' and 'hybrid amalgams' are reinventing tastes, eating utensils and even eating habits. A new eating asserts a free consumer, giving rise to a new food language that changes the food culture.

Keywords

street/food style – style/food surfing – supermarket of style – sampling & mixing – new gastro-trends – food trucks – gastro-markets – gastronomic extravaganzas – hybrid amalgams – 'French Revolution'

1 Introduction: About Fashions

Fashion is not only important in the apparel sector, but in many other fields, such as music, films, cars, sports, holiday destinations, literature, and obviously food and how it is prepared and consumed. Everything that is part of people's lives is subject to fashions and their changes.[1] All these fashions must therefore be ruled by comparable laws and must work in a similar way. They all symbolically express the person's self.[2] The stylistic choices of others show who shares one's values and create a social belonging, while divergent choices tell one's difference from others, preventing one's participation to their groups.[3]

Although the exterior appearance is their most eye-catching quality, fashions are more than an aesthetic style and have an important role as languages or as semiotic statements.[4] Fashions identify oneself and distinguish others. They are a visual vocabulary of signs declaring the persons' identity and making them members of societies and cultures.[5] This membership used to be dependent upon knowing what should be worn or eaten and upon using the appropriate codes, such as: not wearing bright colours at funerals or knowing how to eat 'difficult' foods (clams, snails, sushi) or which utensil to use to convey food to the mouth. This knowledge is a matter of convention[6] and the use of 'correct' behaviours, stands for a cultural, social, national etc. belonging, which expresses identity. However the meanings of this sign-language are constantly re-negotiated while cultures change in time.[7] These changes make cultures 'typically' distinctive of a specific society and time. This text assumes that people's manifestation of identity through dress or food are very similar and are an indicator for the path taken by the evolution of contemporary society.

---

1   This idea is freely inspired by T. Polhemus, 'Style surfing', *Enciclopedia della Moda* (vol. 3), Enciclopedia Italiana, Roma, 2005, p. 361.

2   A.-M. Sellerberg, 'Moda', *Enciclopedia delle Scienze Sociali* (vol. 5), Enciclopedia Italiana, Roma, 1996, pp. 739–746 <http://www.treccani.it/enciclopedia/moda_(Enciclopedia-delle-scienze-sociali)/> (Accessed 10 September 2015).

3   Polhemus, 'Style surfing'.

4   Ibid.

5   Identity is a term used in psychology, sociology and other disciplines to describe individuality. It is the condition of being a specified person and allows one to perceive one's being oneself and one's distinction from the others, while identity construction is the process by which an individual develops a distinct (and recently often chosen) personality and a personal, social, cultural, political *etc.* belonging. Identity is a social construction. The sharing of ideas, knowledge or objects, with a group leads to the construction of a shared identity. See U. Galimberti, 'Identità', *Dizionario di Psicologia*, UTET, Torino, 1992, p. 459; R. Eliott, 'Making Up People: Consumption as a Symbolic Vocabulary for the Construction of Identity', in K. M. Ekström and H. Brembeck (eds.), *Elusive Consumption*, Berg Publishers, Oxford and New York, NY, 2004, pp. 129–143.

6   The term 'convention' is defined by the Cambridge Dictionaries Online as 'a usual or accepted way of behaving, especially in social situations, often following an old way of thinking or a custom in one particular society'. See 'Convention', *Cambridge Dictionary* <http://dictionary.cambridge.org/dictionary/english/convention> (Accessed 6 July 2016).

7   The term 'sign' refers to a semiotic comunication system. For a further analysis of the notion of 'sign', see U. Eco, *A Theory of Semiotics*, Indiana University Press, Bloomington, 1976.

For Ann-Mari Sellerberg, '[f]ashions can attack old areas ... [By...] changing rules about *how* you cook, *how* you attend your garden and *how* you clean ...'[8] In other words, fashions update and 'fashionalize' 'old' practices. This text studies the 'fashionalization' of cooking styles and eating practices.

2   Streetstyle

This text assumes that the theories by the anthropologist Ted Polhemus[9] about dressing styles, are applicable to eating trends (and probably to all consumption trends). A comparative analysis of dress and food helps to better understand both types of consumption. In his studies and in his exhibition *Streetstyle, From Sidewalk to Catwalk, 1940 to Tomorrow*,[10] Ted Polhemus elaborated the concepts of 'streetstyle',[11] 'style surfing',[12] 'supermarket of style',[13] and 'sampling & mixing',[14] which are briefly summarized in the text below. Fashions, Polhemus claims, now arise from the new blends of garments used on the streets of the global metropolis. This 'streetstyle' ensues from a free choice of clothing from designers, ethnic cultures, subcultures and vintage shops, from past and present. 'Streetstyle' allows to invent an individual dressing style and lifestyle. 'Streetstyle' expresses the individuality, freedom and creativity, typical of the present. It replaces a 'traditional' fashion prescribed by customs, designers or marketing strategies.[15] According to Polhemus, people 'style surf'[16] the entire ocean of fashion, choose the items they like and mix them into personal combinations. The history of style of the entire world is today mixed into innovative

8   A.-M. Sellerberg, 'The Practical. Fashion's Latest Conquest', *Free Inquiry in Creative Sociology*, vol. 12, no. 1, 1984, pp. 80–82, p. 80.

9   T. Polhemus, *Streetstyle: From Sidewalk to Catwalk*, Thames & Hudson, London, 1994.

10   T. Polhemus, *Streetstyle, From Sidewalk to Catwalk, 1940 to Tomorrow* [exhibition], Victoria & Albert Museum, London, 16 November 1994–19 February 1995 <http://www.vam.ac.uk/archives/searches?q=exhibition+Streetstyle%2C+From+Sidewalk+to+Catwalk%2C+1940+to+Tomorrow+held+at+the+V%26A+in+1994–5> (Accessed 12 July 2016).

11   Ibid.; T. Polhemus, *Streetstyle*, PYMCA (Photographic Youth Music Culture Archive UK), n.p., 2010.

12   Polhemus, 'Style surfing', pp. 359–364.

13   Polhemus, *Streetstyle*, pp. 209–219.

14   T. Polhemus, 'Sampling & Mixing', in G. Ceriani and R. Grandi (eds.), *Moda: regole e rappresentazioni*, Franco Angeli, Milano, 1995, pp. 109–122.

15   C. Winterhalter, 'The Evolution of the Retail Space: From Luxury Malls to Guerilla Stores: Tracing the Change of Fashion', in B. Brownie, L. Petican, and J. Reponen (eds.), *Fashion: Exploring Critical Issues*, ID Press, Oxford, 2012, pp. 295–309.

16   Polhemus, 'Style surfing', p. 361.

looks, but people are unaware of their promiscuity of styles. In his book *Street-style*, Polhemus[17] shows 26 young people happily mixing contrasting dressing styles (Converse sneakers, skater gear, biker jackets, hoodies, punk hair and bow ties).[18] A very similar phenomenon can be observed in food consumption.

3   'Supermarket of Styles', Globalization Effect and Hybrid Styles

The mentioned 'streetstyle' and 'style surfing' and the theories by Polhemus about a 'supermarket of style' and 'sampling & mixing' contibute to a global-ization effect and to a rise of hybrid styles, visible in the 'new eating'. In today's 'supermarket of styles', theorizes Polhemus,[19] all the clothing styles 'of every world and every era'[20] are on offer on the shelves, like tins of soup, ready to be mixed into new combinations and used at any time: '[j]ust take them ... stir the content and all the flavour of authenticity is yours'.[21] The people creating these mixes do not care about their new meanings. They use them, like 'a pinch of salt',[22] to make their soup taste better.

However the constant change causes a loss of function.[23] Without a meaning there is no contradiction in wearing disparate items (such as a wedding dress with sneakers).[24] All items may be used at any time, to ex-press anything. They become a huge, meaningless repository to plunder to create individual styles.[25] The 'looks of yesterday', says Polhemus, 'are strip mined ... of meaning and ... pounded into an *amalgam*'[26] in which, as in a giant soup pot, all styles mix, fuse and contaminate each other.[27]

---

17   Polhemus, *Streetstyle*.

18   M. Barnard, *Fashion Theory. An Introduction*, Routledge, London and New York, NY, 2014.

19   T. Polhemus, 'In the Supermarket of Style', *Ted Polhemus in the 21st Century* [personal web-site] <http://www.tedpolhemus.com/index.html> (Accessed 11 August 2016); see also Pol-hemus, *Streetstyle*.

20   Polhemus, 'Style surfing', p. 361.

21   Polhemus, 'Sampling & Mixing', p. 119.

22   Polhemus, *Streetstyle*, p. 211.

23   Polhemus, 'Style surfing'.

24   R. Grandi, 'Sottoculture e Moda', *Enciclopedia della Moda* (vol. 3), Enciclopedia Italiana, Roma, 2005, pp. 107–119.

25   Barnard, *Fashion Theory*.

26   Polhemus, *Streetstyle*, p. 211 (emphasis by the author).

27   In this text the term 'contaminate' is used with its Latin meaning: *com* (together) and *tangere* (touch), a modification produced by touching. It is never used with the meaning of pollution or infection, caused by contact.

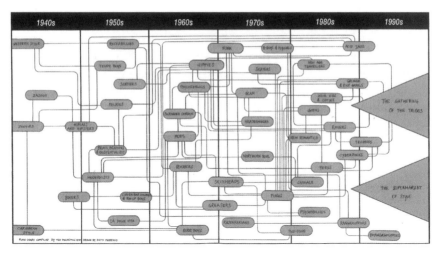

FIGURE 7.1   Flow Chart of Subcultures in T. Polhemus, Streetstyle.
RETRIEVED FROM SIDEWALK TO CATWALK, THAMES & HUDSON, LONDON
1994. USED WITH KIND PERMISSION FROM TED POLHEMUS AND THAMES &
HUDSON, 2018.

The effects of this contact of all styles are depicted by Polhemus on a
diagram in *Streetstyle* (Figure 7.1), which shows that the 'Supermarket of
Styles' and the 'Gathering of Tribes' (the two large, orange triangles with
diverging legs or catheti, on the right), will intersect and invade the entire
space.[28] In other words, these two new ways of dressing will supplant all
the others.

Three elements, which are (i) the simultaneous availability of all styles in
the 'supermarket of style',[29] (ii) the constant mix into countless streetstyles,[30]
and (iii) the increased circulation of cultural diasporas[31] have caused, experts
affirm, the setting of the traditional subcultures and have changed the way in
which society creates its styles.

---

28   Polhemus, *Streetstyle*, pp. 136–137.
29   D. Muggleton and R. Weinzierl, *The Post-Subcultures Reader*, Berg Publishers, Oxford and
      New York, NY, 2003.
30   See Polhemus, *Streetstyle: From Sidewalk to Catwalk*; Polhemus, *Streetstyle*.
31   A. Appadurai, *Modernity at Large. Cultural Dimensions of Globalization*, University of
      Minnesota Press, Minneapolis, MN, 1996. Appadurai speaks of five dimensions of the cul-
      tural flow, that he terms ethnoscape, mediascape, technoscape, financescape and ideos-
      cape. His idea is that '[t]he suffix *–scape* allows ... to point to the fluid irregular shapes, ...
      that characterize International capital as deeply as they do International clothing style'.
      Ibid., p. 33.

The streets of the city have turned into creative workshops, where new styles arise, propounded by the mainstream, subcultures and style tribes, of present and past.[32] While traditional fashion loses its power[33] to dictate how to dress or eat,[34] the new styles grow on the urban streets, by remixing old and new elements.[35] All items and styles, ingredients and tastes are quoted by 'sampling & mixing', a rap, rave and techno music expression, used by Polhemus, to explain how mixing fragments generates completely new items.[36] The globalizing contacts of immigrant communities with local cultures[37] produce hybrid styles.[38]

Nevertheless this globalization is not a worldwide homogenization,[39] but a mutual exchange, which recasts local societies. The globalizing effect of cultural flow changes, Appadurai argues, according to the local culture.[40] For Margaret Maynard, the idea of a globalized sameness is an illusion.[41] All styles modify and are modified by their proximity to neighbouring styles. This constant heterogenization[42] and hybridization [43] generates new styles, but this style change is not a process from an original form to a new one, but a new language with a completely different form.[44] All of these processes are applicable to eating trends.

---

32   A subculture is a group of people who stand out from the mainstream culture, by using new styles in items (or foods) that become like a brand of their identity. See 'Subculture', *Oxford Online Dictionaries* <http://www.oxforddictionaries.com/us/definition/american_english/subculture> (Accessed 7 July 2016). See also Grandi, 'Sottocolture e Moda'. 'Style tribe' is a concept invented by Polhemus and designates a group of people that dress with a distinctive style to show their membership to a group. See Polhemus, *Streetstyle*.

33   Grandi, 'Sottocolture e Moda'.

34   For the cause of this weakening see C. Winterhalter, 'Normcore or a New Desire for Normality: To Be Crazy, Be Normal', *Catwalk: The Journal of Fashion, Beauty and Style*, vol. 5, no. 1, 2016, pp. 21–42, p. 31 (footnote 33).

35   See C. Winterhalter, 'Conclusione', in G. Balbi and C. Winterhalter (eds.), *Antiche novità. Una guida transdisciplinare per interpretare il vecchio e il nuovo*, Orthotes, Napoli and Salerno, 2013, pp. 145–151.

36   Polhemus, 'Sampling & Mixing'.

37   See the five dimensions of cultural flow theorized by Appadurai in footnote 31 of this chapter.

38   What is true for subcultures and their dressing styles is assumed to be valid also for the new eating, see Grandi, 'Sottocolture e Moda'.

39   Barnard, *Fashion Theory*.

40   See the chapter 'Cultural Dimensions of Globalization, Homogenization and Heterogenization' (pp.32–43), in Appadurai, *Modernity at Large*.

41   M. Maynard, *Dress and Globalization*, Manchester University Press, Manchester, 2004.

42   See Appadurai, *Modernity at Large*; Barnard, *Fashion Theory*.

43   Barnard, *Fashion Theory*; Grandi, 'Sottocolture e Moda'.

44   Grandi, 'Sottocolture e Moda'.

4   A Translation from Fashion Theory to the New Ways of Eating

The new eating styles are consistent with today's fashion styles. Food trends work like those concerning clothing. The new ways of eating have also a 'street-style', a 'style surfing', a 'supermarket of style' and a 'sampling & mixing', which illustrate the features of the new eating trends. A 'trend' is 'a general development or change in a situation or in the way that people are behaving'.[45]

People now decide freely and creatively where, when, and what they eat. In fact people consume food everywhere, all the time, on every occasion. Today's food style is a free re-combination of all dishes, of the past and the present, of traditional, ethnic, global flavours, of what is imagined to be preferred by the rich and famous or eaten in foreign countries or on urban streets. In the new eating the entire food history, available in the supermarket of styles, is chosen and recombined to create surprising new dishes and eating habits, just like streetstyles, recombine garments of all kinds into personal looks. In dressing you can be a punk, a hippy, a mod or a mix of all styles. In eating, you can use one ethnic cooking tradition or combine all cuisines into a completely new food. This 'food surfing' mixes all ingredients into unexpected new dishes. It erases all eating rules, such as appropriate table etiquette or religious food prescriptions,[46] allowing a free choice of flavours, ingredients, techniques. It also changes utensils, modes, convivial habits, eating times and places.

All foods today, served as 'local' or 'traditional', are the product of a 'new alimentary folklore',[47] which invents a fictional continuity in time. The seeming recoveries of the past are 'inventions of tradition'[48] or symptoms of innovation, as I have shown elsewhere.[49] All cuisines, even those claiming ancient origins,[50] are new constructions, sampling and mixing tastes from different times or places to create new gastro-trends or a hybrid cuisine.[51]

---

45   'Trend', *Cambridge Dictionaries* <http://dictionary.cambridge.org/dictionary/english/trend> (Accessed 20 March 2016).

46   C. Winterhalter, 'Gastronomic Fashions and the Use of Food in the Construction of New Identities', in J.L. Foltyn (ed.), *Fashions: Exploring Fashion Through Cultures*, ID Press, Oxford, 2012, pp. 151–182.

47   V. Teti, *Il colore del cibo. Geografia, mito e realtà dell'alimentazione mediterranea*, Meltemi Editore, Roma 1999, p. 108.

48   E. Hobsbawm and T. Ranger (eds.), *The Invention of Tradition*, Cambridge University Press, Cambridge, 1983.

49   Winterhalter, 'Conclusione'.

50   Cusines claiming to have ancient origins are for example 'regional cuisine' and the 'Mediterranean diet'. Winterhalter, 'Gastronomic Fashions'.

51   Polhemus, 'Sampling & Mixing'; Grandi, 'Sottoculture e Moda'.

5   Recent Gastro Trends or the New Ways of Eating

In the recent gastro-trends or the new ways of eating the people (consumers, chefs) and the objects (dishes, utensils) are in constant change. This change is visible in recent trends, such as 'food trucks', gastro-markets (especially in Spain), street-food collectives (London's KERB), street-food TV shows (the Canadian *Eat Street* presenting American 'food trucks'), the Italian Ape Piaggio mini-truck invasion, market eating stalls, and high-quality food supermarkets (Oscar Farinetti's Eataly). Related topics are 'clandestine dining' (at supper clubs) and the latest dishes, surprising food preparations and the changes of eating utensils and convivial habits presented by avant-garde chefs at culinary conferences.[52] Distinctive features of the new eating styles are (i) the presumed ancient origin, (ii) a growth of foreign and global influences, (iii) a consumption on the streets, with the hands, (iv) 'gastronomic extravaganzas', which reinvent dishes, techniques, utensils and convivial habits.

5.1   *Presumed Ancient Origin of New Dishes*
Supposedly 'ancient' dishes and invented 'traditional' ways of eating have grown very popular. After the spectacular 'fusion, molecular and destructured (or deconstructed)' cuisine, in recent times consumer demand has returned to simple comfort foods or to known dishes *looking* traditional or home-made. Italy's gastronomic blogs continually publish top ten rankings of the 'very best' *Carbonara* [egg, *pancetta*, parmesan], *Amatriciana* [tomato, *pancetta*, *pecorino* cheese] or *Cacio e Pepe* [cheese, pepper] pasta dishes.[53] A rediscovered, successful Italian 'childhood' dish is *polpette di bollito* [meatballs made by recycling boiled broth meat],[54] which claims to represent the 'poor' or 'circular'[55]

---

52   Culinary conferences are where the lastest food and cooking trends are presented and demonstrated: among many others, see for example *Le Cordon Bleu* in England; *Tastes of the World* in the US; *Indentità Golose, Culinaria* or *Le strade della Mozzarella* in Italy.

53   Among many others see A. Soban, 'Carbonara, Cacio e Pepe, Amatriciana: le migliori di Roma', *Dissapore*, 3 December 2015 <http://www.dissapore.com/ristoranti/roma-migliore-carbonara-cacio-e-pepe-amatriciana/> (Accessed 13 July 2016); 'Best carbonara in Rome, five places', *Puntarella Rossa*, 26 April 2016 <http://www.puntarellarossa.it/2016/04/26/best-carbonara-in-rome-five-places/> (Accessed 13 July 2016).

54   A. Sponzilli, 'La ricetta per le polpette di bollito da mangiare con le mani', *Scatti di Gusto*, 18 November 2011 <http://www.scattidigusto.it/2011/11/18/la-ricetta-per-le-polpette-di-bollito-da-mangiare-con-le-mani/> (Accessed 15 July 2016).

55   The term 'circular kitchen' was invented by the Italian star-chef Igles Corelli. Like a circle, with no beginning and no end, contemporary kitchen should consume and recycle its materials, in an environmentally sustainable way, precisely as our ancestors did. See I. Corelli, 'Filosofia. Dal Trigabolo passando alla Cucina Garibaldina fino ad arrivare alla

cooking of the past. In reality, it quotes a traditional recipe, transforming it with high-quality meat cuts and condiments.

Among the 2016 emerging food trends, the Global Food Forums report accordingly quotes a growth of meatballs, with a stunning increase of 39.7 per cent in meatball mentions. Other emerging foods are stewing or organ meats, ethnic dumplings, vegetable roots and stalks, trash fish species (redfish, mackerel, whiting *etc.*), peasant dishes and smoked or charred foods (charred vegetable sides, smoked cocktails, desserts with burned toppings), all evoking the ancient flavours of 'home-made dishes'.[56] This presumed old-time cuisine is a typical characteristic of the new eating of urban contemporaneity, which gives an ancient, known form to innovative dishes.

5.2   *Foreign and Global Influences*

In the new eating, the multiplication of foreign and global influences assumes great importance. There is a 'nostalgia for the foreign world', growing from the increasing cultural contacts (or contaminations) with the migratory flows and the many urban ethnic diasporas of the globalized cities. Foreign flavours (such as *escargots*, lobster, asparagus for the East, and Indian/Thai curries, South American *chimmichurries*,[57] Korean fermented *kimchees*[58] for the West), foreign dishes (such as French and Italian cuisine in the East and sushi, dim sum, soba and ramen[59] in the West) and new preparation techniques (such as raw ingredients, low-temperature, *sous-vide* cooking,[60] siphon foams), which initially represented a rejection of tradition,[61] capture urbanity and a global

---

Cucina Circolare', *Igles Corelli* [personal website], <http://www.iglescorelli.it/filosofia/> (Accessed 15 February 2018).

56   See '2016 Emerging Food Trends' [report], *Global Food Forums*™ <http://www.globalfood-forums.com/food-news-bites/2016-food-trends/> (Accessed 7 April 2016).

57   *Chimmichurry* is an uncooked sauce in different versions (red or green) for grilled meats.

58   *Kimchee* or *gimchi* is a side dish made of fermented vegtables with various seasonings. The fermented taste seems to be one of the most recent 'rediscovered' tastes.

59   Soba are thin Japanese buckwheat flower noodles and ramen is a Japanese noodle dish, consisting of wheat noodles in broth with various toppings. Ramen is one of the first examples of a globalized food. See S. Brickman, 'The History of the Ramen Noodle', *The New Yorker*, 21 May 2014 <http://www.newyorker.com/culture/culture-desk/the-history-of-the-ramen-noodle> (Accessed 2 June 2016).

60   Both methods use a low, regulated temperature, which is typically around 55–60° C. In the first method the food is prepared in the oven, while in the second it is sealed in an airtight plastic bag and cooked in a water bath or in a temperature-controlled steam environment.

61   K. Latham, 'Afterword. Reflections About China, Consumption and Cultural Change', in K. Latham, S. Thompson, and J. Klein (eds.), *Consuming China. Approaches to*

exoticism. Their exotic quality is not tied to one dish, but to all foods, able to suggest it, to the urban eaters of the world.

'Fusion cuisine' was the first step towards globalized cooking. In the 1970s, different culinary traditions were added or fused (hence the name 'fusion') to create new flavours. Traditions from different regions were added in one dish (such as Indian and South-East Asian cooking) or typical ingredients of one tradition were used in a dish from another tradition (such as pizza made with cheddar and taco ingredients).[62] Fusion cooking added all the flavours, without being able to turn the sum into new foods. Today's new ways of eating are, on the contrary, a global encounter of all cuisines, a contact (or contamination), a mutual exchange, which recombines dishes and techniques, to create new hybrid dishes (such as vegetable hamburgers, 'Thai pizzas' or traditional meals served with Coca Cola).[63] Moreno Cedroni, a two-star chef from Senigallia, is famous for his Italian *susci* (with a 'c' instead of an 'h') made with Mediterranean ingredients and Japanese-style, raw fish.[64] Contemporary eaters are attracted by food's global qualities and are curious to taste new cuisines. Foreign foods, tastes, smells, utensils, and techniques, are considered a culturally enriching encounter[65] and an opportunity to acquire new knowledge.[66]

5.3   *Food Consumption on the Streets, with the Hands*

People eat increasingly on the streets and with their hands. This behaviour probably accounts for the great importance assumed by street- and finger-food. A survey conducted in 2016 by Coldiretti[67] showed that in Italy in 2015 more than one third (76 billion euros) of the alimentary expenditure, a 220 billion euro market, was spent on 'eating out'. In the past ten years this expenditure has risen by 28 per cent, driven by people's habit of lunching on the streets during the week and dining out at the weekends. These figures

---

    Cultural Change in Contemporary China, Routledge, London and New York, NY, 2006, pp. 231–237.

62   Winterhalter, 'Gastronomic Fashions'.

63   E. Scarpellini, *A tavola!*, Laterza & Figli, Roma and Bari, 2012.

64   See I. Fantigrossi, 'Dal sushi al "susci": da Cedroni a Iyo è il momento del crudo all'italiana', *Cucina Corriere – Il Corriere della Sera*, 23 January 2015 <http://cucina.corriere.it/notizie/15_gennaio_23/dal-sushi-susci-momento-crudo-all-italiana_2fa81a1a-a2e8-11e4-9709-8a33da129a5e.shtml> (Accessed 13 March 2016).

65   Scarpellini, *A tavola!*.

66   L. M. Heldke, *Exotic Appetites: Ruminations of a Food Adventurer*, Routledge, London and New York (NY), 2003.

67   Coldiretti or Confederazione Nazionale Coltivatori Diretti is the National Farmers Confederation.

confirm the growing success of street-food.[68] Originally, buying food from street vendors was a practice restricted to poor people. Ancient Rome had so-called *thermopolia* which sold cooked foods to those lacking a proper kitchen at home.[69]

Street-food is sold on the sidewalks all over the world and, according to the Food and Agriculture Organization,[70] 2.5 billion people eat street-food every day.[71] Street-foods are ready-to-eat dishes prepared on the streets (such as French fries, hotdogs, kebabs, noodles, chestnuts). They represent the cheapest meal for millions of consumers and provide an income to millions of vendors.[72] Although today it often extends beyond its region of origin, street-food was always present on the local streets. Pizza, sold since the 18th century in Naples,[73] became to such an extent part of the global cuisine that in the United States children consider it a traditional American dish.[74]

The success of street-food is linked to its fashionalization as 'finger-food', a term used for fancy foods eaten with the hands.[75] Eating with the hands used to be, in the West, an ill-mannered way to eat. In the late 1990s, nevertheless stylish finger foods, that could conveniently be eaten while standing, served in little containers with fancy new utensils,[76] turned it into a fashionable form of eating, used for glamorous openings of flagship stores or fashion show parties.[77] Street-food is today sold at fashionable events all over the

---

68   'Dall'apericena allo street food: 76 miliardi per mangiare fuori', *La Repubblica*, 27 February 2016 <http://www.repubblica.it/economia/2016/02/27/news/coldiretti_consumi_ristoranti_spese_fuori_casa-134346872/?ref=fbpr> (Accessed 11 March 2016).

69   See the *thermopolium* of Vetutius Placidus in Pompeii 79 a C., illustrated in C. Parisi Persicce and O. Rossini (eds.), *Nutrire l'Impero. Storie di alimentazione da Roma a Pompei*, 'L'Erma' di Bretschneider, Roma, 2015, p. 157.

70   FAO is an organization of the United Nations.

71   V. A. Chioma, *The Food Safety Knowledge And Microbial Hazards Awareness Of Consumers Of Ready-To-Eat Street-Vended Foods And Their Exposure To Microbiological Hazard* [M.S. thesis], University of South Africa, October 2015, p. 11 <http://uir.unisa.ac.za/bitstream/handle/10500/21791/dissertation_asiegbu_cv.pdf?sequence=1> (Accessed 15 February 2018).

72   See 'Street Foods', *Foods for the Cities - FAO* <http://www.fao.org/fcit/food-processing/street-foods/en/> (Accessed 8 July 2016).

73   Teti, *Il colore del cibo*.

74   Ibid.

75   Winterhalter, 'Gastronomic Fashions'.

76   'Finger Food', *Oxford Dictionaries* <http://www.oxforddictionaries.com/definition/english/finger-food> (Accessed 9 July 2016).

77   From a conversation with Francesca Sarti, associate of Arabeschi di Latte, a company specialized in food design and eating events. *Arabeschi di Latte* [corporate website] <http://www.arabeschidilatte.org> (Accessed 17 March 2010).

world, such as the Mediterranean Street Food Festival in Trapani, the International Street Food Festival in Cesena, the Los Angeles Street Food Fest or the San Francisco Street Food Festival.[78] In Rome, the premises of the Officine Farneto, originally military warehouses, host street-food events, such as the *This Is Food* catering show devoted to metropolitan food cultures and the most innovative Italian cooking.[79] Another street food event is *Sugo* [Sauce] – *condiments for your home*, a show offering new street foods, as well as novelties in Italian craftsmanship.[80]

Various new eating styles arise from the street-food trend, with London as usual, at the forefront. The city's most exciting, creative meals and an incredible variety of foods and tastes are served from multicoloured food trucks by the KERB Street Food Collective, in the King's Cross area, across the headquarters of Central Saint Martins.[81] 'Food trucks' are licensed vehicles selling food on the streets.[82] They evolved from ice-cream,[83] frozen foods[84] or supermarket products selling[85] and later turned to more fashionable foods, such as freshly squeezed lemonade,[86] high-quality ice cream or frozen cocktails. The trucks no longer sell only sandwiches, hot dogs or hamburgers, but, equipped with on-board kitchens, now serve, like pop-up restaurants,[87] cooked, global, gourmet dishes.

---

78   See for example C. Padovani and G. Padovani, *Street Food all'Italiana*, Giunti, Firenze, 2013.

79   D. Marrazzo, 'Roma, dal barbiere speakeasy al gelaperitivo', *food24 – Il Sole 24 Ore*, 30 May 2015 <http://food24.ilsole24ore.com/2015/05/roma-dal-barbiere-speakeasy-al-gelaperitivo/#0> (Accessed 31 May 2015).

80   R. Myrick, 'Lemonade Fun Facts', *Mobile – Cuisine* <http://mobile-cuisine.com/did-you-know/lemonade-fun-facts/> (Accessed 12 July 2016).

81   Street Food, 'Saturday at Granary Street. Street Food KERB Saturdays' [video], *YouTube*, 26 January 2015 <https://www.youtube.com/watch?v=gFlxdxgStys> (Accessed 12 May 2016).

82   'Food truck', *Urban Dictionary*, 27 May 2016 <http://www.urbandictionary.com/define.php?term=food+truck> (Accessed 12 May 2016).

83   B. Viner, 'Great British Institutions: the Ice Cream Van', *The Telegraph*, 20 August 2013 <http://www.telegraph.co.uk/foodanddrink/10252048/Great-British-Institutions-the-ice-cream-van.html> (Accessed 12 July 2016).

84   *Bofrost* [corporate website] <https://www.bofrost.it> (Accessed 12 July 2016).

85   'Vom Verkaufswagen zum Detailhandel. Geschichte der Migros', *Migros* [corporate website] <https://www.migros.ch/de/geschichte/migros-idee.html> (Accessed 12 July 2016).

86   Myrick, 'Lemonade Fun Facts'.

87   The dynamics of the pop-up restaurant trend are very similar to those of the recent pop-up store trend, but need to be investigated further. For pop-up stores, see C. Winterhalter, 'The Evolution of the Retail Space: From Luxury Malls to Guerilla Stores: Tracing the Change of Fashion', in M. Pedroni (ed.), *From Production to Consumption*, ID Press, Oxford, 2013, pp. 111–132.

An Italian version of the food truck, with worldwide success, is the Gastronomic Ape Piaggio [Piaggio Apecar] trend.[88] These minicars, invented in 1948, are redesigned to sell food on the streets. The Romeo Apecar[89] owned by Fabio Spada and Cristina Bowerman, an inventive chef from Puglia, sells in Rome foods, such as fried chicken, 'cod fish and chicks' [name on the menu] and an award-winning pastrami/mustard sandwich.[90] At the *Be (e) Happy Fest,* held in 2015 at Rome's Officine Farneto, Gastronomic Apecars assembled to sell high-quality, cooked, street foods,[91] such as gourmet sandwiches, fried appetizers, aperitifs, local pizzas or sweets, but also handicraft products and vintage items.[92] Piaggio created a special webpage to satisfy the growing request of customized Apecars,[93] such as the *Pukeko Coffee Apecar,* which sells organic coffee on the streets of Oxford.[94]

A similar eating concept (good food at low prices) powers the 'gastro-market boom'[95] which has turned traditional covered markets, such as the Borough Market in London, the Union Square Greenmarket in New York, the Mercado de Maravillas in Madrid or the Mercado San Juan in Palma de Mallorca,[96] into

88   See C. Scateni, 'La rivincita del cibo da strada: se voglio aprire l'Ape da street food devo emigrare', *Dissapore,* 3 July 2012 <http://www.dissapore.com/media-notizia-2/street-food-mobile-cibo-da-strada-aprire-ape/> (Accessed 20 August 2016); V. Lupia, 'Street Food. 11 Ape votati al panino e al gelato mobile', *Scatti di Gusto,* 9 February 2014 <http://www.scattidigusto.it/2014/02/19/street-food-ape/> (Accessed 20 August 2016); V. Lupia, 'Le 65 Api migliori di street food in Italia', *Scatti di Gusto,* 1 December 2015 <http://www.scattidigusto.it/2015/12/01/street-food-65-ape-migliori-italia/> (Accessed 20 August 2016).

89   *ApeRomeo* [corporate website] <http://www.aperomeo.it> (Accessed 23 June 2016).

90   See TV2000it, 'Siamo Noi' (Interview to Vania Orsini, responsable for Romeo Apecar) [video], *YouTube,* 2 December 2014 <https://www.youtube.com/watch?v=Lyb_-XP4NT0> (Accessed 12 May 2016).

91   See 'Ape mania. Un nuovo simbolo di libera impresa' [video], *RadioColonna,* 11 February 2015 <https://www.youtube.com/watch?v=BpuM1mJ5nkM> (Accessed 12 May 2016).

92   'Be(e) Happy Fest a Roma. Le Officine Farneto aprono le porte a 20 Ape Piaggio per celebrare lo street food su ruota', *Gamberorosso,* 1 February 2015 <http://www.gamberorosso.it/component/k2/item/1021345-be-e-happy-fest-a-roma-le-officine-farneto-aprono-le-porte-a-20-ape-piaggio-per-celebrare-lo-street-food-su-ruota> (Accessed 2 June 2016).

93   *V/S Veicoli Speciali* [corporate website] <http://www.vsveicolispeciali.com/allestimenti-street-food/ape-car-per-street-food-costo/> (Accessed 19 March 2016).

94   For information or pictures see *Pukeko-Coffee* [Facebook page] <https://www.facebook.com/Pukeko-Coffee-542939335723468/> (Accessed 18 August 2016).

95   Fdl, 'I 10 Migliori Mercati Gastronomici Del Mondo', *Fine Dining Lovers,* 6 October 2014 <http://www.finedininglovers.it/blog/news-tendenze/migliori-mercati-gastronomici-del-mondo/> (Accessed 19 March 2016).

96   M. Hegarty, 'What to Eat at the World's Best Food Markets', *From the Grapevine,* 11 May 2015 <http://www.fromthegrapevine.com/israeli-kitchen/what-eat-worlds-best-food-markets> (Accessed 12 July 2016); K. Mokha, 'Top 10 Food Markets in Madrid', *The*

fancy eating places, where cooked foods, tapas or oysters with champagne are eaten at stalls. The gastro-markets resemble the dining opportunities offered at Oscar Farinetti's high-quality food Eataly supermarkets.[97] The Eataly chain has spread in Italy since 2007, and is conquering the world,[98] making good use of 'Made in Italy' products.[99] In Italy's gastro-markets, such as Milan's Santa Maria del Suffragio Market,[100] pizza, raw fish, excellent cold cuts or hot dishes can be eaten.[101] In Rome's food markets,[102] such as the San Teodoro Market, the buyers can request that their purchases be cooked for consumption on the spot. At the fancy Testaccio Market several eating stalls serve creative foods. Cristina Bowerman, for example, runs Cups, a stall where tortellini, salads, soups and ice cream are served in ice cream take-away paper cups.[103]

5.4   *Gastronomic Extravaganzas which Reinvent Dishes, Techniques, Utensils and Convivial Habits*

The assembling of local, traditional food, with global flavours or street food gives rise to 'gastronomic extravaganzas' which reinvent dishes, techniques, utensils and convivial habits. At the Testaccio Market, Marco Morello runs Food Box,[104] a stall that 'assembles' Italian and international street food into a single eating experience. It offers Roman *supplì* [rice balls],[105] fried cream from the Marche region, *cannoli* [a fried sweet from Sicily], but also fried

Guardian, 29 January 2015 <https://www.theguardian.com/travel/2015/jan/29/top-10-food-markets-madrid-spain> (Accessed 12 July 2016).

97   See *Eataly* [official website] <http://www.eataly.net/it_it/> (Accessed 12 July 2016).

98   Eataly has opened in New York, Monaco, Germany, Tokyo and Dubai and is planning to open in Los Angeles, London and Copenhagen.

99   See C. Winterhalter, 'The Re-Invention of Made in Italy Goods: Italian Know-How in Product Innovation in the Work of Three Italian Women Crafters', in E. Mora and M. Pedroni (eds.), *Fashion Tales. Feeding the Imaginary*, Peter Lang, Bern *et. al.*, 2017, pp. 183–201.

100   G. Cannarella, 'Apre il Mercato di Santa Maria del Suffragio, e ne siamo entusiasti', *Fine Dining Lovers*, 16 December 2015 <http://www.finedininglovers.it/blog/news-tendenze/mercato-santa-maria-del-suffragio-milano/> (Accessed 23 June 2016).

101   Fdl, 'Ecco i Tormentoni Food che abbiamo odiato (e amato) nel 2015', *Fine Dining Lovers*, 31 December 2015 <http://www.finedininglovers.it/blog/news-tendenze/tormentoni-food-2015/> (Accessed 31 May 2016).

102   'Roma. Mangiate la Puglia e la puccia nel nuovo Box 5 che apre a Ponte Milvio', *Scatti di Gusto*, 27 April 2016 <http://www.scattidigusto.it/2016/04/27/roma-nuova-apertura-puccia-ponte-milvio/> (Accessed 23 June 2016).

103   I. Mazzarella, 'Cups Testaccio, al Mercato arriva la Bowerman (e apre Foodbox)', *Puntarella Rossa*, 2 January 2016 <http://www.puntarellarossa.it/2016/01/02/cups-testaccio-al-mercato-arriva-la-bowerman-e-apre-foodboox/> (Accessed 19 March 2016).

104   Food box is stall 66 of the Testaccio Market.

105   The *supplì* is an elongated rice dumpling made of rice and tomato meat sauce, with a heart of melting mozzarella, fried in lard or in olive oil. The word probably comes from the French

pimientos [green peppers] with *cajun* ribs, *tacos* or *arepas* [wheat or corn tortillas], stuffed with meat, black beans and avocado.[106]

The freedom to blend ingredients and cooking styles produces a growing series of 'gastronomic extravaganzas'[107] such as Massimo Bottura's *Foie Gras Magnum* or a *Magnum* ice cream stick covered in *foie gras* and hazelnuts from Piedmont, intending to provoke astonishment.[108] The new eating is not an addition of elements (as in fusion cuisine), but an aggregation, a hybrid amalgam of foods (with odd compositions), of eating utensils (such as paper cups), of eating modes (with the hands or new utensils) and of consumption times (such as any time rather than set meal times). All flavours can freely be combined to compose innovative foods. Recent hybrid American desserts are the *Cronut*, a combination of a doughnut and a croissant,[109] or the *Cupcaron*, blending a cupcake with a macaron.[110] The *cono graffa* [*Krapfen* ice cream cone] from Naples is a cone-shaped doughnut filled with ice cream. [111]

Known foods turn into something new, like the *Sushi Burger*, which substitutes the well-known American mincemeat patty with astonishing Japanese ingredients: a rice patty, *teriyaki*-jackfruit rags or raw fish, avocado or cucumber, pickled ginger, vegan mayonnaise, red cabbage, *nori* seaweed, *wasabi*, *ponzu* or *tamari* sauces.[112] Other recent 'transformer' variations of this traditional

---

'surprise' and the surprise is probably the stringy *mozzarella* heart. The first written record of the presence of this fried dish is in 1874 on the menu of the Trattoria della Lepre in Rome as '*rice soplis*'. Marco Morello serves a traditional and an innovative version of this dish.

106   Mazzarella, 'Cups Testaccio'.

107   For more 'extravaganzas', see 'Stravaganze gastronomiche', *Aroma. Il portale gourmet della capitale*, May/June 2010 <http://www.aromaweb.it/articoli/mangiare/stravaganze-gastronomiche/> (Accessed 16 April 2014).

108   C. Meo, *Food Marketing: Creare esperienze nel mondo dei foodies*, Hoepli, Milano, 2015. For the ability to create astonishment as a particular quality of innovative products, see C. Winterhalter, 'Innovative Products: Bags by Tommaso Cecchi De' Rossi', in P. Hunt-Hurst and S. Ramsamy-Iranah (eds.), *Fashion and Its Multi-Cultural Facets*, ID Press, Oxford, 2014, pp. 259–271.

109   Fdl, 'Un Po' Croissant, Un Po' Doughnuts: Ecco i "Cronuts"', *Fine Dining Lovers*, 2 July 2013 <http://www.finedininglovers.it/blog/food-drinks/dolci-americani-cronuts//> (Accessed 17 August 2016).

110   Fdl, 'Cupcake + Macaron = il Cupcaron', *Fine Dining Lovers*, 24 June 2015 <http://www.finedininglovers.it/blog/food-drinks/dolci-ibridi-americani-cupcaron//> (Accessed 24 June 2016).

111   F. Bellofatto, 'Cono graffa, il cono gelato con graffa fritta di Ciro a Mergellina che spopola a Napoli', *Scatti di Gusto*, 16 May 2016 <http://www.scattidigusto.it/2016/05/16/napoli-gelato-cono-graffa-chalet-ciro-mergellina/–/> (Accessed 16 May 2016).

112   S. Galmussi, 'Sushiburger, l'hamburger delle meraviglie è vegano', *Scatti di Gusto*, 4 April 2016 <http://www.scattidigusto.it/2016/04/04/sushiburger-hamburger-vegano//> (Accessed 9 April 2016).

American dish are the *Ramen Burger* which substitutes the bread with noodle disks and a Korean-inspired burger topped with *Kimchi* sauce.[113] We also find variations, adapting the dish to other consumption times, such as the *Hot Fudge Sundae Burger*, which, mingling breakfast and lunch, unites contrasting ingredients, such a beef patty, onions, lettuce, potato chips and an ice cream topping with grilled bacon.[114]

The *Eat Street* TV show, about the food trucks selling America's oddest street foods, reveals the growing hybridization of all the foods sold on the streets. These trucks' dishes not only combine ingredients from different cooking cultures but also increasingly amalgamate the foods, utensils and eating modes, erasing also the different eating occasions (lunch, snack, reception). Surprising preparations are multiplying around the world. The Wicked Witches Truck in Tampa Bay serves eggs, cheese and French fries in a sweet doughnut.[115] The Lucky J's in Austin offers Southern Style fried chicken on waffles.[116] London's On Cafe Truck prepares Japanese-inspired, smoked macarons flavoured with black sesame and jasmine, stuffed with French cheese.[117] Stefano Callegari's *trapizzini* are hybrids of sandwiches and pizza stuffed with typically Roman rustic dishes, such as oxtail in red sauce [*coda alla vaccinara*] or offal with artichokes [*coratella con i carciofi*].[118] Niko Romito's cooking school in Naples serves fried doughnuts with salted cod and buffalo mozzarella.[119] Roman-style fish giblets [*quinto quarto di pesce alla romana*], which are monkfish tripe in a garlic tomato sauce, are served by Giulio Terrinoni and a *maritozzo* [Roman sweet bun] is stuffed with roasted quails by Marco Morello at the Testaccio Market.[120] In Chicago, Luca Montersino sells *frushi*, a

---

113   E. Spens and C. Giland, '10 of the Best London Street Food Stalls', *The Guardian*, 24 April 2012 <https://www.theguardian.com/travel/2012/apr/24/top-10-london-street-food-stalls/> (Accessed 10 May 2016).

114   W. Farnetti, 'I 10 hamburger più assurdi del momento', *Agrodolce –Come cibo comanda*, 13 April 2016 <http://www.agrodolce.it/2016/04/13/10-hamburger-piu-assurdi-del-momento//> (Accessed 14 April 2016).

115   'Tampa Bay All – stars Episode', *Eat Street*, 1 October 2011 <http://eatst.foodnetwork.ca/blog/eat-st-on-location-tampa-bay-all-stars.html/> (Accessed 8 July 2016).

116   'Pounds of Pulled Pork Episode', *Eat Street*, 8 November 2012 <http://eatst.foodnetwork.ca/tvshow/recipe/15/fried-chicken-waffles//> (Accessed 8 July 2016).

117   Spens and Giland, '10 of the Best London Street Food Stalls'.

118   See *Trapizzino* [official website] <http://www.trapizzino.it/> (Accessed 8 July 2016).

119   Fdl, 'News e Tendenze. Rivoluzioni gourmet: i piatti degli chef al supermercato e a domicilio', *Fine Dining Lovers*, 5 February 2016 <http://www.finedininglovers.it/blog/news-tendenze/ristoranti-stellati-a-domicilio/#.VrYWC1rfd8s.email. /> (Accessed 10 March 2016).

120   Mazzarella, 'Cups Testaccio'.

rice roll with fruit.[121] *Treppia*, a squid cooked like tripe but with an addition of squid ink, was served by Giovanni Passerini at Rome's 'clandestine dinner',[122] an exclusive supper club.[123] It organizes monthly dinners to be booked online, in an industrial shed used as a photographic studio in the peripheral suburb Mandrione. The tablecloths are brought by the guests, eating at a very long table and the experimental dishes cooked by foreign chefs.[124] Here the hybrid amalgam regards the food, but also the consumption modes (with strangers, at long tables) and places (in a photographic studio, in the suburbs).[125]

The techniques used to cook traditional dishes are also re-invented. Pasta[126] which should be *al dente* [hard under the teeth, term indicating the cooking stage of pasta] is now sometimes served overcooked or raw. At the *Identità Golose* International Culinary Conference, held in Milan in March 2016, Aimo and Nadia Moroni,[127] the starred chefs of the Milanese restaurant Il Luogo, presented their *paccheri* [short pasta], cooked for over 60 minutes, stuffed with fat oxtail from Carrù.[128] Cristina Bowerman served raw pasta, marinated 48 hours in a *bisque* and then cooked for seconds at low temperature (under 60°C). Riccardo Camanini's *Spaghetti Cacio e Pepe* cooked in a bladder, quote Ducasse's famous dish *Volaille de Bresse en Vessie*.[129] At the Culinary Conference *Strade della Mozzarella*, in April 2016, in Paestum, Antonia Klugmann served spring-scented spaghetti with strawberries cooked with a pressure cooker, while Matteo Baronetto regenerated his overcooked pasta by steaming it for 15 minutes

121   I. d'Aria, 'Frushi: il sushi con la frutta', *D La Repubblica*, 3 March 2014 <http://d.repubblica. it/cucina/2014/03/03/news/frushi_sushi_con_frutta_ricette-2032769//> (Accessed 29 August 2016).

122   The author participated in this clandestine dinner with Giovanni Passerini on 11 January 2015.

123   A supper club is originally a restaurant which functions as a social club, but today the term indicates an underground restaurant.

124   All information was collected by the author during the clandestine dinner with Giovanni Passerini on 11 January 2015.

125   The evolution of the food consumption spaces should be theorized, in the same way as the author's researches on the evolution of the retail spaces. See C. Winterhalter, 'The Evolution of the Retail Space'; C. Winterhalter, 'The Evolution of the Retail Space: From Luxury Malls to Guerilla Stores'.

126   S. Gioia and C. Passera, 'Pasta: frullata, stracotta, cruda. Tecniche inedite a Identità: da Cracco alla Bowerman, e poi Scabin, Perdomo, Sultano ...', *Identità Golose*, 9 March 2016 <http://www.identitagolose.it/sito/it/41/14150/primo-piano/pasta-frullata-stracotta-cruda.html?p=0/> (Accessed 8 July 2016).

127   For more information, see *Il luogo di Aimo e Nadia* [corporate webpage] <http://www. aimoenadia.com/?lang=en/> (Accessed 11 August 2016).

128   Gioia and Passera, 'Pasta'.

129   Ibid.

in a jar of clarified butter.[130] Finally at the new Mama Pasta restaurant in Rome, pasta is seasoned in a cocktail shaker.[131]

The latest gastro-trend is a new way of serving the food used by innovative chefs to modify the eating habits. The avant-garde chef Paolo Lopriore is experimenting, since 2015, with new food sharing modes by introducing little, individual Le Creuset pots.[132] This serving method makes it possible to share the food on the table but also to offer different flavours, according to the taste of each guest. On the same table, oysters can be eaten raw, dipped in hot sauce, with bitter chicory or spring onions.[133] In 2016, at the conference *Culinaria – The taste of Identity*[134] Lopriore and the artist Andrea Salvetti presented their 'Convivial Table Manifesto', which moves the process of cooking from the kitchen to the dining table, where the consumers can now freely assemble their foods.[135] For this purpose two new cooking utensils, were created. 'Mystery' is a heated plate with lid and 'Vaporiera' is a steamer composed of a ceramic egg on a heated metal cone. Both utensils, cook the ingredients at the table, amalgamating the juices to create new flavours. This new way of eating allows the consumer to select, assemble, season and dose the food and creates new tastes and gestures.[136] A further evolution of

130   A. Isinelli, '6 chef per 6 piatti notevoli a LSDM 2016', *Agrodolce*, 21 aprile 2016 <http://www.agrodolce.it/2016/04/21/piatti-notevoli-visti-a-lsdm-paestum//>   (Accessed   23 Aprile 2016).

131   P. Sacchetti, 'Mama Pasta a Roma: siete pronti per la pasta shakerata?', *Dissapore*, 21 May 2016 <http://www.dissapore.com/ristoranti/roma-mama-pasta-shaker//> (Accessed 8 Junly 2016).

132   'Paolo Lopriore fuori da Kitchen che chiude all'improvviso', *Scatti di Gusto*, 18 February 2015   <http://www.scattidigusto.it/2015/02/18/paolo-lopriore-fuori-kitchen-chiude-allimprovviso//> (Accessed 9 April 2016).

133   V. Pagani, 'Ristoranti Milano: Paolo Lopriore di nuovo genio al Tre Cristi', *Scatti di Gusto*, 15 May 2015 <http://www.scattidigusto.it/2015/05/15/ristoranti-milano-paolo-lopriore-tre-cristi//> (Accessed 9 April 2016).

134   For the Culinaria Conference see L. Fumelli, 'Culinaria: 9 cose che non dimenticheremo della 10ª edizione', *Agrodolce*, 23 February 2016 <http://www.agrodolce.it/2016/02/23/il-meglio-di-culinaria-2016//> (Accessed 18 April 2016); L. Torriani, 'Culinaria 2016. A Roma il 20 e 21 febbraio lo spettacolo della cucina futurista', *Universofood*, 27 January 2016 <http://www.universofood.net/2016/01/27/culinaria-2016//> (Accessed 9 March 2016); F. Spadaro, 'Pochi giorni a Culinaria 2016: ecco il programma', *Food Confidential*, 16 February 2016 <http://www.foodconfidential.it/programma-culinaria-2016//> (Accessed 9 March 2016); G. Galeffi, 'Culinaria 2016 al Capitol Club a Roma: Bottura e Caceres alle prese con la cucina futurista', *Puntarella Rossa*, 21 Janaury 2016 <http://www.puntarellarossa.it/2016/01/21/culinaria-2016-al-capitol-club-a-roma-grandi-chef-e-cucina-futurista//> (Accessed 9 March 2016).

135   Fumelli, 'Culinaria'.

136   See P. Lopriore and A. Salvetti, 'Tavola conviviale' [video], *YouTube*, 10 March 2016 <https://www.youtube.com/watch?v=swax6tOgAkU/> (Accessed 12 May 2016).

this new eating is to be expected at Lopriore's restaurant Il Portico, opened in 2016 in Appiano Gentile (Tuscany).[137] A similar serving idea, intending to 'invent something, without inventing anything',[138] is adopted by Giovanni Passerini at his Passerini Restaurant & Co, in Paris. 'I want to cook whole pieces of meat and fish', Passerini explains, 'and serve them in the middle of the table, in order to share the main course and the side dishes along with my cooking experience'.[139] He serves the food, like at home, to a few[140] or to just one table, which share common dishes.[141] The guests share their foods and compose their dishes. By having guests play an active role, choose and combine their food and by letting decisions be taken on the table, instead of in the kitchen, these Italian avant-garde chefs use their restaurant as an eating experiment.[142] This new, but also traditional, way to serve food liberates chef and guests from the acquired restaurant eating modes and from the limited plate service, allowing them to exercise their creativity. The *plat comparti*[143] or 'shared platter', changes the eating habits and moves the eater to the centre of a free consumption. No wonder that the major food guides call this new way of eating a 'French Revolution'.[144]

6   Conclusion

This text seems to have confirmed the hypothesis that the theories of Polhemus are applicable to gastro-trends or the 'new eating' and that in food consumption a 'streetstyle', 'style surfing', 'supermarket of style' and 'sampling & mixing', comparable with fashion, are creating new ways of eating.

---

137   G. Mancini, 'Il grande ritorno di Paolo Lopriore: Il Portico di Appiano Gentile', *Agrodolce*, 5 August 2016 <http://www.agrodolce.it/2016/08/05/il-portico-di-appiano-paolo-lopriore//> (Accessed 5 October 2016).

138   A. De Santis, 'Giovanni Passerini: dopo Rino ecco Céros a Parigi', *Gamberorosso*, 17 April 2015 <http://www.gamberorosso.it/component/k2/item/1021893-giovanni-passerini-dopo-rino-ecco-ceros-a-parigi/> (Accessed 17 April 2105).

139   M. Tonelli, 'Rivoluzione Francese. Giovanni Passerini apre "Restaurant Passerini". E a Parigi cambia tutto', *Gamberorosso*, 16 May 2016 <http://www.gamberorosso.it/it/food/1024647-rivoluzione-francese-giovanni-passerini-apre-restaurant-passerini-e-a-parigi-cambia-tutto/> (Accessed 23 June 2016).

140   De Santis, 'Giovanni Passerini'.

141   Tonelli, 'Rivoluzione Francese'.

142   Ibid.

143   From an interview by the author with Alfonso Isinelli (Rome, 22 April 2016).

144   Tonelli, 'Rivoluzione Francese'.

The taste for foods is a capacity, tied to culturally defined models of choice and preference,[145] which are learnt by consuming. All people like to eat what they have learned to appreciate as children, according to their culture. Food choices are therefore determined by familiar, local and cultural customs. Recently however, people have started experimenting new eating styles. These new gastro-trends are not strange fads which will soon go out of fashion, nor are they just 'another' classifier to 'cook' new identities.[146] The new eating makes it possible to analyse how we meet at the table, how we experience our tastes, face our similarities and differences and our knowledge about the world.[147] In the supermarket of food styles, all the ingredients, lined up like tins of soup, are sampled and mixed. The eaters 'food surf' on the entire gastronomic ocean and assemble all dishes, flavours and techniques into gastronomic extravaganzas or hybrid amalgams.[148]

With the disappearance of binding rules on how, when and what to eat, all the foods, all the food combinations, all the eating modes become an immense repertoire to plunder at any time. Peoples' eating on the street, with their hands, in any place and manner, modifies the tastes and the eating habits. This new eating not only asserts a free and creative consumer, but also gives rise to a completely new, hybrid food language, which is able to change the food culture and to promote new lifestyles. Massimo Bottura, the chef whose Osteria Francescana in Modena won in 2016 and in 2018 the title of world's best restaurant,[149] declares:

> I do not cook to fill the stomach but to feed the mind. We must ensure that our food is actual, local and personal; we must convey emotions. [...] We have come too long a way, to back to the kitchens of our grandfathers and grandmothers; we are all part of a great revolution.[150]

---

145   C. Winterhalter, 'Taste and the Rise of Branded Cult Items: Secondary Lines, Counterfeited and Look-Alike Luxury', in M. Vaccarella and J.L. Foltyn (eds.), *Fashion-Wise*, ID Press, Oxford, 2013, pp. 335–345. See also C. Winterhalter, 'Taste and the Rise of Branded Cult Items: Secondary Lines, Counterfeited and Look-Alike Luxury', in J. Berry (ed.), *Fashion Capital: Style Economies, Sites and Cultures*, ID Press, Oxford, 2012, pp. 3–21.

146   Winterhalter, 'Gastronomic Fashions'.

147   This idea is freely inspired by *Global Food Forums* ™ ('2016 Emerging Food Trends').

148   Polhemus, 'Style surfing'.

149   'N° 1. Osteria Francescana Modena Italy', *The World's 50 Best Restaurants*, June 2016 <http://www.theworlds50best.com/list/1-50-winners/Osteria-Francescana> (Accessed 11 July 2016); 'N° 1. Osteria Francescana Modena Italy', *The World's 50 Best Restaurants*, June 2018 <https://www.theworlds50best.com/The-List-2018/1-10/Osteria-Francescana.html> (Accessed 5 August 2018). In 2017, it was only the world's second best restaurant.

150   F. Martinengo, 'Regine e Re di Cuochi: elogio dello chef moderno', *Agrodolce*, 7 March 2016 <http://www.agrodolce.it/2016/03/07/regine-e-re-di-cuochi-a-stupinigi/> (Accessed 9 April 2016).

Bibliography

'2016 Emerging Food Trends' [report], *Global Food Forums*™ <http://www.globalfoodforums.com/food-news-bites/2016-food-trends/> (Accessed 7 April 2016).

'Ape mania. Un nuovo simbolo di libera impresa' [video], *RadioColonna*, 11 February 2015 <https://www.youtube.com/watch?v=BpuM1mJ5nkM> (Accessed 12 May 2016).

ApeRomeo [corporate website] <http://www.aperomeo.it> (Accessed 23 June 2016).

Appadurai, A., *Modernity at Large: Cultural Dimensions of Globalization*. University of Minnesota Press, Minneapolis, MN, 1996.

Arabeschi di Latte [corporate website] <http://www.arabeschidilatte.org> (Accessed 17 March 2010).

Barnard, M., *Fashion Theory. An Introduction*. Routledge, London and New York, NY, 2014.

'Be(e) Happy Fest a Roma. Le Officine Farneto aprono le porte a 20 Ape Piaggio per celebrare lo street food su ruota', *Gamberorosso*, 1 February 2015 <http://www.gamberorosso.it/component/k2/item/1021345-be-e-happy-fest-a-roma-le-officine-farneto-aprono-le-porte-a-20-ape-piaggio-per-celebrare-lo-street-food-su-ruota> (Accessed 2 June 2016).

Bellofatto, F., 'Cono graffa, il cono gelato con graffa fritta di Ciro a Mergellina che spopola a Napoli', *Scatti di Gusto*, 16 May 2016 <http://www.scattidigusto.it/2016/05/16/napoli-gelato-cono-graffa-chalet-ciro-mergellina/–/> (Accessed 16 May 2016).

'Best carbonara in Rome, five places', *Puntarella Rossa*, 26 April 2016 <http://www.puntarellarossa.it/2016/04/26/best-carbonara-in-rome-five-places/> (Accessed 13 July 2016).

Bofrost [corporate website] <https://www.bofrost.it> (Accessed 12 July 2016).

Brickman, S., 'The History of the Ramen Noodle', *The New Yorker*, 21 May 2014 <http://www.newyorker.com/culture/culture-desk/the-history-of-the-ramen-noodle> (Accessed 2 June 2016).

Cannarella, G., 'Apre il Mercato di Santa Maria del Suffragio, e ne siamo entusiasti', *Fine Dining Lovers*, 16 December 2015 <http://www.finedininglovers.it/blog/news-tendenze/mercato-santa-maria-del-suffragio-milano/> (Accessed 23 June 2016).

Cardoz, F., 'Will Molecular Gastronomy go out of Fashion?', *Forbes*, 10 January 2012 <http://www.forbes.com/2012/01/09/forbes-india-will-molecular-gastronomy-go-out-of-fashion.html> (Accessed 13 May 2013).

Charest, C., *Manufacturing 'Authenticity'. A Case Study of the Niagara Wine Cluster* [Ph.D. Thesis], Brock University, 2009 <https://dr.library.brocku.ca/bitstream/handle/10464/3056/Brock_Charest_Caroline_2010.pdf?sequence=1> (Accessed 29 August 2016).

Chioma, V.A., *The Food Safety Knowledge And Microbial Hazards Awareness Of Consumers Of Ready-To-Eat Street-Vended Foods And Their Exposure To Microbiological Hazard* [M.S. thesis], University of South Africa, October 2015 <http://uir.unisa.ac.za/bitstream/handle/10500/21791/dissertation_asiegbu_cv.pdf?sequence=1> (Accessed 15 February 2018).

'Convention', *Cambridge Dictionary* <http://dictionary.cambridge.org/dictionary/english/convention> (Accessed 6 July 2016).

Corelli, I., 'Filosofia. Dal Trigabolo passando alla Cucina Garibaldina fino ad arrivare alla Cucina Circolare', *Igles Corelli* [personal website], <http://www.iglescorelli.it/filosofia/> (Accessed 15 February 2018).

'Dall'apericena allo street food: 76 miliardi per mangiare fuori', *La Repubblica*, 27 February 2016 <http://www.repubblica.it/economia/2016/02/27/news/coldiretti_consumi_ristoranti_spese_fuori_casa-134346872/?ref=fbpr> (Accessed 11 March 2016).

d'Aria, I., 'Frushi: il sushi con la frutta', *D La Repubblica*, 3 March 2014 <http://d.repubblica.it/cucina/2014/03/03/news/frushi_sushi_con_frutta_ricette-2032769//> (Accessed 29 August 2016).

De Santis, A., 'Giovanni Passerini: dopo Rino ecco Céros a Parigi', *Gamberorosso*, 17 April 2015 <http://www.gamberorosso.it/component/k2/item/1021893-giovanni-passerini-dopo-rino-ecco-ceros-a-parigi/> (Accessed 17 April 2105).

Eataly [official website] <http://www.eataly.net/it_it/> (Accessed 12 July 2016).

Eco, U., *A Theory of Semiotics*. Indiana University Press, Bloomington, IN, 1976.

Eliott, R., 'Making Up People: Consumption as a Symbolic Vocabulary for the Construction of Identity', in K. M. Ekström and H. Brembeck (eds.), *Elusive Consumption*. Berg Publishers, Oxford and New York, NY, 2004, pp. 129–143.

Fantigrossi, I., 'Dal sushi al "susci": da Cedroni a Iyo è il momento del crudo all'italiana', *Cucina Corriere – Il Corriere della Sera*, 23 January 2015 <http://cucina.corriere.it/notizie/15_gennaio_23/dal-sushi-susci-momento-crudo-all-italiana_2fa81a1a-a2e8-11e4-9709-8a33da129a5e.shtml> (Accessed 13 March 2016).

Farnetti, W., 'I 10 hamburger più assurdi del momento', *Agrodolce – Come cibo comanda*, 13 April 2016 <http://www.agrodolce.it/2016/04/13/10-hamburger-piu-assurdi-del-momento//> (Accessed 14 April 2016).

'Finger Food', *Oxford Dictionaries* <http://www.oxforddictionaries.com/definition/english/finger-food> (Accessed 9 July 2016).

Fdl, 'Cupcake + Macaron = il Cupcaron', *Fine Dining Lovers*, 24 June 2015 <http://www.finedininglovers.it/blog/food-drinks/dolci-ibridi-americani-cupcaron//> (Accessed 24 June 2016).

Fdl, 'Ecco i Tormentoni Food che abbiamo odiato (e amato) nel 2015', *Fine Dining Lovers*, 31 December 2015 <http://www.finedininglovers.it/blog/news-tendenze/tormentoni-food-2015/> (Accessed 31 May 2016).

Fdl, 'I 10 Migliori Mercati Gastronomici Del Mondo', *Fine Dining Lovers*, 6 October 2014 <http://www.finedininglovers.it/blog/news-tendenze/migliori-mercati-gastronomici-del-mondo/> (Accessed 19 March 2016).

Fdl, 'News e Tendenze. Rivoluzioni gourmet: i piatti degli chef al supermercato e a domicilio', *Fine Dining Lovers*, 5 February 2016 <http://www.finedininglovers.it/blog/news-tendenze/ristoranti-stellati-a-domicilio/#.VrYWC1rfd8s.email. /> (Accessed 10 March 2016).

Fdl, 'Un Po' Croissant, Un Po' Doughnuts: Ecco i "Cronuts"', *Fine Dining Lovers*, 2 July 2013 <http://www.finedininglovers.it/blog/food-drinks/dolci-americani-cronuts//> (Accessed 17 August 2016).

'Food truck', *Urban Dictionary*, 27 May 2016 <http://www.urbandictionary.com/define.php?term=food+truck> (Accessed 12 May 2016).

Fumelli, L., 'Culinaria: 9 cose che non dimenticheremo della 10ª edizione', *Agrodolce*, 23 February 2016 <http://www.agrodolce.it/2016/02/23/il-meglio-di-culinaria-2016//> (Accessed 18 April 2016).

Galeffi, G., 'Culinaria 2016 al Capitol Club a Roma: Bottura e Caceres alle prese con la cucina futurista', *Puntarella Rossa*, 21 Janaury 2016 <http://www.puntarellarossa.it/2016/01/21/culinaria-2016-al-capitol-club-a-roma-grandi-chef-e-cucina-futurista//> (Accessed 9 March 2016).

Galimberti, U., 'Identità', *Dizionario di Psicologia*. UTET, Torino, 1992, p. 459.

Galmussi, S., 'Sushiburger, l'hamburger delle meraviglie è vegano', *Scatti di Gusto*, 4 April 2016 <http://www.scattidigusto.it/2016/04/04/sushiburger-hamburger-vegano//> (Accessed 9 April 2016).

Gioia, S., and C. Passera, 'Pasta: frullata, stracotta, cruda. Tecniche inedite a Identità: da Cracco alla Bowerman, e poi Scabin, Perdomo, Sultano ...', *Identità Golose*, 9 March 2016 <http://www.identitagolose.it/sito/it/41/14150/primo-piano/pasta-frullata-stracotta-cruda.html?p=0/> (Accessed 8 July 2016).

Grandi, R., 'Sottoculture e Moda', *Enciclopedia della Moda* (vol. 3). Enciclopedia Italiana, Roma, 2005, pp. 107–119.

Hebdige, D., *Subculture. The Meaning of Style*. Routledge, London and New York, NY, 1979.

Hegarty, M., 'What to Eat at the World's Best Food Markets', *From the Grapevine*, 11 May 2015 <http://www.fromthegrapevine.com/israeli-kitchen/what-eat-worlds-best-food-markets> (Accessed 12 July 2016).

Heldke, L. M., *Exotic Appetites: Ruminations of a Food Adventurer*. Routledge, London and New York, NY, 2003.

Hobsbawm, E., and T. Ranger (eds.), *The Invention of Tradition*. Cambridge University Press, Cambridge, 1983.

Il luogo di Aimo e Nadia [corporate webpage] <http://www.aimoenadia.com/?lang=en/> (Accessed 11 August 2016).

Isinelli, A., '6 chef per 6 piatti notevoli a LSDM 2016', *Agrodolce*, 21 aprile 2016 <http://www.agrodolce.it/2016/04/21/piatti-notevoli-visti-a-lsdm-paestum//> (Accessed 23 Aprile 2016).

'La ricetta per le polpette di bollito da mangiare con le mani', *Scatti di Gusto*, 18 November 2011 <http://www.scattidigusto.it/2011/11/18/la-ricetta-per-le-polpette-di-bollito-da-mangiare-con-le-mani/> (Accessed 15 July 2016).

Latham, K., 'Afterword. Reflections About China, Consumption and Cultural Change', in K. Latham, S. Thompson, and J. Klein (eds.), *Consuming China. Approaches to Cultural Change in Contemporary China*. Routledge, London and New York, NY, 2006, pp. 231–237.

Lopriore, P., and A. Salvetti, 'Tavola conviviale' [video], *YouTube*, 10 March 2016 <https://www.youtube.com/watch?v=swax6tOgAkU/> (Accessed 12 May 2016).

Lupia, V., 'Le 65 Api migliori di street food in Italia', *Scatti di Gusto*, 1 December 2015 <http://www.scattidigusto.it/2015/12/01/street-food-65-ape-migliori-italia/> (Accessed 20 August 2016).

Lupia, V., 'Street Food. 11 Ape votati al panino e al gelato mobile', *Scatti di Gusto*, 9 February 2014 <http://www.scattidigusto.it/2014/02/19/street-food-ape/> (Accessed 20 August 2016).

Mancini, G., 'Il grande ritorno di Paolo Lopriore: Il Portico di Appiano Gentile', *Agrodolce*, 5 August 2016 <http://www.agrodolce.it/2016/08/05/il-portico-di-appiano-paolo-lopriore//> (Accessed 5 October 2016).

Marrazzo, D., 'Roma, dal barbiere speakeasy al gelaperitivo', *food24 – Il Sole 24 Ore,* 30 May 2015 <http://food24.ilsole24ore.com/2015/05/roma-dal-barbiere-speakeasy-al-gelaperitivo/#0> (Accessed 31 May 2015).

Martinengo, F., 'Regine e Re di Cuochi: elogio dello chef moderno', *Agrodolce*, 7 March 2016 <http://www.agrodolce.it/2016/03/07/regine-e-re-di-cuochi-a-stupinigi/> (Accessed 9 April 2016).

Maynard, M., *Dress and Globalization*. Manchester University Press, Manchester, 2004.

Mazzarella, I., 'Cups Testaccio, al Mercato arriva la Bowerman (e apre Foodbox)', *Puntarella Rossa*, 2 January 2016 <http://www.puntarellarossa.it/2016/01/02/cups-testaccio-al-mercato-arriva-la-bowerman-e-apre-foodboox/> (Accessed 19 March 2016).

Meo, C., *Food Marketing: Creare esperienze nel mondo dei foodies*. Hoepli, Milano, 2015.

Mokha, K., 'Top 10 Food Markets in Madrid', *The Guardian*, 29 January 2015 <https://www.theguardian.com/travel/2015/jan/29/top-10-food-markets-madrid-spain> (Accessed 12 July 2016).

Muggleton, D., and R. Weinzierl, *The Post-Subcultures Reader*. Berg Publishers, Oxford and New York, NY, 2003.

Myrick, R., 'Lemonade Fun Facts', *Mobile – Cuisine* <http://mobile-cuisine.com/did-you-know/lemonade-fun-facts/> (Accessed 12 July 2016).

'N° 1. Osteria Francescana Modena Italy', *The World's 50 Best Restaurants*, June 2016 <http://www.theworlds50best.com/list/1-50-winners/Osteria-Francescana> (Accessed 11 July 2016).

'N° 1. Osteria Francescana Modena Italy', *The World's 50 Best Restaurants*, June 2018 <https://www.theworlds50best.com/The-List-2018/1-10/Osteria-Francescana.html> (Accessed 5 August 2018).

National Restaurant Association, 'What's Hot Culinary Forecast' [report], *Restaurant. org* <http://www.restaurant.org/Downloads/PDFs/News-Research/WhatsHot2016> (Accessed 7 April 2016).

Padovani, C., and G. Padovani, *Street Food all'Italiana*. Giunti, Firenze, 2013.

Pagani, V., 'Ristoranti Milano: Paolo Lopriore di nuovo genio al Tre Cristi', *Scatti di Gusto*, 15 May 2015 <http://www.scattidigusto.it/2015/05/15/ristoranti-milano-paolo-lopriore-tre-cristi//> (Accessed 9 April 2016).

'Paolo Lopriore fuori da Kitchen che chiude all'improvviso', *Scatti di Gusto*, 18 February 2015 <http://www.scattidigusto.it/2015/02/18/paolo-lopriore-fuori-kitchen-chiude-allimprovviso//> (Accessed 9 April 2016).

Parisi Presicce, C., and O. Rossini (eds.), *Nutrire l'Impero. Storie di alimentazione da Roma a Pompei*. 'L'Erma' di Bretschneider, Roma, 2015.

Piscitelli, M., 'Napoli, Pizzeria Brandi: dell'invenzione della Pizza Margherita nel 1889', *Luciano Pignataro Wine & Food Blog*, 2010 <http://www.lucianopignataro.it/a/pizzeria-brandi-dell'invenzione-della-pizza-margherita-nel-1889/18571/> (Accessed 16 March 2016).

Polhemus, T., 'In the Supermarket of Style', *Ted Polhemus in the 21st Century* [personal website] <http://www.tedpolhemus.com/index.html> (Accessed 11 August 2016).

Polhemus, T., 'Sampling & Mixing', in G. Ceriani and R. Grandi (eds.), *Moda: regole e rappresentazioni*. Franco Angeli, Milano, 1995, pp. 109–122.

Polhemus, T., *Streetstyle*, PYMCA (Photographic Youth Music Culture Archive UK), n.p., 2010.

Polhemus, T., *Streetstyle: From Sidewalk to Catwalk*. Thames & Hudson, London, 1994.

Polhemus, T., *Streetstyle, From Sidewalk to Catwalk, 1940 to Tomorrow* [exhibition], Victoria & Albert Museum, London, 16 November 1994–19 February 1995 <http://www.vam.ac.uk/archives/searches?q=exhibition+Streetstyle%2C+From+Sidewalk+to+-Catwalk%2C+1940+to+Tomorrow+held+at+the+V%26A+in+1994–5> (Accessed 12 July 2016).

Polhemus, T., 'Style surfing', *Enciclopedia della Moda* (vol. 3). Enciclopedia Italiana, Roma, 2005, p. 361.

'Pounds of Pulled Pork Episode', *Eat Street*, 8 November 2012 <http://eatst.foodnetwork.ca/tvshow/recipe/15/fried-chicken-waffles//> (Accessed 8 July 2016).

Pukeko-Coffee [Facebook page] <https://www.facebook.com/Pukeko-Coffee-542939335723468/> (Accessed 18 August 2016).

'Roma. Mangiate la Puglia e la puccia nel nuovo Box 5 che apre a Ponte Milvio', *Scatti di Gusto*, 27 April 2016 <http://www.scattidigusto.it/2016/04/27/roma-nuova-apertura-puccia-ponte-milvio/> (Accessed 23 June 2016).

Sacchetti, P., 'Mama Pasta a Roma: siete pronti per la pasta shakerata?', *Dissapore*, 21 May 2016 <http://www.dissapore.com/ristoranti/roma-mama-pasta-shaker//> (Accessed 8 Junly 2016).

Scarpellini, E., *A tavola!* Laterza & Figli, Roma and Bari, 2012.

Scateni, C., 'La rivincita del cibo da strada: se voglio aprire l'Ape da street food devo emigrare', *Dissapore*, 3 July 2012 <http://www.dissapore.com/media-notizia-2/street-food-mobile-cibo-da-strada-aprire-ape/> (Accessed 20 August 2016).

Sellerberg, A.-M., 'Moda', *Enciclopedia delle Scienze Sociali* (vol. 5). Enciclopedia Italiana, Roma, 1996, pp. 739–746 <http://www.treccani.it/enciclopedia/moda_ (Enciclopedia-delle-scienze-sociali)/> (Accessed 10 September 2015).

Sellerberg, A.-M., 'The Practical. Fashion's Latest Conquest', *Free Inquiry in Creative Sociology*, vol. 12, no. 1, 1984, pp. 80–82.

Soban, A., 'Carbonara, Cacio e Pepe, Amatriciana: le migliori di Roma', *Dissapore*, 3 December 2015 <http://www.dissapore.com/ristoranti/roma-migliore-carbonara-cacio-e-pepe-amatriciana/> (Accessed 13 July 2016).

Spadaro, F., 'Pochi giorni a Culinaria 2016: ecco il programma', *Food Confidential*, 16 February 2016 <http://www.foodconfidential.it/programma-culinaria-2016//> (Accessed 9 March 2016).

Spens, E., and C. Giland, '10 of the Best London Street Food Stalls', *The Guardian*, 24 April 2012 <https://www.theguardian.com/travel/2012/apr/24/top-10-london-street-food-stalls/> (Accessed 10 May 2016).

Sponzilli, A., 'La ricetta per le polpette di bollito da mangiare con le mani', *Scatti di Gusto*, 18 November 2011 <http://www.scattidigusto.it/2011/11/18/la-ricetta-per-le-polpette-di-bollito-da-mangiare-con-le-mani/> (Accessed 15 July 2016).

'Stravaganze gastronomiche', *Aroma. Il portale gourmet della capitale*, May/June 2010 <http://www.aromaweb.it/articoli/mangiare/stravaganze-gastronomiche/> (Accessed 16 April 2014).

Street Food, 'Saturday at Granary Street. Street Food KERB Saturdays' [video], *YouTube*, 26 January 2015 <https://www.youtube.com/watch?v=gFlxdxgStys> (Accessed 12 May 2016).

'Street Foods', *Foods for the Cities – FAO* <http://www.fao.org/fcit/food-processing/street-foods/en/> (Accessed 8 July 2016).

'Subculture', *Oxford Online Dictionaries* <http://www.oxforddictionaries.com/us/definition/american_english/subculture> (Accessed 7 July 2016).

'Tampa Bay All – stars Episode', *Eat Street*, 1 October 2011 <http://eatst.foodnetwork.ca/blog/eat-st-on-location-tampa-bay-all-stars.html/> (Accessed 8 July 2016).

Teti, V., *Il colore del cibo. Geografia, mito e realtà dell'alimentazione mediterranea*. Meltemi Editore, Roma, 1999.

Tonelli, M., 'Rivoluzione Francese. Giovanni Passerini apre "Restaurant Passerini". E a Parigi cambia tutto', *Gamberorosso,* 16 May 2016 <http://www.gamberorosso.it/it/food/1024647-rivoluzione-francese-giovanni-passerini-apre-restaurant-passerini-e-a-parigi-cambia-tutto/> (Accessed 23 June 2016).

Torriani, L., 'Culinaria 2016. A Roma il 20 e 21 febbraio lo spettacolo della cucina futurista', *Universofood,* 27 January 2016 <http://www.universofood.net/2016/01/27/culinaria-2016//> (Accessed 9 March 2016).

Trapizzino [official website] <http://www.trapizzino.it/> (Accessed 8 July 2016).

'Trend', *Cambridge Dictionaries* <http://dictionary.cambridge.org/dictionary/english/trend> (Accessed 20 March 2016).

TV2000it, 'Siamo Noi' (Interview to Vania Orsini, responsable for Romeo Apecar) [video], *YouTube,* 2 December 2014 <https://www.youtube.com/watch?v=Lyb_-XP4NT0> (Accessed 12 May 2016).

Viner, B., 'Great British Institutions: the Ice Cream Van', *The Telegraph,* 20 August 2013 <http://www.telegraph.co.uk/foodanddrink/10252048/Great-British-Institutions-the-ice-cream-van.html> (Accessed 12 July 2016).

'Vom Verkaufswagen zum Detailhandel. Geschichte der Migros', *Migros* [corporate website] <https://www.migros.ch/de/geschichte/migros-idee.html> (Accessed 12 July 2016).

V/S Veicoli Speciali [corporate website] <http://www.vsveicolispeciali.com/allestimenti-street-food/ape-car-per-street-food-costo/> (Accessed 19 March 2016).

Winterhalter, C., 'Conclusione', in G. Balbi and C. Winterhalter (eds.), *Antiche novità. Una guida transdisciplinare per interpretare il vecchio e il nuovo*. Orthotes, Napoli and Salerno, 2013, pp. 145–151.

Winterhalter, C., 'Gastronomic Fashions and the Use of Food in the Construction of New Identities', in J.L. Foltyn (ed.), *Fashions: Exploring Fashion Through Cultures*. ID Press, Oxford, 2012, pp. 151–182.

Winterhalter, C., 'Innovative Products: Bags by Tommaso Cecchi De' Rossi', in P. Hunt-Hurst and S. Ramsamy-Iranah (eds.), *Fashion and Its Multi-Cultural Facets*. ID Press, Oxford, 2014, pp. 259–271.

Winterhalter, C., 'Normcore or a New Desire for Normality: To Be Crazy, Be Normal', *Catwalk: The Journal of Fashion, Beauty and Style,* vol. 5, no. 1, 2016, pp. 21–42.

Winterhalter, C., 'Taste and the Rise of Branded Cult Items: Secondary Lines, Counterfeited and Look-Alike Luxury', in J. Berry (ed.), *Fashion Capital: Style Economies, Sites and Cultures*. ID Press, Oxford, 2012, pp. 3–21.

Winterhalter, C., 'Taste and the Rise of Branded Cult Items: Secondary Lines, Counterfeited and Look-Alike Luxury', in M. Vaccarella and J.L. Foltyn (eds.), *Fashion-Wise*. ID Press, Oxford, 2013, pp. 335–345.

Winterhalter, C., 'The Evolution of the Retail Space: From Luxury Malls to Guerilla Stores: Tracing the Change of Fashion', in B. Brownie, L. Petican, and J. Reponen (eds.), *Fashion: Exploring Critical Issues*. ID Press, Oxford, 2012, pp. 295–309.

Winterhalter, C.,'The Evolution of the Retail Space: From Luxury Malls to Guerilla Stores: Tracing the Change of Fashion', in M. Pedroni (ed.), *From Production to Consumption*. ID Press, Oxford, 2013, pp. 111–132.

Winterhalter, C., 'The Re-Invention of Made in Italy Goods: Italian Know-How in Product Innovation in the Work of Three Italian Women Crafters', in E. Mora and M. Pedroni (eds.), *Fashion Tales. Feeding the Imaginary*. Peter Lang, Bern *et. al.*, 2017, pp. 183–201.

PART 3

Educating

..

CHAPTER 8

Collaborative Learning in Fashion Education

Ines Simoes and Mario Matos Ribeiro

Abstract

Conventionally the Fashion Design senior students of the University of Lisbon present to the public their final collections. Accordingly, until 2005 the graduation shows
comprised solely the individual projects by the senior students of the 5-year BA programme. Therefore, with the implementation of the 'Bologna Process' (and the split
of the former BAS into two study cycles) the graduation shows would also involve the
senior students of the 3-year BA programme. However, we realized that they were not
sufficiently creatively mature and technically competent, as each one tended to design
basic and uninspiring collections. In 2015 we devised a strategy with the purpose of
including third-year students in the graduation show, dividing each class into small
teams, who respectively have to structure, design and make one capsule collection under a common theme. The main goal was to engage each class 'in a coordinated effort
to solve a problem together',[1] i.e., to develop a cohesive, complex and appealing collection together. The idea behind the adoption of the collaborative learning approach
was also to oppose the enduring model adopted by fashion schools 'all over the world
[that] keep training students to become catwalk designers, highly individual stars and
divas'.[2] Instead we endorse the pedagogical practice of other creative disciplines that
'have acknowledged the need in their students to cooperate and form groups [and]
teams'.[3] The impact of the three collaborative collections realized until now was perceived by most of the students as a 'golden period, during which they learned from
teachers and classmates more than they had learned the previous years of the course',
as one student stated. In fact, 95 per cent of them acknowledged how much the created collaborative environment contributed for their personal achievements, capabilities and competencies.

---

1   E.R. Lai, 'Collaboration: A Literature Review' [research report], Pearson, 2011 <http://images.
    pearsonassessments.com/images/tmrs/Collaboration-Review.pdf> (Accessed 14 July 2016).
2   L. Edelkoort, 'Anti_Fashion: A Manifesto for the Next Decade'[platform], Union Trend, Par-
    is, 2015.
3   Ibid.

© KONINKLIJKE BRILL NV, LEIDEN, 2019 | DOI:10.1163/9789004382435_010

Keywords

fashion education – problem solving – pedagogical approaches – collaborative
learning – Generation Z

1   Introduction: The Portuguese Context

From 1933 to 1974 Portugal was led by a dictatorial regime, which did its very
best to obstruct progress and modernity.

After the fall of the dictatorship due to the 1974 revolution, the country started to experiment democracy, freedom and social development. For the first
time, Portuguese were allowed to travel and purchase items as common as blue
jeans (forbidden until then), a truly iconic symbol of youth and modernity.

Due to the incredibly low production costs, the almost inexistent textile
and apparel industries had a boom, and myriad factories started producing for
the international market. Nevertheless, the globalisation and integration in
the UE along with the global economic crisis brought new challenges to Portugal because most of the international clients looked for cheaper markets; as
a result, roughly 90 per cent of the factories bankrupted and unemployment
increased.

At the turn of the millennium, a lot of changes occurred. The manufacturing industry recovered due to the implementation of strategies to improve
technological innovation and specialization in production. Despite keeping
production almost exclusively for international labels, the new generation of
manufacturers adjusted their scale of production to respond to the demands
to produce goods for smaller brands, such as Raf Simons and Études.

In fact, while the knitwear and wool weaving industries nearly disap-
peared, the menswear production and the footwear industry grew enormous-
ly (the latter 300 per cent in the last 20 years). The value of the textile and
apparel industries grew 3.5 per cent in the first semester of 2015 and 8.4 per
cent in the second trimester of 2015, compared to the corresponding 2014
semesters.[4]

Regarding fashion education, it was almost non-existent until the 1990s,
except for CITEM, a private vocational and technical school, Italian oriented,

---

4 Centro de Inteligência Têxtil, 'Estudo de Conjuntura Junho 2015' [report], *Portugal Textil*,
   2015 <http://www.portugaltextil.com/docs/econjuntura-junho-2015/?wpdmdl=60645> (Accessed 14 July 2016).

launched in Oporto and Lisbon in 1984. A one-time instance before, a group of Portuguese art students was awarded government scholarships to study fashion at Central Saint Martins, with the purpose of bridging the gap between an industry with untrained designers and an industry with educated designers.

In 1991, the former Technical University of Lisbon (named University of Lisbon since 2013, following its merger with another University), a public institution, offered the first BA in Fashion Design. Students applied from all over the country even though fashion was not their first study option – they had not been admitted to the Architecture degree programme because of insufficient GPA. No portfolio and interview were required for admission, an instance that still exists.

At the time, teachers were selected from a range of fashion designers – running their own small fashion brands/houses of *demi*-couture – based on professional experience. The programme comprised a wide range of courses of study, from project to the humanities, along with technical ones. The teachers' role was to deliver knowledge, make students interested in the fashion field, and impart basic methodological tools – mostly 'the same draconian methods employed from [their] former college professors'.[5]

Regrettably, when entering the professional world, the huge lack of opportunities in the domestic market has been driving alumni to take internship after internship in some fast-fashion brands like Zara or small studios of local designers and brands. The alternative is to venture into the international market, and interestingly, most of the students that acquired the firsts BA in Fashion Design landed a career in the international market, some holding important positions in the global fashion industry.

2   The Problem Solving Metaphor

For some time now, fashion was accepted as a design discipline, taught and learned at higher education institutions. Is fashion, thus, 'about changing existing situations into preferred ones',[6] as Herbert Simon defined design?

Despite being from 1969, this definition is the most cited one because it fits any design discipline or even any type of human activity that requires planning

---

5   S. Faerm, 'Why Art and Design Higher Education Needs Advanced Pedagogy', *MISC*, 13 November 2013 <https://miscmagazine.com/why-art-and-design-higher-education-needs-advanced-pedagogy/> (Accessed 20 January 2016).

6   H.A. Simon, *The Science of the Artificial*, MIT Press, Cambridge, MA, 1996, p. 111.

toward a desired, foreseeable end, to use the words chosen by Victor Papanek in 1963.[7]

On the one hand, and however the phrasing is, the definition seems to follow Alexander Christopher, as he suggested in 1964 that designers start always from past forms to derive new, provisional, ones.[8] On the other hand, the definition suggests that design is a process, i.e., it is about discovering and assembling sequences of actions to solve problems.

Albeit its broadness, Simon's definition urged designers to move from an intuitive process (typically adopted by them) into a more rigorous science. In contrast, and surely more sensibly, Papanek believed that designers work within two modes of activity, i.e., logical reasoning and intuitive perception.

Possibly the current (re-)consideration that design, all disciplines included, is mainly a problem-solving activity has two causes: one, rather prosaic, might come from the academic jargon designers are required to use in their PhDs; the other, utterly idealistic, might be a revival of Gui Bonsiepe's humanistic philosophy – or, to be more precise, what he considered to be the true mission of design – widening it from the 'focus on the excluded, the discriminated, and economically less-favoured groups'[9] to the focus on sustainability and usability.

But as Alberto Zamarrón puts it, 'first, we should know what we are calling a problem'.[10] Does it only apply to noble causes and the strictly functional? Or, like Simon's broad definition of design, can 'problem' be roughly applied to almost anything, therefore also to the (supposedly) whimsical or unfunctional?

How else does someone outside the discipline interpret some garments designed, for example, by Rei Kawakubo?

If fashion design seems to despise functionality and looks like it is drawn to the ephemeral and quickly obsolete, Anne Hollander, among other fashion researchers, reminds us that 'tedium in fashion is much more unbearable than

---

7   V. Papanek, *Designing for the Real World: Human Ecology and Social Change*, Thames & Hudson, London, 2006 <https://monoskop.org/images/c/c2/Papanek_Victor_Design_for_the_Real_World_2nd_ed.pdf> (Accessed 14 July 2016).

8   J. Michl, 'E.H. Gombrich's Adoption of the Formula Form Follows Function: A Case of Mistaken Identity?', *Human Affairs*, vol. 19, 2009, pp. 274–288 <http://janmichl.com/eng.gombrich-fff.pdf> (Accessed 16 December 2011).

9   G. Bonsiepe, 'Design and Democracy', *Design Issues*, vol. 22, no. 2, 2006, pp. 27–34, p. 30.

10   A. Zamarrón, 'The Problem of Identifying with Problem Solving', *UX Collective*, 9 April 2015 <https://uxdesign.cc/the-problem-of-identifying-design-with-problem-solving-e5fb88d7d640> (Accessed 14 July 2016).

any sort of physical discomfort, [therefore] a certain amount of trouble and effort is a defining element of dress, as it is of all art'.[11]

Of course, fashion design aspires to become recognized as an art form. As such, its functional aspect is primarily to provide a pleasurable aesthetic experience, to stimulate the senses; secondly, it is 'a sign of its need, at times, to conceal its mass production and mass-market roots',[12] two circumstances that are inherent to design.

In spite of this, fashion design is concerned with the creation of tangible products for everyday life, ranging from workwear to leisurewear, from informal to formal wear. As such, its functional aspect is primarily focused on the experience of the user, whatever the situation may be. How else would we interpret the garments designed, for example, by Madeleine Vionnet?

Thus, the quest of fashion design, and also of all other design disciplines, has always been to improve the formal and functional (along with the recently added usage and sustainable) elements of the existing situations (objects or systems), or engender new, necessary, ones, in order to satisfy the user. How else would we interpret the emergence and evolution of pants since ancient times?

Given the above, another question arises: how should fashion design be now taught and learned at higher education institutions, particularly in the first-study cycle?

3   The Challenges of the Bologna Framework

In 2003, the European Union organized the 'Bologna Convention for the European Higher Education Area', more commonly known as the 'Bologna Process', with the intention of creating identical systems of higher education in Europe.

After 2005 the previous 5-year BA programmes were split into a first-study cycle (3 years), and a second-study cycle (2 years); moreover, the academic year system was converted into the semester system (14 weeks each) and the contact hours were reduced drastically (24 per week), stipulations that have been challenging for teachers and students alike, as the 'fleeting' stressful semesters (Portuguese people don't like to be hurried), the amount of work done outside the classroom (Portuguese students are not very able to manage alone), the constant resets and peaks on top of the long school breaks disrupt the flow of teaching/learning.

---

11   A. Hollander, *Sex and Suits: The Evolution of Modern Dress*, Claridge Press, Brinkworth, 1994, p. 48.

12   P. Sparke, *The Genius of Design*, Quadrille Publishing, London, 2009, p. 10.

Manifestly the new framework demanded that substantial alterations were made to the curricula of the courses and that the objectives of the two cycles were clearly different. Accordingly, the BA in Fashion Design (the focal point of this chapter) offered by the University of Lisbon was designed to provide a basic understanding of the fashion world as well as basic skills in product development (subject to given briefs), and the master's degree was designed to let students follow their own design interests and methods.

In 2014 the BA coordinator outlined a new programme of study similar to that of art education (no longer based on copying the works of renowned artists nor in the production of artworks for a particular audience), so as to develop a range of cognitive and practical skills and to rouse the expression of creativity in students (even if it may be embryonic in the first-study cycle).

Accordingly, the BA in Fashion Design is not grounded on consumption; instead, it is grounded on the experience of the user (reminding the students that they, too, have an experience as a dressed body).

The course is organized in a gradual system of complexity, similar to the process of learning how to 'read and write' because, in the same way as we begin by processing letters, translate them into sounds, and connect this information with a known meaning, fashion is based on the organization of visual and tactile (not to mention audible) elements and the construction of relationships among them.

In practical terms, first-year students focus on details and garments, moving from parts to wholes; second-year students focus on garment families and looks, moving from objects to relationships; third-year students focus on capsule collections and line ups, moving from concept to narrative.

Overall, the BA favours experimental creative processes as opposed to fixed, mechanical methods, so as to incite a fondness for discovery and to assure students that,

> [t]here is no 'right' way to approach design; there are no 'wrong' turns. Everything matters. Designers are problem-solvers. Problems present challenges that require solutions and these often lead to the most original design, or at least one the designer hadn't thought of initially. Mistakes must also be embraced for they often lead to the most glorious discoveries that one could not have predicted, yielding fresh concepts that drive silhouette and form forward. Innovation often happens on the heels of error in the midst of chaos and complexity.[13]

---

13   F. Dieffenbacher, *Fashion Thinking: Creative Approaches to the Design Process*, Ava Publishing, London, 2012, p. 10.

To be honest to dare the students to think outside the box is not an easy deed because the Portuguese are generally conservative – possibly an effect of the 'sort of 'grey age', a monochromatic standstill that lasted for 4 decades', as Baptista described the dictatorship.[14]

4   The Portuguese Generation Z

With the new millennium, many students entering college choose Fashion Design above all other study options, because, unlike their 1990s peers, 'they find the fashion world better than any other job'.[15] This shift in career preference should mean that teaching Fashion Design is easier, as students would be more willingly involved in learning the implicated skills. However, we have been observing that Generation Z students – born from the mid-1990s to early 2000s – today's undergraduates, seem to be unable to relate their own experiences as dressed bodies with the process of designing fashion products.

The reasons for this apparent lack of tacit knowledge – i.e., what we know how to do unthinkingly, e.g., how to get dressed and undressed, how to dress for cold or warm weather – may lay in the fact that fast fashion, a phenomenon that came to the fore in the late 1990s, is the current consumption practice. For one thing, the quick manufacturing of clothes based on current, high-cost luxury fashion trends, sold at an affordable price encourages a 'throwaway' attitude among users.[16] The constant need for stimulation explains, to some extent, why both fast fashion and users embrace obsolescence. Youngsters, in particular and unsurprisingly, are the perfect 'victims', as they are 'continually evolving temporary identities'.[17] New clothes are available every few weeks and correspondingly discarded, a pace that results in long-run indifference (as though old clothes cannot be affectionately regarded) and excludes from consciousness much of the details (as though clothes are merely perceived as inkblots).

Although Portuguese Generation Z students aren't different from their peers around the world (they are also technologically savvy, connected 24 hours a day,

---

14   J. Baptista, 'What Was It Like to Live Under Estado Novo?', *Quora*, 6 March 2016 <https://www.quora.com/What-was-it-like-to-live-under-Estado-Novo> (Accessed 14 July 2016).

15   R. Hameed, 'The Effects of Fashion on Teenagers', *Voice of Journalists*, 26 May 2016 <http://www.voj.news/the-effects-of-fashion-on-teenagers/> (Accessed 24 April 2017).

16   A. Joy, J. Sherry, A. Venkatesh, J. Wang, and R. Chan, 'Fast Fashion, Sustainability, and the Ethical Appeal of Luxury Brands', *Fashion Theory*, vol. 16, no. 13, 2012, pp. 273–296.

17   Ibid., p. 276.

follow and participate in a wide range of social media), they entirely depend economically and emotionally on their parents, who pamper their offspring and keep 'protecting' them from the social reality (the excess of graduates, the lack of employment opportunities, the short-term employment practices *etc.*) until their 30s or more. Consequently, many of them don't feel hurried to leave their parents' 'nest' and only do it after they 'collected' several degrees (entirely sponsored by their progenitors).

As first-time college students, they are under-prepared as the great majority doesn't 'read' or attend any art shows and performing arts events, except for pop and electronic music festivals. Smartphones and other technological devices are their best friends; social media dominates their lives. The information they search on the Internet is very shallow and they are not particularly concerned with issues like validity or ethics: research, for instance, is normally developed using Google or Pinterest (as they consider analogical research boring).

In order to rethink the way fashion design is taught, educators must be prepared to understand and face the characteristics of Generation Z, or else we risk increasing the gap between the way we teach and the way this generation learns. Obviously to avoid this barrier requires thinking of and embracing alternative learning approaches.

In defence of these students' self-centeredness, the enduring model adopted by fashion schools 'all over the world keep training students to become catwalk designers, highly individual stars and divas'.[18]

But since 'fashion is not created by a single individual but by everyone involved in the production of fashion, and thus fashion is a collective activity',[19] it isn't sufficient to think that

> [i]n truth, learning is almost always a collaborative event, whether from author to reader, teacher to student, or student to student [...] essentially, we learn in dialogue, in relationship – in community. So, we must rethink what our idea of a design school means, in light of creating a learning community.[20]

---

18   Edelkoort, 'Anti_Fasion'.

19   Y. Kawamura, *Fashion-ology: An Introduction to Fashion Studies*, Berg Publishers, Oxford and New York, NY, 2004, p. 1.

20   M. DeKay, 'Systems Thinking as the Basis for an Ecological Design Education'[conference paper], *Proceedings of the 21st National Passive Solar Conference*, April 1996 <https://www. academia.edu/people/search?utf8=✓&q=Systems+Thinking+as+the+Basis+for+an+Ecological+Design+Education> (Accessed 5 June 2017).

5 Collaborative Learning in Fashion Design

Considering that third-year students are not yet creatively mature and technically competent – as each one tends to design basic and uninspiring collections – and since the University of Lisbon established long ago that senior students must be part of the DEMO graduation shows, an alternative to the enduring model adopted by fashion schools was to develop a culture of collaboration in the teaching and learning process, beginning by adopting the pedagogical approach of other creative disciplines that 'have acknowledged the need in their students to cooperate and form groups [and] teams'[21] so they understand more easily the importance of working together toward a common goal.

This approach goes along with the European Qualifications Framework for Lifelong Learning (EQF), as it recommends that higher education students should acquire a variety of competencies, such as, to 'adapt own behaviour to circumstances in solving problems ... exercise self-management within the guidelines of work or study ... review the performance of self and others ... manage individuals and groups'.[22] Actually the competencies acquired through collaborative learning, a pedagogical approach experienced by our third-year students since 2015, correspond with the ones highlighted by the neuroscientist and psychologist Alma Dzib Goodin, which comprise the 'ability to solve group and not only personal [problems] ... to act as an element of a group ... the ability to accept and learn with critics'.[23]

The first collaborative learning project was carried out throughout the second semester of 2015 and involved third-year students and teachers. Both classes of 30 students were divided into teams of five, each having the responsibility of designing and make a capsule collection of six looks to be presented in the DEMO'15 graduation show. The teachers' role was not only to ensure that the teams' dynamics was positive but also to guide the students toward directions recognized as potential (regarding the concepts/themes chosen by each group). Part of the materials and colours were common to ensure harmony among the collections.

21 Edelkoort, 'Anti_Fasion'.

22 European Commission, 'European Qualifications Framework for Lifelong Learning (EQF)' [document], *ecompetences.eu*, 2008 <www.ecompetences.eu/site/objects/download/4550_EQFbroch2008en.pdf> (Accessed 27 October 2017).

23 A. Dzib Goodin, 'Successful at the Academy, Less So at Finding Employment: Different Skills Needed', *The Evolllution*, 1 June 2012 <http://www.evolllution.com/curriculum_planning/successful-at-the-academy-less-so-at-finding-employment-different-skills-needed/> (Accessed 19 September 2017).

The second collaborative learning project took place in 2016, also involved the two classes of third-year students and teachers throughout the second semester. This time the complexity of the problem increased, as each class – divided into five teams of four/five students – had to design and make one sole collection under the teachers' creative guidance to be presented in the DEMO'16 graduation show. In both classes the process was similar: every team worked on a distinct capsule or category, namely, surface design and accessories, menswear, knitwear, womenswear, streetwear/sportswear. The final collections – which included capsules with 10 to 12 looks (totalizing 85 garments), 25 accessories and 5 prints – were developed from the overarching concept/themes discussed in class. Materials and colours were the starting point for the design process, including the surface design.

The third collaborative learning project occurred in 2017, comprising the two classes of third-year students and teachers as well. Unlike the previous years, the two collections started to be developed in the first semester because the teachers believed that expanding the duration of the process would bring to full development the students' ideas and consequently improve their results. However, the school break (from mid-December to mid-February) disrupted the flow of work and forced the students of each class to reset their ideas for the two collections of 40 looks. As perceived in the DEMO'17 graduation show, the 'wasted time' had no negative effect on the outcomes.

In the three instances described previously each team comprised students with different skills (drawing, pattern cutting, sewing *etc.*) so as to balance the end results. Since students had never had to design and make so many garments in a short period of time, they planned the various implicated activities.

Of course, some groups didn't team-up as well as others, due to conflicting aesthetic ideas or the disorganization of some members. Nevertheless, it was really exciting to observe the interaction among students while engaged in discussion, involved in learning to 'negotiate', develop/share skills and teach their peers (as valuable qualities in the professional context).

If in the beginning it was hard for them to adjust their creative and technical skills to a shared project, they rapidly became aware of the many advantages of collaborative work and coordinated efforts to solve a problem together. If at first they seemed unable to surpass dull and basic design solutions, to go beyond a 'grey' colour palette and to envisage the applicability of the selected fabrics, they soon opened up their minds due to the environment of active, involved, exploratory process they were able to create.

After each DEMO, the teachers collected the students' opinions about the collaborative experience so as to analyse the strengths and weaknesses of the implemented pedagogical approach. On the whole, the strengths are summarized in statements like, '[w]ith this methodology, there was a better use of each member's capabilities'. Actually, for most of the students, the experience was a 'golden period, during which they learned from teachers and classmates more than they had learned the previous years of the course', as one stated; for another, 'it was a period of discovery', one where they realized that the design process is not 'closed' when the drawings are apparently concluded. By moving from the 2D thinking process into the actual making of the clothes and accessories they found solutions they hadn't thought of initially.

By eagerly spending nearly 18 hours a day together – sharing concepts, ideas and patterns, deciding on the best finishes and details, editing, styling and line-up – students did their very best for a cohesive, complex and appealing collection. All things considered, 'the feeling of a job well done', as stated by one student, is a fact not a misconception regarding the three experiments.

Nevertheless, just like in any project or experience, we identified one weakness in 2017. By developing a collaborative collection, the dozens of garments are essentially the product of aesthetic, formal and technical compromises. That being the case, some students (20 per cent) of one class stated that did not identify themselves with the final edited collection. Although this single instance was viewed by us as a result of a consequence of the ineffectual dynamic created among students, due to the fact that 5 per cent of them did not drop the wannabe diva attitude.

6   Conclusion

The majority of the third-year students involved in the collaborative learning projects considered that the high point of the experience was that it 'increased their notions of compromise and responsibility toward the group', and the feeling of having never felt 'so close to one another'.

Notwithstanding the students' praise, it was important to observe whether the implemented pedagogical approach had had an impact on their development as designers. So, in 2015, after the semester was over, the students were asked to design a small collection on their own. Unfortunately, only a few projects were turned in (as the majority of students were enjoying their holidays), but they displayed an increased formal quality albeit having traces of the collaborative collections.

The validity of the collaborative learning process was also evident after observing the attitudes of the former third-year students while first-year master students: despite having to design individual collections they kept sharing/helping one another. In a conversation with us, some of them acknowledged that the collaborative learning approach (experienced the year before) had put an end on the selfish pose they once had, a circumstance that made them grow as designers and individuals.

It should be said that supervising collaborative projects instead of individual projects is far more arduous for teachers, as they have to organize teams with distributed skills, manage the participation/interaction within each team and between all teams, oversee the students' discussions and mediate negotiations, constantly check if activities are carried out according to the devised schedules, and so on.

Nevertheless, the worth of collaborative learning compensates the effort, as it is a way to counter the obsessive virtual connectedness Generation Z have and to develop their cognitive and practical skills, on top of their creative and technical aptitudes. Owing to those aspects, the fourth collaborative learning project is now being designed (to be presented in June 2018) to expand the collaboration among the students of both classes, so that they create and produce a single collection instead of two different ones. The intention is to further the students' adaptability and flexibility to and toward others, besides having to tackle a much more complex problem and to face broader challenges.

Having proven to be positive, a combination of flipped teaching and collaborative learning has been implemented in other study courses, namely, pattern cutting, enabling second-year and third-year students to overcome their fear of the technical elements of fashion design and acquire a creative approach to clothing construction.

The benefits that this combination of approaches brought to the students who present publically their collections in the DEMO graduation shows are substantial: it enhanced their ability to solve team problems and to know how to act as a team element instead of wannabe divas. Another plus is that it prepares students for real social life and employment situations. Unfortunately, it is not yet possible to know the impact of the collaborative teaching/learning process on the apparel industry, because part of the students has enrolled in MA programmes (in Portugal and abroad). However, an increasing number of graduate students are being scouted by multinational clothing companies, such as the Inditex Group, and fashion online platforms like Farfetch.

Bibliography

Baptista, J., 'What Was it Like to Live Under Estado Novo?', *Quora*, 6 March 2016 <https://www.quora.com/What-was-it-like-to-live-under-Estado-Novo> (Accessed 14 July 2016).

Bonsiepe, G., 'Design and Democracy', *Design Issues*, vol. 22, no. 2, 2006, pp. 27–34.

Centro de Inteligência Têxtil, 'Estudo de Conjuntura Junho 2015' [report], *Portugal Textil*, 2015 <http://www.portugaltextil.com/docs/econjuntura-junho-2015/?wpdm-dl=60645> (Accessed 14 July 2016).

DeKay, M., 'Systems Thinking as the Basis for an Ecological Design Education' [conference paper], *Proceedings of the 21st National Passive Solar Conference*, April 1996 <https://www.academia.edu/people/search?utf8=✓&q=Systems+Thinking+as+the+Basis+-for+an+Ecological+Design+Education> (Accessed 5 June 2017).

Dieffenbacher, F., *Fashion Thinking: Creative Approaches to the Design Process.* Ava Publishing, London, 2012.

Dzib Goodin, A., 'Successful at the Academy, Less So at Finding Employment: Different Skills Needed', *The Evolllution*, 1 June 2012 < http://www.evolllution.com/curriculum_planning/successful-at-the-academy-less-so-at-finding-employment-different-skills-needed/> (Accessed 19 September 2017).

Edelkoort, L., 'Anti_Fashion: A Manifesto for the Next Decade' [platform], Union Trend, Paris, 2015.

European Commission, 'European Qualifications Framework for Lifelong Learning (EQF)' [document], *ecompetences.eu*, 2008 <www.ecompetences.eu/site/objects/download/4550_EQFbroch2008en.pdf> (Accessed 27 October 2017).

Faerm, S., 'Why Art and Design Higher Education Needs Advanced Pedagogy', *MISC*, 13 November 2013 <https://miscmagazine.com/why-art-and-design-higher-education-needs-advanced-pedagogy/> (Accessed 20 January 2016).

Hameed, R., 'The Effects of Fashion on Teenagers', *Voice of Journalists*, 26 May 2016 <http://www.voj.news/the-effects-of-fashion-on-teenagers/> (Accessed 24 April 2017).

Hollander, A., *Sex and Suits: The Evolution of Modern Dress.* Claridge Press, Brinkworth, 1994.

Joy, A., J. Sherry, A. Venkatesh, J. Wang, and R. Chan, 'Fast Fashion, Sustainability, and the Ethical Appeal of Luxury Brands', *Fashion Theory*, vol. 16, no. 13, 2012, pp. 273–296.

Kawamura, Y., *Fashion-ology: An Introduction to Fashion Studies.* Berg Publishers, Oxford and New York, NY, 2004.

Lai, E. R., 'Collaboration: A Literature Review' [research report], Pearson, 2011 <http://images.pearsonassessments.com/images/tmrs/Collaboration-Review.pdf> (accessed 14 July 2016).

Michl, J., 'E.H. Gombrich's Adoption of the Formula Form Follows Function: A Case of Mistaken Identity?', *Human Affairs*, vol. 19, 2009, pp. 274–288 <http://janmichl.com/eng.gombrich-fff.pdf> (Accessed 16 December 2011).

Papanek, V., *Designing for the Real World: Human Ecology and Social Change.* Thames & Hudson, London, 2006 <https://monoskop.org/images/c/c2/Papanek_Victor_Design_for_the_Real_World_2nd_ed.pdf> (Accessed 14 July 2016).

Simon, H. A., *The Science of the Artificial*. MIT Press, Cambridge, MA, 1996.

Sparke, P., *The Genius of Design*. Quadrille Publishing, London, 2009.

Zamarrón, A., 'The Problem of Identifying with Problem Solving', *UX Collective*, 9 April 2015 <https://uxdesign.cc/the-problem-of-identifying-design-with-problem-solving-e5fb88d7d640> (Accessed 14 July 2016).

CHAPTER 9

Clothing and Body: Case Studies in 'Slow Fashion' in Fashion Education

Lan Lan and Peng Liu

Abstract

'Same bed, different dreams'[1] is a Chinese expression which reflects the ambivalent relationship in the collaboration between Chinese and Italian fashion corporations in the early years of 2000. More than a decade later, with the economic boom slowing down in China, the manufacturers have shifted focus to designer-driven product in order to better position themselves in the increasingly competitive market. It reflects the rise of 'creative economy' in China. Meanwhile, fashion schools in China have also realized the industrial shift in demanding highly innovative and creative designers who can turn 'imagination into a product'.[2] In response to the market, for example, the curriculum of the School of Fashion at Beijing Institute of Fashion Technology (BIFT) focuses on the engagement between body and clothing to provoke sensations which allows 'a reflexive and elective sense of self'[3] to be activated during the process of making, so called 'slow fashion'. This paper draws rich discussions from body study and fashion study to further elaborate the idea of 'slow fashion' applied in Chinese fashion education. It delineates the relationship between body, as historical inherited and cultural embodied being,[4] and clothing, as 'performative aspect of self'[5] or a 'given identity' through case studies at BIFT. Particularly, the investigation demonstrates how

---

1 R. S. Segre, 'China and Italy: Fast Fashion Versus Pret a Porter. Towards a New Culture of Fashion', *Fashion Theory: The Journal of Dress, Body & Culture*, vol. 9, no. 1, 2005, pp. 43–56, p. 43.

2 A. Bill, 'Blood, Sweet and Shears: Happiness, Creativity, and Fashion Education', *Fashion Theory: The Journal of Dress, Body & Culture*, vol. 16, no. 1, 2012, pp. 49–65, p. 50.

3 A. Briggs, 'The Fashioned Body: Fashion, Dress and Modern Social Theory, Joanne Entwistle', *Fashion Theory: The Journal of Dress, Body & Culture*, vol. 5, no. 2, 2001, pp. 225–228, p. 227.

4 C. Shilling, *The Body and Social Theory*, Sage Publications, London, 1993; S. B. Turner, *The Body & Society, Second Edition: Explorations in Social Theory*, Sage Publications, London, 1996; M. Douglas, 'The Two Bodies', in M. Fraser and M. Greco (eds.), *The Body: A Reader*, Routledge, New York, NY, 2005, pp. 68–78; M. Mauss, 'Techniques of the Body', in M. Fraser and M. Greco (eds.), *The Body: A Reader*, Routledge, New York, NY, 2005, pp. 73–77.

5 J. Entwistle, 'Fashion and the Fleshy Body: Dress as Embodied Practice', *Fashion Theory: The Journal of Dress, Body & Culture*, vol. 4, no. 3, 2000, pp. 323–347, p. 324.

© KONINKLIJKE BRILL NV, LEIDEN, 2019 | DOI:10.1163/9789004382435_011

Chinese fashion students realize and develop a sense of individuality through 'slow fashion' reflecting to their traditional culture, while living in an urban lifestyle.

Keywords

fashion education – slow fashion – body – clothing

1   Introduction

Given the changing environment of global economy, the economic transition, shifting from manufacturing economy labelled as 'Made in China' to creative economy seen as 'Designed in China', has been promoted by the central government underlined with several policies. The movement has taken place in China for nearly a decade. Undertaking economic transition has caused impact on various social aspects, particularly in product/fashion design. Chinese designers need to reflect the new demands in their design work achieving sustainable economy, thereby the economic transition aims to sustain the constant economic growth that leads to a re-consideration of design aesthetic and technique.

Specifically, there is a top-down intention to embrace Chinese traditional and cultural elements in design work which the authorities believe would benefit the economy in the long run. Despite being inscribed with cultural meaning as one aspect of so called 'slow fashion' in the field of fashion design, 'everything [every intention] came from a position, and every position was political'.[6] However, the political implication of promoting Chinese culture in design, seen as a Chinese version of 'slow fashion', is not the focus of the chapter, neither of the impact of the policies on actual economy. Rather we are interested in the implementation and impact of the cultural promotion in fashion design education in Chinese institutes. In other words, how fashion institutes interpret and convey the cultural/traditional orientated concept of 'slow fashion' into curriculum teaching.

Due to the 'Cultural Revolution', Chinese tradition and culture had been interrupted and depressed for a decade long with a sluggish economy afterwards. Since the economy 'open-up' policy came to effect this has lifted China in economic capital. The cultural capital however is declining as Western culture and

6 R. Solnit, *Wanderlust: A History of Walking*, Penguin Books, New York, NY, 2000, p. 72.

product occupy everyday life so that Chinese tradition and culture has been largely overlooked. In contextualizing with fashion students graduated in the last ten years, there has been a strong presence of Western aesthetic domination in their design work.

Under the State's culture promotion, it is hoped that the phenomenon of the Chinese fashion industry of being merely an advocate of the Western fashion cycle would be withdrawing, at the same time, the characteristic of its own is forming at global stage. Specifically, the concept of 'slow fashion' is interpreted as the revival of 'spirit of the craftsman' which has been advocated by all levels of the government aiming to slow down the process of designing and making. This approach implies a sense of attitude toward a slow lifestyle that would improve the quality of the design and the final product. Delivering the concept requires a change in thought among the fashion educators working at art/fashion institutes, to redefine its role as contemporary fashion educator and re-consider how the concept of 'spirit of the craftsman' could be applied in contemporary fashion design which is to ask how 'inheritance and innovation' can be better fused and implemented in fashion education.

2   Fashion Education in China

Fashion educators in Chinese higher education institutes can be categorised into three, namely: 'traditional', 'market driven', and 'overseas'. Firstly, the 'traditional' educators are recognized as post war 'baby-boom' generation and started teaching during 1980s and 1990s with emphasis in traditional handmade techniques. Secondly, the 'market driven' educators have a strong connection with the fashion market, playing several different roles alongside educator, for example providing consultancy to fashion companies or running fashion brands themselves. Their teaching styles lean toward the taste of the current fast-fashion market and encourage students to conduct designs and drawings by software (Computer Aided Design), such as Adobe Illustrator and which are widely used in fashion companies. Thirdly, the educators who have foreign study or work experience are named 'overseas' those who started teaching in late 2000. They have brought Western modules, concepts of fashion education and most importantly social theories into their teaching content that make up the majority of staffing along with the 'market driven' people.

Given that graduation employment rate has always been the priority in Chinese higher education systems the graduate needs to acquire concrete skills in order to be competent in surviving and accommodating the labour market, the institutions encourage 'market driven' staff to bring in their industry experience and connections to teach essentials in the way that fashion companies would appreciate in the way of mass produce and fast fashion. However, the changing of the outer global economic environment results in the market detailing segmentations which require the design and final product to be sophisticated and at the same time, diversified to meet the demand of customers who come from various backgrounds. The potential customers are not blank canvases, but in Foucault's words, bodies acted upon by institutions[7] as a representation of their class, gender, race and so on, who are increasingly demanding the right product made to match who they are. The awareness of cultural embodiment and social relation of the body become prominent factors in terms of both designer and customer that cultivating a contemporary fashion designer needs to reflect.

The body can be understood in terms of a physical entity and a cultural embodiment, as well as an interrelationship between these two conceptual understandings. Shilling regards the body '...as a material, physical and biological phenomenon which is irreducible to immediate social processes or classifications ... our senses, knowledgeability and capability to act are integrally related to the fact that we are embodied beings'.[8] The interrelationship is further noted by Turner that human beings are 'simultaneously part of nature and part of culture ... and culture shapes and mediates nature ... [and] nature constitutes a limit on human agency'.[9] Particularly, culture shapes the physical entity so that 'a certain type of social identification or label can be read on the body in society'.[10] And culture mediates the physical entity so that every move of the body in interacting with others in society (as in affecting and being affected by others) has its cultural perspective. Through the framework of body theories, every fashion student, in their every thought, every bodily movement, and every reaction, delineates an image of being Chinese. Both their physical appearance and their approach to the world has been affected by their cultural position, including the place they went to, their family members, their education, and the societies.

Therefore, the course of Fashion Design in higher education starts focusing on students' individuality, originality and creativity in terms of broad

7   M. Foucault, *Discipline and Punish: The Birth of the Prison*, trans. A. Sheridan, Penguin Books, London, 1991.

8   Shilling, *The Body and Social Theory*, pp. 10–12.

9   Turner, *The Body & Society*, p. 197.

10   P. Liu, 'The Impact of Space Upon the Body in the Forbidden City: From the Perspective of Art', in K. Buccieri (ed.), *Body Tensions: Beyond Corporeality in Time and Space*, Brill, Leiden, 2014, pp. 23–35, p. 26.

social and cultural contexts, for which it is hoped that graduates can drive the Chinese fashion market in developing an innovative market embedded with a strong sense of Chinese character. During the transitional period, fashion institutions need to keep the balance between the existing market that favours fast and low-cost product, and new tides that focuses on personalized product.

For instance, Beijing Institute of Fashion Technology (BIFT), as the only Chinese institute named in fashion with majors in Fashion Design, has re-thought its role under the current circumstance by asking questions on how educators can better motivate students in engaging with Chinese tradition, culture, and techniques in design and how students translate their individual cultural understating and original research findings into design language.[11]

The current concern is, through my observation, that the majority of the enrolled students in fashion design primarily copy traditional forms and elements into their design work without re-construction. Lacking in research methods and critical analysis during the design process sabotages the output which is the major concern for Chinese students, thereby the interaction between the physical body and cultural body through material manipulation remains passive. This is a common problem not only to Chinese students but also foreign students studying fashion at BIFT, such as students from Turkmenistan and South Korea who are enthusiastic in using their native cultural elements. However, the premature use of Turkmenistan traditional embroidery pattern and South Korean traditional *hanbok* reflects neither thoughtful input in the students' design, nor the engagement of the interaction between material and the body. In addition, students maybe point out terms like 'deconstruction' and 'postmodernism' during the supervision, however, the insufficient theoretical understanding has led to unclear thought process and haphazard methodological approaches resulting in failure to achieve the proposed initial goal. Traditional patterns borrowed into their design look aesthetically awkward and the critical thinking is always absent in their design process.

---

11   The office for teaching and learning of the university issued a statement of 'Practice and Training Scheme' to improve learning quality. IMSUE, 'Practice and Training Scheme', *Beijing Institute of Fashion and Technology* [official website] <http://jwc.bift.edu.cn/tzgg/sjjxglk_tz/61536.htm> (Accessed 14 January 2018). Programmes have been facilitated by faculties to extend students' learning experience, such as the International Workshop initialled in 2014. 'International Workshop', *Beijing Institute of Fashion and Technology* [official website] <http://fzy.bift.edu.cn/pages/message/messagehd/266.html> (Accessed 14 January 2018).

3   Chinese Traditional Clothing

The concept of 'slow fashion' has its roots in Chinese culture and tradition. The connection between body, material and spirit is advocated in Chinese traditional art and culture, in particular the making of traditional clothing of ethnic groups. As Douglas notes: 'the physical body is a microcosm of society, its experience always sustaining a particular set of cultural meanings, a particular social order'.[12] Women in ethnic Miao for example, the cloth making conducted by the bodies reflect the cultural embodiment, material culture and social hierarchy. They start learning embroidery techniques at eight years old, and begin making their own wedding dress two years later. They are persistent in practicing the techniques on a daily basis with a minimum of one hour spent each day even during busy farming seasons. While practicing, they always imagine themselves wearing it on the wedding day, thereof, every needle and thread is embedded with expectation for the future and nostalgia from the past that the body is engaged with the material through actions saturated with cultural belonging.

Although there is no school training provided, the forms and patterns created in making dress by women of ethnic Miao are culturally inherited as well as personalized in comparison to the students' work at fashion school. The design of embroidery in ethnic Miao use daily narratives or myths to form scenarios. The composition is carefully structured in a two dimensional format and stories are visualized in personal needle and thread (Figure 9.1). Such a process of making reflects the conversation between the body, material and culture that the outcome is much appreciated.

In contrast, body feelings and emotions are overlooked in fashion education in China whilst mimicking Western aesthetic and style on the surface. Therefore, despite the latest technology and fashion tendency inevitably impacting on design, the role of the body in creative practice shall be re-emphasised in cloth making in fashion education that the concept of 'slow fashion' gradually gains momentum.

4   Case Study at BIFT

Experts from various backgrounds point out that a good design is more than just a piece of beautiful garment, creative director Shaldon Kopman's suggests

---

12   Douglas, 'The Two Bodies', p. 68.

FIGURE 9.1   'Hundreds of Birds' cloth, depicting traditional dragons, various birds and fish,
               worn for rituals, made from silk, 144.5 cm × 71.5 cm.
               USED WITH KIND PERMISSION FROM ETHNIC CLOTHING MUSEUM, BEIJING
               INSTITUTE OF FASHION AND TECHNOLOGY.

'designing is not about creating beautiful garments, it is about commercialis-
ing design and selling and producing it'.[13] Apart from a commercial perspective, the idea of 'body first' in terms of sociology is that clothing is created to
complete the body by wearing it, rather than using the body as a hanger to display cloth. Regardless the understanding and interpretation of a good design
changes over time, space and cultural context, nevertheless, designers need to
spend quality time in research, analysis of relevant factors and the practice of
making. Body as a culturally embodied being is deeply involved in the making
process.

By encouraging students to think and develop the design process thoroughly, lecturers at BIFT revised the grading system to allow more emphasis on the
design process rather than rely on the design output only. There is an example
from a student's work as the case study shown below. The student was a Maison
Lesage Paris Award winner[14] at Arts of Fashion Foundation (AOF) during 2013,
who further expanded the design work in her final year undergraduate project

13   S. Kopman, 'Design Is More Than Just Beautiful Garments, It Must Sell: Fashion
       Designers', *ENCA.com*, 4 February 2017 <http://www.enca.com/life/design-is-more-than-
       just-beautiful-garments-%E2%80%93-it-must-sell-say-fashion-designers> (Accessed 7
       October 2017).
14   Q. Wei, 'Resilience', *Arts of Fashion Foundation* <http://www.arts-of-fashion.org/AoFCom-
       petition/2013/pages/selected/+Qinwen%20Wei.html> (accessed 14 January 2018).

in 2014. Furthermore, she studied a postgraduate course at Royal College of Art (RCA) afterwards and became a staff member at BIFT in late 2016. Seeking overseas study experience for postgraduates is an ideal path for a large proportion of undergraduate art/design students. The phenomenon is also a force to push the revision to happen. Her initial idea is about Chinese shadow puppetry and grandma. Instead of printing the image of shadow puppetry straight onto the cloth which would look primitive, the student firstly plays around with the images of the shadow puppetry in free hand illustration which is the intimate method her body trained up. The visual dairy is mandatory and used to document the design process during the course, which is beneficial of having it for a period of time. The process of sketching is considered part of the research which allows the student to testify various possibilities and better understand the visual representation of the shadow puppetry (Figure 9.2). All these experiments help the student to form her own language in the design later.

The student spends a tremendous amount of time to do research and practice (Figures 9.3–9.4) with no rush to finalise the design work. The students did not refer to the visual information of current fashion elements in her design, but rather spent time in talking and observing professional shadow puppetry makers, whose body will always be the inheritor of the techniques, and experimenting the making process. New social and cultural experience is added into her body which is going to make an impact on her physical activities, precisely her design. According to Douglas, '[t]he physical body is never immediately perceived, but always experienced through the mediation of cultural categories …'[15]

Cultural categories can also be understood as cultural perspectives that allow the physical body to be perceived through. In other words, 'the physical body is always perceived partly and temporarily through one or more of these perspectives'.[16] In this case, the social experience of talking, observing and making shadow puppetry is a new cultural experience and perspective added to the body's framework of understanding.

Through the newly added cultural perspective, there could be some unknown aspects of the physical body unveiled. According to Liu, after a piece of information has been newly received by the body, it would cause a reshuffle of the existing information in relation to one another in the body.[17] Enriching the body becomes one of the focuses in contemporary education emphasised at BIFT. The focus is to promote bodily experience of students

---

15   Douglas, 'The Two Bodies', p. 68.
16   Liu, 'The Impact of Space Upon the Body', p. 26.
17   Ibid.

FIGURE 9.2 A page of visual dairy reflects how this student has translated the visual image of
Chinese shadow puppetry into a clothing design. 'Chinese shadow puppetry and
Grandma left: Grandma in aquarium with dragon and turtle, right Grandma with
horse in jungle'.
PHOTOGRAPHER/DESIGNER: WEI QINWEN, 2014.

and translate such experience into fashion language through various art practices they are familiar with. Ideally, the greater the number of different social environments which the physical body experiences, the more cultural categories and information gained results in the body acquiring greater complexity and sophistication.[18] The body becomes more capable of creating new things.

During the research, the student acquires better bodily understanding in regards to the making process and the materials of the shadow puppetry, thereafter, she is able to reconcile the visual representation of the shadow puppetry and her emotional expression toward to her grandma through the language of design. The design also demonstrates strong individual style through manipulating the techniques of embroidery and beading which the student reinforces with certain feelings and emotions. The tactility is actualized through the use of textile.

18   Ibid.

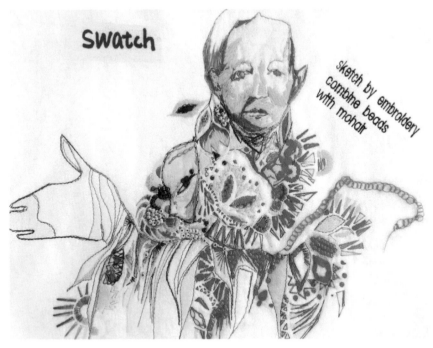

FIGURE 9.3   Reconciliation between the patterns of the shadow puppetry and the image of
her grandma.
PHOTOGRAPHER/DESIGNER: WEI QINWEN, 2014.

5   Conclusion

With focus in fashion education, BIFT amplifies students' ability in critical
thinking and to promote the concept of slow design through restructuring existing courses. Moreover, the fashion school has also conducted various short
courses and study camps offering hands-on experience in relation to Chinese
traditional art and culture with the aim to stimulate their students, precisely
their bodies, to become sensitive to and sophisticated in translating their bodily
experience into the language of design. Such programmes also involve experts
from the fashion industry that allows students to see things through multiple
perspectives, at the same time, balance the graduates with a sense of demanding from the current market, for example, a joined course with Marisfrolg.[19]

---

19   'Industrial Collaborated Programmes – Marisfrolg and School of Fashion and Engineering' [Faculty News Announcement], *Beijing Institute of Fashion and Technology* [official
website] 2014 <http://fzy.bift.edu.cn/pages/message/messagehd/292.html> (Accessed 14
January 2018); *Marisfrolg* [corporate website] <http://www.marisfrolg.com>(Accessed 14
January 2018).

FIGURE 9.4 A part of the design collection with model Dominika.
PHOTOGRAPHER/DESIGNER: BOLIN STUDIO /WEI QINWEN, 2014.

Bibliography

Bill, A., 'Blood, Sweet and Shears: Happiness, Creativity, and Fashion Education', *Fashion Theory: The Journal of Dress, Body & Culture*, vol. 16, no. 1, 2012, pp. 49–65.

Briggs, A., 'The Fashioned Body: Fashion, Dress and Modern Social Theory, Joanne Entwistle', *Fashion Theory: The Journal of Dress, Body & Culture*, vol. 5, no. 2, 2001, pp. 225–228.

Douglas, M., 'The Two Bodies', in M. Fraser and M. Greco (eds.), *The Body: A Reader*. Routledge, New York, NY, 2005, pp. 68–78.

Entwistle, J., 'Fashion and the Fleshy Body: Dress as Embodied Practice', *Fashion Theory: The Journal of Dress, Body & Culture*, vol. 4, no. 3, 2000, pp. 323–347.

Foucault, M., *Discipline and Punish: The Birth of the Prison*. Trans. A. Sheridan. Penguin Books, London, 1991.

IMSUE, 'Practice and Training Scheme', *Beijing Institute of Fashion and Technology* [official website] <http://jwc.bift.edu.cn/tzgg/sjjxglk_tz/61536.htm> (Accessed 14 January 2018).

'Industrial Collaborated Programmes – Marisfrolg and School of Fashion and Engineering' [Faculty News Announcement], *Beijing Institute of Fashion and*

Technology [official website], 2014 <http://fzy.bift.edu.cn/pages/message/message-hd/292.html> (Accessed 14 January 2018).

'International Workshop', *Beijing Institute of Fashion and Technology* [official website] <http://fzy.bift.edu.cn/pages/message/messagehd/266.html> (Accessed 14 January 2018).

Kopman, S., 'Design is More Than Just Beautiful Garments, It Must Sell: Fashion Designers', *ENCA.com*, 2017 <http://www.enca.com/life/design-is-more-than-just-beautiful-garments-%E2%80%93-it-must-sell-say-fashion-designers> (Accessed 7 October 2017).

Liu, P., 'The Impact of Space Upon the Body in the Forbidden City: From the Perspective of Art', in K. Buccieri (ed.), *Body Tensions: Beyond Corporeality in Time and Space*. Brill, Leiden, 2014, pp. 23–35.

Marisfrolg [corporate website] <http://www.marisfrolg.com>(Accessed 14 January 2018).

Mauss, M., 'Techniques of the Body', in M. Fraser and M. Greco (eds.), *The Body: A Reader*. Routledge, New York, NY, 2005, pp. 73–77.

Segre, R. S., 'China and Italy: Fast Fashion Versus Pret a Porter. Towards a New Culture of Fashion', *Fashion Theory: The Journal of Dress, Body & Culture*, vol. 9, no. 1, 2005, pp. 43–56.

Solnit, R., *Wanderlust: A History of Walking*. Penguin Books, New York, NY, 2000.

Shilling, C., *The Body and Social Theory*. Sage Publications, London, 1993.

Turner, S. B., *The Body & Society Second Edition*. Sage Publications, London, 1996.

Wei, Q., 'Resilience', *Arts of Fashion Foundation* <http://www.arts-of-fashion.org/AoFCompetition/2013/pages/selected/+Qinwen%20Wei.html> (accessed 14 January 2018).

CHAPTER 10

Making It Real: Engaging the Consumer in Sustainable Fashion Consumption

Natalie C. McCreesh, Christopher R. Jones, Alex McIntosh and Helen Storey

Abstract

With moves towards improving sustainability within the retail sector and a growing requirement to conform to existing and emerging legislation, retailers from ostensibly disparate sectors face the common challenge of encouraging the reduced consumption of saleable products, while simultaneously maintaining their prosperity. Project TRANS-FER was initiated to investigate how efforts to promote sustainable consumption within retail is received and responded to by consumers. Consumers and partners in the retail sector were engaged with throughout the research which culminated in three consumer facing outputs; a workshop ('Put a Better Foot Forward', The Moor retail destination, Sheffield, UK), installation ('Making in Real', pop-up T-Shirt factory, Trinity Shopping Centre, Leeds, UK) and animated short film (*Nothing to Wear?* available via YouTube and launched at the Sheffield Shorts film screening, Sheffield, UK). Each of the outputs were designed to allow consumers to reflect on their shopping and consumption habits in an engaging, stimulating environment. The key aim was to promote mindfulness and engage consumers in discussion and debate. All the output events were free for the general public to attend/participate in. This paper will discuss the role of engaging the consumer in sustainable fashion research and the impact of consumer facing outputs in education and awareness of sustainable issues in shopping and consumption.

Keywords

sustainable fashion – fashion – consumer – retail – public engagement – fashion film

1　Project Transfer

The 'Trading Approaches to Nurturing Sustainable consumption in Fashion and Energy Retail' (TRANSFER) knowledge exchange project was a collaboration between the University of Sheffield (UoS) and the London College of Fashion (LCF), at the University of the Arts London.[1] The key aim of the project was to facilitate knowledge exchange between energy and fashion retailers regarding the promotion of sustainable consumption. Due to the interest of numerous additional parties the project went on to include utilities companies including regional water providers and retailers from areas outside of fashion with an invested interest in sustainability.

Retailers are increasingly confronted by a common challenge, they must encourage the reduced consumption of their saleable product in order to promote sustainability and conform to existing and emerging environmental legislation, while simultaneously maintaining growth and financial prosperity. Energy retailers are experienced in such practices having been legally required to promote energy-efficiency to consumers for some years (e.g., loft and cavity wall insulation).[2] This is paired with a growing recognition among fashion retailers of the need to engage in activities that help to promote sustainable consumption among consumers (e.g., in-store recycling schemes).[3]

With this in mind, the aims of this research were twofold: (i) to bring together representatives of the energy and fashion retail sectors, with academic experts in psychology, management and fashion, to exchange best practice around the promotion of sustainable consumption to consumers; and (ii) to investigate how efforts to promote sustainable consumption within these sectors is received and responded to by consumers. In fulfilling these aims we hoped to foster a more complete understanding of how initiatives in both sectors can be successfully designed and implemented in order to have maximum positive impact on the behaviour of consumers (e.g., energy use and clothing purchase practices).

---

1   Funded by the Economic and Social Research Council (ESRC) as part of the Retail Sector Initiative 2013 (Grant number ES/L005204/1). With thanks to Prof. Lenny Koh and Prof. Dilys Williams collaborative members of the TRANSFER team.

2   This is being achieved, in part through an on-going series of programmes, e.g., the Energy Efficiency Commitment (EEC, 2005–08), the Carbon Emissions Reduction Target (CERT, 2008–12), the Community Energy Saving Programme (CESP, 2009–12) and more recently the Energy Company Obligation (ECO, 2012–15).

3   A number of UK high-street retailers now offer schemes where customers can return unwanted clothes to stores for recycling in exchange for store gift vouchers. For example, see: 'Clothes for Life', *Monsoon* [corporate website] <http://uk.monsoon.co.uk/view/content/tandc-clothes-for-life> (Accessed 18 October 2016); 'Sustainability', *H&M* [corporate website] <http://about.hm.com/en/sustainability.html> (Accessed 18 October 2016); 'Shwopping, Ordinary Clothes Made Extraordinary', *M&S* [corporate website] <http://www.marksandspencer.com/s/plan-a-shwopping> (Accessed 18 October 2016).

With regards to addressing the first aim (i) a collaborative one-day partner workshop event was planned, to bring diverse stakeholders together in a synergistic, collaborative context, in order to promote in-depth, problem-solving discussion on key issues. Workshops provide forums where different options can be considered and knowledge and expertise exchanged but where increased consensus on solutions (i.e. best practice) can be achieved. Prior to this workshop event interviews were held with delegates to address a series of questions relating to the opportunities and challenges of promoting sustainable consumption (SC), how they currently promote SC (if relevant), what specifically they wish to achieve from engaging with project TRANSFER, and what format they would wish the workshop to take. The responses from these interviews were analysed in order to generate a formal discussion framework for the workshop. By allowing partners to participate in the design of the workshops and by providing them with an advanced framework for the discussions, we hoped to tailor the workshop so as to maximise the benefit to them in participating.

The second aim (ii) was met in the first instance by holding a series of consumer focus groups. A total of five focus groups were conducted (three at Meadowhall, Sheffield; two at Westfield Centre, Shepherd's Bush, London) each with an average of eight participants. Participants for these focus groups were a convenience sample of shoppers at the respective shopping centres. If facilitated carefully, focus groups can provide a useful context for establishing 'why' people feel the way they do about issues and to learn more about how such issues become represented and socially shared. To stimulate discussion on these topics at the workshop, participants were shown video recordings of the partner discussions (selected to illustrate the main points of the discussion and edited to maintain the anonymity of workshop participants), thus creating an indirect 'fishbowl' method.[4] A series of set questions were used to structure and guide conversations however the discussions were left to progress naturally with minimum prompting from the facilitators. Focus group discussions were analysed by the academic team using thematic analysis in order to identify central themes in responding and how these map to psychological models of trust and consumption (see forthcoming publications from the authors).[5]

The results of this analysis would provide the commercial and academic partners with feedback on the current level of understanding and importance that consumers place on the issue of SC and how the efforts made by retailers

---

4   R. Sutherland, K. Reid, D. Kok, and C. Collins, 'Teaching a Fish Bowl Tutorial: Sink or Swim', *The Clinical Teacher*, vol. 9, no. 2, 2015, pp. 80–84.

5   V. Braun and V. Clarke, 'Using Thematic Analysis in Psychology', *Qualitative Research in Psychology*, vol. 3, no. 2, 2006, pp. 77–101.

to promote the issue within each sector affect (e.g., levels of trust in the retailer, intentions to purchase from the retailer).

Using the set questions to guide the discussion participants were first asked about their shopping habits in relation to fashion (clothing/apparel/accessories) and feelings/emotions surrounding this. Secondly participants were asked the same relating to energy and water utility shopping. They were then asked to compare the two, noting similarities and differences in the process and emotions surrounding the topics. A clear distinction was made between shopping for a specific item which was perceived as a 'need'. One participant stated:

> I panic-buy everything. So it's usually off ASOS. We're going on holiday, therefore I need holiday stuff. Or we've got a wedding, therefore I need an outfit. There's no planning or, 'Oh, it's a nice Saturday afternoon, let's go into the shops'. *It's all panic buying.*

In contrast shopping as a pass time or hobby for pleasure with no specific aim to purchase were classed as spontaneously desired or 'wants'. One participant describes her spontaneous purchase:

> I bought this fabulous necklace. It was ants in gold, which I never buy gold but I really loved it, and it's these crazy ants. It was in the sale and I had been watching it and going I'm going to get it and then I went, 'Just buy it'. So I did and felt not at all guilty, and I normally feel guilty. I'm just going to have it.

Items regarded as 'needs' were generally those required for specific occasion or purpose such as clothing items for work, special occasions, holidays or seasonal, for example a new dress for a friend's wedding or a new white shirt for a job interview. The purchasing process of 'need' garments was often considered stressful, due to difficulties of finding the exact item required. Problems included finding the correct size, colour, style and price were listed as main issues preventing purchase in addition to practicalities such as store opening times and time afforded to look around a number of different stores. In this type of scenario the faster the needed item could be located and purchased the more appeased the consumer was. This participant describes how stressful shopping can feel

> [f]inding something specific is really difficult. I had to find a white shirt last year, a collared white shirt that would fit ... I was getting really stressed because I had offered to do this job and I just couldn't find a shirt.

In contrast, shopping as a pass time was viewed as a leisure activity that was pleasurable, often done with friends as a mode of entertainment. With regards to the shopping environment malls were seen as more stressful, but a necessity during bad weather and as a convenience due to later opening hours in comparison with the high street. Charity and vintage shops were seen as the most pleasurable places to shop in addition to the cheaper prices, buying second hand was considered more 'guilt free' as consumerism was viewed as being offset by donating to charity. Overall price was the main signifier in purchasing choice with the lower price often sought out and purchase delayed in some instances until there was a price reduction from sales or discount events.

> I think the last thing I bought, clothing-wise, was something from a charity shop. So something a bit like recycling. The area that I live in has a really nice charity shop. I tend to get things that I wouldn't buy myself, because they're usually quite expensive from Monsoon. So it makes me feel good if I've bought something a) to recycle and b) I haven't spent a fortune.

Energy and water utility purchasing was not viewed as 'shopping', it was seen as paying for necessities which participants felt they had little choice over doing so. The process of choosing or changing supplier was viewed as a chore, which was time consuming and overly complicated. Participants admitted to a general lack of knowledge with regards to different energy suppliers and tariffs. Finding the option with the lowest price was seen as highest priority and price was the only important feature. There was a lack of trust towards energy companies, with participants feeling 'cheated' and forced to pay more for something perceived as a basic human right. Whilst there was agreement that saving energy/water was important there was little understanding of the metrics employed to measure their usage. One participant explains:

> I find bills very confusing ... and they've got, like, a read out of all the kilowatts per second. I just don't understand any of it. I don't know why they don't make it simple, it's so complicated. Even on the phone, she's like 'This is how much you pay per hour, and these are the rates for water, this is the rate for electricity', and I'm like, 'I don't know what this means, I've got no idea', so I just sort of give up.

It was generally presumed that discussing bills was a taboo subject to bring up with friends which may be a result of lack of knowledge. A smaller number of participants had educated themselves on energy tariffs by using online comparison websites to find the cheapest energy deals. They admitted that they felt a sense of pride in 'getting one over' on the energy companies by making savings. Some had noticed the option of 'green energy tariffs' but admitted that price was the only priority for them. They felt that producing and providing green energy was the responsibility of the suppliers.

> I've been really savvy with making sure the stuff ... so it's like all the energy saving, water saving devices, everywhere, and I love that. Shopping around, I leave that to my husband because he'll quite happily do the Money Supermarket thing because he likes to beat them, I say beat them like it's a game but, yes, get the best deal. We use all the different cash back ones, find out what's the best deal via them ... The idea of actually having to pay for energy and water I think is an absolute rip off.

When asked to compare the similarities and differences between shopping for fashion and energy, predominant trends were that both types of shopping can be stressful however due to the items to be purchased being perceived as 'needs' it could not be avoided. The element of 'bargain hunting' was one method of counteracting the induced stress, with feelings of 'getting one over' on energy companies and retailers. It was agreed that both sectors offered a lot of choice and competition, however this was not always a positive factor with too much choice and competition leaving shoppers feeling confused and unaware of all their potential options. The key differences between shopping for fashion and energy were that (i) there was generally no pleasure element to shopping for energy, unlike fashion; and (ii) the lack of a high-street brick-and-mortar presence for energy and water companies was viewed as a huge issue for fostering trust in them i.e., trust in fashion retailers was facilitated by the presence on the high-street energy retailers having no physical presence for shopping i.e., no retail outlet can result in a lack of personal approach. Consumers felt reassured when they could go into a physical store and speak to someone in person regarding any problems or questions they might have. The energy and water companies were only available to contact over the phone and online which left a feeling of unease to many shoppers. People would like help with energy saving but would like a more personal approach, tailored to meet their specific needs. With regards to fashion retailers who already had a physical presence it was suggested that they could offer tailoring/alterations to improve their services. In addition to this extending garment life cycle it was felt that if something had been made/tailored specially to fit you then it would hold more non-intrinsic value and you would be encouraged to wear it more and keep it longer.

2   **Partner Concept Feedback**

Prior to the commercial partner workshop we interviewed a number (15) of the attendees in order to elucidate some of the key challenges facing businesses as they seek to promote sustainability. Interviewees were asked to comment on (i) the opportunities and challenges of promoting sustainable consumption; (ii) how sustainable consumption is currently promoted in their company; (iii) what specifically participants wished to achieve from participating in TRANSFER; these responses were used to help set an agenda for the workshop. Despite the diversity in the partners interviewed, a number of commonalities arose in the comments provided.

2.1   *Cost*
It was recognised that more environmentally sustainable products (e.g., renewable energy, organic cotton) would tend to come at a financial premium compared with more 'traditional' alternatives. There was concern that these costs might have to be passed to consumers and uncertainty as to how this could be achieved without losing their custom.

2.2   *Communication*
It was noted that at present there is no common language when talking about sustainability within business-to-business and business-to-consumer interactions. It was felt that the indiscriminate use of the term 'sustainability' had led to the term losing some of its meaning and that the 'green-washing' of the general public had left consumers confused and/or skeptical about pro-environmental claims made by retailers.

2.3   *Customer*
The importance of good retailer-customer relations was recognised as key to the success of business and consumer satisfaction. It was also noted that having a good awareness of customer profile (e.g., demographic, motivation for purchase) could help in the development and delivery of efforts to promote sustainable consumption.

With this in mind the two broad aims of the commercial partner workshop were:

(i)   To discuss the challenges and benefits of promoting sustainable consumption, while maintaining competitiveness. It was hoped that these discussions should highlight key (un-) common ground between the partners.

(ii)   To identify and develop novel solutions for encouraging more conscientious consumption among members of the general public. Partners were invited to think about how utility sector interventions might apply to fashion and vice versa.

During the partner workshop, delegates were asked to design a concept which could promote sustainability through combining the fashion and utilities industries. Delegates were divided into three groups and each designed a concept: 1. 'Wash Less, Wear More'; 2. 'Passing On Savings'; 3. 'Making it Real / Scan your Life'. These concepts were presented to the consumer focus groups for participants to feedback on.[6]

2.4   'Making It Real'

It was recognised that consumers likely feel detached from the people and processes that bring electricity, gas and water into their homes and put clothes on the shop floor for them to buy. It was reasoned that this detachment in itself might promote over-consumption due to a lack of awareness of the consequences associated with purchasing decisions. It was argued that if retailers could more clearly elucidate how these goods and services are 'manufactured', that this could enhance awareness and responsibility for change. It was also recognised that communications (e.g., the metrics used) should be tailored to map to things of personal relevance to the consumers. The commercial partner generated concept to offer consumers the opportunity to 'Scan their Life' was, for example, suggested. This would involve providing consumers with a barcode/QR code on their clothes/energy bills which can be scanned using a mobile device, which would then present them with a picture or narrative as to where and how that good or service was sourced and/or transported. Suggestions of how to appropriately affect lifestyle change in order to reduce impact would also be provided.

2.5   'Wash Less, Wear More'

Many clothing items are washed more often than actually needed, which can be due to the social stigma of being perceived as 'dirty' or 'lazy' if one does not wash them frequently. Whilst frequent washing might be appropriate for items worn close to the body, such as underwear or shirts, many items can be worn for longer periods without the need for laundering. Denim jeans, for example, are often washed far more than they need to be and, in fact, excessive washing actually damages the fabric. One suggested solution to this problem could be to bring fashion and water companies together to encourage consumers

---

6   For further details on the other concepts please see Project TRANSFER Team, 'Workshop 1', *Project TRANSFER* <http://www.project-transfer.group.shef.ac.uk/index.php/research-activities/partner-workshop-1/> (Accessed 18 October 2016).

to 'wash less, wear more'. If successful, this could cut down on the laundering process, saving detergent, water and electricity and prolong the life of clothes (reducing the need for repurchase). The possibility of a PR strategy or bespoke labeling could be explored to promote such a campaign, which could also serve to between buying and caring for clothes.

2.6   *'Passing on Savings'*

Questions relating to consumers understanding of the impact their sustainable actions have 'in the real world' were brought into discussion. For example, water companies specified that their consumers can find it hard to grasp the concept that water needs to be conserved when they see it raining outside. It was suggested that consumers might be more willing to live more sustainably if they could 'see' what difference their behaviours had for others. A way to approach this could be to design and deliver an initiative with, for example, an NGO, where more conscientious consumption (i.e., the use of less by 'us') would result in direct benefits to others (e.g., those living in poverty or drought prone areas) in other words, making the benefit of savings made by consumers more tangible and meaningful. This could be achieved through an App linked to the energy/water consumption of a household. Savings could be represented by credits, which could be saved up and donated to select charities.

The 'Making it Real' concept, the idea that overconsumption could be stemmed by more explicitly sharing the social/ environmental impacts of consumer choice with consumers, resonated most with the consumer participants. Therefore this was the concept chosen to expand on for the next stage of research taking the concepts and making them consumer facing.

3   Engaging with Consumers

Taking the information gathered from both the partner workshops and consumer focus groups, the aim of the project was to then devise ways of communicating findings with the general public, especially those visiting retail destinations. The challenge was to use the 'Making It Real' concept to promote thoughtful and sustainable consumption in a positive way by both consumers and retailers. This culminated in three consumer facing outputs; a workshop ('Put a Better Foot Forward', The Moor retail destination, Sheffield, UK), an interactive installation ('Making in Real', pop-up T-Shirt factory, Trinity Shopping Centre, Leeds, UK) and an animated short film (*Nothing to Wear?* available via YouTube and launched at the Sheffield Shorts film screening, Sheffield, UK).

The first output was held November 2014, members of the TRANSFER team were involved in hosting a half-day workshop as part of the ESRC Festival of Social Science.[7] The 'Put a Better Foot Forward' workshop was an interactive event designed to promote more conscientious consumption of fashion, focusing on people's footprints. A number of activities were designed to highlight the back-story to where and how shoes are made; and what impact our shoes have upon environmental, economic and social sustainability. These activities included: (i) a creative thinking exercise where people thought of innovative ways to make more sustainable shoes, (ii) two socio-dramas where people were invited to step into the shoes of people involved in the shoe supply chain and (iii) a life-cycle analysis where people were asked to think about the relative impacts of the different parts of the shoe supply chain. The workshop was held at a former Woolworths store at The Moor retail destination in the centre of Sheffield. This store is now being used to host a series of cultural events designed to encourage shoppers back to the high street through the provision of non-retail events and activities.

The second output, 'Making it Real' an interactive installation was held at Leeds Trinity Shopping Centre (7–8 February 2015) in association with DED and ANTIFORM.[8] Developing from the idea that overconsumption of clothing is driven in part by a disconnection from the processes that produce the products we buy, this exhibition sought to highlight the backstory to our clothing by showcasing the steps involved in the manufacture of a simple t-shirt. Present at the exhibition was Dr. Rob Speranza of the South Yorkshire Filmmakers Network, who shot a documentary style video of the event. This documentary comprises interviews with the academic team, the manufacturing team and some members of the public who interacted with the exhibition and has been used to further promote the message of the installation after the event.[9]

For the third output project TRANSFER worked with Emily&Anne Animations and Dr. Rob Speranza to create a short animated video stemming from some of the key themes arising from the research. *Nothing to Wear?* follows Jasmine, a 20-something fashion conscious individual, on her journey to work. It explores how the pressures of living in a consumerist society can easily make us look past the things we already own and prompt a never-ending desire to acquire (Figures 10.1–10.4). The animation can be viewed on the project website as before.

7 Core project TRANSFER team in collaboration with Teo Greenstreet and Nick Nuttgens.

8 DED Associates Graphic Designers founded by Nic and Jon Daughtry and ANTIFORM, a UK based fashion company founded by Lizzie Harrison.

9 The video can be watched here: Project TRANSFER Team, 'Public Engagement and Impact', *Project TRANSFER* <http://www.project-transfer.group.shef.ac.uk/index.php/public-engagement-impact/> (Accessed 18 October 2016).

FIGURE 10.1 Title screen, still from 'Nothing to Wear?'
DESIGNER: EMILY & ANNE ANIMATIONS, 2016.

FIGURE 10.2 The main character is concerned about her fashion image as she hasn't received
as many 'likes' on social media as her friends, still from 'Nothing to Wear?'
DESIGNER: EMILY & ANNE ANIMATIONS, 2016.

4 Conclusion

Project TRANSFER was designed to facilitate discussion and knowledge-transfer between academics, industry and consumers in the context of how to sustainably promote sustainable consumption. The aim of the consumer

FIGURE 10.3 Receiving emails with discount offers the protagonist starts to question
             if protagonist needs 'something new', still from 'Nothing to Wear?'
             DESIGNER: EMILY & ANNE ANIMATIONS 2016.

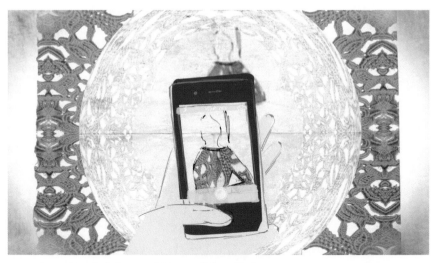

FIGURE 10.4 Detail of phone and fabric, still from 'Nothing to Wear?'
             DESIGNER: EMILY & ANNE ANIMATIONS, 2016.

focus groups and industry workshops was to promote discussion and gain an
understanding of how people feel about their consumption and shopping habits in light of sustainability. The consumer focused engagement activities were
then designed with the intent of showcasing some of the key results of these
discussions.

It was evident that while partners did understand the unique challenges facing their companies and/or their sector, there was a shared belief that issues of cost (limiting/not passing costs onto the customer), communication (lack of a common language to talk about sustainability) and customer relations (awareness of consumer profile) were central to efforts to successfully establish initiatives designed to promote more conscientious consumption. These factors, in addition to business transparency, were seen as essential in fostering consumer trust and brand loyalty.

While partners did note that the nature of their business models and sectors would to some extent necessitate bespoke approaches towards nurturing more sustainable consumption; there was also a strong sense of the value that could be generated from working together. It was reasoned that successful promotion of environmental sustainability requires lifestyle change and that the collaboration and cross-pollination of ideas between ostensibly different retail sectors could help to more clearly communicate this message to consumers.

The first consumer facing activity was the 'Put a Better Foot Forward' workshop. This workshop built upon the 'Making it Real' theme – the idea that overconsumption might be driven by an inherent disconnection between products and the processes by with they are generated and supplied, that pervaded our stakeholder discussions. The concept was to connect consumers with their clothing by engaging workshop participants in a series of interactive tasks designed to illustrate the social, economic and environmental footprint of our shoes.

The second consumer facing activity (the interactive exhibition at Trinity Shopping Centre in Leeds) similarly built upon the 'Making it Real' theme; showcasing the steps, resources and personnel involved in the manufacture of a simple t-shirt. The intention with the installation was not to tell people where to shop or what to buy but rather to get people to begin to understand the embedded costs in the clothing we often take for granted (often because of how cheap it is). In doing so, we hope that we would begin to get people to think twice before making a spontaneous or spurious purchase; to ask themselves: 'is this something that I will value and wear?'

The installation yielded considerable interest and engagement from passing shoppers. Those we spoke to typically bought into the aims and objectives of the project, recognising the importance of making more considered clothing purchase decisions. While it often takes more than the raised awareness of issues and the formation of good intentions to affect change; these things make a good starting point and can be a catalyst for change.

The final consumer facing activity was the production of the *Nothing to Wear?* animated film, designed to again, prompt consumers to consider what they are buying and why they are doing so. Is there a genuine need or is it to fill other social and psychological needs and desires? The animation has met with a good response, receiving in excess of 3,600 unique views on YouTube (correct at the time of publication) and has been positively engaged with via social media. We hope that it will continue to be shared and provide as a reminder for us to be more considerate consumers.

Project TRANSFER succeeded in achieving its stated aims. While the project officially ended in March 2015, it has yielded a rich, diverse dataset and a number of legacy outputs, which we hope will ensure continued academic and non-academic impacts into the future.

Acknowledgements

The authors would like to thank ESRC for funding. Our project partners: Antiform, ASOS PLC, Co-operative Energy, DED Associates, Dots Printhaus, Ecotricity, Emily&Anne Animation, E.ON UK, Jessica Brinton (journalist Sunday Times), Katherine Goodwin (womenswear design consultant), Leeds College of Art and the manufacturing team, LUST Cosmetics, Marion Hulme (journalist), Marks & Spencer, Meadowhall Sheffield, MK Things Happen, National Grid PLC, Neals Yard, Retail Centric, Reve en Vert, ReWardrobe, Rob Speranza (South Yorkshire Film Makers), Susie Stone Ltd, Thames Water, Trinity Leeds, United Untilities, Westfield London, WRAP. All the members of the public who interacted so positively in the workshops, exhibition and focus groups.

Bibliography

Braun, V., and V. Clarke, 'Using Thematic Analysis in Psychology', *Qualitative Research in Psychology*, vol. 3, no. 2, 2006, pp. 77–101.

'Clothes for Life', *Monsoon* [corporate website] <http://uk.monsoon.co.uk/view/content/tandc-clothes-for-life> (Accessed 18 October 2016).

Project TRANSFER Team, 'Public Engagement and Impact', *Project TRANSFER* <http://www.project-transfer.group.shef.ac.uk/index.php/public-engagement-impact/> (Accessed 18 October 2016).

Project TRANSFER Team, 'Workshop 1', *Project TRANSFER* <http://www.project-transfer.group.shef.ac.uk/index.php/research-activities/partner-workshop-1/> (Accessed 18 October 2016).

'Shwopping, Ordinary Clothes Made Extraordinary', *M&S* [corporate website] <http://www.marksandspencer.com/s/plan-a-shwopping> (Accessed 18 October 2016).

'Sustainability', *H&M* [corporate website] <http://about.hm.com/en/sustainability.html> (Accessed 18 October 2016).

Sutherland, R., K. Reid, D. Kok, and C. Collins, 'Teaching a Fish Bowl Tutorial: Sink or Swim', *The Clinical Teacher*, vol. 9, no. 2, 2015, pp. 80–84.

PART 4

Communicating

∴

Fashioning a Soviet Narrative: Jean Paul Gaultier's Russian Constructivist Collection, 1986

Doris Domoszlai-Lantner

Abstract

As the Soviet Union neared its demise, major design houses created collections that included garments and accessories that drew upon its impending collapse. The year 1986 was particularly significant, as the Soviet Premier Mikhail Gorbachev's complementary policies, *perestroika* and *glasnost*, found their place on some of fashion's greatest runways as what we can refer to as 'fashnost'. Although a handful of designers created 'fashnost', Jean Paul Gaultier's pieces were arguably the most expressive, focusing on the early period in the USSR's history during which the Russian Constructivist art movement formed and thrived. In his collection, Gaultier utilized many of the techniques and motifs from the Constructivists' body of work, capturing the essence of their aesthetic by integrating Cyrillic letters and numbers in block type, linear and geometric forms, and photomontage in his garments and accessories. Gaultier delved into the precarious social and political climate of the Soviet Union, drawing numerous connections between his own work and that of the Constructivists, and the USSR's policies. This paper presents the preliminary research for the author's master thesis at the Fashion Institute of Technology.

Keywords

constructivism – fashion – history – Russian – Jean Paul Gaultier – art – ideology – politics – *glasnost* – *perestroika* – 'fashnost'

1 Setting the Stage: The Soviet Union and Jean Paul Gaultier

French designer, Jean Paul Gaultier has long been known for his pioneering, provocative fashion collections. Drawing upon themes of fetishism, theatricalism, and art, Gaultier's collections were highly topical both within and outside of the fashion industry. His ability to effectively capture the zeitgeist of the time by translating the climate around him into objects of fashion was especially evident in his Fall/Winter 1986 collection. In this collection, Gaultier delved into the precarious social and political climate of the Soviet Union, putting it in conversation with its early, state-sponsored art movement, Russian Constructivism. In doing so, Gaultier drew numerous connections between his own work and that of the Constructivists, and the Soviet Union's political policies at the time.

The former Soviet Union (USSR) was a product of the 1917 Revolution, which brought the Communist movement and its leaders to the forefront of Russian life. The majority of the USSR's history passed under the auspices of the Cold War, a conflict against United States and its Western allies that was never formally declared. After surviving numerous revolts and uprisings from its member and allied nations, the Soviet Union faced its greatest crisis in the late 1980s and early 1990s, to which it ultimately succumbed. By the late 1980s, the social and political climate of the Soviet Union was ripe for change as the public, as well as its leaders, called for reform.

One leader who recognized the need for change was the General Secretary of the Communist Party, Mikhail Gorbachev. In an effort to revive and preserve the Soviet Union, Gorbachev launched the concept of *uskorenie*, which aimed to accelerate socio-economic development after the stagnation that occurred during his predecessor, Leonid Brezhnev's, term. More significantly, *uskorenie* was the foundation of the two major concepts that Gorbachev introduced in 1985 and in 1986 at the Party's 27th Congress, respectively: *perestroika* and *glasnost. Perestroika*, or 'restructuring', and *glasnost*, 'openness and transparency', were complementary concepts that aimed to revitalize the USSR by working within the framework of Soviet socialism. Gorbachev argued that the USSR could remain successful if it returned to its roots and thus, Lenin's teachings, of the 1910s and 1920s, while continuing to pursue policies of *detente* with its foes.[1] Shockwaves from the implementation of *perestroika* and *glasnost* were felt around the world, and had wide-reaching effects, including on the fashion industry. The year 1986 was particularly significant, as these parallel concepts made their way to some of fashion's greatest runways.

In the June 1989 issue of *Vogue* magazine, contributor Page Hill Starzinger summarized some of the most recent runway and street-style fashion trends. Amongst them was 'fashnost', a conglomeration of the words *glasnost* and fashion, stating:

---

1   M. Gorbachev, *Perestroika: New Thinking for Our Country and the World*, Harper and Row, New York, NY, 1987.

[g]lasnost may be a success, but will fashnost? Young Russian designers eager to cash in on the new openness are rushing to American shores (and stores) weighed down by what they consider to be the latest: punked-out clothes exploding with studs and chains. Ironically, what American youth are already buying at Unique Clothing Warehouse (New York City and Philadelphia) is the complete opposite : kitschy Russian military uniforms, government-produced wool coats.[2]

Starzinger specifically used the term 'fashnost' to refer to the disconnect between Soviet designers' offerings and the demands of their new Western audiences. Her focus on the aesthetic details of the clothing, without unpacking the deeper political and social meanings behind them, brings me to advocate for a broader interpretation of the term. I, therefore, use 'fashnost' to refer to design during the end of the Soviet era that was born out of, or referenced, Gorbachev's policies. Moreover, my research indicates that 'fashnost' originated not when Starzinger's article was published, but rather, at least three years earlier.

In fact, in 1986, another fashion journalist, George Leslie, had written about the Soviet-inspired garments and accessories that he had witnessed on the runways, without giving it any special moniker. In his *Women's Wear Daily* editorial, 'Accessories: From Paris: Soviet Chic', Leslie presented the fashions into which Gorbachev's policies had permeated.[3] As the Soviet Empire was drawing its last breaths, major design houses such as Thierry Mugler, Yves Saint Laurent, and fashion's so-called *enfant terrible*, Jean Paul Gaultier, created collections that drew upon its impending collapse. Creators of both couture and ready-to-wear showcased 'fashnost' in the form of Soviet-inspired fashions that encompassed various design motifs, such as Cyrillic text and Soviet symbols.

Without explicitly referencing the USSR, Saint Laurent's Fall/Winter collection was characterized by a general militarism that was juxtaposed with exaggerated pelts of fur and large, imposing pieces of costume jewelry, an ornate reference to the pre-Revolutionary splendor of the tsarist period. Contrastingly, Mugler's militarism was combined with Cyrillic text that spelled out his name, and streamlined silhouettes with broad shoulders that represented power and authority.

Jean Paul Gaultier's collection that season was aesthetically more similar to Mugler's than Saint Laurent's. Gaultier also incorporated Cyrillic text, but

---

2 P.H. Starzinger, 'Overseen and Overheard', *Vogue*, vol. 179, no. 6, June 1989, p. 52.
3 G. Leslie, 'Accessories: From Paris: Soviet Chic', *Women's Wear Daily*, vol. 151, no. 66, 4 April 1986, p. 9.

brushed past the overt Soviet militarism that his colleagues had drawn upon. Instead, he focused on the early part of the 20th century, during which the USSR and Russian Constructivist art movement formed and thrived. That year, Gaultier presented a collection as an homage to, and dialogue with, some of the Soviet Union's most devoted, and politically-charged artists.

The Russian Constructivist movement and the Soviet regime shared common ideological roots: Marxist Communist thought. As the movement developed, the artists helped create, and participated in, the greater Soviet narrative. The Constructivists' group included acclaimed artists such as Liubov Popova, Vladimir Mayakovsky, and the husband and wife duo, Aleksandr Rodchenko and Varvara Stepanova, amongst others. Through the use of geometric shapes, sharp angles, decisive text, and their pioneering photomontage technique, the Constructivists created art that was designed to serve the Communist cause as a tool of political propaganda to encourage the masses to collectively work to achieve the Communist goals. According to curator Peter Noever

> for the Constructivists, 'art'– if they acknowledged such a category at all – consisted in making life worth living, work in the factory or the household more satisfying, and not just in providing an 'escape' from the grim reality of the routine of daily life.[4]

Rodchenko's assessment of his role as an artist is especially pertinent to our understanding of the Constructivist philosophy. As Aleksandr Lavrent'yev, executor of the Rodchenko estate declared,

> Rodchenko began to use a new word to denote the value of artistic work: 'inventiveness'. Accordingly, he was of the opinion that 'inventors are artists, and the artist is essentially an inventor'.[5]

From the Constructivists' point of view, the term *l'art pour l'art*, or 'art for art's sake', was simply invalid; all the work they engaged in and constructed served a utilitarian purpose.

Born in Paris in 1952, in a world far removed from that of the Constructivists, Jean Paul Gaultier grew up in the Parisian suburbs in a working-class

---

4   P. Noever, 'Introduction', in P. Noever, A.M. Rodchenko, V. Stepanova, and A.N. Lavrent'yev, *The Future is Our Only Goal*, ed. A. Volker, Prestel-Verlag, Munich, 1991, p. 7.

5   A.N. Lavrent'yev, 'The Future is Our Only Goal', in P. Noever, A.M. Rodchenko, V. Stepanova, and A.N. Lavrent'yev, *The Future is Our Only Goal*, ed. A. Volker, Prestel-Verlag, Munich, 1991, pp. 9–21, p. 13.

neighborhood, which his biographer, Colin McDowell described as 'gritty and grey'.[6] Gaultier's career in fashion design began at an early age in the ateliers of the avant-garde designer, Pierre Cardin.[7] Next, he briefly worked under the designer Jacques Esterel, whose fantastical creations had a far-reaching impact on his own design philosophy, and eventually at the House of Patou.[8] Gaultier opened his eponymous design house in 1976, stunning his audiences and critics with his ostentatious designs.

To an extent, Gaultier's design philosophy ran parallel to that of Rodchenko and the Constructivists, in that they did not consider themselves to be artists creating art objects. During an interview, journalist Jim Boulden was surprised to hear Gaultier insist that '... he is not an artist, though he said he can be inspired by art'.[9] Gaultier and the Constructivists were creators and inventors whose goals included the provocation of their audiences.

2   Gaultier's Russian Constructivist Collection

The invitation to Gaultier's Fall/Winter 1986 show was made of printed cardboard. Against a black background, muted primary colors that spelled out Gaultier's name in Cyrillic that suggested a Russian subject matter were surrounded by an assemblage of collaged images of women's heads.[10] Once guests arrived, they came across the runway on which Gaultier would present his collection. Designed to resemble construction scaffolding, the runway was made out of metal poles and was certainly an appropriate background for a collection that was based on Russian Constructivist movement.[11] It was open, uncluttered, and resembled some of the Constructivists' 'constructions', or, their three-dimensional works of experimental art, including Vladimir Tatlin's Monument to the Third Communist International, and Liubov Popova's stage

6   C. McDowell, *Jean Paul Gaultier*, Penguin Group, New York, NY, 2000, pp. 9–10.

7   Ibid.

8   Ibid.

9   J. Boulden, 'Gaultier: A Modest Provocateur Who Might Be Slowing Down', *CNN*, 10 April 2014 <http://www.cnn.com/2014/04/09/business/jean-paul-gaultier-retrospective/index.html> (Accessed 20 February 2016).

10   J.P. Gaultier, 'Invitation' [paper], *Jean Paul Gaultier: Be My Guest*, Fashion Space Gallery, London College of Fashion, 1986 <http://www.fashionspacegallery.com/exhibition/jean-paul-gaultier/> (Accessed 3 March 2016).

11   'View: The Cutting Edge', *Vogue*, vol. 176, no. 7, July 1986, p. 134.

sets for the play *The Magnanimous Cuckold*.[12] Moreover, the stage symbolized the open society that Gorbachev was trying to achieve in the USSR.

Within his collection, Gaultier captured the essence of the Constructivist movement by integrating design elements that emulated their body of work. Arguably, the most noticeable of these aesthetic references was the block-type Cyrillic letters and numbers, which drew a close visual comparison to the suspense-filled fonts that were utilized in the Constructivists' printed art. Highly angular font can be seen throughout the covers and pages of their print publication, *Lef*, whereas more rounded fonts can be seen in *New Lef*. According to Lavrent'yev, very angular typography was characteristic of the Constructivists' early and 'classical' work, and was gradually replaced in the 1920s by more rounded, softer typefaces.[13]

Gaultier utilized aspects of both the Constructivists' early and later typography in his designs. His name, either in its entirety or just as 'Jean', in addition to a few other words, appears in transliterated Cyrillic on many of the garments and accessories from the collection. Of the five objects from this collection in the Metropolitan Museum of Art's holdings, four of them have Cyrillic letters in their design. One of these dresses is notable for its large-scale lettering that spells out fragments of Gaultier's name across the chest. Paired with the term 'N 6', and large areas of sequined decoration, the piece is a glossy reimagining of Constructivist art.[14] Also in the Metropolitan Museum of Art collection, a pair of black and turquoise-colored gloves spell out what is likely the word 'audience' (публика) woven in white along the cuffs. Gaultier's use of the word 'audience' served multiple purposes.[15] Firstly, it reaffirmed his personal work ethic of creating diverse fashions that drew upon, and were reflective of the experiences and lives of his audience, including those who may have been in the Soviet and Eastern Bloc nations. Secondly, it also reaffirmed the connection between the Constructivists' goals and the means through which they achieved them by utilizing frenzied, agitated text to incite revolutionary action amongst their own audience.

Yet another thought-provoking choice of terminology can be seen on the torso of a sweater that was for sale on *The Salvages*, an e-commerce

---

12   C. Lodder, *Russian Constructivism*, Yale University Press, New Haven (CT) and London, 1983.

13   Lavrent'yev, 'The Future is Our Only Goal'.

14   J.P. Gaultier, *Dress* [wool, synthetic, silk, and metal], The Metropolitan Museum of Art, 1986 <https://www.metmuseum.org/art/collection/search/185755> (Accessed 8 February 2016).

15   J.P. Gaultier, *Gloves* [cotton and synthetic], The Metropolitan Museum of Art, 1986 <https://www.metmuseum.org/art/collection/search/121225> (Accessed 8 February 2016).

website that specializes in the sale of high-end, private fashion collections.[16] On this piece, the Russian word 'ИЗБРАНЬ' is strategically knitted in the same large-scale, block-type Cyrillic font, providing the wearer with multiple historic references. The word 'ИЗБРАНЬ' can be used to mean 'selected', which was part of the title of the book of selected poems written by the author and *Lef* editor, Nikolai Aseev in 1923. Rodchenko designed the first edition of Aseev's *Избрань: Стихи 1912–1922* ('Selected: Poems 1912–1922').[17]

The word 'ИЗБРАНЬ' can also be used to mean 'election'. In this regard, as elections in the former USSR were notorious for being staged and manipulated, Gaultier's use of this word underscored the necessity for political reform, and Gorbachev's eventual call for multi-candidate, free elections in the coming years. Through the use of this double entendre, Gaultier's was simultaneously engaging in discourse with the Constructivists and the Soviet regime, strengthening Gorbachev's notion that in order for the USSR to survive, it must revive its early history, when such artists and the state prospered.

Utilizing the same block-type font, Gaultier also integrated numbers into the designs of his collection. The text 'N 6' is a design component on several of Gaultier's pieces, including one of the Metropolitan Museum of Art's dresses, and a knitted sweater. The Cyrillisized capital letter 'N', (a letter found in the Latin alphabet, but not in the Cyrillic), was used by the Constructivists as an abbreviation for the word 'number'. For example, 'N 2' was printed on the front cover of the April-May issue of *Lef* in 1923 to indicate that it was the second issue of their journal. Likewise, Liubov Popova utilized a variation of this abbreviation, 'No.', and various numbers in her costume designs for a theatrical production in 1921. Although another artist's designs were ultimately chosen for the play, Popova's exemplify the extent to which art and dress were related within the Constructivist movement.[18] Popova and her colleagues sought to

---

16   'A/W85-86 Jean Paul Gaultier Knit Turtleneck from the "Russian Constructivist" Collection by Jean Paul Gaultier', *The Salvages* <https://thesalvages.com/products/a-w85-86-russian-contructivist-zip-cardigan> (Accessed 6 June 2017). The same sweater, in a different size, was also recently sold on the e-commerce website, eBay, but unfortunately, none of them have been accessioned into the collections of any major museums as of yet. Although The Metropolitan Museum of Art has a few pieces from this collection, their holdings are by no means representative of the prevalence of such pieces in other museums. Thus, a fair amount of my research on this collection has been focused on pieces that have been vetted and offered for sale at various auctions worldwide.

17   N. Aseev, *Izbran: Stkihi 1912–1922*, Krug, Moscow and St. Petersburg, 1923.

18   M. Dabrowski, *Liubov Popova*, The Museum of Modern Art, New York, NY, 1991, p. 23.

merge the concepts of art and production in order to create alluring, expressive objects that were applicable to the new Soviet way of life. As Magdalena Dabrowski, a curator at the Museum of Modern Art in New York, explained:

> ... in designing for the theater and executing commissions for various propagandistic projects in celebration of Communist events that many Constructivist artists, Popova among them, found the opportunity to realize their utopian visions of art for the masses.[19]

In addition to the use of highly recognizable typography, among the other design elements that were characteristic of Russian Constructivist art was the integration of dynamic linear elements, as well as the technique of photomontage. In his observations on the Constructivists' advertisements for the Soviet government's retail products, Lavrent'yev explained the artists' design philosophy behind the use of these techniques. He stated that

> exclamation marks and arrows were intended to attract the attention of passersby, make them curious about the text, and encourage them to read it in full. A further unusual feature of this advertising was its documentary character. The artists included photographs of the products or of people shown in full-face in the design concept.[20]

The covers of the second and third issues of *Lef* in 1923 contain both the linear and photographic elements that Lavrent'yev described. They allude to socialism's triumph over capitalism by depicting a photomontage of capitalists and their propaganda (Issue 2), and a plane, emblazoned with the *Lef* logo, deploying a weaponized fountain pen that battles a spear-wielding ape, representative of the simple-minded bourgeoisie.

Just as the Constructivists used such vivid visual elements in their art, Gaultier did as well. Densely packed horizontal stripes sharply contrast a large downward facing arrow – one of Gaultier's undisguised sexual references – in a slim-fitting dress in the Met's collection.[21] Similarly, on a dress sold by Kerry Taylor Auctions in 2015, Gaultier utilized a large-scale combination of stripes

---

19   Ibid.
20   Lavrent'yev, 'The Future is Our Only Goal', p. 15.
21   J.P. Gaultier, *Dress* [cotton and synthetic], *The Metropolitan Museum of Art*, 1986 <https://www.metmuseum.org/art/collection/search/150527> (Accessed 8 February 2016).

and an arrow, creating the illusion that the wearer is fully in motion even as she stands still.[22]

Photomontage also figured prominently in Gaultier's garments, notably on a knitted, greyscale sweater at the Metropolitan Museum of Art, which features the printed, vertical image of a surly young boy riding a bicycle.[23] A similar visual language, albeit with an older subjects, is seen on another sweater featuring the chiseled, disjointed faces of male models.[24] These pieces bring to mind Rodchenko's later photographic work, in which he captured scenes of everyday life, and gave it a sense of movement by shooting the image at an angle, or often, on the diagonal. At one point, Rodchenko spent a lot of time engaging in portraiture, including children in his long list of subjects.[25] Photomontages of Vladimir Lenin were also a common aspect of the Constructivists' work, with many of them having been published in *Lef* and *New Lef*, alongside literature extolling the virtues and triumphs of the revered leader. Gorbachev himself felt strongly about Lenin's work and wanted to simultaneously reinvigorate his legacy while tying it into his own by advocating for the types of semi-capitalistic reforms that eventually took place under both men. As evidenced by his use of collage and photomontage, Gaultier seemed to have grasped the similarities between the documentary aspect of the Constructivist artists' *oeuvre* and Gorbachev socioeconomic program; he did not, however, include any direct references to Lenin in his collection.

3   Gaultier's Constructivist Legacy

Gaultier's Russian Constructivist collection only graced the fashion world's runway and stores for a short period of time, yet it has had a longstanding legacy that underscores its importance in fashion and Soviet history. Years after his Fall/Winter 1986 show, Gaultier still had remnants of Constructivism on his

---

22   'A Good Jean Paul Gaultier "Russian Constructivist"', *Kerry Taylor Auctions* <https://www. liveauctioneers.com/item/37628805_a-good-jean-paul-gaultier-russian-constructivist> (Accessed 10 March 2016).

23   J.P. Gaultier, *Sweater* [wool, synthetic, and plastic], *The Metropolitan Museum of Art*, 1986 <https://www.metmuseum.org/art/collection/search/137474> (Accessed 3 March 2016).

24   'Jean Paul GAULTIER pour Equator (automne/hiver 1986–87, collection "French Gigolo")' [sweater], *Artcurial*, 29 October 2014 <http://www.artcurial.com/en/asp/fullCatalogue. asp? salelot=2498++++++11+&refno=10499502> (Accessed 12 March 2016).

25   For a selection of Rodchenko's children's photography, see A. Monteil, *Rodtchenko*, Friedrich Reinhardt, Basel, 2009, pp. 159–168.

mind. In 1989, Gaultier released a music album. *Aow Tou Dou Zat*, his comical, accent-ridden pronunciation of the phrase 'How to do that', was released as the designer's experimental foray into the music industry. Different editions of the album with different covers were created; amongst them, at least one of them was Constructivist-inspired. On this cover, Gaultier's bodiless head is the target of the linearly-oriented wrath of a pair of scissors.[26] Against the backdrop of the muted red and teal color scheme, this image was a symbolic extension of his Constructivist collection during the year the Eastern Bloc tore away from its Soviet master.

Unsurprisingly, nearly 30 years later, Gaultier asserted his high regard for this collection. In an editorial for *Harper's Bazaar* magazine, he placed it amongst his top ten most daring runway looks. In the article, Gaultier stated that that the very least, '… Cyrillics became very popular' as a result of his work that year.[27] Although Gaultier was not the only major designer to debut a 'fashnost' collection, he certainly helped initiate a new trend by analyzing and interpreting the zeitgeist around him. On the occasion of the opening of his retrospective exhibition at the Brooklyn Museum in 2013, Gaultier affirmed the modest, yet contemplative disposition that resulted in such a historically and contemporarily reflective collection in 1986. Speaking about his career-long experiences in an interview for *Vogue*, Gaultier stated that he '… think[s] that real fashion always comes from things that are happening in society. We are not, in reality, prophets'.[28] This collection was not born out of a prophetic vision of things to come in the following years; rather, it was a reflection on the Soviet Union's then-contemporary society, its history, and its slow journey towards demise.

Perhaps the significance of this collection was best explained by the commemorative 15th anniversary issue of *Harper's Bazaar Russia* in 2011, in which garments from the runway and Gaultier's face are featured prominently on the cover and in a multi-page editorial.[29] Founded in 1996, this Western, capitalist magazine would never had been permitted to open had Gorbachev not introduced his reform program, thus escalating the USSR's crisis of survival,

---

26   'Jean Paul Gaultier – Aow Tou Dou Zat', *Discogs* <https://www.discogs.com/Jean-Paul-Gaultier-Aow-Tou-Dou-Zat/master/79794> (Accessed 10 March 2016).

27   J.P. Gaultier, '#theLIST: My Most Daring Runway Looks', *Harper's Bazaar*, 27 September 2014 <http://www.harpersbazaar.com/fashion/designers/g3049/jean-paul-gaultier-daring-looks/> (Accessed 19 February 2016).

28   K. Andersen, 'Jean Paul Gaultier: "My Purpose Is Not To Shock"', *Vogue*, 23 October 2014 < http://www.vogue.com/13264210/jean-paul- gaultier-purpose- shock/.17> (Accessed 19 February 2016).

29   *Harper's Bazaar Russia*, vol. 15, no. 11, November 2011.

and eventually, its collapse. By featuring the designer and his collection on the cover of this momentous issue, the editors of the magazine highlighted the relationship between his rendering of 'fashnost', and Gorbachev's policies of *glasnost* and *perestroika*, reminding us of Gaultier's ability to transform the rumblings of discontent into a visually-triumphant conversation with the past.

Acknowledgments

I gratefully acknowledge the support and generosity of the following individuals at the Fashion Institute of Technology: Dr. Mary E. Davis, the Dean of Graduate Studies, Denyse Montegut, the Department Chair of Fashion and Textile Studies, and Rebecca Jumper Matheson, Adjunct Professor of Advanced Theory: Professional Seminar.

Bibliography

'A Good Jean Paul Gaultier "Russian Constructivist"', *Kerry Taylor Auctions* <https://www.liveauctioneers.com/item/37628805_a-good-jean-paul-gaultier-russian-constructivist> (Accessed 10 March 2016).

Andersen, K., 'Jean Paul Gaultier: "My Purpose Is Not To Shock"', *Vogue*, 23 October 2014 <http://www.vogue.com/13264210/jean-paul- gaultier-purpose- shock/.17> (Accessed 19 February 2016).

Aseev, N., *Izbran: Stikhi 1912–1922.* Krug, Moscow and St. Petersburg, 1923.

'A/W85-86 Jean Paul Gaultier Knit Turtleneck from the "Russian Constructivist" Collection by Jean Paul Gaultier', *The Salvages* <https://thesalvages.com/products/a-w85-86-russian-contructivist-zip-cardigan> (Accessed 6 June 2017).

Boulden, J., 'Gaultier: A Modest Provocateur Who Might Be Slowing Down', *CNN*, 10 April 2014 <http://www.cnn.com/2014/04/09/business/jean-paul-gaultier-retrospective/index.html> (Accessed 20 February 2016).

Dabrowski, M., *Liubov Popova.* The Museum of Modern Art, New York, NY, 1991.

Gaultier, J.P., *Dress* [cotton and synthetic], *The Metropolitan Museum of Art*, 1986 <https://www.metmuseum.org/art/collection/search/150527> (Accessed 8 February 2016).

Gaultier, J.P., *Dress* [wool, synthetic, silk, and metal], *The Metropolitan Museum of Art*, 1986 <https://www.metmuseum.org/art/collection/search/185755> (Accessed 8 February 2016).

Gaultier, J.P., *Gloves* [cotton and synthetic], *The Metropolitan Museum of Art*, 1986 <https://www.metmuseum.org/art/collection/search/121225> (Accessed 8 February 2016).

Gaultier, J.P., 'Invitation' [paper], *Jean Paul Gaultier: Be My Guest*, Fashion Space Gallery, London College of Fashion, 1986 <http://www.fashionspacegallery.com/exhibition/jean-paul-gaultier/> (Accessed 3 March 2016).

Gaultier, J.P., *Sweater* [wool, synthetic, and plastic], *The Metropolitan Museum of Art*, 1986 <https://www.metmuseum.org/art/collection/search/137474> (Accessed 3 March 2016).

Gaultier, J.P., '#theLIST: My Most Daring Runway Looks', *Harper's Bazaar*, 27 September 2014 <http://www.harpersbazaar.com/fashion/designers/g3049/jean-paul-gaultier-daring-looks/> (Accessed 19 February 2016).

Gorbachev, M., *Perestroika: New Thinking for Our Country and the World*. Harper and Row, New York, NY, 1987.

Harper's Bazaar Russia, vol. 15, no. 11, November 2011.

'Jean Paul Gaultier – Aow Tou Dou Zat', *Discogs* <https://www.discogs.com/Jean-Paul-Gaultier-Aow-Tou-Dou-Zat/master/79794> (Accessed 10 March 2016).

'Jean Paul GAULTIER pour Equator (automne/hiver 1986–87, collection "French Gigolo")'[sweater], *Artcurial*, 29 October 2014 <http://www.artcurial.com/en/asp/fullCatalogue.asp? salelot=2498++++++11+&refno=10499502> (Accessed 12 March 2016).

Lavrent'yev, N.A., 'The Future is Our Only Goal', in P. Noever, A.M. Rodchenko, V. Stepanova, and A.N. Lavrent'yev, *The Future is Our Only Goal*. Ed. A. Volker. Prestel-Verlag, Munich, 1991, pp. 9–21.

Leslie, G., 'Accessories: From Paris: Soviet Chic', *Women's Wear Daily*, vol. 151, no. 66, 4 April 1986.

Lodder, C., *Russian Constructivism*. Yale University Press, New Haven (CT) and London, 1983.

McDowell, C., *Jean Paul Gaultier*. Penguin Group, New York, NY, 2000.

Monteil, A., *Rodtchenko*. Friedrich Reinhardt, Basel, 2009.

Noever, P., 'Introduction', in P. Noever, A.M. Rodchenko, V. Stepanova, and A.N. Lavrent'yev, *The Future is Our Only Goal*. Ed. A. Volker. Prestel-Verlag, Munich, 1991, p. 7.

Starzinger, P.H., 'Overseen and Overheard', *Vogue*, vol. 179, no. 6, June 1989.

'View: The Cutting Edge', *Vogue*, vol. 176, no. 7, July 1986.

CHAPTER 12

Fashion, Fantasy, Power and Mystery: Interpreting Shoes through the Lens of Visual Culture

Naomi Joanna Braithwaite

Abstract

The high-heeled shoe has often been subjected to a myriad of cultural interpretations. Provoking connotations of power, eroticism, fragility and femininity, the high heel swings metaphorically between the objectification of female empowerment and a more negative association with the subordination of women. That shoes have an integral, fascinating and controversial place in culture is without doubt. Within a commercial sphere, shoe sales generate millions worldwide. Culturally their roles in stories such as *Cinderella* and *The Wizard of Oz* exemplify the transformative, magical and sometimes dark powers that they can hold. As fashion accessories high heels transform wearers aesthetically, physically and emotionally. It is as meaningful physical objects that high-heeled shoes have been most frequently scrutinised.

In response this chapter takes a different approach by exploring meaning through the lens of visual culture. By discussing how shoes are represented in fashion photography, in particular through the work of the French fashion photographer Guy Bourdin, the paper brings further understanding to Western culture's obsession with the mysterious and paradoxical nature of high heels. Bourdin was famed for his surrealist approach to fashion photography, focusing on theatrical composition and vivid colour use; he combined narrative storytelling with dark fantasy. Through the 1970s and into the 1980s Bourdin created campaigns for the renowned French shoe designer, Charles Jourdan, maker of exquisite high-heeled shoes. Drawing from semiotics, the author assumes the role of *voyeur* and observes the immersion of Jourdan's shoes within Bourdin's mysterious and sometimes sinister photographic world of storytelling. Bourdin's stylistic placement of shoes captures the imagination of viewers, drawing them into stories of femininity, mystery and eroticism. Key to the chapters argument is how the medium of fashion photography enables the cultural interrogation of the high heel, and, in so doing, reveals how images create and disseminate meaning.

Keywords

high heels – Guy Bourdin – Charles Jourdan – image – fashion – fantasy – femininity

1   Introduction

> Aomame pulled in her chin, kept her gaze fixed straight ahead, her
> back straight, and her pace steady. Her chestnut-colored Charles
> Jourdan heels clicked against the road's surface, and the skirts of
> her coat waved in the breeze.[1]

This extract comes from Murakami's *1Q84* as one of his key characters, Aomame
begins her transition from an expressway in Tokyo, 1984, into the parallel universe
of 1Q84. Her high-heeled Charles Jourdan shoes carry her on the journey that she
takes between Murakami's two worlds, and through them we can almost feel her
presence in these worlds. Aomame's passage to *1Q84* is down the expressway's
emergency staircase and before descending she slips off her high heels and rolls
up her skirt, liberating her body from the restrictions of these garments, and
then, once descended, she steps back into her shoes, moving forward towards
the unknown.[2] Murakami's sensory description of Aomame's movement within
and without the shoes prompts the reader to imagine the transformative power
that the shoes have on her physicality. As she strides across the expressway they
become metaphoric representations of femininity, but rather than the more ste-
reotypical notions of feminine fragility there is empowerment.

Cultural interpretations of high heels swing between female empowerment
and subordination.[3] The shoe's transformative effect on the wearer's body,
tightening calves and buttocks, projecting breasts forwards, has resulted in its
associations with the erotic and fetishism.[4] In the case of Aomame, Murakami's descriptions of her toned and lean physique lead the reader to imagine
how the heel serves to exaggerate this disciplined feminine silhouette, combined with the clicking of the heel against the ground indicating a determined,
empowered gait. The high heels present a more modern femininity, where the
heel is a metaphor for confidence, empowerment and freedom. Murakami's

---

1 H. Murakami, *1Q84*, Vintage Books, London, 2012, p. 13.
2 Ibid.
3 L. Gamman, 'Self-Fashioning, Gender Display, and Sexy Girl Shoes: What's at Stake – Female
   Fetishism or Narcissism?', in S. Benstock and S. Ferriss (eds.), *Footnotes: On Shoes*, Rutgers
   University Press, New Brunswick (NJ) and London, 2001, pp. 93–115.
4 V. Steele, *Fetish: Fashion, Sex and Power*, Oxford University Press, Oxford and New York, NY, 1996.

rendering of the high-heeled shoe resonates with fairy tales, such as *Cinderella* or the *Wizard of Oz*, where shoes have magical, transformative powers as they sit on the 'thresholds between worlds or states of being'.[5] As one reads the opening passages of *1Q84* there is a feeling of mystery and a sense of foreboding darkness to follow.

Through the descriptions of these shoes' relationship to the wearer's physique and demeanour, Murakami's extract sets the context of the paper which explores the cultural interpretations of the high heel. Theoretical meanings of the high heel are prolific and as they are culturally constructed they are open to shifting interpretations of femininity.[6] That the high heel has been subjected to interrogation from a myriad of theoretical perspectives is without doubt and it is these which have led to its role in creating a particular image of the wearer's persona. While it is not the intention to challenge these different meanings, the paper intends to explore how the presentation of shoes in image fashion advertising may serve to create and disseminate further meaning to shoes.

Perusing the *Vogue* archives confirms the prominence that shoes have had from brand advertisements through to accessories in fashion spreads.[7] During the 1970s fashion advertising became more experimental with the creation of darker and sinister themes, evident in the pages of French *Vogue*[8] and the work of French photographer Guy Bourdin.[9] In addition to his work with *Vogue*, Bourdin created the advertising campaigns for the French shoe designer Charles Jourdan. Bourdin's images for Jourdan invited the observer into a world of dark, mysterious, often sinister stories, posing the question: what's happened here? Although the shoe is always there, it is the story being told around it that captures the imagination of the viewer.

While considering the cultural meanings of high heels, the chapter draws from particular Jourdan campaign images with the intention of questioning the role shoes play in fuelling the imagination and constructing stories in the viewer's minds:

> Bourdin's pictures mesmerized us with their views of a world of impossible glamour, impossible pleasure, impossible danger, a world of high

---

5   H. Davidson, 'Shoes as Magical Objects', in H. Persson (ed.), *Shoes: Pleasure and Pain*, V&A Publishing, London, 2015, pp. 24–35, p. 26.

6   E. Semmelhack, 'The Allure of Power', in H. Persson (ed.), *Shoes: Pleasure and Pain*, V&A Publishing, London, 2015, pp. 39–51.

7   C. Probert, *Shoes in Vogue: Since 1910*, Thames & Hudson, London, 1981.

8   Also known as *Vogue Paris*.

9   H. Marriot, 'Inside the Surreal World of Guy Bourdin', *The Guardian*, 5 March 2015 <https://www.theguardian.com/fashion/2015/mar/05/surreal-world-guy-bourdin> (Accessed 10 August 2016).

adventure in which you never knew whether the boudoir door would open onto the rooftop, the desert, the palazzo, or the ditch.[10]

It is this sense of impossibility which sets in motion a desire to enter his photographic world and explore these images further.

2   Coming to Bourdin and Jourdan: A Reflective Approach

The impact that Guy Bourdin (1928–1991) has had on the world of photography, fashion and visual culture is significant. During the 1960s and 1970s he was a photographer for French *Vogue* and designer Charles Jourdan. Bourdin was credited for disrupting the norms of fashion imagery. Moving away from traditional representations of beauty and the stylised representations of products, to create instead double page spreads filled with complex, compelling and often dark narratives.[11] Biographical accounts of Bourdin tell how he came to photography in his twenties, being heavily inspired and later tutored by Man Ray. This accounts for the surrealist approach evident in his use of vivid colours and artistic experimentation with compositions.[12]

In 1954 Bourdin presented his work to *Vogue* where it caught the eye of Edmonde Charles-Roux, assistant to the editor-in-chief. Charles-Roux was recorded as saying that his images '... were men and women in the nude, showing only their back and bottom and sitting. The subject matter was extremely far from what could be of interest at *Vogue*',[13] but the quality was 'exceptional'.[14]

Chapeau-Choc (translated as 'Hat Shocker') was to be Bourdin's first commission for *Vogue* in 1955, where models posed in front of dead cows' heads and slabs of meat hanging from hooks, in the meat market of Paris's Les Halles.[15] Despite a barrage of complaints, Bourdin continued to produce images for *Vogue* and by 1967, under the guidance of accessories editor

---

10   L. Sante, 'Foreword', in S. Bourdin and G. Bourdin, *Exhibit A*, Jonathan Cape, London, 2001, p. 4.

11   R. Brooks, 'Sighs and Whispers', in C. Cotton and S. Verthime (eds.), *Guy Bourdin*, V&A Publishing, London, 2003, pp. 126–133.

12   A. Gingeras, *Guy Bourdin*, Phaidon Press Ltd., London, 2006.

13   A. Haden-Guest, 'The Return of Guy Bourdin', *The New Yorker*, 7 November 1994 <https://www.newyorker.com/magazine/1994/11/07/the-return-of-guy-bourdin> (Accessed 20 November 2017).

14   Ibid.

15   Gingeras, *Guy Bourdin*.

Francine Crescent, every issue of *Vogue* had at least 20 pages of Bourdin's photographs.[16]

It was through Crescent that Bourdin was introduced to the French shoe designer Roland Jourdan, son of Charles Jourdan, in 1964.[17] At the time Jourdan was looking for a different type of vitality in their advertising; something that went beyond the product.[18] There was already a distinct shift in the nature of advertising imagery, evident in the work of other photographers like Helmut Newton, who was moving away from traditional product shots to a more explicit portrayal of narratives around fashion.[19] The Jourdan brand was founded in 1919 by the shoemaker Charles. Jourdan's shoes were renowned for luxury, quality and innovative design, comparable with today's designers such as Christian Louboutin and Jimmy Choo.

In 1966 Bourdin shot his first campaign for Jourdan in New York. Their partnership was unique as Bourdin had control of artistic direction. For this campaign Bourdin requested giant shoes which Jourdan duly crafted. In one shot a model is seen running by the Brooklyn Bridge, while being chased by two gun toting New York cops. In another, the same shoe is pictured in a hotel corridor amidst lots of normal sized men's shoes. These images are almost fairytale-esque in their composition and resonate with the work of more contemporary images makers such as Tim Walker. Gérard Tavernas, Jourdan's head of Paris Office, recalled the resulting fervour from these images:'[i]t was if we were publishing not advertisements but a paperback novel or a comic strip ... People were hungry to see what was next'.[20] What did come next were 15 years and over 30 campaigns for Jourdan which encompassed Bourdin's distinct and often sinister narratives. Fascination for these images still holds significance today, yet the focus for analysis is more usually centred on the images themselves with less attention given to the role that the Jourdan shoes may play in the narrative's significance.

In 1979 Bourdin, with a case full of Charles Jourdan sample shoes, a pair of female mannequin legs (cut off at the knees) and a Cadillac, came to the UK, taking a road trip, from Poole to Hadrian's Wall. Using the mannequin legs instead of a live model, he created the *Walking Legs*

---

16   Ibid.

17   Haden-Guest, 'The Return of Guy Bourdin'.

18   Y. Aubry, 'Guy Bourdin et Charles Jourdan', *Zoom*, vol. 83, 1981, pp. 78–85.

19   C. Cotton, 'The Falsity of the Image', in C. Cotton and S. Verthime (eds.), *Guy Bourdin*, V&A Publishing, London, 2003, pp. 142–149.

20   Haden-Guest, 'The Return of Guy Bourdin', p. 140.

campaign: extraordinary images in ordinary settings – bus stops, gardens, by the sea front. It was seeing these images at the *Guy Bourdin: Image Maker* exhibition, Somerset House (London) in 2015, that initiated my intrigue in exploring further the work of Guy Bourdin and his photographic representation of shoes.

The motives for this paper are self-indulgent, having both a great passion for shoes and for Charles Jourdan. I have previously researched the meaning of shoes from the perspective of the designers who create them, through to the particular relationship women have to their high-heeled shoes. Before coming to academia, I worked for many years for a designer shoe brand that had been created by ex-Jourdan employees. I was fortunate enough to have worked with the designer who created the shoes featured in Bourdin's imagery and I spent years learning the Jourdan way of creating and selling shoes. This instigated a particular passion for the unique craftsmanship of Jourdan shoes, and I was to become an avid collector of vintage designs. My most treasured pair are black suede, high-heeled ankle boots with a distinctive metallic blue leather insignia on the outside edge, found in a vintage store called Resurrection in New York. My approach to shoes stems from material culture and explores how they objectify meaning in the lives of the women I have researched. More recently I have taken a self-reflective approach to material culture by cataloguing my own archive of shoes and recording how they each represent my biography. It was during this process that I visited the Bourdin exhibition and saw a photograph of my black ankle boots on a pair of mannequin legs, standing on the seafront, as if the absent body of the wearer was looking out to sea as a ship passes by. The role of fashion advertising has always been to manufacture desire for the product with a promise of an aspirational life.[21] Yet here I was faced with an image of a product that was already part of my own biography and seeing it in the context of image brought to the fore the fact that these shoes had their own history and context which was contained within the realms of visual culture. It seemed important to explore then how images could become a medium for understanding what shoes mean both culturally and subjectively, and it is this that the paper will question. As a researcher of material culture, I was intrigued to see what examining shoes in images might bring to an understanding of heels as cultural signifiers and the role of advertising in transmitting meaning through culture.

---

21   E. Shinkle, 'Introduction', in E. Shinkle (ed.), *Fashion as Photograph: Viewing and Reviewing Images of Fashion*, I.B. Tauris, London and New York, NY, 2012, pp. 1–13.

3   From Product to Image: Interpreting High
        Heels through Bourdin's Images

Whether on or off, the body shoes express identity and gender.[22] This is strikingly evident with the high heel, which is feminine, sexy, and eroticizes the body.[23] When worn, the heel transforms the wearer physically, tilting the pelvis back, pronating the bottom and breasts, creating a wiggle or even totter.[24] In 'Techniques of the Body', the anthropologist Mauss noted the technical ability that was needed to walk in high heels, one that he found incomprehensible.[25]

The high heel has had an illustrious history from being worn foremost by men, to an emblem of femininity and elevated status, to associations with fetishism and more recently the choice of an empowered female. For feminists the high heel represents disempowerment and links to subordinate status.[26] Although the heel is usually worn through choice and pleasure, its cultural interpretation fluctuates between empowerment and disempowerment.[27] Stories of women being expected to wear high heels in the work place, for example, frequently appear in the media.[28] It is in this contradictory context that a clear link can be seen between a cultural interpretation of the high heel and the presentation of femininity in advertising imagery which veers between that of being sexually degrading to a more modern approach encapsulating sexual empowerment.[29] The high heel is vested with cultural meaning and different interpretations of femininity. While the paper does not intend to solve these contradictions, it does use them to explore how they may aid the interpretation of Bourdin's images.

22   A. Brydon, 'Sensible Shoes', in A. Brydon and S. Niessen (eds.), *Consuming Fashion: Adorning the Transnational Body*, Berg Publishers, Oxford and New York, NY, 1998, pp. 13–38.

23   V. Steele and C. Hill, *Shoe Obsession*, Yale University Press, New Haven (CT) and London, 2012.

24   Ibid.

25   M. Mauss, 'Techniques of the Body', *Economy and Society*, vol. 2, no. 1,1973, pp. 70–89.

26   S. Jeffreys, *Beauty and Misogyny: Harmful Cultural Practices in the West*, Routledge, London, 2005.

27   Gamman, 'Self-Fashioning, Gender Display, and Sexy Girl Shoes'.

28   N. Khomami, 'London Receptionist Sent Home from PwC for Not Wearing High Heels', *The Guardian*, 11 May 2016 <https://www.theguardian.com/uk-news/2016/may/11/receptionist-sent-home-pwc-not-wearing-high-heels-pwc-nicola-thorp> (Accessed 18 August 2016).

29   R. Gill, 'Empowerment/Sexism: Figuring Female Sexual Agency in Contemporary Advertising', *Feminism and Psychology*, vol. 18, no. 1, 2008, pp. 35–60.

In a visually saturated world, images are central in making meaning through culture.[30] Meaning is encoded into images. Through their production and the context in which they are viewed, this meaning is then decoded both culturally and subjectively. Meaning, Berger stated, comes not just from what is known about the image and its message, but importantly the more mysterious, unknown qualities.[31] Advertising imagery is explicit in its use of coded signs, and the fashion system depends on the spectacle of images to fuel consumer desire through codes that signify aspirational lifestyles.[32] When it comes to a methodology for analysing images, Barthes' semiotic approach towards what the signifiers in the image are, in other words what it is of, and then what that signifies culturally, is the most usual point of reference.[33] However, given the complexity of fashion images it may be more relevant to take a nuanced approach to the methodology.[34] While the image analysis here has applied elements from semiotics to consider meaning, what has been fundamental to their understanding is what Hall terms 'negotiated reading',[35] implying some form of subjective analysis on the part of the researcher, which is informed by cultural connotations.

Many of the Jourdan images presented a distorted perspective of femininity, often containing some element of eroticism. An image from 1977 shows a maid with her *maitresse de la maison* fastening the ankle strap of her high-heeled strappy sandals, encapsulating the idea of both dominance and submission that surrounds the high heel.[36] In other campaigns, Bourdin invites the viewer to be a voyeur of an unsettling, crime scene. The key image for analysis here is from Jourdan's 1975 campaign. Taking a semiotic approach to describe the image, a blue car sits behind a chalk outline of a female silhouette, stains on the street allude to blood and a pair of pink high heel wedges are abandoned on the pavement. It signifies that something bad has happened and that a woman, the fragile female perhaps, is the victim of an illicit crime. Yet there is not a trace of her bar the chalk line and her discarded pink shoes. Although the shoes are not central to the image, they are an important signifier of who she

30   M. Sturken and L. Cartwright, *Practices of Looking: An Introduction to Visual Culture*, Oxford University Press, Oxford and New York, NY, 2001.

31   J. Berger, *Understanding a Photograph*, Penguin Classics, London, 2013.

32   Shinkle, 'Introduction'.

33   R. Barthes, *Image, Music and Text*, William Collins, Sons & Co, London, 1964.

34   Shinkle, 'Introduction'.

35   Sturken and Cartwright, *Practices of Looking*, p. 57.

36   J. Crump, 'Shoot to Thrill: Fetishism and Fashion Photography in the 1970s', in I. Vartanian (ed.), *High Heels: Fashion, Femininity, Seduction*, Thames & Hudson, London, 2011, pp. 36–57.

was. Taking a more nuanced and questioning approach perhaps the fragile female victim is not really what it is about, could the shoes belong to someone else, a *femme fatale* or a witness to the scene. In this context the more obvious meanings are immediately clouded by the mystery and incompleteness of the scenario presented. Bourdin's image triggers the imagination allowing minds to wander and create their own stories. The cultural meanings of high heels enable a reading of who the absent female might be.

Cotton argues that shoes rarely have a primary place in Bourdin's narratives.[37] Yet the fact that they are not central perhaps makes them even more pertinent to the narrative. Bourdin was a proponent of Alfred Hitchcock's 'Macguffin technique' where inanimate objects, in this case shoes, serve as catalysts to the plot.[38] What Bourdin achieves is the creation of a different image of fashion, with connotations of the erotic, fetishized femininity, dominance and submission, and somewhere within either on or off the body is a pair of high-heeled shoes. Although the shoes are not central to the image they have a role in the narrative that ultimately fulfilled the needs of advertising by selling product.[39]

Returning to Bourdin's *Walking Legs* campaign, what is striking here is the absent body, yet the mannequin legs are positioned in such a way that you can almost imagine the wearer's physicality. Bourdin has captured a sense of movement and the styles of the different shoes are imparting particular postures, where you can almost feel the resulting movement. Decoding images brings forth the ideas of journeys, resonating with Murakami's Aomame and fairy tales, where shoes guide movement between different places and senses of being.[40] These images suggest the place that shoes have in imparting the wearer's physical presence in the world, dictating posture, movements and persona, which in these images seems to be that of an empowered but contemplative woman. Culture is undoubtedly significant in influencing the interpretation of images, however, we unavoidably decode subjectively, imparting our own ideals and emotions on what we read into the image. We see what we want to see and believe what we want, but culture does influence the choices that are made.

---

37   Cotton, 'The Falsity of the Image'.
38   Marriot, 'Inside the Surreal World of Guy Bourdin'.
39   Ibid.
40   Davidson, 'Shoes as Magical Objects'.

4   Conclusion

By its very nature looking at images instigates an expectation of meaning.[41] Perception as a situated bodily practice means that images are not only seen they are felt.[42] It is this which triggers a more emotive and subjective interpretation. Shoe expert and academic, Valerie Steele, states that the meaning of the high-heeled shoe, 'is not inherent in the object itself. It's entirely something that's constructed by people in the society around it'.[43] This strikes a chord with how meaning is interpreted through images, where it stems from not just from what it portrays and the context in which it is seen but also the observer's cultural and subjective position.[44]

The volume of images that Bourdin created for Jourdan are immense, making it impossible to explore them all here, but what they each have is their own distinctive, mysterious, uncertain narrative which alludes to some reading of femininity. Whether on the live body, the disembodied mannequin legs or discarded in the corner of the image the high heel has a role to play in the images fuelling the narrative, stimulating the viewer's imagination and presenting a cultural perspective on femininity. The high heel is vested with conflicting cultural interpretations from subordination to empowerment and it is this which influences the subjective reading of the anonymous characters in Bourdin's narratives. Exploring the shoe's presentation in visual culture confirms its metaphoric role in the complexity of modern femininity and its ability to further stimulate culture's fascination with the high-heeled shoe.

Bibliography

Aubry, Y., 'Guy Bourdin et Charles Jourdan'. *Zoom,* vol. 83, 1981, pp. 78–85.
Barthes, R., *Image, Music and Text.* William Collins, Sons & Co, London, 1964.
Berger, J., *Understanding a Photograph.* Penguin Classics, London, 2013.
Bourdin, S., and G. Bourdin, *Exhibit A.* Jonathan Cape, London, 2001.

---

41   Berger, *Understanding a Photograph.*

42   E. Shinkle, 'The Line Between the Wall and the Floor: Reality and Affect in Contemporary Fashion Photography', in E. Shinkle (ed.), *Fashion as Photograph: Viewing and Reviewing Images of Fashion,* I.B. Tauris, London and New York, NY, 2012, pp. 214–226.

43   V. Steele, 'In Conversation', in I. Vartanian (ed.), *High Heels: Fashion, Femininity, Seduction,* Thames & Hudson, London, 2011, pp. 58–104, p. 58.

44   Sturken and Cartwright, *Practices of Looking.*

Brooks, R., 'Sighs and Whispers', in C. Cotton and S. Verthime (eds.), *Guy Bourdin*. V&A Publishing, London, 2003, pp. 126–133.

Brydon, A., 'Sensible Shoes', in A. Brydon and S. Niessen (eds.), *Consuming Fashion: Adorning the Transnational Body*. Berg Publishers, Oxford and New York, NY, 1998, pp. 13–38.

Cotton, C., 'The Falsity of the Image', in C. Cotton and S. Verthime (eds.), *Guy Bourdin*. V&A Publishing, London, 2003, pp. 142–149.

Crump, J., 'Shoot to Thrill: Fetishism and Fashion Photography in the 1970s', in I. Vartanian (ed.), *High Heels: Fashion, Femininity, Seduction*. Thames & Hudson, London, 2011, pp. 36–57.

Davidson, H., 'Shoes as Magical Objects', in H. Persson (ed.), *Shoes: Pleasure and Pain*. V&A Publishing, London, 2015, pp. 24–35.

Gamman, L., 'Self-Fashioning, Gender Display, and Sexy Girl Shoes: What's at Stake – Female Fetishism or Narcissism?', in S. Benstock and S. Ferriss (eds.), *Footnotes: On Shoes*. Rutgers University Press, New Brunswick (NJ) and London, 2001, pp. 93–115.

Gill, R., 'Empowerment/Sexism: Figuring Female Sexual Agency in Contemporary Advertising', *Feminism and Psychology*, vol. 18, no. 1, 2008, pp. 35–60.

Gingeras, A., *Guy Bourdin*. Phaidon Press Ltd., London, 2006.

Haden-Guest, A., 'The Return of Guy Bourdin', *The New Yorker*, 7 November 1994 <https://www.newyorker.com/magazine/1994/11/07/the-return-of-guy-bourdin> (Accessed 20 November 2017).

Jeffreys, S., *Beauty and Misogyny: Harmful Cultural Practices in the West*. Routledge, London, 2005.

Khomami, N., 'London Receptionist Sent Home from PwC for Not Wearing High Heels', *The Guardian*, 11 May 2016 <https://www.theguardian.com/uk-news/2016/may/11/receptionist-sent-home-pwc-not-wearing-high-heels-pwc-nicola-thorp> (Accessed 18 August 2016).

Marriot, H., 'Inside the Surreal World of Guy Bourdin', *The Guardian*, 5 March 2015 <https://www.theguardian.com/fashion/2015/mar/05/surreal-world-guy-bourdin> (Accessed 10 August 2016).

Mauss, M., 'Techniques of the Body', *Economy and Society*, vol. 2, no. 1, 1973, pp. 70–89.

Murakami, H., *1Q84*. Vintage Books, London, 2012.

Probert, C., *Shoes in Vogue: Since 1910*. Thames & Hudson, London, 1981.

Sante, L., 'Foreword', in S. Bourdin and G. Bourdin, *Exhibit A*. Jonathan Cape, London, 2001.

Semmelhack, E., 'The Allure of Power', in H. Persson (ed.), *Shoes: Pleasure and Pain*. V&A Publishing, London, 2015, pp. 39–51.

Shinkle, E., 'Introduction', in E. Shinkle (ed.), *Fashion as Photograph: Viewing and Reviewing Images of Fashion*. I.B. Tauris, London and New York, NY, 2012, pp. 1–13.

Shinkle, E., 'The Line Between the Wall and the Floor: Reality and Affect in Contemporary Fashion Photography', in E. Shinkle (ed.), *Fashion as Photograph: Viewing and Reviewing Images of Fashion.* I.B. Tauris, London and New York, NY, 2012, pp. 214–226.

Steele, V., 'In Conversation', in I. Vartanian (ed.), *High Heels: Fashion, Femininity, Seduction.* Thames & Hudson, London, 2011, pp. 58–104.

Steele, V., and C. Hill, *Shoe Obsession.* Yale University Press, New Haven (CT) and London, 2012.

Steele, V., *Fetish: Fashion, Sex and Power.* Oxford University Press, Oxford and New York, NY, 1996.

Sturken, M., and L. Cartwright, *Practices of Looking: An Introduction to Visual Culture.* Oxford University Press, Oxford and New York, NY, 2001.

CHAPTER 13

Fashion Plates: Rudolph Ackermann and Paul Poiret: The Relationship between Classical Revival and Feminist Expressions

Jill M. Carey and Lindsay E. Feeney

Abstract

The Ackermann Repository, published by Rudolph Ackermann between 1809 and 1829, depicted detailed fashion plates which focused on female dress styles. These fanciful illustrations did not feature a particular individual but instead served as generalized portraits to capture classical elements of the Regency Period. In these images, the designs, fabrics, and embellishments that were favored are indicative of a deeper meaning than trends alone as women stepped through the threshold of civil liberties.

The Regency Period, after the fall of Napoleon and the rise of Queen Victoria, provides insights into fashion; however, this era is often overlooked regarding the history of costume.[1] This oversight seems questionable given the significant relationship between fashion styles within an emerging marketplace of classical revival as indication of social transformation. As capitalism and industrialization occupied Western society, Rudolph Ackermann's depictions of the empire silhouette, for example, correspond both to Lord Byron's literary acknowledgment of romanticized ruins in Greece and Egypt, and the resurgence of Napoleon's political structure as a means to stabilize reform.

Nearly a century later, the plate-work of fashion visionary Paul Poiret as a marketing tool, proved that Ackermann's groundwork, though laid during a historical hiatus, achieved a level of intricacy and anonymity that suited modernity and female activism. Like Ackermann, Poiret promotes his visionary creations, inspired by classical themes, through progressive fashion illustrations that mark feminist desires and independence.

Keywords

fashion plates – Ackermann Repository of Arts – Regency Period – Classical Revival – Vertical Epoch – Edwardian mode – feminism – Art Nouveau – Orientalism – Paul Poiret

---

1 R. Ackermann and S. Blum, *Ackermann's Costume Plate: Women's Fashions in England, 1818–1828*, ed. S. Blum, Dover Publications, New York, NY, 1978.

1   Introduction

The derivation of societal insights through fashion has been accomplished in many forms, but a significant moment in the expressiveness of female style was realized in French culture during the 17th century, through the invention of fashion plates. Artfully illustrated from wood cuts and engravings, these representations embodied a form of material cultural through fashion compositions with a focus on style, body type and behaviour. As one examines these exquisite renderings, compelling insights arise from simply observing an article of clothing and its wearer and considering the relationship between the two. The engravings go 'so far as to intimate that if consumers acquired the new outfit being depicted they might at the same time acquire a share in the lifestyle of the person shown wearing it'.[2] Artful documentation of women would continue to be prolific in England during the years following the French Revolution.

Rudolph Ackermann, a German-born entrepreneur, further capitalized on the emerging industrial period by documenting the marriage between trends and societal cues, publishing more than 1,400 detailed and vibrant fashion plates between 1806 and 1828: a time when feminist concerns were emerging concurrently with Napoleon Bonaparte's classical revival. The pendulum of an appreciation for fashion innovation swung again a century later during the early 1900s. Designer Paul Poiret, known for his exotic social styles, abandoned Edwardian modes for a feministic approach, which liberated the female form from layers of petticoats and corsets focusing on draping rather than tailoring. In this case, the classical influence is brought to the forefront of aesthetic considerations regarding the connection between individual freedom and fashion restoration. Poiret, like Ackermann, saw the value of fashion plates as a means to advertise la *mode* in the form of suggestive interpretations to articulate the contemporary merging of wearable art and shifting roles of women.

2   Revolution, Feminism and Dress

During the French Revolution, ideas about female rights beyond domestic life rose to the surface and were debated without consequence. However, the roles of women did not evolve, nor did their position as decision makers within

---

2 J.E. DeJean, *The Essence of Style: How the French Invented High Fashion, Fine Food, Chic Cafés, Style, Sophistication, and Glamour*, Free, New York, NY, 2006, p. 68.

politics or social forums. What did develop during this radical period was the use of women in allegorical forms as symbols of virtue. These depictions, such as that of Liberty, appeared on currency, letterhead, swords, and playing cards.[3] The use of this type of imagery without a realistic connection to an individual was a means to limit actual power; therefore, female figures were dressed in classical Greek or Roman styles, clothing not necessarily worn by the public during the latter part of the eighteenth century.

As Napoleon restored the Empire, this notion of allegorical interpretations would evolve and was further supported through the rebuilding of France as a fashion capital. Bonaparte travelled with his army to ruins in Rome, Greece, and Egypt. The remnants of these cultures, since their demise, created intricate landscapes of vegetation and stone that held centuries of stories, scenery that was unlike anything Bonaparte's troops had experienced. The men sketched and documented the vestiges, and when they returned to France, their compositions and accounts were powerful enough to start a revival of classical antiquity regarding female fashion.[4]

The timing of this extreme style shift was significant, given European society's mistrust of past aristocratic expressions of excess and body restraint through dress. According to Jane Austen, '[a] woman, especially if she has the misfortune of knowing anything, should conceal it as well as she can'.[5] In this case, Austen is referring not only to the mind, but also to concealment in all aspects. The complacency of years of these societal views created the desire to shed layers of confinement that were synonymous with female suppression. Whether Austen was a feminist or not continues to be a long-debated question and was most recently contemplated in England, as she is the new face of Britain's ten-pound note. Austen was born on the brink of the Revolution, a time 'propelled by capitalism and industrialization where fashion became the barometer of change. Looking for the first time beyond the decorative, it embodied the philosophical, political, and practical issues of the day'.[6] Austen capitalized on diversity in dress in her portrayal of characters during this era. Generally speaking, women were not encouraged to document events during

---

3 'Liberty, Equality, Fraternity: Exploring the French Revolution', *Centre for History and New Media* <chnm.gmu.edu/revolution.chap5d.html> (Accessed 5 March 2014).

4 P.G. Tortora and K. Eubank, 'Part Five: The Nineteenth Century', *Survey of Historic Costume: A History of Western Dress*, Fairchild, New York, NY, 2010, pp. 295–350.

5 D. Widger, *Northanger Abbey, Author: Jane Austen* [EBook #121], 21 January 2010 <http://www.gutenberg.org/files/121/121-h/121-h.htm> (Accessed 27 February 2014).

6 S.J. Downing, *Fashion in the Time of Jane Austen*, Shire Publications Ltd., Long Island City, NY, 2010, p. 5.

this time period; however, Austen was able to illustrate varying roles and opinions of women by translating behaviour and societal details into situational garments and adornment: 'Austen adeptly used the newfound diversity of fashion to enliven her characters',[7] which would come to life in fashion plates.

An acknowledged feminist, Mary Wollstonecraft included a more systematic analysis of women and their condition in her *Vindication of the Rights of Women*, published in 1792. In essence, Wollstonecraft

> perceived women's inferior intelligence was not something inborn, but was a result of women's lack of education. Wollstonecraft become strongly associated with the idea of women's rights, its social effects, and the emergent movement on its behalf.[8]

Wollstonecraft was a philosopher of women's rights and was vehemently criticized for living her life openly; she carried on numerous affairs and bore a child out of wedlock, rendering her a taboo figure. Despite Wollstonecraft's criticism of women and their irrational concern for trivial things like fashion, she herself embraced the styles of the period and was commonly depicted in muslin fabrications, empire gowns, and turban head wraps, perhaps worn as a means to garner public support for her principles.

By the 1820s, the classical revival was widely embraced in numerous aspects of life, including literature and fashion. In England, Rudolph Ackermann's proficiency in both artistic design and printing methods established his *Repository of Arts*,[9] a worthy time capsule of culture and creativity reflecting Bonaparte's antiquarian influence. Though Ackermann's publications focused on a variety of topics, women were the main subjects when he profiled fashion. The images depict a stylized character modelled in a somewhat static form, based on Greek and Roman statues as a means to maintain a level of anonymity. A trend named the 'Grecian bend', deriving from female portrayal in ancient Grecian artwork, was created by 'placing a bustle-like padded roll underneath the gown at the back of the waistline, which gave the body the appearance of an S-shaped silhouette on the women who executed

---

7   Ibid.

8   A.F. Scott, 'Nineteenth-Century Feminist Writings', *The Gilder Lehrman Institute of American History*, 2006 <https://new.gilderlehrman.org/.../topics/womens-history/essays> (Accessed 10 March 2014).

9   R. Ackermann, *The Repository of Arts, Literature, Commerce, Manufactures, Fashions and Politics* (1809–1829) <https://archive.org/details/repositoryofarts109acke> (Accessed 5 April 2014).

the fad'.[10] Additionally, lightweight chemises, also inspired by classical an-
tiquities, hugged women's natural curves and revealed more of their bodies
than the modern world had seen before:[11] '[f]ashion's dramatic response was
to make women reed-slender, their waistlines clinging to their bosoms as
though for comfort, their silhouette sleek and etiolated'.[12] Popular colours in
fashion were given names such as 'Dust of Ruins' and 'Egyptian Earth', and
hairstyle names such as the 'Apollo Knot' truly reflected their inspiration.[13]
As stated by an anonymous writer, when a woman

> steps inquiringly into the 19th century she assumes a bolder air. She starts
> by discarding her sentiment and a good deal of her clothing. Inevitably a
> certain coolness is marked by the younger woman of the Vertical Epoch.[14]

Often Neoclassical themes melted into the Empire period, which gave way to
the fine detailing of the Romantic era. Jean-Jacques Rousseau's love affair with the
English political system also encouraged the adoption of Anglo-fashions in
France, as their studied casualness was regarded as elegantly democratic.[15] This
period of exhibitionism was amply documented by contemporary comments:

> 'What delicate mind can view with unconcern the nudes we meet every-
> where'. 'The arm once covered is now bare nearly to the shoulder the bo-
> som shamefully exposed and far more the ankle', was a wail in 1806. The
> evening dresses of the following year, with 'the bosom cut lower in the
> compliment to the back, and shoulders which still continue their public
> exhibition, braving both moral and physical declamation', provoked an
> outcry, 'The ladies of the first fashion, in order to set all competition at
> defiance, actually appeared in public more than half naked; but instant-
> ly the whole necks, arms, shoulders and bosoms in the kingdom were
> thrown open to the eye of the gazer'.[16]

---

10   Tortora and Eubank, 'Part Five: The Nineteenth Century', p. 315.
11   S. Pendergast, T. Pendergast, and S. Hermsen, 'The Nineteenth Century', *Fashion, Costume,
      and Culture: Clothing, Headwear, Body Decorations, and Footwear Through the Ages* (vol. 3),
      UXL, Detroit, MI, 2004, pp. 605–652.
12   Downing, *Fashion in the Time of Jane Austen*, p. 11.
13   P. N. Stearns, *Encyclopedia of European Social History from 1350 to 2000* (vol. 5.), Scribner,
      New York, NY, 2001.
14   C. W. Cunnington, *Fashion and Women's Attitudes in the Nineteenth Century*, Dover Publi-
      cations Inc., Mineola, NY, 2003.
15   Downing, *Fashion in the Time of Jane Austen*, p. 9.
16   Cunnington, *Fashion and Women's Attitudes in the Nineteenth Century*, p. 40.

This style appears to have disrupted the balance between sentimentalism and exhibitionism. These two attitudes of the female mind during the Vertical Epoch were essentially antagonistic during this period, as there was an imbalance in the relationship between the internal and external self. Therefore, during times of environmental extremes, exhibitionism seems to prevail. The classical forms admired for their frankness and unemotional simplicity tended to dominate during the Empire and the Romantic eras.

3   Fashion Plates

It seems the public was able to identify with fashion plates as covetable depictions for their symbolic status, without adding to the influence of a particular person. The notion of the private and the public self in dress was a feature of the marketplace, with concepts associated with specific garments regarding secret and modest layers. The secret layer closest to the body, became a symbol of personal indulgence and sexuality and was identified with individuality. The modest layer was one of concealment and provided a barrier between self-expression and environmental regulations as a means to garner social approval. Ackermann's fashion plates pushed the envelope by breaking down traditional barriers regarding the depiction of female dress and by focusing on a progressive design trend referred to as 'undress'. Indications of feministic expression are evident in many illustrations that reveal the undercurrent of a more liberal attitude in terms of the relationship between mind, body, and society. For example, in Ackermann's figure titled 'Dancing Dress' from February 1809, the female figure gazes out openly toward the viewer while raising her arms in a vulnerable physical position. The light, sheer layers of her empire gown cascade delicately over her feminine form, displaying freedom in a fairly exotic sense:

> [i]t is impossible to underestimate how important dancing was to the Regency lady ... so much competition in the flooded marriage market that every ball or assembly had to be approached strategically with the perfect gown as the most important element.[17]

The figure in this provocative representation embodies a cunning display of beauty and grace as a type of Neoclassical goddess, celebrating her new range of physical expression (Figure 13.1).

---

17   Downing, *Fashion in the Time of Jane Austen*, p. 18.

DANCING   DRESS.

FIGURE 13.1   *N.2 Dancing Dress, Feb.1809, Ackermann's Repository of Arts, Plate,29 Vol XIII.*
PHOTOGRAPHER: DAVID PARNES. USED WITH KIND PERMISSION FROM
LASELL COLLEGE, AUBURNDALE, MA. GIFTED TO THE LASELL FASHION
COLLECTION BY MR. VIRGILIUS DIBIASE. 2013.

In another example providing insight, an Ackermann plate titled 'Carriage
Dress', from June 1815, features the profile of an anonymous woman seated
with her head turned away from the viewer; she is gazing at a piece of art. In
her hand she holds a book, as she appears engaged entirely with imagination
and education, in contrast to the reality of her banality. Modelled in a relaxed

position, her shoulders slumped and her legs separated, the woman in this illustration remains unfazed by patriarchal judgment of her body positioning and her environment. Her white-satin *pelisse*, simplistic in its empire silhouette, is highly ornamented around her neck and bust, mirroring the opulence of her satin hat complete with Pomona green plumes:

> [t]he pelisse was a welcome outer layer for warmth and being a heavier fabric – velvet or wool in the colder months, and sarsnet or silks in summer – it provided a new scope for decoration. Although in Paris the high-waisted silhouette was lauded as the apex of refinement, in England the waist-less gown was frequently greeted as an abomination, especially by men[18]

... as the concealment of the female form in an unstructured sense was threatening. 'The divergence of the lives of men and women was marked entirely by their clothes',[19] and Ackermann continued to concentrate on the Empire styles despite public debate about this fashion. He recognized the capitalistic value of these representations as emblematic of the industrial period and the progression toward egalitarian enlightenment, which appealed to the female demographic: '[b]oth the French and Industrial Revolutions had precipitated a headlong dash into a "better" future against a growing dissatisfaction for the present'.[20] Female rights did not dramatically change in the early part of the 19th century, but concepts related to women's educational and political rights lingered during the so-called 'cult of domesticity' prior to the 20th century (Figure 13.2).

4   Vertical Epoch

Women's fashions demanded novelty and rapid cycles of change, as an indication of the desire to escape the banalities of an evolving capitalist social order:[21] '[m]en could no longer compete with women in this arena. Women's clothing, in comparison to that of men, was more complicated and more

---

18   Ibid., p. 16.
19   Ibid.
20   Ibid., p. 23.
21   D. D. Hill, *An Abridged History of World Costume and Fashion*, Pearson Education Inc., Upper Saddle River, NJ, 2011.

CARRIAGE DRESS.

FIGURE 13.2 *N.78 Carriage Dress, June.1815, Ackermann's Repository of Arts, Plate, 29 Vol XIII.*
PHOTOGRAPHER: DAVID PARNES. USED WITH KIND PERMISSION FROM
LASELL COLLEGE, AUBURNDALE, MA. GIFTED TO THE LASELL FASHION
COLLECTION BY MR. VIRGILIUS DIBIASE. 2013.

subject to change'.[22] It would seem Ackermann's prolific renderings of female
style influenced writers such as Lord Byron, who wrote some of the time's
best-known work, setting his poetry in classical antiquity[23] within a melancholy gothic framework. Byron and the Romantic poets 'took on the air of the
"blighted being" overtly displaying their sensitivity as an ethereal mark of "oth-
erness." '[24] The imagery created by written works such as Byron's elevated the

---

22   Tortora and Eubank, 'Part Five: The Nineteenth Century', p. 315.
23   Ibid.
24   Downing, *Fashion in the Time of Jane Austen*, p. 24.

importance of experiencing the notion of democratic republics, whether by first-hand account or by fantasy. This literary approach coincided seamlessly with the desire for something other than the comfort of complacency, whether it was in the intangibility of a person, a place, or an attitude: '[h]eroines like Emily in *The Mysteries of Udolpho* spend an inordinate amount of time wearing a white veil whilst being chased through romantic ruinous European landscapes'.[25] The culture shift featured a group of people who were enamoured of another time period, ignoring current social conventions of the Romantic era.[26] Women were so committed to the Vertical Epoch that they were willing to compromise their health when wearing the diaphanous gown made of lightweight, sheer fabrics, which they would douse with water for public display, revealing much more than a new silhouette. Known as the 'muslin disease', countless individuals succumbed to consumption, and those who didn't took their own measures to embrace a fragile appearance by drinking vinegar and dropping belladonna into their eyes: 'Women had been left on the side-lines as their world was changed around them',[27] and attaining such an appearance of romanticized illness and ethereal physicality certainly attracted the public's attention. The simple, democratic muslin style that had become the mainstay of fashion, according to Ackermann's *Repository of Arts*, would give way to the Victorian approach of severe body shaping and multiple layers.

The decline of the 'Grecian bend' was inevitable, given its provocative nature and the measures women took to embody a look that displayed outerworldly stylistic sophistication:

> [m]en and women were becoming further polarized ... Women lost any freedoms they may have gained with the rise of evangelicalism and sentimentality, when it was remembered that women were 'inherently sinful' and the only way they could redeem themselves was through a life of modesty, sobriety, charity, and silence.[28]

The backlash from the 'Grecian bend' would result in years of corseted layers and heavy petticoats, not to mention frequent and intense silhouette modifications. From crinolines to bustles, women emerged time and time again in varying states of configurations based on defined fashion cycles, economic conditions, politics, and Victorian attitudes that made females the moral

---

25   Ibid., p. 27.
26   Stearns, *Encyclopedia of European Social History from 1350 to 2000*.
27   Downing, *Fashion in the Time of Jane Austen*, p. 26.
28   Ibid., p. 62.

gauges of social stability. Even physical features of women such as hands and feet were celebrated at times for unrealistic *petite* sizing, forcing women to alter what was natural. Their feet coerced into tiny shoes and their hands covered with tight gloves, women emulated Queen Victoria, who sat at the centre of Western ideals related to style, the household, family, motherhood, and respectability.[29] From Europe to the United States, women were layered, laced, and lacquered with body covers defining them as objects of ornamentation, in environments that continued to offer limited access to education and decision making beyond the domestic sphere, despite organizations and movements in the public arena that paved the way for gender reform.

5   Modernistic Style Shift

With the advent of the 20th century, La Belle Époque marked a period in history in which the public celebrated significant advances in technology, the arts, cutting-edge fashion, and the integration of exotic cultures. In a top-down structure, dress was the symbol of lifestyle during this era and was identified as a mark of civility and achievement. As in the early 19th century, patriarchal systems were in transition and on the brink of accelerated changes. Women in America were making great strides towards a suffrage movement to take their newfound equalization further than fashion and into their personal rights as citizens. Inspired by their English sisterhood, who adopted tactics such as hunger strikes and picketing to draw attention to women's liberation, activists Alice Paul and Lucy Burns laid the groundwork in 1913 for America's first National Women's Party.

In France, women's lives and identities underwent alteration as this culture developed into a more urban, market-oriented society. Modernization altered the fabric of daily life, and newly mobilized females became consumers of goods, fashion, and literature designed to please this population.[30] French fashion designer Paul Poiret would capitalize on the direction of this trend by creating fashion in fluid forms connected to classical revival and Art Nouveau:

> [i]n freeing women from corsets and dissolving the fortified grandeur
> of the obdurate, hyperbolic silhouette, Poiret effected a concomitant

29   L. Abrams, 'Ideals of Womanhood in Victorian Britain', *BBC History*, 2001 <http://www.bbc.co.uk/history/trail/vistorian/women home/ideals womanhood ol.shtml> (Accessed 5 March 2014).

30   D. Holmes, and C. Tarr (eds.), *A Belle Epoque?: Women and Feminism in French Society and Culture 1890–1914*, Berghahn Books, Oxford and New York (NY), 2007.

revolution in dressmaking, one that shifted the emphasis away from the skills of tailoring to those based on the skills of draping.[31]

Despite France's New Republic, the status of women was limited with respect to political and basic human rights. This set of circumstances recalled the classical revival of the early nineteenth century for its articulation of change, though it was the contradiction between the impetus toward emancipation and the reality of gender discrimination that fuelled the growth of an organized political feminism.[32]

6   Poul Poiret/Inspired Fashion

Notable designers emerged to drive female fashion in industrialized societies into new but familiar territory. These individuals responded to dominant aesthetic influences and the opportunity to use dress as a means of artistic expression, in response to shifting gender roles. Fashion plates would resurface in the form of illustrations to document and market trends. Paul Poiret, known in America as 'The King of Fashion' or le Magnifique in Paris, 'changed the course of costume history but also steered it in the direction of modern design history'.[33]

Poiret liberated the female body, dissolving years of traditional dressmaking: '[r]estrictive, uncomfortable clothes were soon identified with restrictive social systems, and they too were rejected. After about 1908 women abandoned confining corsets and impractical long gowns',[34] which enabled Poiret's columnar silhouettes, directly influenced by the Greek chiton and the Japanese kimono, to establish a connection between feminism and this corresponding style: '[t]he cylindrical wardrobe replaced the statuesque, turning three dimensional representations into two dimensional abstraction',[35] a perfect complement as the first wave of feminism was coming to a close, with a modern appeal for health reform and, soon, the right to vote. Poiret's work built from straight lines and geometric rectangles hung from the shoulder, creating

---

31   H. Koda and A. Bolton, Paul Poiret (1879–1944) – Thematic Essay – Heilbrunn Timeline of Art History, The Metropolitan Museum of Art, New York, NY, 2000 <https://www.metmuseum.org/toah/hd/poir.htm> (Accessed 5 March 2014).

32   Holmes and Tarr, A Belle Epoque?, p. 22.

33   Koda and Bolton, Paul Poiret (1879–1944).

34   K. Mulvey and M. Richards, Decades of Beauty: The Changing Image of Women, Octopus, New York, NY, 1998, p. 666.

35   Koda and Bolton, Paul Poiret (1879–1944).

multiple effects of the relationship between the body and a woman's choice to liberate her wardrobe. His high-waisted, Directoire-revival silhouettes, although similar in their composition to the images in Ackermann's plates, went a step beyond, with acidic colours and exotic accessorizing connected to Orientalism:

> [i]n 1908 Poiret began printing the designs he commissioned in limited-edition catalogs, which he sent to his customers. The manner in which these catalogs were laid out influenced the evolution of the fashion magazine.[36]

Poiret commissioned a number of fashion artists, including Paul Iribe and George Lepape, to capture and market the luxury, ornamentation, and sensual aspects of his design work in an eclectic and compelling manner.

Le Robes de Paul Poiret, illustrated by Paul Iribe, set the stage for the *Gazette du Bon Ton, Journal des Dames et des Modes*, a limited edition of fashion plates of which approximately 250 copies were published in 1909 (Figure 13.3). The *pochoir* plates feature various black-and-white backgrounds; colour is reserved for the female figures and their fashions: '[a]ll these clothes appeared in a shocking and bright new palette of rich and sumptuous Eastern colour, even stockings changed from dreary Victorian black to red and gold'.[37]

Generally speaking, the women were dressed in empire gowns, embellished and textured with a combination of Art Nouveau and elements that would appear in the Art Deco movement. The erogenous zone was portrayed discreetly, a slight departure from Ackermann's revealing plates. Instead of plunging necklines and sheer fabrics, Poiret opted for 'the richness of pattern which was particularly suited to the simpler draped styles, and became working surfaces on which the designers could introduce more and more opulence'.[38] Iribe specifically illustrated women as caricatures of reality in images that suggested detachment from any real person, as women in groups appeared to be less threatening than notable individuals of consequence. Compositions included images of multiple women posed before paintings or admiring sculpture, in varying postures and with elaborate head wraps; unique facial expressions and cutting-edge classical-revival silhouettes suggested an opaque type of sexuality. Depicting not a singular woman but groups of women in a plate reflected

---

36   Pendergast, Pendergast, and Hermsen, 'The Nineteenth Century', p. 667.
37   Mulvery and Richards, p. 52.
38   Ibid.

FIGURE 13.3 *Pochoir Illustration by Paul Iribe "Les Robes de Paul Poiret" (Plate II) 1908.* Retrieved
from: Artophile Gallery, http://www.artophile.com.
USED WITH KIND PERMISSION FROM RICHARD J. ROBERTS OWNER OF THE
ARTOPHILE GALLERY PORT PERRY, CANADA.

a sense of independence within the community of other women, as feminism
was being defined and the movement was now well positioned.

In addition to Iribe, Poiret commissioned Georges Lepape to illustrate his
landmark book, *Les Choses de Paul Poiret*, published on 15 February 1911. Poiret
and Lepape combined their design ingenuity and marketing genius to create

fashion plates that not only displayed prevailing trends in fashion but also offered insights into interior decorating, textiles, and Art Deco furnishings. In
fact, one illustration featured *chaises longues* named after Josephine Bonaparte,
Napoleon's wife, further suggesting similarities between the Empire Period and
La Belle Époque. Generally speaking, Lepape's designs featured women in dramatic settings, emphasizing 'the New Woman' in a robust environment and,
according to Elsie Clews Parsons, a feminist anthropologist, portraying

> a woman not yet classified and perhaps not classifiable; the Woman, New
> not only to men, but to herself. In short the New Women were about
> breaking away from the more traditional limitations set upon them.[39]

Lapape's use of dramatic gesturing, moody cosmetics, and striking associations to exotic compositions helped to capture the likes of silent film stars such
as Theda Bara, who lived out this fantasy. Unlike her 19th century counterparts
from the Directoire period who favoured vinegar and belladonna, Bara, considered the first sex symbol, 'wore indigo makeup, which emphasized her death-
like pallor'.[40] Lepape's artistic chronology further established Poiret's mission,
which was to link art and fashion as a means toward iconic commercial success
while providing a platform for feminist ideals.

7   Conclusion

There is a striking resemblance between the fashion plates of Ackermann and
those of Poiret as documentation of female fashion and expression at historic
moments of egalitarian desires. The term 'reading in between the lines' comes
to life when one is evaluating the parallels between a single fashion plate and
the corresponding attitude of societal acceptance of feminist lifestyles at the
time of the plate's publication. Ackermann and Poiret worked nearly a century apart, allowing one to articulate the connection with classical revival
from both behavioural and stylistic perspectives: when la mode and societal
discernments went too strongly in the direction of liberation. The opportunity to dissect the illustrative cues and observe the subliminal correspondenc-
es between the works of two individuals who were influential in fashion and

---

39   S. Glenn, *Female Spectacle: The Theatrical Roots of Modern Feminism*, Harvard University
      Press, Cambridge, MA, 2000, p. 5.
40   Mulvery and Richards, p. 59.

lifestyle represents an unprecedented opportunity to examine the internal and external evolution of classical revival and feministic expression.

Bibliography

Abrams, L., 'Ideals of Womanhood in Victorian Britain', *BBC History*, 2001 <http://www. bbc.co.uk/history/trail/vistorian/women home/ideals womanhood ol.shtml> (Accessed 5 March 2014).

Ackermann, R., *The Repository of Arts, Literature, Commerce, Manufactures, Fashions and Politics* (1809–1829) <https://archive.org/details/repositoryofarts109acke> (Accessed 5 April 2014).

Blum, S., *Ackermann's Costume Plates: Women's Fashions in England 1818–1828*. Dover Publications Inc., New York, NY., 1978.

Botting, E. H., 'Making an American Feminist Icon: Mary Wollstonecraft's Reception in US Newspapers, 1800 – 1869', *History of Political Thought*, vol. 34, no. 2, 2013, pp. 273–295.

Boyle, L., 'Rudolph Ackermann and His Repository of Arts', *Jane Austen Centre*, 11 December 2013 <http://www.janeausten.co.uk/rudolph-ackermann-and-his-repository-of-arts/> (Accessed 5 March 2018).

Cunnington, C.W., *Fashion and Women's Attitudes in the Nineteenth Century*. Dover Publications Inc., Mineola, NY, 2003.

DeJean, J.E., *The Essence of Style: How the French Invented High Fashion, Fine Food, Chic Cafés, Style, Sophistication, and Glamour*. Free, New York, NY, 2006.

Downing, S.J., *Fashion in the Time of Jane Austen*. Shire Publications Ltd., Long Island City, NY, 2010.

Fischer, G.V., *Pantaloons and Power*. The Kent State University Press, Kent, OH, 2001.

Gayle, J., *Fashions in the Era of Jane Austen*. Publications of the Past Inc., Columbia, MO, 2012.

Glenn, S., *Female Spectacle: The Theatrical Roots of Modern Feminism*. Harvard University Press, Cambridge, MA, 2000.

Hill, D. D., *An Abridged History of World Costume and Fashion*. Pearson Education Inc., Upper Saddle River, NJ, 2011.

Holmes, D., and C. Tarr (eds.), *A Belle Epoque?: Women and Feminism in French Society and Culture 1890–1914*. Berghahn Books, Oxford and New York, NY, 2007.

Koda, H., and A. Bolton, *Paul Poiret (1879–1944) – Thematic Essay – Heilbrunn Timeline of Art History*. The Metropolitan Museum of Art, New York, NY, 2000 <https://www. metmuseum.org/toah/hd/poir.htm> (Accessed 5 March 2014).

'Liberty, Equality, Fraternity: Exploring the French Revolution', *Centre for History and New Media* <chnm.gmu.edu/revolution.chap5d.html> (Accessed 5 March 2014).

Looser, D., 'Jane Austen, Feminist Icon', *LareviewofBooks.org*. <https://lareviewofbooks. org/article/jane-austen-feminist-icon/#!> (Accessed 5 March 2014).

Mulvey, K., and M. Richards, *Decades of Beauty: The Changing Image of Women*. Octopus, New York, NY, 1998.

Pendergast, S., T. Pendergast, and S. Hermsen, 'The Nineteenth Century', *Fashion, Costume, and Culture: Clothing, Headwear, Body Decorations, and Footwear Through the Ages* (vol. 3). UXL, Detroit, MI, 2004, pp. 605–652.

Scott, A.F., 'Nineteenth-Century Feminist Writings', *The Gilder Lehrman Institute of American History*, 2006 <https://new.gilderlehrman.org/.../topics/womens-history/ essays> (Accessed 10 March 2014).

Stearns, P.N., *Encyclopedia of European Social History from 1350 to 2000* (vol. 5.). Scribner, New York, NY, 2001.

Tortora, P.G., and K. Eubank, 'Part Five: The Nineteenth Century', *Survey of Historic Costume: A History of Western Dress*. Fairchild, New York, NY, 2010, pp. 295–350.

Widger, D., *Northanger Abbey, Author: Jane Austen* [EBook #121], 21 January 2010 <http://www.gutenberg.org/files/121/121-h/121-h.htm> (Accessed 27 February 2014).

CHAPTER 14

Fashion Icons in Photography: American Magazine Turning to Iconic Representations from the 1960s On

Alice Morin

Abstract

In the 1960s, fashion started to shift focus on the fluidity of identity. This impacted American magazines such as *Vogue* and *Harper's Bazaar* which are the corpus of this study. In magazines of seemingly unlimited means and growing readership, feminine role-models multiplied and became strongly polarized in their photographs. Some of these figures have been endlessly re-staged in fashion editorials from the 1960s onward (and even before that) – such as the working single girl, the *femme fatale* or the chic socialite – to whom was granted an enduring iconic quality. *Vogue* and *Harper's Bazaar* represent a platform between fashion's artistic temptation and the commercial necessities commanding their production. The emergence, repetition and dissemination of such iconic figures through their pages can thus be analysed as an avant-garde-inspired game on stereotypes, ironically detaching itself from the consumer culture that it was embracing – a stance derived from the Pop Art revolution. The readers' compulsive fascination for these images was in the process deeply stimulated. Yet the new norms set by such iconic models proved anything but subversive. My purpose here is to question the making of these fashion iconic figures and to show that they inaugurated new, modern, programmatic narrative and visual discourses, in which the collaboratively-constructed narrative ultimately failed to offer readers a space for negotiation.

Keywords

fashion photography – fashion magazines – *Vogue* – *Harper's Bazaar* – feminine models – commodification – avant-garde – Pop Art

1   Introduction

'Icon' is a term commonly used when talking about fashion, for instance when referring to a person as a 'fashion icon' and to clothes or fashion photographs as 'iconic'. It was the case for Yves Saint-Laurent's *Mondrian Dress*, Richard Avedon's photograph of *Dovima with Elephants* shot at the Cirque d'Hiver for *Harper's Bazaar* in 1955, and Helmut Newton's take on Yves Saint-Laurent *Le Smoking* (again for *Vogue* in 1975), amongst many examples.

This chapter focuses on such photographs, but not necessarily on iconic ones. Instead, it is interested in the formation of iconic *figures*, in American culture and beyond, and in the way they are disseminated through photography in fashion publications.

However, observing the traits which most of the aforementioned recognised icons of fashion culture share, we can posit a few of their common characteristics. First, icons are easily recognisable by a reader or viewer, because they are familiar to him or her, in a manner that can be very personal – everyone usually agrees on an icon's *iconic* quality. In turn icons are easily appropriated by one and all. Furthermore, this wide recognition gives icons a 'sacred aura', echoing its evocative power. The term 'icons' is thus self-explanatory, and widely accepted as such. It is however seldom used as a critical tool.

A landmark in research about icons, Marie-Josée Mondzain's study of Byzantine imagery and of the iconoclastic controversy develops on the position of iconoclasts and iconophiles, whose attitude toward images has finally been adopted – and is still today shaping the relationship we have with images. Mondzain also states that icons are the articulation between the invisible (which, by definition, cannot be represented) and the visible, to sum it up very roughly.[1]

It is undeniable that in the past decades, the term 'icon' has gained popular and especially journalistic favour, somehow sparking the appearance of a 'modern turn' (or even 'post-modern turn') of the concept of 'icon', as we are about to discuss.

Camille Rouquet – writing also of photographic icons, but referring to photojournalism in the 1970s United States – provided a clear recap of the recent critical fortune of the term in academia. Before 1990s, 'iconic' as an adjective was rarely used by historians to categorize pictures. They used 'classic' or 'memorable' instead. In 1991, Vicki Goldberg's influential *The Power of Photography* defined icons as 'representations that inspire some degree of awe – perhaps mixed with dread, compassion, or aspiration – and that stand for an epoch or a system of beliefs' adding that 'icons almost instantly acquired symbolic overtones'.[2] Rouquet goes on to underline the adoption of the word in the research

---

1   M.-J. Mondzain, *Image, icône, économie. Les sources byzantines de l'imaginaire contemporain*, Seuil, Paris, 2000.
2   V. Goldberg, cit. in C. Rouquet, 'Creation and Afterlife of the Iconic Photographs of the Vietnam War', *Arts of War and Peace*, vol. 2, no. 1, 2014, pp. 1–14, p. 7.

community, leading, 20 years later, to a number of academic publications on the topic such as 'No Caption Needed by Robert Hariman and John Louis Lucaites, a book entirely dedicated to the study of photojournalistic icons'.[3]

Such a 'modern turn of the icon' is acknowledged when it comes to the visual (as a broad category), and I would like to use this tool to talk about fashion photography, starting by taking a look at Pop Art uses (and maybe abuses) of icons and iconic figures. Indeed, I believe this 'turn of the icon' is triggered by Pop Art's upheavals, mobilizing aesthetic, political and social stakes, just as fashion photography does, rather than merely reflecting these changes.

2   The '(Post-)Modern Turn of the Icon': Of Pop Art and Fashion

2.1   Pop Art Mechanisms and Influence

Much has been written and said about Pop Art, its mechanisms and its influence up to today. In this chapter, I will focus on some relevant aspects: first its 'dehierachisation' of the arts, or its introduction of 'low culture' into 'high culture', which allows in particular a strategic association with fashion, but which also hugely influences the perception of icons, and their cultural success. I will also use the concept of 'new sensibility' Pop Art manifests, as explained by Susan Sontag in the 1966 essay One Culture and the New Sensibility, in which she notes that wit, nostalgia, and a fascination for ephemerality are all characteristic of the new relationship an audience entertains with icons.[4]

Thus, Pop artists' ambiguous relationship to history, on the one hand, and to consumer culture, on the other, resulted in their ambiguous position towards icons, and ultimately in the latter's undisputed omnipresence in the public sphere.

To pursue on that note, it might be useful to specify that the tradition of appropriation goes back a very long way – the Modernists' multiple borrowings, for instance, are famous; and yet appropriation, as Benjamin Buchloh reminds us, is bound to fail, especially when it comes to low culture, which is co-opted as soon as it is reused[5] – in a way which strikingly mirrors the proceedings of fashion itself. Furthermore, parodistic appropriation, which is the form

---

3   Ibid.

4   S. Sontag, 'One Culture and the New Sensibility', in S. Sontag, Against Interpretation and Other Essays, Farrar, Strauss & Giroux, New York, NY, 1966, pp. 303–304.

5   B. H. D. Buchloh, 'Parody and Appropriation in Francis Picabia, Pop, and Sigmar Polke', in B. H. D. Buchloh (ed.), Neo-Avantgarde and Culture Industry. Essays on European and American Art from 1955 to 1975, The MIT Press, Cambridge, MA, 2001, pp. 343–364.

adopted by Pop Artists, necessarily results in creating an ambiguous (as always with Pop Art) space that acknowledges the necessity to fail, but points out the defaults of the society wherein it has developed.[6]

Catherine Bernard's description of Andy Warhol's treatment of icons (such as Marilyn Monroe or Jackie Kennedy) serves as an example of this appropriation and iconisation process. It consists of saturating space with an already existing image, thus cementing it in memories, allowing altogether for its endless reproduction and for the dilution of its essence along this reproduction process.[7]

2.2 Fashion and (Pop) Art

A figure very close to the fashion world,[8] Andy Warhol more generally exemplifies the ties between fashion and art. In the 1960s, both fields (the former with ready-to-wear and the latter with Pop Art) underwent comparable upheavals, as evidenced by a burst of creativity, the embrace of consumerism, and the aforementioned adoption of diverse influences from all surrounding domains.

Sara Doris, in her 2014 book *Pop Art and the Contest over American Culture*, points out that the connection between Pop Art and Pop Culture, and especially fashion, is established quickly, even by critics of the time, through youth (and youth culture). Fashion (and youth culture)'s defining characteristics are its 'fast paced' quality, and its swift process of recycling appropriated elements into a new cycle of trends.[9]

Although links between art and fashion have long been noted (and have been discussed at length by fashion scholars),[10] something more was at stake during the 1960s. If fashion has always looked up to art (artistic collaborations of the 1920s such as Man Ray's with *Vogue*[11] stand out amongst many examples), and has often tried to be accepted as an artistic form, such an ambition seldom reached such an articulated status as when Pop artists claimed they were closer to 'Pop culture managers'. Elizabeth Currid tells us that '[Andy Warhol] also understood the inverse: that art and culture could be translated

---

6   Ibid.

7   C. Bernard, 'Spectres d'Andy Warhol', *Sillages Critiques*, no. 8, 2006, pp. 133–144.

8   A. Krause-Wahl, 'Between Studio and Catwalk – Artists in Fashion Magazine', *Fashion Theory*, vol. 13, no. 1, 2009, pp. 7–27.

9   S. Doris, *Pop Art and the Contest over American Culture*, Cambridge University Press, Cambridge, 2007, pp. 156–167.

10   On this subject, see for example S. B. Kim, 'Is Fashion Art?', *Fashion Theory*, vol. 2, no. 1, 1998, pp. 51–71.

11   See, for instance, his portrait of Kiki de Montparnasse in *Vogue* Paris (published in May 1926), titled 'Noire et blanche'.

into a commodity form – what he called "business art." '[12] At the same time, stylists unabashedly 'borrowed' from trendy artistic motives of Pop and Op Art for their designs, sold as 'lifestyle' symbols[13] – an uninhibited connection. Sara Doris' contention that the decisive turn stemming from Pop Art practices is about who is allowed to make culture is thus verified through the period's fashion.

2.3   *Pop Art and the Treatment of American Icons in Fashion Magazines*

This shift in artistic production happened through a subversion of mainstream codes, and through the ironic/iconic deconstruction 'turned into a cultural success' as Buchloh puts it.[14] There is a complicity between ad and art which eventually ensures, ironically, (both) their iconic success. Key elements of this process, shared by both Pop Art and (Mod) fashion are the emphasis on surface as an expression in, and of itself, and the use of the process of repetition.[15]

About the collaboration of art and fashion media, James Meyer talks about 'cross-pollinisation' through a circle in which actors from all creative industries operate and interact.[16] It was very much the case in New York from at least the beginning of the 20th century; the city being a place wherein cultural webs and networks could develop. Therein, Elizabeth Currid sees the starting point of what she calls 'the Warhol economy', merging cultural production with business through a social scene, noting the 'transformation of New York's art and culture from bohemia to a creative economy'.[17]

In this case, I would argue that fashion and art collaboration was rather about blurring boundaries and making the positions unclear in a social circle fuelled by exchanges between photographers, musicians, socialites, and journalists. The exchanges in this closed circle resulted in the creation of a certain atmosphere of subversion in art and fashion, a sort of *bricolage* with an added sexiness, benefiting both from the elegance of the avant-garde, from its edge,

---

12   E. Currid, *The Warhol Economy: How Fashion, Art, and Music Drive New York City*, Princeton University Press, Princeton, NJ, 2008, pp. 15–16.

13   J. Walford, *Sixties Fashion, From 'Less Is More' to Youthquake*, Thames & Hudson, London, 2013.

14   Buchloh, 'Parody and Appropriation', p. 351.

15   On repetition and the practice of repetition, see Buchloh, 'Parody and Appropriation'; Doris, *Pop Art and the Contest over American Culture*; on the 60s' notion of 'play', see P. Braunstein, 'Forever Young, Insurgent Youth and the Sixties Culture of Rejuvenation', in P. Braunstein and M. W. Doyle (eds.), *Imagine Nation, the American Counterculture of the 1960s & 70s*, Routledge, New York, NY, 2002, pp. 243–274.

16   J. Meyer, 'The Mirror of Fashion: Dale McConathy and the Neo-Avant Garde', *Artforum*, vol. 39, no. 9, 2001, pp. 134–138, p. 135.

17   Currid, *The Warhol Economy*, p. 36.

and from the seductiveness of fashion's feverishness in a way I would even link to earlier phenomena of exoticisation. This creative atmosphere and the public adhesion to this upheaval of culture and creative zeitgeist did benefit the dissemination of iconic figures.

It seems important to note the collective dimension in this process and that the participation of the audience was growingly expected – a dimension palpable in all the avant-garde theories of the time, for that matter. This is where the fashion magazines came into play, as the importance of mediation increased in art and social practices, a shift duly noted by critics.[18] Fashion magazines provided this most-needed mediation with the audience, unfolding a space in which people felt they could interact with (artistic) creation. Their pages also provided the ideal medium for the aforementioned emphasis on surface. Their firmly established position as beloved cultural artefacts (a position obtained through the flourishing of the publishing industry in the U.S. from the 1890s onwards), their large readership (estimate numbers of circulation in the early 1970s were approximately 1.2 million copies for *Vogue*, and 430,000 copies for *Harper's Bazaar*)[19] and their unlimited means directed at the production of fashion photographs. Photographs also proved crucial in the development and diffusion of iconic figures. All in all, fashion publications provided the distortion of the relationship to reality necessary to the birth of icons, as demonstrated by a more precise case study of the American editions of *Vogue* and *Harper's Bazaar* from the 1960s until the 1980s.

3   Iconic Figures in American Magazines, from the 1960s On

3.1   *Recurrences and Persistence of Iconic Figures*
        in Fashion Photography
While taking a look at this photographic production, it is important to observe the historical recurrence of certain *clichés* in fashion imagery, which resonate with the tradition of appropriation in fashion (a phenomenon similar to the one observed in art). Figures of the *passante* (the 'passer-by'), of the *Parisienne*, or the 1960s 'Single Girl', to name just a few, have all been the subject

---

18   On mediation, see Doris, *Pop Art and the Contest over American Culture*; Currid, *The Warhol Economy*; A. Marwick, *The Sixties, Cultural Revolution in Britain, France, Italy, and the United States, c.1958-c. 1974*, Oxford University Press, Oxford, 1998.

19   Association of National Advertisers, *Magazine Circulation and Rate Trends, 1940–1971*, A.N.A, New York, NY, 1972.

of extensive studies, respectively by Agnès Rocamora, Helena Ribeiro, Hilary Radner.[20] Thus, we could contend that the solid implantation of fashion magazines such as *Vogue* or *Harper's Bazaar* allowed them to create and disseminate a certain fashion mythology, along with a large common basis of visual references, strengthened over time.

How can one recognise iconic figures in fashion magazines? Interestingly, magazine icons are often self-proclaimed, as evidenced by features' titles such as 'Marilyn, Fashioning an Icon' (*Vogue U.S.*, October 1999) or 'The Power of a Legend [Jackie Kennedy's] iconic legacy' (*Vogue U.S.*, March 2001) – whether the iconic character of women represented has withstood the test of time or not. As we can infer from the study of fashion magazines, generational icons coexist with timeless ones, but often differ from one another, the latter being generally widely recognised beyond the realm of fashion.

An attempt at a typology of icons, undertaken for practical research reasons, could divide them into three categories. First, historical, cultural icons, such as the *femme fatale*, the *ingénue*, etc., are the imaged translation of archetypes eventually becoming recognisable through their distinctive features (for example, the *ingénue* is always represented wide-eyed, with long legs and child-like short dresses). A second category similarly displays more recent and often more precise stereotypes (often national stereotypes) spread though popular imagery – the all-Natural outdoor loving American, the sophisticated composed chic Parisian are famous examples. Conversely, a third category of embodied icons emerge when real-life persons reportedly incarnate an idea, as was the case in the 1960s of Jackie Kennedy or Marilyn Monroe who became icons through the resonance of their public *personae*.

Icons are thus diverse and originate from different sources (a mix in itself reminiscent of Pop Art): from literature (for example the 'passer-by'), from cinema (inspiring the *femme fatale* or revealing certain movie stars), and sometimes from several genres throughout time (as with the *ingénue*).

The way they are disseminated is once again through the repetition of a signifying surface. Indeed, there is a visual recurrence of these figures (or persons) which could be roughly deconstructed as follows: first a lingering of key

---

20   See A. Rocamora, 'La femme des foules: la passante, la mode et la ville', *Sociétés*, vol. 95, no. 1, 2007, pp. 109–119; H. Ribeiro, 'Made in America: Paris, New York and Postwar Fashion Photography', in E. Paulicelli and H. Clark (eds.), *The Fabric of Cultures. Fashion, Identity, and Globalization*, Routledge, New York, NY, 2009, pp. 41–52; H. Radner, 'On the Move: Fashion Photography and the Single Girl in the 1960s', in S. Bruzzi and P. C. Gibson (eds.), *Fashion Cultures; Theories, Explorations and Analysis*, Routledge, New York, NY, 2000, pp. 128–142.

elements (borrowed from these diverse sources); then a crystallisation and a codification of these distinctive traits to make the icon widely recognisable; the success at a certain time of one or several photo-series establishing subjects as memorable figures, followed by the declination of these figures in other photo-series (often using lookalike models) reinforcing this success through a game of references and/or the collage of original photographs into trend pages, whereby original icons lend their aura to all other images around them.

For instance, in the 1960s copycat 'Jackie Kennedy' models became a regular feature in numerous fashion series (and still are today), while the 1990s saw the recurring use of archives-pulled photographs of Marilyn Monroe to lend some star-quality to, in no specific order, Kate Moss and Johnny Depp's relationship, Stephanie Seymour (also notably disguised as Marilyn in 'The Straight and the Narrow' by Herb Ritts for *Vogue U.S.*, September 1989), or Yves Saint-Laurent's newest designs. In another interesting example, Lauren Hutton came to incarnate 'the American woman' in the 1970s (sporty, natural, blue-eyed blonde, smiley, open, casually chic). Her image was thus modelled in this way by and through magazines (which featured her a lot between the late 1960s and the 1970s; today, with 26 occurrences, she is the model who appeared the most often on *Vogue* covers). She came to *signify* such a vision of Americanness, in which issues of class, political influence and economic power struggles were embedded, to a large number of readers. Such an association was effective to the point that she is today herself emulated in photoshoots using models 'playing' her, and more specifically her 1970s all-American self (as did for example, Natalia Vodianova in 'The Great Pretender' shot by Steven Meisel for *Vogue U.S.* in May 2009).

The final step of the iconisation of these figures is their appropriation by popular culture which reinterprets them, ultimately reusing them in advertisement widely disseminated in public space, making them more likely to enter the collective psyche. Once again in those cases, hinting to already-famous, titillating personalities such as Jackie Kennedy and Marilyn Monroe is a frequent recourse. The latter's sexy, platinum blond, languid, sensual character proved a *topos* for ads of all sorts such as, amongst many examples, the 2009 Dolce & Gabbana Beauty Campaign starring Scarlett Johansson photographed by Solve Sundsbo, or the 2011 Guess Fall Campaign starring Amber Heard photographed by Ellen Von Unwerth.

Such an exposition puts icons forth and turns them into the subject of many more mis- and re- appropriations, of all kinds, more or less commercial.[21]

---

21   Pertaining to this subject, there would be much more to be added on the 'artification' of fashion photography at the time of the emergence of these icons (with the mainstream

However, the most notable effect of all these re-readings, taken together with semantic recurrences (for example 'fun', 'fresh', 'dashing', 'daring' are often associated with images of the *ingénue*), is that they create standards, ultimately setting norms in femininity.

3.2   *The Adoption of Iconic Figures*

Looking back to the 'Pop Art turn' of the icon, the success of fashion visual icons, as they are constructed in American magazines, can definitely be read through the prism of the mechanisms raised earlier: subversion, ambiguity of the endorsement of popular and consumerist culture, tension between 'high and low cultures', repetition, power of the surface's appeal, nostalgia and irreverence, all of which being, in this context, particularly efficient.

Interestingly, an undeniable and growing erasure of the fashion dimension in iconic figures' representations takes place in parallel with the codification of these figures, whereby clothes become a uniform rather than fashion, so that the fashion dimension is progressively rubbed out, to the benefit of two other powerful categories to which it (tries to) pertain(s): art and popular culture.

Also relevant is the question of the incarnation. Retrospectively, we can assess that icons make visible the invisible and thus incarnate elements of the society in which they develop, as recent critics such as Hariman and Lucaites have noted, writing that iconic photographs

> are thought to have had distinctive influence on public opinion [...] the iconic image combination of mainstream recognition, wide circulation and emotional impact is a proven formula for reproducing a society's social order.[22]

All these elements also contribute to explain their public success.

Thus, incarnation manifests a crystallisation of social and cultural currents. In the case of fashion, it has indeed been demonstrated by sociologists that clothing was, roughly until the late 1950s, a class signifier. With the changes mentioned earlier in who can dictate what is fashionable, theories of Simmel,

---

success of photographers such as Avedon and Penn), as well as on the increasingly close ties between fashion and ad photography, which significantly strengthened during the same period.

22   R. Hariman and J. L. Lucaites, *No Caption Needed – Iconic Photographs, Public Culture and Liberal Democracy*, University of Chicago Press, Chicago, IL, 2007, pp. 7–9.

Veblen and Tarde,[23] without being less relevant, are completed with new ideas of fashion 'from the bottom up' as a way of expressing one's individuality and identity, which should be reflected in fashion pages.

However, magazines, which have presented themselves as advocators of a fluid, renewed identity from the 1960s on,[24] have, by using icons, failed instead to really emancipate readers by offering diverse, alternative models. Indeed, recurring iconic figures and the symbols they summon set new norms and thus unattainable ideals. In doing so, the subversive space of negotiation suggested in the wake of Pop Art as one of the elements presiding over iconic creation is apparently invalidated, trapped within its own inability to distance itself from the system it stands out to criticize.

4   Conclusion

In spite of this apparent failure, I would like to underline the amazing resilience of iconic figures which emerged and crystallized in the 1960s – one can still encounter them today while perusing a fashion magazine. My research ends with the 1980s,[25] a period infused with visual influences from the 1960s, and which saw the full deployment of the power of icons for several reasons, including but not limited to the realisation of postmodernism through camp, nostalgia and irreverence,[26] the obsession with remix, and the scopophiliac embrace. But in the 1990s, with the notable spread of the Internet, relationships to the visual shifted, as did the reinterpretation of cultural icons, which multiplied and became more personal – the rise of amateur photoshoots on the Internet being one example of these new forms.

Thus, I would argue that in the icon's distortion of one's relationship to reality there still emerges a space for projection and fantasy, which fuels in turn a desire to keep watching them. This potential unfolded and unfolds in

---

23   G. Simmel, *Philosophie de la mode*, Allia, Paris, 2013 [1905]; T. Veblen, *The Theory of the Leisure Class: An Economic Study in the Evolution of Institutions*, Dover Publications, New York, NY, 1994 [1899]; and G. Tarde, *Les Lois de l'Imitation*, Kimé, Paris, 1993 [1890].

24   L. W. Rabine, 'A Woman's Two Bodies: Fashion Magazines, Consumerism and Feminism', in S. Benstock and S. Ferriss (eds.), *On Fashion*, Rutgers University Press, New Brunswick, 1994, pp. 59–75.

25   The reason my study ends with the 1980s is because I consider that between the 1960s and the 1980s, fashion images have completed an aesthetic and symbolic cycle, before the rise of the Internet in the 1990s shifted the power dynamics between the press and their audience.

26   Doris, *Pop Art and the Contest over American Culture*.

a world witnessing the raise of intericonicity,[27] the saturation and growing accessibility of the visual, and its increasing power is also widely commented upon.[28]

In that way, I would say that the model upon which icons are constructed is still very much topical. Moreover, through these endless remediation's and through a growing involvement of the public (a phenomenon also rooted in the 1960s avant-garde art movements), iconic images with their continuous success may today finally be granted the power to offer a much needed space for negotiation.[29]

Bibliography

Association of National Advertisers, *Magazine Circulation and Rate Trends, 1940–1971.* A.N.A, New York, NY, 1972.

Bernard, C., 'Spectres d'Andy Warhol', *Sillages Critiques*, vol. 8, 2006, pp. 133–144.

Braunstein, P., 'Forever Young, Insurgent Youth and the 60s Culture of Rejuvenation', in P. Braunstein and M. W. Doyle (eds.), *Imagine Nation, the American Counterculture of the 1960s & 70s.* Routledge, New York, NY, 2002, pp. 243–274.

Buchloh, B.H.D., 'Parody and Appropriation in Francis Picabia, Pop, and Sigmar Polke', in B.H.D. Buchloh (ed.), *Neo-Avantgarde and Culture Industry. Essays on European and American Art from 1955 to 1975.* The MIT Press, Cambridge, MA, 2001, pp. 343–364.

Chéroux, C., 'Le déjà-vu du 11-Septembre, Essai d'intericonicité', *Etudes photographiques*, vol. 20, 2007, pp. 148–173.

Currid, E., *The Warhol Economy: How Fashion, Art, and Music Drive New York City.* Princeton University Press, Princeton, NJ, 2008.

---

27   On intericonicity, see C. Chéroux, 'Le déjà-vu du 11-Septembre, Essai d'intericonicité', *Etudes photographiques*, vol. 20, 2007, pp. 148–173. On intericonicity and fashion, see J. Morère, 'Intericonicity in Disguise in Madame Yevonde's Goddesses Series and Cindy Sherman's History Portraits/Old Masters', *E-Rea. Revue Électronique d'Études Sur Le Monde Anglophone*, vol. 13, no. 1, 2015 <https://erea.revues.org/4659?lang=fr> (Accessed 12 December 2015).

28   See, for example W. J. T. Mitchell, *What Do Pictures Want?*, University of Chicago Press, Chicago, IL, 2004; M. E. Hocks and M. Kendrick (eds.), *Eloquent Images: Word and Image in the Age of New Media*, The MIT Press, Cambridge, MA, 2005.

29   This is what Thompson and Haytko suggest empirically in their 1997 study. See C. Thompson and D. Haytko, 'Speaking of Fashion: Consumers' Uses of Fashion Discourses and the Appropriation of Countervailing Cultural Meanings', *Journal of Consumer Research*, vol. 24, no. 1, 1997, pp. 15–42.

Doris, S., *Pop Art and the Contest over American Culture*. Cambridge University Press, Cambridge, 2007.

Hariman, R., and J. L. Lucaites, *No Caption Needed – Iconic Photographs, Public Culture and Liberal Democracy*. University of Chicago Press, Chicago, IL, 2007.

Harper's Bazaar U.S. (issues from 1962 through 1987), Hearst Corporation, New York, NY.

Hocks, M. E., and M. R. Kendrick (eds.), *Eloquent Images: Word and Image in the Age of New Media*. The MIT Press, Cambridge, MA, 2005.

Kim, S. B., 'Is Fashion Art?', *Fashion Theory*, vol. 2, no. 1, 1998, pp. 51–71.

Krause-Wahl, A., 'Between Studio and Catwalk – Artists in Fashion Magazine', *Fashion Theory*, vol. 13, no. 1, 2009, pp. 7–27.

Marwick, A., *The Sixties, Cultural Revolution in Britain, France, Italy, and the United States, c.1958-c.1974*. Oxford University Press, Oxford, 1998.

Meyer, J., 'The Mirror of Fashion: Dale McConathy and the Neo-Avant Garde', *Artforum*, vol. 39, no. 9, 2001, pp. 134–138.

Mitchell, W. J. T., *What Do Pictures Want?* University of Chicago Press, Chicago, IL, 2004.

Mondzain, M.-J., *Image, icône, économie. Les sources byzantines de l'imaginaire contemporain*. Seuil, Paris, 2000.

Morère, J., 'Intericonicity in Disguise in Madame Yevonde's Goddesses Series and Cindy Sherman's History Portraits/Old Masters', *E-Rea. Revue Électronique d'Études Sur Le Monde Anglophone*, vol. 13, no. 1, 2015 <https://erea.revues.org/4659?lang=fr> (Accessed December 2015).

Rabine, L.W., 'A Woman's Two Bodies: Fashion Magazines, Consumerism and Feminism', in S. Benstock and S. Ferriss (eds.), *On Fashion*. Rutgers University Press, New Brunswick, 1994, pp. 59–75.

Radner, H., 'On the Move: Fashion Photography and the Single Girl in the 1960s', in S. Bruzzi and P. C. Gibson (eds.), *Fashion Cultures; Theories, Explorations and Analysis*. Routledge, New York, NY, 2000, pp. 128–142.

Ribeiro, H., 'Made in America: Paris, New York and Postwar Fashion Photography', in E. Paulicelli and H. Clark (eds.), *The Fabric of Cultures. Fashion, Identity, and Globalization*. Routledge, New York, NY, 2009, pp. 41–52.

Rocamora, A., 'La femme des foules: la passante, la mode et la ville', *Sociétés*, vol. 95, no. 1, 2007, pp. 109–119.

Rouquet, C., 'Creation and Afterlife of the Iconic Photographs of the Vietnam War', *Arts of War and Peace*, vol. 2, no. 1, 2014, pp. 1–14.

Simmel, G., *Philosophie de la mode*. Allia, Paris, 2013 [1905].

Sontag, S., 'One Culture and the New Sensibility', in S. Sontag, *Against Interpretation and Other Essays*. Farrar, Strauss & Giroux, New York, NY, 1966, pp. 293–304.

Tarde, G., *Les Lois de l'Imitation*. Kimé, Paris, 1993 [1890].

Thompson, C. J., and D. L. Haytko, 'Speaking of Fashion: Consumers' Uses of Fashion Discourses and the Appropriation of Countervailing Cultural Meanings', *Journal of Consumer Research*, vol. 24, no. 1, 1997, pp. 15–42.

Veblen, T., *The Theory of the Leisure Class: An Economic Study in the Evolution of Institutions*. Dover Publications, New York, NY, 1994 [1899].

Vogue U.S. (issue from 1962 through 1987), Condé Nast, New York, NY.

Walford, J., *Sixties Fashion, From 'Less Is More' to Youthquake*. Thames & Hudson, London, 2013.

PART 5

Embodying

∴

CHAPTER 15

Transcending the Traditional: Fashion as Performance

Jennifer Richards

Abstract

From fashion's inception, there has been an intrinsic link between clothing, performance and the body. This dialogue has been evident throughout the last century and into the present. This paper will examine contemporary examples of the pose through fashion shows, fashion displays and fashion performances. It will discuss the work of Daphne Guinness and Viktor and Rolf, and how their work seeks to reflect the historical associations of the pose but updates this mode within the 21st century fashion climate. It will also consider Olivier Saillard's work which examines the use of the pose with the contemporary fashion industry. His trilogy of work with the actress Tilda Swinton examines the history of couture, its process and creation, and the viewer's relationship within the body and garment. These examples seek to break the barriers of the traditional modes of the pose within the fashion context. They ask questions as to our own relationship with clothing and the body, imbuing meaning and symbolism into their work. This paper will argue that these new modes help to raise the profile of the pose as performance, raising their status to work in part as a spiritual medium, evoking emotional responses in our own readings of the work.

Keywords

performance – pose – body – meaning – symbolism

1 Introduction

In recent years, there has been an increasing number of collaborations between the visual arts and the world of fashion. Major fashion houses have sought out collaborations with performance-based artists such as Marina Abramović (co-art directing Givenchy's shows) and Vanessa Beecroft for Yeezy.

© KONINKLIJKE BRILL NV, LEIDEN, 2019 | DOI:10.1163/9789004382435_017

Most recently Clare Waight Keller included hip-hop ballet dancers within her debut for Givenchy S/S18. These particular catwalk shows have become art installation pieces, more akin to the ideas behind the rise of conceptual art or the Fluxus movement. These parallels although interesting and engaging, are not wholly new. Andy Warhol famously collaborated with many artists and designers in his Factory studio in the 1960s. So why this re-emergence of interest in performance and fashion?

Steven Sebring's *Study of Pose – A 1000 poses of Coco Rocha* demonstrates the growing interest in the dialogue between the traditional uses of the pose in fashion from the Salon through to the more contemporary uses of the pose in fashion photography, film and performance. Historically in the traditional use of the fashion pose, the Parisian Salon was the location for the parade of fashion where clients and buyers could view items displayed by a model in the precursor to today's modern catwalk shows. The growing interest in performance demonstrates that the use of movement or stillness can be seen as an important vessel to begin a dialogue around the importance of the pose within a 21st century climate. Throughout the digital age and social media in particular, this interest has steadily grown and the use of the body and the pose has become more relevant than ever. Platforms such as Instagram visualise key influencers in fashion and are an archive for anyone who wishes to document their extensive 'selfie' collection. You can also now buy an app to help to create the perfect image and the ideal pose to capture.

2   Guinness and Saillard

There are also a wide range of creative individuals within fashion that are exploring ideas surrounding the use of the pose. Daphne Guinness creates performance pieces inspired by her friends and her love of fashion. The designers Viktor and Rolf have evolved the traditional use of the catwalk show into a new space in which art and fashion collide. Olivier Saillard's curatorial and performative work, particularly with the actress Tilda Swinton, seeks to create a dialogue between the traditional and more contemporary face of fashion. All three collaborators works are an attempt to try and elevate the status of the pose within their work, imbuing each work with a sense of spirituality. They are all transcending the traditional boundaries of the pose and use of movement in fashion into something more esoteric and otherworldly.

The British artist and socialite Daphne Guinness created her piece *Remembrance of Things Past* in 2011. Guinness referred to the performance as a 'poetic gesture'[1] to both Alexander McQueen and Isabella Blow. Blow was both daring and provocative and established a legacy within the fashion industry. This work was an attempt to represent Blow's personality and *joie de vivre*. An unusual location was selected, this being Barney's store front window. It became a location to both curate and showcase work from Alexander McQueen's and Isabella Blow's collections. At this time, Guinness was custodian for Blow's collection and agreed with Barney's to showcase key items on the six-week build up to the Costume Institute Gala. As a finale to this installation, she was to perform a one-off show which saw her undress and dress in the window in her finest Alexander McQueen gown. Invites were sent out to a select crowd so that fashionistas and the public alike could share in this unique and momentous occasion.

Walking into the window in a McQueen jumpsuit, Guinness' head is covered. She poses outstretched onto a table, then undresses behind a screen (the viewer can see her gyrating in silhouette). She then reappears in front of the crowd in one of McQueen's signature gowns. She removes the scarf from her head, reveals her face then exits. This performance totals eight minutes in length.

This work is a love letter to her two friends. It is an attempt to demonstrate her ability to create a tribute to both Blow and McQueen in her unique and highly imaginative way. The element of transformation is a key part of the performance, and resonates with the viewer. McQueen used many different tropes and transformations throughout his collections, and had a particularly fondness for the macabre and the gothic. This sense of drama and melancholy is present when viewing the work. The audience can sense this emotional connection between the three collaborators through Guinness' presence, and by omission, the absence of both Blow and McQueen. Guinness herself states that the work seeks to 'transform the wearer and in turn, it transforms the piece – it locks'.[2]

Daphne Guinness went on that year to collaborate on another performance with jeweller Shaun Leane. This work titled *Contra Mundum* (translated as 'Against the World'), manifested itself in the form of an armoured glove. Guinness suggested this piece represented a means of armouring the self against the outside world. The glove had the aesthetics of an evening glove and was made from 18ct white gold but visually sought to replicate lace or silk, due to the intricate jewel work by Leane. Articulated fingers and detailed birds were worked into the piece. This piece became symbolic of their collaboration, the

1   L. Carpenter, 'Daphne Guinness on Her Friend Alexander McQueen's Tragic Death', *The Telegraph*, 30 April 2016 <http://www.telegraph.co.uk/fashion/people/daphne-guinness-on-her-friend-alexander-mcqueens-tragic-death-i/> (Accessed 8 May 2016).
2   B. Stasiewicz (dir.), *Contra Mundum* [DVD], UK, 2011.

piece therefore transformed into an *objet d'art*. It was both a reflection of their friendship and homage to McQueen who contributed to the initial idea.

The work was showcased with Guinness lying on a stone plinth, surrounded by candles, shrouded and veiled wearing the glove. Her arm was the only part of her body that was on show and exposed to the viewer. Members of the party could then step forward to gaze upon her, revering her as if she were a knight lying in state after a great battle. Like a medieval warrior, the performance allows Guinness to become a modern-day Joan of Arc. Dressed in the bespoke glove and shrouded in white silk tulle, her lie-in state as her gloved hand lay over the tulle and rested on her upper-body, symbolising the concept of the *objet d'art*.

This work like *Remembrance of Things Past* was highly theatrical. An installation piece, reminiscent of the works of the Fluxus era it sought to evoke both the past and the future simultaneously. It engaged with the public actively, not just in a passive manner as an audience would traditionally view a performance work. Here individual members of the party were invited to step forward and view Guinness in her lie-in state. Each individual had their own unique experience of the work, and they became part of both Guinness' process and outcome.

3   Viktor and Rolf

Avant-garde designers Viktor and Rolf chose to revolutionise the catwalk show by removing it completely when showing their collection in 1999. For their *Russian Doll* collection, they used just one model to display the collection. Model Maggie Rizer was placed onto a revolving turntable, a barrage of clothes layered onto her body in excess of 70 kilogrammes.

The audience became active participants in the performance. Like Guinness' works, they became an intrinsic part of this new spectacle. They were audible gasps of adoration and amazement whilst the designers performed the act of adding more and more garments to their model. These items began with lighter fabrics such as slips and shirts to a final over-sized and intricately patterned coat. The overall effect of this mass of clothing was in the finale, the creation of a real-life Russian doll. Critic André Leon Talley called the collection, 'the Viagra of couture week'.[3]

---

3   A.L. Talley, 'Fall 1999 Couture – Viktor and Rolf', *Vogue*, 1999 <https://www.vogue.com/fashion-shows/fall-1999-couture/viktor-rolf> (Accessed May 2016).

This example of Viktor and Rolf's work pushes the boundaries of fashion within this period of time, and questions how we as the audience view fashion and fashion shows. Viktor and Rolf purposefully mock the traditional constructs of the fashion show in order to create their own vision of what contemporary fashion should be. This is a major part of their design philosophy, and they have continued to do this in subsequent works. For example, their A/W 2015 fashion show they took on the role of performance artists. They removed the items from each of the models once they had walked the catwalk then hung them on the white wall which enclosed the catwalk. Here the garments became art objects to be revered by the establishment. The final look was reminiscent of a Dutch master painting, although somewhat deconstructed in the guise of Conceptual Art. Both these works demonstrate what Viktor and Rolf's work is all about. The ideas and concepts are paramount to the two designers as they continue to push the boundaries of what is expected.

4   Swinton and Saillard

Like Viktor and Rolf before him, Olivier Saillard has continued this dialogue with the pose in his own performance pieces. As a high-profile fashion curator and fashion historian, he has the opportunity and platform to explore his ideas further. Throughout his work, he has sought to create a discourse transforming our preconceived notions associated with the pose in fashion and the fashion industry. An example of this is his work *Models Never Talk* (2014). This work seeks to uncover the relationship between the model and the designer. Traditionally, a model can be a muse, helping to develop how a designer may envisage that season's fashion from the conception of an idea through to the final collection. Saillard uses this particular performance to demonstrate the difference when models enter the catwalk. Here the models fall silent and the dialogue is lost. They are viewed only as a prop for the clothing to be displayed.

Further to this, his subsequent trilogy of work with the actress Tilda Swinton examines the history of couture, its process and creation, and the viewer's relationship within the body and garment. These three works also attempt to examine our deep-seated desires and responses to clothes.

The first collaboration with Swinton was *The Impossible Wardrobe* (2012). Here Saillard and Swinton combine to give the viewer a glimpse into a museum collection, he as caretaker and she as model. There are around 54 items displayed for the viewer including garments and accessories by designers such as Lanvin and Schiaparelli. Napoleon Bonaparte's jacket also makes an appearance. Swinton takes on the role as model and walks along a catwalk which ends with a full-length mirror. Here she uses her body as a gesture, imbuing the clothing with expression or movement. She interacts with each garment or accessory differently, as if she can feel their emotional needs and desires. There is a sense of tension in the piece, as these items have been housed in museum collections for years, static and untouched, preserved for the public to view. Swinton carefully constructs the narrative of each item, demonstrating the close connection we have with beauty, craft and the previous wearer of these exquisite pieces. Each piece is also described above Swinton's head as she collects it from Saillard. This again emphasises the connection we make with the knowledge of an item. Our aesthetic desire to see items lost amongst the centuries is revived. Some items are lovingly caressed, others held aloft as art objects. There is a tension between our needs as a viewer to be visually enthralled, but also the experience of these items is somewhat tinged with a sense of loss. The items become a type of a *memento mori*; they become ghosts of the past.

Their second collaboration was for the work titled *Eternity Dress* (2014). This performance follows the design process of creating a dress from initial sketch to finished garment. Saillard examines the historical use of the haute couture dress making process. He examines this mode through the fine art process, drawing comparisons with garment making and the creation of artworks. Swinton works as muse throughout the process and inspiration, posing throughout the garment making process. Swinton is measured; the pattern is drawn and cut as Saillard tests out a range of sleeves, collars and details for the dress.

Saillard adds additional pockets, and then Swinton seeks to remove them as his back is turned. Swinton also removes or dismisses certain items as the process evolves. Here she interacts with the design process, which is highly unusual within traditional haute couture dressmaking techniques. Traditionally, the model is static, they are the hanger. There is no need to speak with them or an opinion to be formed of the designers' vision. The next stage demonstrates the selection of the chosen cloth, which is then draped across Swinton. Swinton then sews herself into the canvas toile. When the dress is complete, she models this 1930s-inspired gown as if it were an item by Balenciaga, posing in the iconic shapes and gestures of the designer. Within her performance of the garment she also makes nods to Yves Saint Laurent's *Le Smoking*, with her hand in her pocket and then removes her shoes in homage to Rei Kawakubo.

The work can be seen as a statement alluding to the contemporary fashion system, Saillard seeking to bring back the traditional haute couture methods in opposition to the desire for fast fashion items created at incredible speed due to increasing consumer demand. This works asks us to look at the craftsmanship and artistry that goes in to the creation of a bespoke item. Saillard and Swinton seek to emphasise each in individual stage of the process, the meticulous accuracy and painstaking development of each stage. We as the audience are asked to re-think our preconceived notions of the garment making process. This has been an on-going dialogue with fashion, with the growth of sustainability and eco-friendly fashion at the forefront of many ethical and social discussion within the fashion industry. Most recently, issues surrounding couture's use of fur within their designs has been highlighted in the media with big name brands and designers removing all traces from their collections. Also, the desire for the acquisition and display of couture garments has increased in recent years which in turn demonstrates the public's desire. Recent exhibitions such as Balenciaga's at the V&A, highlight the interest in the examination of clothing and the role in which fashion has to offer a platform for discussion and debate.

Their final collaboration was for the work *Cloakroom Vestiaire* (2015). This work embraces the interactive qualities of the performance piece. Members of the public are asked to deposit items of clothing to the 'coat check lady' in this case, Swinton. Swinton carefully selects an item to interact with. As with Saillard's previous works, the emphasis is on the interaction of Swinton with the clothing. With some items she speaks to them, with others she carefully scrutinises their details. She also places items in pockets of garments, kissing tissue paper with her lipstick and placing it into a jacket pocket. She also includes flowers, poems and written fragments, adding her own personality or experience into each item, changing it forever after her time with the item. Swinton forcibly imposes herself on these items, changing them forever within a few minutes of interaction.

This work asks us to question our relationship with the clothes we wear, the clothes we love, and the ones with memories of significant events. It is a way to examine ourselves, what we as individuals project out into the world, our innermost desires expressed through our clothes. This work adds another dimension to the experience within this trilogy of work as it involves the audience more directly. They are less passive observers; they become an important part of the performance. Their personal items become both the process and outcome of the work. Saillard states that the work is about 'how one day our own clothing will be granted meaning in a museum context, purely because it is ours'.[4]

---

4 D. Thawley, 'Tilda Swinton Wears Your Sleeve on Her Heart', *Interview*, 25 November 2014 <https://www.interviewmagazine.com/art/tilda-swinton-wears-your-sleeve-on-her-heart> (Accessed July 2016).

Examining the trilogy of work Saillard has created, *Eternity Dress* and *The Impossible Wardrobe* are more passive, and they are more akin to the traditional fashion show. In both works, items are displayed for the audiences' pleasure; they are examined or showcased as you would see them in a Salon. Swinton uses traditional poses to display the items, gestures which are associated with the high fashion poses. *Cloakroom Vestiaire* breaks the fourth wall of theatre, affecting the audience with the performance, rather than as a passive observation on aesthetics such as the garments colour or use of craft.

5   Conclusion

In conclusion, Daphne Guinness, Viktor and Rolf and Olivier Saillard seek to investigate how clothes are inhabited. They attempt to look at ways of reinventing clothing with our experience of viewing items on models. They try to change the perception of the fashion show from a passive spectacle to a personal and more individual experience. It can be argued that the fashion industry itself is built on façade, emphasising the aesthetic beauty or visual as of paramount importance. Therefore, these works force us as individuals to begin to look internally at ourselves and not rely on our external qualities. They attempt to celebrate the individuality of an item, the person, or the designer. These examples seek to break the barriers of the traditional modes of the pose within the fashion context. They ask questions as to our own relationship with clothing and the body, imbuing meaning and symbolism into their work. They all continue to raise the importance of performance-based works to evoke emotional responses in our own readings of the work.

Saillard's work is a reflection of this continuing dialogue. His work has evolved throughout the trilogy creating a new space in which to discuss fashion and performance. Throughout the journey of the three performances discussed, Saillard has systematically moved away from the more tradition notions of the museum context and fashion history, into something more contemporary. This new way of seeing is more akin to the performance artists, breathing life into the fashion system, creating new and exciting possibilities and sources of inspiration for the next generation of visual artists. In December 2017, Saillard was confirmed as curator of the Fondation Alaia, which will celebrate the brand's heritage and identity. The exhibition is titled *Azzedine Alaïa: Je Suis Couturier.*

This move highlights new possibilities for collaboration and interdisciplinary modes of working for a wide range of practitioners and disciplines. Long may it continue.

Bibliography

Brand, J., *Fashion and Imagination: About Clothes and Art.* ArtsEZ Press, Arnhem, 2010.

Carpenter, L., 'Daphne Guinness on Her Friend Alexander McQueen's Tragic Death', *The Telegraph*, 30 April 2016 <http://www.telegraph.co.uk/fashion/people/daphne-guinness-on-her-friend-alexander-mcqueens-tragic-death-i/> (Accessed 8 May 2016).

Issac-Goize, T., 'The Fondation Alaïa Will Open With an Olivier Saillard–Curated Exhibition at the January Haute Couture Shows', *Vogue*, 18 December 2017 <https://www.vogue.com/article/fondation-alaia-opens-olivier-saillard-exhibition> (Accessed 15th January 2018).

Miller, S., 'Fashion as Art: Is Fashion Art?', *Fashion Theory: The Journal of Dress, Body & Culture*, vol.1, 2007, pp. 25–40.

Saillard, O., *Cloakroom Vestiarie, Eternity Dress, The Impossible Wardrobe*. Rizzoli International, London, 2015.

Sebring, S., *Study of the Pose – 1,000 Poses by Coco Rocha*. Harpers Collins, London, 2014.

Stasiewicz, B. (dir.), *Contra Mundum* [DVD]. UK, 2011.

Talley, A.L., 'Fall 1999 Couture – Viktor and Rolf', *Vogue*, 1999 <https://www.vogue.com/fashion-shows/fall-1999-couture/viktor-rolf> (Accessed May 2016).

Thawley, D., 'Tilda Swinton Wears Your Sleeve on Her Heart', *Interview*, 25 November 2014 <https://www.interviewmagazine.com/art/tilda-swinton-wears-your-sleeve-on-her-heart> (Accessed July 2016).

CHAPTER 16

Visual Impairment and Fashion: Breaking Barriers

Nádia Fernandes

Abstract

People with visual impairment encounter a number of difficulties in their daily living activities, which can be overcome through the use of adaptive strategies. Garment, fashion and style are concepts frequently put forward in the daily lives of vision-impaired people. Assistive technology and low vision aids are used to support visual information and for selection and combination of clothes.

The aim of this qualitative study is to describe and analyse the awareness of three vision-impaired women regarding fashion and their strategies used in dressing alongside aesthetic acceptance of assistive technologies. A structured interview was applied to collect information about their identity, difficulties choosing clothes and make-up, the use of assistive technologies and barriers to fashion. Videos and photos were collected to assess these everyday scenarios. Based on the interviews it was possible to realize that as a form of self-expression and communication, style is more important than being fashionable. These women believe that it is essential to wear clothes that reflect their own personality, lifestyle and values. Visual impairment did not affect their concern of self-image. The colour and lighting in shops were identified as the main barriers for garment activities. The use of assistive technology causes some aesthetic embarrassment in public situations. Strategies to overcome difficulties include the use of speaking colour identifiers; magnifiers to read tags and absorptive filters for lighting glare control.

This study shows that vision-impaired women care about dressing and can overcome fashion barriers, inspiring other women who have difficulties in improving or accepting their self-image.

Keywords

aesthetic – assistive technologies – fashion – identity – garment – style – visual impairment

1   Introduction

People with visual impairment encounter a number of difficulties in their daily living activities, which can be overcome through the use of adaptive strategies. There are numerous pathologies that cause loss of vision and it is important to consider two main aspects in this field: the structural and the functional changes. According to the World Health Organization, an estimated 253 million people live with visual impairment, 36 million are blind and 217 million have moderate to severe vision impairment.[1] Low vision is an irreversible vision loss that cannot be corrected with standard glasses or contact lenses and reduces a person's ability and performance in activities of daily living. According to the visual impairment guide outlined by the World Health Organization's International Classification of Diseases (ICD), vision function is classified in four categories: (i) Normal Vision; (ii) Moderate Visual Impairment; (iii) Severe Visual Impairment; (iv) Blindness. Functional vision is a qualitative description of vision loss and categories (ii) and (iii) are included in the low vision group.[2] Visual rehabilitation plans allow the vision-impaired person to acquire new strategies and improve skills in specific daily activities. The low-vision multidisciplinary team works with the purpose of giving better quality of life to the patient.

As stated by Sandra Lee Evenson in her chapter 'Forms of Dress Worldwide', '[d]ress is a visual form of communication'.[3] For vision-impaired people significant accessibility barriers in fashion exist and some of them can be overcome by the use of assistive technology to access visual information and for selection and combination of clothes. Low vision devices are designed to improve visual performance in visual impaired people, and these devices can be optical, non-optical and electronic. These options are available to maximize reading activities and enhance contrast and colour vision, which are important in dressing and clothing management. Conventionally, optical and electronic devices such as microscopes, stand or handheld magnifiers, tele-microscopes and electronic magnification are included in low vision rehabilitation programs because they are the 'gold standard' for visually impaired patients. However, there are limitations or disadvantages with these devices such as short working distances,

---

1   S.P. Mariotti, 'Global Data on Visual Impairments 2010', *World Health Organization*, 2012 <http://www.who.int/blindness/GLOBALDATAFINALforweb.pdf.> (Accessed 30 October 2017).

2   Ibid.

3   S.L. Evenson, 'Dress and Identity', *Berg Encyclopaedia of World Dress and Fashion*, vol.10 <https://doi.org/http://dx.doi.org/10.2752/BEWDF/EDch10007> (Accessed 10 March 2016).

postural discomfort, limited fields of view, dexterity in handling and high cost. Beyond these limitations,

> patients do not always view the devices as being socially acceptable and many patients do not want to be identified as visually impaired and feel that using optical devices uncommon among normally sighted individuals would expose their impairment.[4]

With vision-impaired women the problem could be aesthetic acceptance when the devices are used in a store or in other public situations with psychological impact. Fashion and style are present in our daily life and garments reflect our values, preferences, identity and lifestyle.[5] Some women with low vision rehabilitation have goals related to clothing and their combination in daily life, such as combining clothes, combining colors, distinguishing different types of garments and displaying labels. The aim of this qualitative study is to describe and analyse the awareness of three vision-impaired women in fashion, strategies used in dressing and aesthetic acceptance of assistive technologies.

2   Case Studies

Design
The need to capture the personal experiences of participants impelled consideration of a descriptive design incorporating a qualitative research methodology based in case studies to better understand the patient's life. The questions were formed based on the difficulties patients refer to in the low vision rehabilitation practice, the challenges themselves present when they need to purchase clothing, their difficulties in identifying some colors and visualizing labels, as well as their self-perception of style and image. Some preliminary studies revealed accessibility barriers in clothing for vision-impaired people and mentioned possible ways to overcome the dificulties.

---

4   D. Irvine, A. Zemke, G. Pusateri, L. Gerlach, R. Chun, and W. M. Jay, 'Tablet and Smartphone Accessibility Features in the Low Vision Rehabilitation', *Neuro-Ophthalmology*, vol. 38, no. 2, 2014, pp. 53–59, p. 54.
5   Z. Arvanitidou, *Fashion, Gender and Social Identity* [Ph.D. dissertation], University of the Aegean, 2011 <http://www.fashion.arts.ac.uk/media/research/documents/zoi-arvanitidou.pdf> (Accessed 8 March 2016).

Participants

Three adult women with different visual loss in the range of low vision were randomly asked to participate in this study. Clinical, demographic and identity data was collected for case description.

Material and Procedures

An interview with each participant was undertaken individually during January and February 2016 in Topcare Clinic in Oeiras (Portugal). The duration of each interview varied from 20 to 30 minutes. The purpose of this study was explained and an informed consent form was filled out. To portray the quotidian scenario, videos and photos were collected with previous authorization for image collection (Figure 16.1–16.4).

A structured interview was applied to collect the following information:
– The main difficulties in choosing clothes at the shop, in wardrobe and make-up
– The use of assistive technology in public and aesthetic embarrassment
– Concern with self-image
– Define personal style
– If the clothes used reflect their personality, lifestyle and values
– Self-confidence in their clothes style
– If they are afraid to be the first to wear something different

FIGURE 16.1 VI simulator (relative central vision loss).
PHOTOGRAPHER: LUÍS RODRIGUES.

FIGURE 16.2 Make-up session with a magnifying mirror.
PHOTOGRAPHER: LUÍS RODRIGUES.

FIGURE 16.3 VI simulator (total central vision loss).
PHOTOGRAPHER: LUÍS RODRIGUES.

FIGURE 16.4 Outdoor glare control with special filters.
PHOTOGRAPHER: LUÍS RODRIGUES.

- What is more important: style or fashion
- Taste for clothes that promote the feminine side
- The main visual difficulties and barriers in the fashion world
- If the visual impairment influenced concern for the style and physical appearance

Videos and photos were collected to portray the quotidian scenario: style, closets, dressing and make-up activities using assistive technologies.

3   Discussion

From the functional point of view, each woman has their own visual needs taking into account the pathology that caused the vision loss. This reflects in the difficulties of their daily life and also in the type of strategies and visual aids that are more effective for each of them. On the other hand, their differences also reside in their identity factors, in their age, lifestyle, religion, aesthetic concepts, which in one way or another will influence their acceptance not only of visual impairment, but also the construction of self-image. Despite this, it is possible to perceive that the existence of a visual impairment does not imply carelessness or lack of concern with fashion and style issues, with the following aspects being emphasized in each case.

Fashion, Style and Strategies for Breaking Barriers

Based on the interviews, it was possible to realize that colour, lighting in shops, catalogues and clothes tags are the main barriers in garment activities. Taking into account the functional vision of each patient, it is important to refer the individual strategies adopted to overcome the difficulties in the choice of clothes and make-up: for example in case 1, the patient only uses lipsticks in shades of red because it is the only colour that she recognizes; in case 2, the patient uses a portable electronic magnifier to be able to see prices in a clothing store and takes an accompanying person to help her choosing clothes; in case 3, difficulties happen only when the lighting in stores is dim which makes it difficult to distinguish the dark and bright tones.

In all cases the strategies used included organizing the closet with label hangers for textures, patterns and seasons, using speaking colour identifiers, magnifiers to read tags and special filters for lighting glare control. In both cases 1 and 2 using make-up was rated as difficult – only lipstick and eyeliner. As a form of self-expression and communication, style is more important than being fashionable. They believe that it is essential to wear clothes that reflect their own personality, lifestyle and values. For them, visual impairment did not affect their concern of self-image and is not a reason to stop worrying about style and have a refined image: 'I'm not in a group, this it is my own style'; 'my clothes reflect some values. Wanting to be accepted in a particular place reflects what we will use'. A second participant explained: 'there was a time when I dressed in a more irreverent way, showing my rebellion, but now I'm more contained'.

Finally, one participant confided: 'I have a very unique style, but because of my profession I cannot keep my style at work; my preferred style is hippie and funk, but professionally I adopt a more classic style (hippie chic)'.

Assistive Technology, Low Vision Aids and Aesthetic Embarrassment

Assistive technology and low vision aids improve visual performance and ability in clothing activities. The low vision aids used by patients were absorptive filters (glasses with special coloured lenses that enhanced contrast vision and reduced glare), handheld magnifier (optical device for near tasks), electronic magnifier (for better contrast and high levels of magnification) and voice software in mobile phone (screen reader). However, an aesthetic embarrassment is caused by the use of some types of assistive technology in public environment. This issue can affect people differently according to the social acceptance and beauty standards of each person. With regards to the public use of a handheld magnifier once participant explained: 'people question and usually do not understand. It depends on my availability and state of mind'. About public use of voice software in mobile phone, a participant explained: 'currently I don't use it. I don't feel well using the mobile phone because of the voice software'. Finally, with regards to the public use of indoor filters 'I felt ugly and hideous, because everybody was looking at me and questioned me about it. I do not care what others say but I have to feel good'.

4   Conclusion

The results of this study show that vision-impaired women care about dressing and can overcome some fashion barriers through the use of low vision aids and assistive technology. Although, there was some aesthetic problems when these devices are used in public. It is a fact that many vision-impaired people think that when using low vision aids in public places are exposing their impairment and this has a psychological impact, but these devices and assistive technology are very important in the daily living of these women and other patients. In the three cases the public use of some types of low vision aids was a problem, maybe because of social acceptance. Patients felt like 'strange objects' when out and about in Portuguese society, since the distinction between blindness and low vision is still not well known to the general public – low vision aids are uncommon and can seem alien to those without knowledge of their purpose.

Recent studies suggest that including smartphones and tablets into low vision rehabilitation programs could be a versatile alternative because many people have these devices for other reasons.[6] Combining this inclusive and socially acceptable technology with or without conventional low vision aids, mainly in specific daily living activities, could be a useful strategy to overcome the aesthetic embarrassment. The medical community must be aware about dressing and clothing needs in visual rehabilitation programs. The psychological factor is present in these descriptions and warrants further investigation.

Based on difficulties reported in the interviews by these three women, special attention should be given for colour, lighting in shops, catalogues and clothes tags that were referred to as the main barriers in garment activities. In vision rehabilitation programs we have guidelines to introduce some strategies that improve closet organisation and matching clothes. For example, to label make-up colours, lighting adaptations (right position), using white light without brightness or natural light could help to identify, match colours and allow better navigation of stores. Large print tags are easier to read. Some of these

---

6   Irvine *et al.*, 'Tablet and Smartphone Accessibility Features in the Low Vision Rehabilitation'.

strategies and environmental adaptations may be used in store context in an attempt to overcome these barriers. This revealed the importance of promoting open forums that involve schools of fashion and low vision rehabilitation services to talk about fashion barriers in clothing and make-up daily activities. Introducing the use of assistive technology in the fashion world, for example, as a resource available in clothes shops for visual impaired people used to read price tags and other ideas to promote autonomy for their own fashion choices is important. For example, the use of more inclusive options like apps related with closet organisation and fashion style.[7]

In conclusion, these three case studies show that vision-impaired women care about dressing and can overcome fashion barriers through specific strategies and devices, inspiring other women who have difficulty in improving or accepting their self-image. Smartphones and tablets apps could be inclusive and aesthetically acceptable devices. Fashion stores may adopt some inclusive environmental modifications in order to enhance the visual performance of people with low vision in their clothing process.

Acknowledgments

First, I would like to thank my three participants for their participation and for having accepted this challenge. I also want to thank Carla Lança for the technical review and Luis Rodrigues for the photographs.

Bibliography

Arvanitidou, Z., *Fashion, Gender and Social Identity* [Ph.D. dissertation], University of the Aegean, 2011 <http://www.fashion.arts.ac.uk/media/research/documents/zoi-arvanitidou.pdf > (Accessed 8 March 2016).

Burton, M.A., J. Beser, C. Neylan, and A. Hurst, 'Making Fashion Accessible for People with Vision Impairments' <http://web.ist.utl.pt/tiago.guerreiro/pervasive-accessibility/docs/1.pdf> (Accessed 8 March 2016).

Evenson, S.L., 'Dress and Identity', *Berg Encyclopaedia of World Dress and Fashion* (vol.10), pp. 1–9 <https://doi.org/http://dx.doi.org/10.2752/BEWDF/EDch10007> (Accessed 10 March 2016).

---

7   M.A. Burton, J. Beser, C. Neylan, and A. Hurst, 'Making Fashion Accessible for People with Vision Impairments' <http://web.ist.utl.pt/tiago.guerreiro/pervasive-accessibility/docs/1.pdf> (Accessed 8 March 2016).

Irvine, D., A. Zemke, G. Pusateri, L. Gerlach, R. Chun, and W.M. Jay, 'Tablet and Smartphone Accessibility Features in the Low Vision Rehabilitation', *Neuro-Ophthalmology*, vol. 38 no. 2, 2014, pp. 53–59.

Mariotti, S.P., 'Global Data on Visual Impairments 2010', *World Health Organization*, 2012 <http://www.who.int/blindness/GLOBALDATAFINALforweb.pdf.> (Accessed 30 October 2017).

PART 6

Positioning

..

CHAPTER 17

Sustainable Kate? Wear-Again Anne?: The Recycled Fashions of the Duchess of Cambridge and the Princess Royal

Jacque Lynn Foltyn

Abstract

The marriage of Kate Middleton and Prince William introduced an international audience not only to a non-aristocrat who married a direct heir to the British throne but to a Duchess who recycles her wardrobe. While the Duchess' habit of re-wearing clothing is treated as a novelty, Anne, Princess Royal, daughter of Queen Elizabeth II, has long been associated with the practice. Using the semiotics of fashion and a qualitative methodology based on content, textual, and visual analyses of two articles from the *Daily Mail*, a study of news coverage and reader comments about their wear-again behaviour was conducted. The results suggest that reader reaction depends upon how one interprets the responsibilities of royal status and values British thrift and the monarchy. While some posters deem outfit repeats as 'normal', others view it as a cynical public relations ploy designed to present the royal family as 'middle class' and ecologically oriented. An anti-royal narrative argues that publicity about recycled garments is rubbish, a diversionary tactic to assuage concerns voiced by taxpayers about the financial costs of the monarchy. Another narrative argues for royal privilege, endorsing the conspicuous consumption and waste of one-wear fashion. The analysis presented is framed by theories of consumption, social status, identity, authenticity, social agendas, and patterns of emulation in the era of social media.

Keywords

fashion – Kate Middleton – Catherine, Duchess of Cambridge – Anne, Princess Royal – British Royal Family – *Daily Mail* – sustainable – social class – social media – authenticity – brands

1   Introduction

The marriage of Kate Middleton and Prince William in 2011 not only introduced an international audience to the first non-aristocratic commoner to
marry a British prince in close succession to the throne in 350 years[1] but also
to a newly designated royal, Catherine, Duchess of Cambridge, who re-wears
articles of clothing at official appearances. The Duchess is the only member
of the Royal Family to emerge as an icon of fashion since the death in 1997 of
Princess Diana, another chosen bride who, like Queen Marie Antoinette, wife
of Louis XVI, became not only a fashion star but famous in her own right.[2] In
part because of her personal style, the public reception of the Duchess has
been overall positive, though she has her detractors. In popularity polls, Catherine ranks as one of the most admired members of the Royal Family.[3] One
third of Britons view her as a 'fantastic ambassador for the UK', 30 per cent
claim she has 'reinvigorated public perception of the royals', and 40 per cent
admire her 'down-to-earth nature' and dedication to family and charity work.
Significantly, 20 per cent of those polled view the Duchess as a positive role
model for girls.[4]

---

1   Since Anne Hyde wed the Duke of York, later James II, in 1660. S. Bates, 'Profile: Kate Middle-
    ton', *The Guardian*, 16 November 2010 <http://www.guardian.co.uk/uk/2010/nov/16/profile-
    kate-middleton> (Accessed 29 January 2012). Earlier versions of this chapter were presented
    in 2015 at two conferences: J. L. Foltyn, 'Eco-Kate? The Recycled Fashions of the Duchess
    of Cambridge' [abstract], *7th Global Conference Fashion: Exploring Critical Issues*, Mansfield
    College, Oxford University, Oxford, 24–26 September 2015, pp. 8–9; J. L. Foltyn, 'Sustainable
    Kate? The Recycled Fashions of Kate Middleton, the Duchess of Cambridge' [conference
    presentation], *Fashion Tales: Feeding the Imaginary, International Conference*, ModaCult –
    Centre for the Study of Fashion and Cultural Production, Università Cattolica, Milan, 18–20
    June 2015.
2   P. C. Gibson, 'New Patterns of Emulation: Kate, Pippa and Cheryl', *Celebrity Studies*, vol. 2,
    no. 3, 2011, pp. 358–360.
3   In a YouGov poll, the Duchess was voted the fourth most popular member of the British
    Royal Family, after Prince Harry, Queen Elizabeth II, and Prince William. YouGov/Newsweek
    Survey Results, 'Which One of the Following, If Any, Would You Consider to be Your Favourite
    Member of the Royal Family?', *YouGov*, 2014 <https://d25d2506sfb94s.cloudfront.net/cumu-
    lus_uploads/document/40pfhhdrcv/Newsweek_Results_140909_Kate_Middleton_Website_
    140929.pdf> (Accessed 10 Dec 2014).
4   R. Styles, 'It Might Be Kate's Birthday but Harry is the Nation's Favourite Royal ... Prince
    is Number One While the Duchess Languishes in Second Place', *Daily Mail*, 9 January
    2015 <http://www.dailymail.co.uk/femail/article-2903281/It-Kate-s-birthday-HARRY-nation-
    s-favourite-royal-Prince-number-one-Duchess-languishes-second-place.html#ixzz4wkGip-
    dtS> (Accessed 20 May 2015).

A worldwide force for fashion, Catherine is responsible for pumping billions of pounds into the UK's economy and boosting sales of British fashion.[5] As a media object, she has become an international brand of modern 'consumer society',[6] with documentable social cultural effects, and has surpassed Princess Diana as a global fashion influencer.[7] Those who have made the Duchess a fashion icon sell-out within hours whatever dress, coat, jeans, or boots she wears, in a phenomenon known as the 'Duchess Effect', 'Kate Middleton Effect', or 'Kate Effect'. Whatever one calls it, economists have noted its unprecedented impact on the British economy,[8] including the fuelling of a 'repliKate' industry of knockoffs and 'copyKates', for similar more affordable garments and accessories.[9]

An important aspect of the 'Kate Effect' is that the majority of the clothing the Duchess wears is off the rack, a first in the British Royal Family known for wearing bespoke garments.[10] Moreover, at press events Catherine mixes designer brands like Alexander McQueen with high-street brands like L.K. Bennett, and fast fashion brands like Zara and Topshop; and is responsible for helping relax long-established rules of royal dress that arose with sumptuary laws and protocols driven more by social structure than individual taste and identity.[11]

With her bespoke and expensive ready-to-wear garments from British fashion houses, the Duchess' garments reinforce the still useful Veblenian and Simmelian theories of 'trickle-down' fashion, whereby ordinary people emulate

5   By 2012, already $1.5 billion. Naughty But Nice Rob, 'Kate Middleton's Far-Reaching Fashion Influence', *HuffPost*, 29 May 2012 <https://www.huffingtonpost.com/2012/05/29/kate-middleton-fashion_n_1553975.html> (Accessed 12 June 2012).

6   J. Baudrillard, *The Consumer Society: Myths and Structures*, Sage Publications, Thousand Oaks, CA, 1998.

7   T. Sykes, 'How Duchess Kate Middleton Stole Princess Diana's Crown', *Daily Beast*, 11 April 2016 <https://www.thedailybeast.com/how-duchess-kate-middleton-stole-princess-dianas-crown> (Accessed 29 October 2017).

8   A. Logan, 'Netnography: Observing and Interacting with Celebrity in the Digital World', *Celebrity Studies*, vol. 6, no. 3, 2015, pp. 378–381. Two examples: for the Preen dress, see E. Barsamian, 'Kate Middleton's Preen Dress Is Already Sold Out, Less Than 24 hours Later', *Vogue*, 14 July 2017 <https://www.vogue.com/article/kate-middleton-duchess-of-cambridge-preen-prada-natural-history-museum-celebrity-royal-style> (Accessed 23 October 2017); for Banana Republic skirt, see C. Kratofil, 'Everything Kate Touches Turns to "Sold"', *People*, 18 May 2016 <http://people.com/style/everything-kate-touches-turns-to-sold/banana-republic-skirt> (Accessed 25 October 2017).

9   Logan, 'Netnography'.

10   Princess Diana wore bespoke clothing at her official engagements.

11   For more on this, see D. Crane, *Fashion and Its Social Agendas: Class, Gender and Identity in Clothing*, University of Chicago Press, Chicago, IL, 2000.

the fashions of their 'social betters'. That said, the Duchess disrupts, as well as reinforces, the 'trickle-down' rule, for when she wears high-street and fast-fashion garments she disturbs the traditional fashion diffusion rule with a pastiche of brand signifiers she has re-arranged to serve in her performance as a 'relatable Duchess' in the construction of an authentic identity. Responsive to trends created by non-elites in the 'bubble-up' manner described by Polhemus and the 'open fashion' manner described by Lipovetsky,[12] the Duchess is both trend follower and trendsetter. Her 'trickle-down'/'bubble-up' style is part of the 'Kate brand' and is driven not only by traditional news coverage but also by social media[13] and an army of style bloggers who document her every outfit.[14]

Though a variety of newspapers, fashion and lifestyle magazines, blogs, and polls regularly chronicle what the Duchess wears, including her multiple wearings of a garment,[15] Anne, Princess Royal, is another member of the British monarchy who regularly repeats her garments, and has done so for decades. The difference in attention paid to the two wear-again royals can be attributed to a number of factors, including the obvious one that Catherine is a new member of the Royal Family with a Cinderella story, is glamorous, is 32 years younger than the princess, and is known for her love of fashion, while Anne,

---

12   T. Veblen, *The Theory of the Leisure Class: An Economic Study in the Evolution of Institutions*, Macmillan, New York, NY, 1902 [1899]; G. Simmel, 'Fashion', *International Quarterly*, vol. 10, 1904, pp. 130–143; T. Polhemus, *Streetstyle*, Thames & Hudson, New York, NY, 1994; G. Lipovetsky, *The Empire of Fashion: Dressing Modern Democracy*, trans. C. Porter, Princeton University Press, Princeton, NJ, 1994.

13   Logan, 'Netnography'.

14   For example: *KatesCloset.com*; *KateMiddletonStyle.com*; *WhatKateWore.com*; *DuchessKate.com*; *HRHDuchessKate.com*.

15   On the day this chapter was originally submitted, the *Daily Mail* published yet another account of Middleton as the recycling duchess: S. Linning, 'Lovely in Lace! Kate Displays a Hint of a Baby Bump in Black Designer Gown that She Also Wore While Pregnant with Princess Charlotte as She Attends a Glittering Kensington Palace Charity Gala', *Daily Mail*, 8 November 2017 <http://www.dailymail.co.uk/femail/article-5058895/Pregnant-Kate-displays-hint-baby-bump-charity-gala.html?ito=email_share_article-top> (Accessed 8 November 2017). See also A. Graafland, 'Thrifty Kate Middleton Strikes Again as She Recycles Cream Alexander McQueen Coat for Royal Garden Party', *Mirror*, 24 May 2016 <http://www.mirror.co.uk/3am/style/celebrity-fashion/thrifty-kate-middleton-strikes-again-8041704> (Accessed 5 October 2017); B. London, 'Thrifty Kate Strikes Again! Duchess of Cambridge Recycles a £2,500 Scarlet Gown by Her Favourite Designer Jenny Packham for the Buckingham Palace Reception', *Daily Mail*, 9 December 2016 <http://www.dailymail.co.uk/femail/article-4016370/Kate-Middleton-recycles-2-500-gown-favourite-designer-Jenny-Packham-Buckingham-Palace-reception.htmlWhatKateWore.com covers every detail of the duchess' fashion> (Accessed 30 October 2017).

the Queen's daughter, is characterised as a non-nonsense royal with an enthusiasm for horses, not fashion.[16]

2   The Study: Methodology

Duchess Catherine and Princess Anne are public figures and most of what is
known about them comes through mass media representations. Through content analysis of accounts of their fashion recycling, this exploratory study seeks
to answer the following questions: are there similarities and differences in the
ways in which the wardrobe repeats of Catherine and Anne are reported? How
do readers respond to such coverage? Is royal 'wear-again' behaviour a sign of
the times, a nod to changing patterns of consumption, the sustainability trend,
and a challenging economic climate? What social-cultural-economic-political
factors shape the content of reader comments?

   This chapter presents a comparative analysis of two articles focussed on the
Duchess and the Princess Royal as 'wear-again royals', published in the online
version of the *Daily Mail*.[17] The reporting, photographs, vocabulary, and tone
of the articles, and relevant reader comments serve as sources of data for the
study. The online version of the *Daily Mail* was chosen not only because of its
non-stop coverage of the British royal family but because it is the most widely read news publication in the world, ahead of *The New York Times* and *The
Guardian*.[18]

---

16   Catherine, born 9 January 1982, and Anne, born 15 August 1950. R. Lewis, 'Anne, the Prin-
      cess Royal', *Encylopaedia Britannica*, 24 October 2017 <https://www.britannica.com/biog-
      raphy/Princess-Anne-British-royal> (Accessed 31 October 2017).
17   The online version is more celebrity-focussed than its parent print version and shares
      only 25 per cent of the print version's content. L. Collins, 'Mail Supremacy: The Newspa-
      per That Rules Britain', *The New Yorker*, 2 April 2012 <https://www.newyorker.com/maga-
      zine/2012/04/02/mail-supremacy> (Accessed15 January 2018).
18   'Monthly Reach of National Newspapers and Their Websites in the United Kingdom (UK)
      from April 2016 to March 2017 (in 1,000 individuals)', *Statista*, 2017 <https://www.statis-
      ta.com/statistics/246077/reach-of-selected-national-newspapers-in-the-uk/> (Accessed
      29 October 2017); 'Top 10 Most Read Newspapers in the World', *Trending Top Most*, 2017
      <http://www.trendingtopmost.com/worlds-popular-list-top-10/2017-2018-2019-2020-
      2021/world/most-read-newspapers-world-best-selling/> (Accessed 3 January 2018). The
      online version attracts an audience that is a younger, wealthier reader, and focusses less
      on right-wing politics than the print version. This readership is not only more comfort-
      able with online platforms but is perhaps one that is less deferential to the Royal Family.
      See Collins, 'Mail Supremacy'; 'A Political History of the Daily Mail', *The Week*, 11 October
      2017 < http://www.theweek.co.uk/88935/a-political-history-of-the-daily-mail> (Accessed
      18 January 2018).

3   Catherine, Duchess of Cambridge

The focus of the first article, 'Thrifty Kate Strikes Again: Pregnant Duchess Wears Designer Dress for the THIRD Time as She Attends Gala Dinner with Prince William in New York', is Catherine's re-wearing in early December 2014 of an ink blue silk tulle gown with a black velvet sash belt, from Jenny Packham's 2013 Fall collection. The Duchess wore the dress to an event held at the Metropolitan Museum of Art, New York, to raise funds for St Andrews University in Scotland, the Prince and Duchess' Alma Mater. Published on 10 December 2014, the article features ten photographs of the Duchess wearing the gown, six images at the New York event and four documenting the two prior wearings.[19]

Relevant text from the article, emphasising the multiple wearings, appears below:

> [s]he's known for recycling her favourite outfits, often opting to wear the same piece on two occasions. ... Catherine, Duchess of Cambridge has done it again by choosing to wear a favourite Jenny Packham dress for a third time during a public appearance in New York on Tuesday.
>
> Her look was remarkably elegant but incited a touch of déjà vu in her most devoted fashion followers, who would no doubt notice she has worn the stunning dress twice before in public. ... Kate is known for her sensitivity to the economic climate, and has gained a huge fashion following thanks to her knack for classic style, embracing the high street and often recycling her expensive gowns. ... Blending her thrifty sensibilities with a respect for the royal institution, Kate caused a stir by pairing the dress with a priceless diamond necklace on loan from the Queen. ... At a cost of £2,000 it is little wonder the frugal Duchess was keen to get yet another event out of the flattering and easy to wear dress. ... Despite having worn the eye-catching garment before ... the effect was still suitably regal and the most formal outfit she had sported during their three-day visit to America.[20]

---

19   In October 2013, at the Women in Hedge Funds Gala at Kensington Palace, and in February 2014, at an event at the National Portrait Gallery.

20   L. Mapstone and R. English, 'Thrifty Kate Strikes Again: Pregnant Duchess Wears Designer Dress for the THIRD Time as She Attends Gala Dinner with Prince William in New York', *Daily Mail*, 10 December 2014 <http://www.dailymail.co.uk/femail/article-2867909/Thrifty-Kate-strikes-Pregnant-Duchess-wears-designer-dress-time-steps-Prince-William-gala-dinner-New-York.html> (Accessed 15 June 2015).

The headline and the article itself highlight the Duchess' multiple wearings of the gown, with words such as the capped THIRD, 'déjà vu', and 'favourite', and phrases like 'a third time', 'done it again', 'twice before'. Motivation is assigned to the multiple wearings, with the reporters describing the Duchess as 'thrifty' and 'frugal', noting her 'sensitivity to economic climate', while emphasising the cost of the 'designer dress' and 'the priceless diamond necklace'.

The article provoked 309 comments and 1.9K content shares. Posters overwhelmingly supported the Duchess wearing the dress more than once, with 112 positive responses. The most common response (52) was to mock and condemn the *Daily Mail* for its 'rude', 'pathetic', snobbish reporting. Liz,[21] whose comments received the most reader votes, with 1103 upward arrows and 29 downward arrows: 'OH MY GOD!!! What are we ever going to do????', she wrote, '[i]t's the end of the world!! The Duchess wore this same dress 3 times already!!!! Get over it DM. She's a real woman'.

Twenty-two readers wrote the Duchess 'can't win'. According to Susan, '[e]ither she's extravagant buying expensive clothing or she's penny pinching because she's wearing an outfit more than once'.

Eleven praised the Duchess' restraint, sensibility, frugality, and for setting a good example. 'It means shes not wasteful on useless vanity. It shows class and temperance. She isn't extravagant and frivolous', wrote Isolde Nightengale. Nine readers observed that re-wearing the gown is evidence of the Duchess' normality. 'One is allowed to wear ones dresses more than once it's not being thrifty it's being normal', wrote Her opinions only. Two contrasted the normalcy of the duchess wearing the gown three times with the profligacy of celebrities like 'the Kardashian Klowns'.

Five readers praised the Duchess for her sustainable approach, demonstrating that garments are not disposable. Elizabeth Ng wrote that she respects the Duchess: '[s]he is showing the rest of the world to be normal n not be ashamed of saving the earth'. One reader sarcastically condemned the consumer-industrial-fashion system and entertainment-consumer-celebrity complex that produces such profligacy:

> [o]h no! She wore the same dress THREE times?! What a terrible role model for young women, doesn't she realise in this capitalist hellscape we reside in we must only wear expensive designer clothes once and then forever relegate them to the back of our wardrobe?!
>
> (LEÃ¡ MAC)

---

21   The names used for the individuals commenting below are user IDs or 'handles', and are quoted as written.

There were critiques, as well, about the sexism or classism underlying the article's editorial content. Mookins007 noted, 'I bet Will wears the same Dinner Suit dozens of times without anyone mentioning it', and KAtkin suggested, '[w]e'll be calling her the peasant princess next'. In line with the latter comment, DW noticed a bias against Catherine:

> So DM slams her for wearing a £1500 coat and then slams her for wearing a designer dress 3 times. She can't win can she? I'd like DM to do an article on Diana and her 'thriftiness' because I don't recall there ever being an article on her wearing things more than once. She seemed to have a new outfit on no matter what the occasion (including playing with the children!!).

The article provoked 36 reader comments critical of the Duchess' decision to wear the same dress again. Twenty-three readers said the gesture was calculated, insincere, and hypocritical:

> [s]he could have bought a off the peg £25 number from the high street and wore it three times...& gained some real and genuine credibility.
>   BRY23

> 'Kate is known for her sensitivity to the economic climate' Hahahahaha-hahahahahaha, excuse me a moment, hahahahahahahahahaha hahaha-haha hahahahahahahahahahahaha. Thanks for the laugh.
>   PETER

> [a]m I the only one thinking there's something absolutely nuts about a world/country where we read that, when we have increasing numbers of food banks and hear of pensioners dying of the cold, a Duchess is 'thrifty' because she wears a £2000 designer dress/gown three times?
>   GJEDGAR

> I want them to pay their own way in life especially her. She was not even born into it and she CAN afford it. Because she uses taxpayers money she wants to show she is so humble and not above herself.
>   MOTHACOOLA07

Five readers remarked that wearing the same gown more than once was inappropriate and undermined the monarchy.

[s]he is a 'royal', a 'duchess', perhaps a future queen consort. She was representing her country, her family, her 'subjects'. These are not the occasions to be 'thrifty'

KATE

some might argue that this selfless act harms the mystique of the Monarchy. I'd be insulted if I had queued for hours to get a glimpse and saw her in a dress she's worn twice before.

BROBRI

4   Anne, Princess Royal

The second *Daily Mail* article used for the study, 'And the Gold Star for Thrift Goes to Anne: Princess Royal Recycles Outfit She First Wore in 1980 for the First Day of Royal Ascot', was published on 17 June 2015. With text and photographs, it documents the five wearings by Anne of an ensemble she wore in 1980, 1983, 1991, 2011, and 2015.

[s]he is the royal best known for her frugal fashion, regularly recycling handbags, dresses and hats from the past for state occasions. ... But it was her appearance at Royal Ascot yesterday that truly cemented her reputation as the thriftiest royal of all. For her high-necked silk print dress, caramel-coloured coat and belt were all part of an identical outfit she first wore 35 years ago. Since then, the Princess Royal has sported her colourful combination on no less than four occasions ... she's worn it to race meetings three times in the past – first at the Epsom Derby in 1983, and then to Royal Ascot in 1991 and 2011. ... Its debut came at the Trooping the Colour in June 1980. ... That photograph could easily be mistaken for yesterday's look. ... The outfit has been worn so many times it must be getting rather worn by now, but nobody can accuse Princess Anne of being a spendthrift when it comes to fashion. Or, indeed, changing with the times.

If history is anything to go by, it won't be long before we get another glimpse of this very frugal royal's favourite wardrobe staple.[22]

---

22   S. Rainey, 'And the Gold Star for Thrift Goes to Anne: Princess Royal Recycles Outfit She First Wore in 1980 for the First Day of Royal Ascot', *Daily Mail*, 17 June 2015 <http://www.dailymail.co.uk/femail/article-3127219/And-gold-star-thrift-goes-Anne-Princess-Royal-recycles-outfit-wore-1980-day-Royal-Ascot.html> (Accessed14 July 2015).

Textual analysis of the language and phrases in the article highlights the Princess' wear-again practice. 'Regularly recycling', 'from the past', 'identical outfit she first wore 35 years ago', 'no less than four occasions', 'three times in the past', 'its debut', 'could easily be mistaken for yesterday's look', 'getting rather worn', 'favourite wardrobe staple', and [not] 'changing with the times'. Motivations for the multiple wearings are imputed to Anne's character: 'very frugal royal', 'the thriftiest royal of all', and [not] 'a spendthrift when it comes to fashion'.

There were 8.9K shares of the article, and the vast majority of the 528 readers who posted were impressed that the Princess had kept her figure and could still wear the outfit. As with the Duchess, some readers simply noted that the Princess would be criticised either way and the *Daily Mail* should focus on more important topics. Two readers noted that the press only recently taken notice of 'wear-again' Anne:

> [a]t least this photographic evidence proves that the Duchess of Cambridge wasn't the first thrifty Royal. The Daily Mail and the Royal PR machine are going to have to come up with something better to make her interesting now.
>
> FUNKYSTAR

In all, 148 readers directly praised the Princess' 'wear-again' practice. Fourty-three applauded her classic taste, tailoring, and the quality of her long-lasting clothing. An Angel observed that the princess' clothes 'aren't throwaway like the cheap rubbish that is supposed to be "fashionable" these days', and Marshall Folsh praised her for 'doing her part saving British Taxpayers money. Very honorable'. Thirty-one readers praised Anne's frugality:

> [w]ell done Anne. When people knock the Royal Family they forget about people like you who are happy to stick with classic clothes that are never out of date and save money and our lovely Queen who goes around turning unwanted lights off and keeping a tight hold on the household purse.
>
> DINKIE1993

Twenty-eight readers approved of the Princess' lack of concern about being fashionable. According to codswollop kid, '[s]he's the one Royal who doesn't give a hoot about being a clothes horse or follower of fashion, good on her I say'.

Nine readers noted that wearing garments more than once is 'normal' not recycling, and the subject of environmental recycling was raised by four readers. Honey noted: 'it's highly relevant to our times of excessive consumer

habits that a person of considerable means has the good grace financially, ecologically'.

Sexism was cited by two readers: '[w]onder how many times the men in the
family have worn the same suits and no one seems to comment', wrote gimsara.

Twenty-nine readers contrasted recycling Anne favourably with the wastefulness and frivolity of other members of the Royal Family, including her sib-
lings; her niece, Princess Beatrice; Sophie, Countess of Wessex; and, especially,
Catherine.

> Someone's got to compensate for kate and wills' frivolous waste of money
> NEMO

> [o]nly the nouveaux have to have everything brand new and shiny. It's
> why Carole Middleton won't be seen in the same outfit/car twice but
> someone like Princess Anne will.
> EH

> Her clothes fit, they are tailored to her figure and she's kept herself
> healthy. She isn't like the average person who is constantly bombarded by
> media telling them that they are only somebody because they are wear-
> ing something with an ostentatious label or it's been endorsed by a Z list
> celebrity. Whilst I am not a monarchist, I applaud her – now compare this
> to the middle class must have must have NOW Middletons.
> LUCIFERS SISTER

Among the negative comments posted, 61 criticised Anne as a frumpy, outdat-
ed repeat offender. Anne is 'stuck in a time warp', wrote Erim. Elly-May Clam-
pett wondered, '[h]ow old will the dress be, before Anne gives it to a charity
shop? Will they want it?' Eighteen argued that the Princess needs a makeover,
six criticised her for not being interested in fashion, and one condemned her
for not measuring up to proper standards of royal presentation. 'What an embarrassment, she doesn't deserve to be royal, its wasted on her', wrote Countess
Crumpet.

Politics and the economy shaped the critiques of ten reader comments.
According to Sarah B,

> [t]he rich and obscenely rich – cue the Princess Royal – strive to be seen
> as 'thrifty' and 'frugal' and 'down to earth' and 'normal' while the palace
> PR machine work round the clock to convince a gullible public that's the
> case. Hence, the press release that lo and behold 'thrifty' Anne has worn

the same frock and coat more than thrice in 35 years! ... Salute this per-
snickety poseur if you like, but I'll reserve my salutes for those who are
worthy of them.

5   Discussion

The results of this exploratory study suggest that most readers of the *Daily Mail*
are not bothered by the wear-again fashions of the Duchess and the Princess
but are offended by the reporting of what they view as 'normal' behaviour.
Readers called the publication on its 'clickbaiting', provocative, ironic, snarky,
and sniggering headlines, usual practices in an era of online news consumption and tabloidization in which revenue is driven by advertisements rather
than by reader subscriptions.[23]

Articles about the Duchess' clothing are laden with lures, with links to the
designers she wears, 'copyKates', and 'repliKates'. Readers in both articles complained the royals 'can't win', and several noted the sexism underlying the emphasis on the repeated wearings, when no such reporting is done about male
members of the royal family. Both women were praised for setting a good
example and compared favourably with once-wear celebrities like 'the Kardashian Klowns'. Their frugality was appreciated, as was their saving of taxpayer money. Anne, especially, was lauded for being 'thrifty' like her mother, the
Queen. Thrift is part of a long-established and distinctive British value system,
with origins in Protestant Christianity and an ethic that values prudence, par-
simony, and discipline.[24]

The Duchess and the Princess were also lauded for not viewing clothing as
disposable and, to a lesser extent, for their sustainable approach to fashion, as
'waste not' royals, ethical-fashion-consumer role models for green consumption. In this narrative, they not only wear their garments again and again,
breaking from contemporary celebrity protocols of one-wear conspicuous
consumption that treat each wearing as a runway show, and past royal protocols that allow for repeated wearings of jewels and ceremonial robes associated with the prestige of the crown but not mere fashionable garments. In the
Veblenian sense, Catherine and Anne flout the conspicuous display of 'waste'

---

23   Readers of 'Thrifty Kate' took the bait they were directed to not only the article itself but
to the designs of Jenny Packham; the article also featured a video of the duchess wearing
Burberry ('Kate Wears Burberry for Visit to Youth Organization With William').

24   I. Bradley, *Believing in Britain: The Spiritual Identity of 'Britishness'*, I.B. Tauris, New York,
NY, 2007; M. Weber, *The Protestant Ethic and the Spirit of Capitalism*, Scribner, New York,
NY, 1958 [1905].

associated with their social class, i.e., the flaunting of what wealth can buy[25] and support an ideological approach to sustainable fashion, as well as the British economy, when they buy locally crafted British garments.[26] The sociologist Diana Crane has noted that Britain has always been ahead of the sustainable fashion trend, which has become a worldwide social movement.[27]

That said, some readers could not care less about eco-fashion and ethical consumption, and complained that the Duchess and Princess insult, embarrass, and do not live up to proper royal expectations when they wear the same garments more than once. Veblen's concept of 'the doll',[28] whereby women become idle trophy wives of wealthy men, as a vicarious form of conspicuous waste, is useful for explaining this attitude towards the Duchess.

Some who criticised Catherine's and Anne's multiple wearings viewed the generally royalist-leaning *Daily Mail* articles as participating in a carefully crafted public relations campaign on the part of the British Crown to cast Royals as moderate not profligate, to mould the Duchess, in particular, as a 'waste-not' future queen of England, and to position Anne as part of the old guard of frugal, hardworking royals. Those readers were not buying the propaganda and argued the women live like *pashas* with opulent lifestyles of conspicuous waste, consumption, and leisure that parade medieval-like displays of inequality. For republic-minded responders, the monarchy is an archaic institution, based on a traditional, no longer legitimate authority, as Weber would characterise it, bankrolled by British taxpayers who are trying to make ends meet in an economy that has suffered a downturn and in a time of austerity politics.[29]

The category of class deserves a discussion of its own, for the social-economic origins of the Duchess and the Princess informed the responses of

---

25   T. Veblen, *The Theory of the Leisure Class.*

26   The ready-to-wear garments the Duchess wears, of course, are not all made in Great Britain.

27   D. Crane, 'Fashion Tales: Feeding the Imaginary' [keynote speech], *International Conference*, ModaCult – Centre for the Study of Fashion and Cultural Production, Università Cattolica, Milan, 18-20 June 2015. For more on this worldwide trend in fashion, see: D. Crane, *Fashion and Its Social Agenda*; K. Niinimäki (ed.), *Sustainable Fashion: New Approaches*, Aalto University, Helsinki, 2013; M. Sahakian and H. Wilhite, 'Making Practice Theory Practicable: Towards More Sustainable Forms of Consumption', *Journal of Consumer Culture*, vol. 14, no. 1, 2014, pp. 25-44.

28   T. Veblen, *The Theory of the Leisure Class.*

29   Sovereign Grant is costing the taxpayer £ 43 million per year. Lovemoney.com, 'How Much Does the UK Royal Family Cost?', *BT*, 20 July 2016 <http://home.bt.com/lifestyle/money/mortgages-bills/how-much-does-the-royal-family-cost-11363982445194> (Accessed 23 October 2017); M. Weber, *On Charisma and Institution Building*, ed. S. N. Eisenstadt, University of Chicago Press, Chicago, IL,1968.

some readers. The Princess was born royal, and for some, that fact alone, explains why she thinks nothing of repeatedly wearing the same garments, for decades if she so desires, whether in pristine condition or in tatters. For them, her behaviour is not 'embarrassing', it is expected of one who has 'nothing to prove', is secure in her social station, and who could care less about being fashionable.[30] By wearing the same ensemble since 1980, the princess is seen as 'marching to her own drum', conduct that can also be interpreted as eccentric. The British are known to be tolerant of unconventional and unusual individuals, especially in the upper classes. 'Even today, eccentricity is often seen as an obligatory component of the English national character. The eccentric ... provides others with a pleasant diversion from the tedium of everyday life', notes the literary critic Miranda Gill.[31]

The social origins of the Duchess also informed the attitudes of responders, especially those who criticised her. Since the reign of Queen Victoria, the British monarchy has attempted to create an image of itself as ordinary and possessing middle-class values.[32] Queen Elizabeth II carries on aspects of that value system and is routinely characterised as a family-oriented, hardworking sovereign; the fact that she and her husband, Philip, Duke of Edinburgh, have an off-duty cottage on the Sandringham estate where they live and behave like ordinary people is emphasised. With the goal of being more ordinary, Princess Anne insisted that royal titles not be conferred on her children, and Princess Diana defied royal traditions by giving birth to her sons in hospital, sending them to nursery, taking them to theme parks, and allowing them to eat fast-food and to befriend ordinary children. Much has been made in the coverage of the royal family about its transformation in a time of social change where it is now possible for Kate Middleton, the great-granddaughter of a coalminer, to marry Prince William, the future King. Like Princess Diana, the Duke and Duchess of Cambridge have defied some aspects of royal convention and live in ways more 'middle class', including the Duchess wearing high-street brands

---

30   Consider the following anecdote, shared with me by a member of the Italian aristocracy in Milan, which underscores the attitude of the Windsors. When Margaret Thatcher queried a staff member of Queen Elizabeth's staff about the possibility of the two of them wearing the same colour at an event, she was told: 'The Queen is unconcerned about what commoners wear.'

31   M. Gill, 'Rethinking Eccentricity', *University of Cambridge – Research*, 1 May 2009 <http:// www.cam.ac.uk/research/news/rethinking-eccentricity> (Accessed 15 May 2015); see also M. Gill, *Eccentricity and the Cultural Imagination in Nineteenth-Century Paris*, Oxford University Press, Oxford, 2009.

32   M. Homans, *Royal Representations: Queen Victoria and British Culture, 1837-1876*, University of Chicago Press, Chicago, IL, 1998.

to official functions more than once. Prince Harry, too, is often portrayed as 'down-to-earth' and ordinary, and, at the time of this writing, is engaged to marry the biracial American actress Meghan Markle, a descendent of slaves.[33] The younger royals are part of a growing phenomenon of royal families in Europe not only behaving in ways deemed 'middle-class' but exogamously selecting grooms and brides outside of royal and aristocratic circles.[34]

With a birth surname laden with meanings, the Duchess' style has a language of its own. Her fashion choices and self-presentation signal clues about her gender, sexuality, age, nationality personality, character, and past, as well as present, socio-economic status.[35] She has struck a balance of fashionable moderation, a middle ground between two extremes, neither excessive nor deficient, and her success can be viewed in line with the ancient doctrine of the 'middle way', 'middle path', or 'golden ratio', as propounded by Confucius, Buddha, and Aristotle. Beyond this, the Duchess' 'middle way' can be read as a calming public relations and political strategy, necessary for a royal family of the 21st century seeking to remain in favour with a public divided about inherited royal privilege and a republic-oriented social movement that would end the monarchy.[36] Her 'wear-again' practice is viewed as a symbol of a more relevant, modern British monarchy, 'middle-class' in its sensitivities, taste, and interests. Circumspect about her wardrobe, the Duchess dresses modestly and purportedly will not accept free clothes.[37] Since she first attracted the attention of the mass media, Catherine has known 'the true potency of dress', claims Pamela Church Gibson, the historian of fashion, and 'has had to tread carefully, and this has affected her chosen model of self-presentation'.[38]

---

33   B. Little, 'Henry VIII Beheaded Meghan Markle's Ancestor', *History*, 27 November 2017 <https://www.history.com/news/henry-viii-beheaded-meghan-markles-ancestor> (Accessed 14 March 2018).

34   M. Luckel, 'Move Over, Kate Middleton: These Commoners All Married Royals, Too', *Vogue*, 8 December 2016 <https://www.vogue.com/article/royals-who-married-commoners-kate-middleton-prince-william> (Accessed 8 October 2017).

35   R. Barthes, *The Fashion System*, trans. M. Ward and R. Howard, University of California Press, Berkeley, CA, 1990; M. Rampley, *Exploring Visual Culture: Definitions, Concepts, Contexts*, Edinburgh University Press, Edinburgh, 2005; F. Davis, *Fashion, Culture, and Identity*, University of Chicago Press, Chicago, IL, 1994.

36   J. L. Foltyn, 'The Middle Way: The Duchess of Cambridge and the Politics of Fashionable Moderation' [abstract], *4th Global Conference Fashion: Exploring Critical Issues*, Mansfield College, Oxford University, 16-19 September 2012, p. 12.

37   D. Mau, 'Kate Middleton Won't Accept Free Clothes, is Striking "Private Agreements" with Designers', *Fashionista*, 21 June 2011 <https://fashionista.com/2011/06/kate-middleton-wont-accept-free-clothes-is-striking-private-agreements-with-designers> (Accessed 17 June 2014).

38   Gibson, 'New Patterns of Emulation'.

While the image projected by the Duchess has been generally received positively, in part because of her ordinariness, those who reject her, including some fashion editors and bloggers, do so for the same reasons, proclaiming her personal style not special, matronly, and too cautious. In this narrative, the evocatively named Middleton's 'middle-class' origins are not easily shed; this leads to class-based explanations of her fashion 'commonness', reflected in her passion for off-the-rack garments and unwillingness to part with 'perfectly good clothing', which she re-wears. Portrayed as down-market, social climbing, *nouveau riche*, disrespectful of her position, the Crown and the British people, the Duchess, not surprisingly, is often contrasted unfavourably with Princess Diana, the former Lady Diana Spencer, an aristocrat.

It is worth noting that in a companion article about the Duchess, published on the same day as 'Thrifty Kate', the royal correspondent remarked, '[d]isappointingly, perhaps, for fashion watchers, Kate has worn the stunning dress twice before in public'.[39] Six readers posted contemptuous comments about the Duchess' background. Katra referred to her as 'the daughter of a shopkeeper'. Under Lord said she 'would not look out of place at the fish counter at TESCO's'. TheGreatAppeaser described her as 'working class rough woman acting suspiciously, very upper class'. Ferguson1 wrote 'Wills married well below himself. He could have married a "real" Princess & NOT a commoner'. Victoria claimed the Duchess 'and her family manipulated a foolish weak man into marrying her when his first choice turned him down'. Fluffball claimed, '[r]oyalty must marry royalty, -Kate Middleton has NO class. Class is pedigree NOT money'.

By marrying the Prince, Middleton trumped her detractors, 'social betters' and class 'shamers', who snobbishly look down upon the Middletons as arriviste multi-millionaires, whose ancestors worked in coal mines and shops, and whose present fortune was founded by her mother's Party Pieces business, an activity frequently still referred to contemptuously in the UK, as 'trade'. Not surprisingly, this entrepreneurial activity has been a source of derision in the UK, by the same press focussed on the fashion choices of the Duchess. A parliamentary democracy, under a constitutional monarchy, the social stratification of the UK has historically been highly influenced by the concept of social

---

39   R. English, 'Kate Saves the Best for Last! Pregnant Duchess Dazzles in Formal Gown as Royal Couple Join William's Cousin Princess Eugenie to Complete New York tour at Star-Studded Manhattan Fundraiser', *Daily Mail*, 10 December 2014 <http://www.dailymail. co.uk/news/article-2867757/Kate-saves-best-Pregnant-Duchess-dazzles-blue-gown-royal-couple-attend-glitzy-Manhattan-fundraiser-university-fell-love.html#ixzz4wpwh-Krgb> (Accessed 15 July 2015).

class, and one's socioeconomic origins remain a resilient social classification system.[40] The social status the Duchess was ascribed at birth remains a powerful form of social distinction and cultural capital.[41] Compared to a country like the USA, where social mobility is admired, there is a persistent ambivalence about social mobility in the UK, and resentment of people like the Middletons who move above the circumstances of their birth, a remnant of British class system snobbery.

In the *Daily Mail*, there is sometimes pushback to such characterisations of the Duchess, such as the one posted by Lili Sings, in the article about 'wear-again' Anne, when the Duchess was compared unfavourably to the Princess Royal:

> [n]othing the beautiful Kate does will ever satisfy the UK commoners. There is too much jealousy!...1) That she had no 'royal blood'. 2) That her parents were not at least aristocrats. 3) That she has fulfilled her duty as a Princess admirably. 4) That she has filled her duty of producing the 'heir and a spare', at great personal sacrifice, and danger to her own life. 5) That both she and Prince William have a marriage of love.

6   Conclusion

In conclusion and summary, discourse about clothing reflects changing social structure, relationships, and times, and can mirror tensions between social groups.[42] Consider the below passage by Denny, who while responding to the article about the Princess Royal, turned his attention to both the Duchess and her deceased mother-in-law, Princess Diana:

> [i]t seems apparant to me that KM does not spend nearly so much on clothes as her late mother in law did for similar functions. If that had

---

40   Unlike Continental European countries, the UK never experienced the democratic revolutions that dispossessed the nobility and royalty of their estates; the British upper class remains small and consists of a hereditary peerage, gentry, hereditary landowners, and, in some cases, hugely wealthy industrialists. A. Biressi and H. Nunn, *Class and Contemporary British Culture*, Palgrave Macmillan, Basingstoke, 2013.

41   P. Bourdieu, *Distinction: A Social Critique of the Judgement of Taste*, Harvard University Press, Cambridge, MA, 1984; P. Bourdieu, 'The Forms of Capital' in J. E. Richardson (ed.), *Handbook of Theory of Research for the Sociology of Education*, Greenwood Press, Westport, CT, 1986, pp. 241-258.

42   Crane, *Fashion and Its Social Agendas*.

been Princess Diana, she would have worn lavish new haute coutier dress by Bruce Oldfield costing £30K and also decked out in priceless fine gems given to her by Prince of ... of Saudi Arabia etc.. Mind you, she would have looked a lot more regal too. Diana didn't do high street for formal occasions and she didn't wear the same evening clobber time and again in a few short years. KM is clearly trying to carve out a role as a money conscience, UK industry promoting royal.[43]

DENNY

Not surprisingly, *Daily Mail* articles about the British Royal Family and reader responses to them reflect cultural, social, and political divisions in the UK population. Founded in 1896 and modelled after US newspapers that appealed to working people, the *Daily Mail* has always been at the centre of the political life of Britain[44] and is the only newspaper in the UK with a female majority readership, albeit slightly.[45] According to a profile in *The New Yorker*, 'the *Mail* presents itself as the defender of traditional British values, the voice of an overlooked majority whose opinions inconvenience the agendas of metropolitan élites'.[46] Known for its moral rectitude, the *Daily Mail* is described as a 'middlebrow juggernaut that can slay knights and sway Prime Ministers'.[47] While doing this, it nimbly balances a variety of topics and moods that hold the attention of readers, i.e., a smorgasbord of subjects from the serious to the frivolous, mixing ordinary people and celebrity. Evoking a variety of emotions, the *Daily Mail* gives voice to concerns of the suburban, patriotic, middle class, who are concerned about immigration, crime, education, and welfare abuse.[48]

---

43   Rainey, 'And the Gold Star for Thrift Goes to Anne'.

44   'A Political History'.

45   Approximately 52-55 per cent. H. Fearn, 'The *Daily Mail* has a Mainly Female Readership – So Why Do Women Enjoy Those "Who Won Legs-it" Headlines?', *The Independent*, 28 March 2017 <https://www.independent.co.uk/voices/daily-mail-brexit-legs-it-theresa-may-nicola-sturgeon-female-readershop-women-feminism-a7654326.html> (Accessed 17 January 2018). According to 'Where Men and Women Differ in Following the News', *Pew Research Center*, 6 February 2008 <http://www.pewresearch.org/2008/02/06/where-men-and-women-differ-in-following-the-news/> (Accessed 17 January 2018), women readers are thought to be more interested in family, the arts, and entertainment than men. These are related fields like fashion and celebrity, which the *Daily Mail* serves its readers every day amid its serious reporting on other topics. Articles about the Duchess and the Princess Royal – typically written by women journalists, focus on their appearance, families, and fame, and reader reaction to them. See also Collins, 'Mail Supremacy'.

46   Collins, 'Mail Supremacy'.

47   Ibid., 'A Political History'.

48   Collins, 'Mail Supremacy'.

An unreliable supporter of the Conservative Party, or for that matter, any cause,[49] it has campaigned for liberal and environmental causes (e.g., 'Banish the Bags')[50] while railing against the EU, BBC, NHS, wind turbines, and 'benefits scroungers'. The *Daily Mail* shows no deference for the famous, including the well-born, and delights in exposing 'spongers', hypocrites, overpaid, or depraved.[51] Its position on celebrity is sceptical,[52] and no target is exempt, including members of the British monarchy, a tactic that reels in royalists and republicans, conservatives and progressives, and royal admirers and haters.

Bibliography

'A Political History of the Daily Mail', *The Week*, 11 October 2017 <http://www.theweek. co.uk/88935/a-political-history-of-the-daily-mail> (Accessed 18 January 2018).

Barsamian, E., 'Kate Middleton's Preen Dress Is Already Sold Out, Less Than 24 hours Later', *Vogue*, 14 July 2017 <https://www.vogue.com/article/kate-middleton-duchess-of-cambridge-preen-prada-natural-history-museum-celebrity-royal-style> (Accessed 23 October 2017).

Barthes, R., *The Fashion System*. Trans. M. Ward and R. Howard. University of California Press, Berkeley, CA, 1990.

Bates, S., 'Profile: Kate Middleton', *The Guardian*, 16 November 2010 <http://www.guardian.co.uk/uk/2010/nov/16/profile-kate-middleton> (Accessed 29 January 2012).

Baudrillard, J., *The Consumer Society: Myths and Structures*. Sage Publications, Thousand Oaks, 1998.

Biressi, A., and H. Nunn, *Class and Contemporary British Culture*. Palgrave Macmillan, Basingstoke, 2013.

Bourdieu, P., *Distinction: A Social Critique of the Judgement of Taste*. Harvard University Press, Cambridge, MA, 1984.

Bourdieu, P., 'The Forms of Capital', in J. E. Richardson (ed.), *Handbook of Theory of Research for the Sociology of Education*. Greenwood Press, Westport, CT, 1986, pp. 241–258.

Bradley, I., *Believing in Britain: The Spiritual Identity of 'Britishness'*. I. B. Tauris, New York, NY, 2007.

---

49   Ibid.
50   P. Wilby, 'Paul Dacre of the *Daily Mail*: The Man Who Hates Liberal Britain', *New Statesman*, 2 January 2014 <https://www.newstatesman.com/media/2013/12/man-who-hates-liberal-britain≥ (Accessed 18 January 2018).
51   Ibid.; J. Lloyd, 'John Lloyd Responds to Dacre's Attack', *Press Gazette*, 9 February 2007 <https://web.archive.org/web/20070907013140/http://www.pressgazette.co.uk/story.asp?storyCode=36759&sectioncode=12 (Accessed 17 January 2018).
52   Collins, 'Mail Supremacy'.

Collins, L., 'Mail Supremacy: The Newspaper That Rules Britain', *The New Yorker*, 2 April 2012 <https://www.newyorker.com/magazine/2012/04/02/mail-supremacy> (Accessed 15 January 2018).

Crane, D., *Fashion and Its Social Agendas: Class, Gender and Identity in Clothing*. University of Chicago Press, Chicago, IL, 2000.

Crane, D., 'Fashion Tales: Feeding the Imaginary' [keynote speech], *International Conference*, ModaCult – Centre for the Study of Fashion and Cultural Production, Università Cattolica, Milan, 18–20 June 2015.

Davis, F., *Fashion, Culture, and Identity*. University of Chicago Press, Chicago, IL, 1994.

English, R., 'Kate Saves the Best for Last! Pregnant Duchess Dazzles in Formal Gown as Royal Couple Join William's Cousin Princess Eugenie to Complete New York tour at Star-Studded Manhattan Fundraiser', *Daily Mail*, 10 December 2014 < http://www.dailymail.co.uk/news/article-2867757/Kate-saves-best-Pregnant-Duchess-dazzles-blue-gown-royal-couple-attend-glitzy-Manhattan-fundraiser-university-fell-love.html#ixzz4wpwhKrgb> (Accessed 15 July 2015).

Fearn, H., 'The *Daily Mail* has a Mainly Female Readership – So Why Do Women Enjoy Those "Who Won Legs-it" Headlines?', *The Independent*, 28 March 2017 <https://www.independent.co.uk/voices/daily-mail-brexit-legs-it-theresa-may-nicola-sturgeon-female-readershop-women-feminism-a7654326.html> (Accessed 17 January 2018).

Foltyn, J. L., 'The Middle Way: The Duchess of Cambridge and the Politics of Fashionable Moderation' [abstract], *4th Global Conference Fashion: Exploring Critical Issues*, Mansfield College, Oxford University, 16–19 September 2012, p. 12.

Foltyn, J. L., 'Eco-Kate? The Recycled Fashions of the Duchess of Cambridge' [abstract], *7th Global Conference Fashion: Exploring Critical Issues,* Mansfield College, Oxford University, Oxford, 24–25 September 2015, pp. 8–9.

Foltyn, J. L., 'Sustainable Kate? The Recycled Fashions of Kate Middleton, the Duchess of Cambridge' [conference presentation], *Fashion Tales: Feeding the Imaginary, International Conference*, ModaCult – Centre for the Study of Fashion and Cultural Production, Università Cattolica, Milan, 18–20 June 2015.

Gibson, P. C., 'New Patterns of Emulation: Kate, Pippa and Cheryl', *Celebrity Studies*, vol. 2, no. 3, 2011, pp. 358–360.

Gill, M., *Eccentricity and the Cultural Imagination in Nineteenth-Century Paris*. Oxford University Press, Oxford, 2009.

Gill, M., 'Rethinking Eccentricity', *University of Cambridge – Research*, 1 May 2009 < http://www.cam.ac.uk/research/news/rethinking-eccentricity> (Accessed 15 May 2015).

Graafland, A., 'Thrifty Kate Middleton Strikes Again as She Recycles Cream Alexander McQueen Coat for Royal Garden Party', *Mirror*, 24 May 2016 <http://www.mirror.co.uk/3am/style/celebrity-fashion/thrifty-kate-middleton-strikes-again-8041704> (Accessed 5 October 2017).

Homans, M., *Royal Representations: Queen Victoria and British Culture,1837–1876*. University of Chicago Press, Chicago, IL, 1998.

Kratofil, C., 'Everything Kate Touches Turns to "Sold" ', *People*, 18 May 2016 <http://people.com/style/everything-kate-touches-turns-to-sold/banana-republic-skirt> (Accessed 25 October 2017).

Lewis, R., 'Anne, the Princess Royal', *Encylopaedia Britannica*, 24 October 2017 <https://www.britannica.com/biography/Princess-Anne-British-royal> (Accessed 31 October 2017).

Linning, S., 'Lovely in Lace! Kate Displays a Hint of a Baby Bump in Black Designer Gown that She Also Wore While Pregnant with Princess Charlotte as She Attends a Glittering Kensington Palace Charity Gala', *Daily Mail*, 8 November 2017 <http://www.dailymail.co.uk/femail/article-5058895/Pregnant-Kate-displays-hint-baby-bump-charity-gala.html?ito=email_share_article-top> (Accessed 8 November 2017).

Lipovetsky, G., *The Empire of Fashion: Dressing Modern Democracy*. Trans. C. Porter. Princeton University Press, Princeton, NJ, 1994.

Little, B., 'Henry VIII Beheaded Meghan Markle's Ancestor', *History*, 27 November 2017 <https://www.history.com/news/henry-viii-beheaded-meghan-markles-ancestor> (Accessed 14 March 2018).

Lloyd, J., 'John Lloyd Responds to Dacre's Attack', *Press Gazette*, 9 February 2007 <https://web.archive.org/web/20070907013140/http://www.pressgazette.co.uk/story.asp?storyCode=36759&sectioncode=1> (Accessed 17 January 2018).

Logan, A., 'Netnography: Observing and Interacting with Celebrity in the Digital World', *Celebrity Studies*, vol. 6, no. 3, 2015, pp. 378–381.

London, B., 'Thrifty Kate Strikes Again! Duchess of Cambridge Recycles a £2,500 Scarlet Gown by Her Favourite Designer Jenny Packham for the Buckingham Palace Reception', *Daily Mail*, 9 December 2016 <http://www.dailymail.co.uk/femail/article-4016370/Kate-Middleton-recycles-2-500-gown-favourite-designer-Jenny-Packham-Buckingham-Palace-reception.html WhatKateWore.com covers every detail of the duchess' fashion> (Accessed 30 October 2017).

Lovemoney.com, 'How Much Does the UK Royal Family Cost?', *BT*, 20 July 2016 <http://home.bt.com/lifestyle/money/mortgages-bills/how-much-does-the-royal-family-cost-11363982445194> (Accessed 23 October 2017).

Luckel, M., 'Move Over, Kate Middleton: These Commoners All Married Royals, Too', *Vogue*, 8 December 2016 <https://www.vogue.com/article/royals-who-married-commoners-kate-middleton-prince-william> (Accessed 8 October 2017).

Mapstone, L., and R. English, 'Thrifty Kate Strikes Again: Pregnant Duchess Wears Designer Dress for the THIRD Time as She Attends Gala Dinner with Prince William in New York', *Daily Mail*, 10 December 2014 <http://www.dailymail.co.uk/femail/article-2867909/Thrifty-Kate-strikes-Pregnant-Duchess-wears-designer-dress-time-steps-Prince-William-gala-dinner-New-York.html> (Accessed 15 June 2015).

Mau, D., 'Kate Middleton Won't Accept Free Clothes, is Striking "Private Agreements" with Designers', *Fashionista*, 21 June 2011 <https://fashionista.com/2011/06/kate-middleton-wont-accept-free-clothes-is-striking-private-agreements-with-designers> (Accessed 17 June 2014).

'Monthly Reach of National Newspapers and Their Websites in the United Kingdom (UK) from April 2016 to March 2017 (in 1,000 individuals)', *Statista*, 2017 <https://www.statista.com/statistics/246077/reach-of-selected-national-newspapers-in-the-uk/> (Accessed 29 October 2017).

Naughty But Nice Rob, 'Kate Middleton's Far-Reaching Fashion Influence', *HuffPost*, 29 May 2012 <https://www.huffingtonpost.com/2012/05/29/kate-middleton-fashion_n_1553975.html> (Accessed 12 June 2012).

Niinimäki, K. (ed.), *Sustainable Fashion: New Approaches*. Aalto University, Helsinki, 2013.

Polhemus, T., *Streetstyle*. Thames & Hudson, New York, NY, 1994.

Rainey, S., 'And the Gold Star for Thrift Goes to Anne: Princess Royal Recycles Outfit She First Wore in 1980 for the First Day of Royal Ascot', *Daily Mail*, 17 June 2015 <http://www.dailymail.co.uk/femail/article-3127219/And-gold-star-thrift-goes-Anne-Princess-Royal-recycles-outfit-wore-1980-day-Royal-Ascot.html> (Accessed 14 July 2015).

Rampley, M., *Exploring Visual Culture: Definitions, Concepts, Contexts*. Edinburgh University Press, Edinburgh, 2005.

Sahakian, M., and H. Wilhite, 'Making Practice Theory Practicable: Towards More Sustainable Forms of Consumption', *Journal of Consumer Culture*, vol. 14, no. 1, 2014, pp. 25–44.

Simmel, G., 'Fashion', *International Quarterly*, vol. 10, 1904, pp. 130–143.

Styles, R., 'It Might Be Kate's Birthday but Harry is the Nation's Favourite Royal ... Prince is Number One While the Duchess Languishes in Second Place', *Daily Mail*, 9 January 2015 <http://www.dailymail.co.uk/femail/article-2903281/It-Kate-s-birthday-HARRY-nation-s-favourite-royal-Prince-number-one-Duchess-languishes-second-place.html#ixzz4wkGipdtS> (Accessed 20 May 2015).

Sykes, T., 'How Duchess Kate Middleton Stole Princess Diana's Crown', *Daily Beast*, 11 April 2016 <https://www.thedailybeast.com/how-duchess-kate-middleton-stole-princess-dianas-crown> (Accessed 29 October 2017).

'Top 10 Most Read Newspapers in the World', *Trending Top Most*, 2017 <http://www.trendingtopmost.com/worlds-popular-list-top-10/2017-2018-2019-2020-2021/world/most-read-newspapers-world-best-selling/> (Accessed 3 January 2018).

YouGov/Newsweek Survey Results, 'Which One of the Following, If Any, Would You Consider to be Your Favourite Member of the Royal Family?', *YouGov*, 2014 <https://d25d2506sfb94s.cloudfront.net/cumulus_uploads/document/40pfhhdrcv/Newsweek_Results_140909_Kate_Middleton_Website_140929.pdf> (Accessed 10 December 2014).

Veblen, T., *The Theory of the Leisure Class: An Economic Study in the Evolution of Institu-tions*. Macmillan, New York, NY, 1902 [1899].

Weber, M., *The Protestant Ethic and the Spirit of Capitalism*. Scribner, New York, NY, 1958 [1905].

Weber, M., *On Charisma and Institution Building*. Ed. S. N. Eisenstadt. University of Chicago Press, Chicago, IL, 1968.

'Where Men and Women Differ in Following the News', *Pew Research Center*, 6 Feb-ruary 2008 <http://www.pewresearch.org/2008/02/06/where-men-and-women-differ-in-following-the-news/> (Accessed 17 January 2018).

Wilby, P., 'Paul Dacre of the *Daily Mail*: The Man Who Hates Liberal Britain', *New States-man*, 2 January 2014 <https://www.newstatesman.com/media/2013/12/man-who-hates-liberal-britain> (Accessed 18 January 2018).

CHAPTER 18

Clothing Issued the Enslaved on the Monticello Plantation

Gaye S. Wilson

Abstract

This study began with a question. Can clothing that is largely uniform and issued systematically on a bi-annual basis function within the parameters of 'fashion' as defined
by Veblen? The historic clothing in question is that issued to the enslaved people who
lived and worked on a central Virginia plantation, Monticello, in the late 18th – early
19th centuries. Little remains as visual or physical evidence of the clothing beyond
buttons, buckles and a few beads; therefore, this study relies primarily upon the farm
records and correspondence of Monticello owner, Thomas Jefferson. His records are
most complete for the year 1794, when he began recording clothing allotments that
then continue through 1824, though some of the later lists contain less detail. His
lists and letters provide information as to what, how much and to whom textiles and
clothing accessories were issued. This still leaves unanswered the actual appearance
of the slave garments as to cut and style, nevertheless the recorded allotments provide
a basis for discussion of how the clothing functioned within the Monticello enslaved
community.

Keywords

enslaved people – Thomas Jefferson – Monticello – Thorstein Veblen – field workers –
tradesmen – house slaves – knaps and half-thicks – osnaburg – calamanco

1   Introduction

A study of African-American slave clothing is problematic in the very temporal
nature of clothing never intended for survival but rather to be used up with
repeated wearing. Thomas Jefferson's central Virginia plantation, Monticello,
is not an exception, as there are no textile items known to remain from the
enslaved community. What does survive are the written records: farm records,

accounts, correspondence and memoranda. These form a skeletal outline of this lost clothing and even more importantly allude to the role of clothing within the plantation structure.

Critical theories on the nature and function of fashion did not begin to appear until later in the 19th century, many decades after Thomas Jefferson entered his first inventory of slave clothing in his *Farm Book*. An early work that included clothing in an analysis of social structure was economist Thorstein Veblen's *The Theory of the Leisure Class*, first published in 1899. Here he coined his lasting phrase 'conspicuous consumption'. Early in his discussion he states:

> [i]n order to gain and to hold the esteem of men it is not sufficient merely to possess wealth or power. The wealth or power must be put in evidence, for esteem is awarded only on evidence.[1]

In his chapter 'Dress as an Expression of the Pecuniary Culture', he applies this theory to clothing and asserts that fashion becomes a means for the moneyed, leisure class to visually affirm their superior social position. Veblen explains that as clothing is always in evidence, it serves as an instant indicator of status.

The relationship of the wealthy with their servants entered Veblen's discussion. He saw the appearance and presence of the personal or body servant integral to the image of the rich employer that he identified as 'master'. He stated, '[t]he master's person, being the embodiment of worth and honour, is of the most serious consequence both for his reputable standing in the community and for his self-respect'.[2] Veblen believed these personal servants to be as much for public show as for service and recognized the distinction in the personal servant and those who worked at a distance.

> [P]ersonal service and attendance on the master becomes the special office of a portion of the servants while those who are wholly employed in industrial occupations proper are removed more and more from all immediate relation to the person of their owner.[3]

Rather than chattel slavery Veblen was motivated by his observations of 19th century industrialism and the class inequalities that the Industrial Revolution created. Though there can never be an equation of even the poorest yet free industrial worker with those held enslaved, Veblen's observations do provide a

---

1   T. Veblen, *The Theory of the Leisure Class*, Modern Library, New York, NY, 2001 [1899], p. 29.
2   Ibid., p. 43.
3   Ibid., p. 42.

framework for considering the role of clothing within an enslaved community on an 18th century plantation. Enslaved peoples, with so few personal choices, were hardly examples of conspicuous consumption themselves, nevertheless a study of clothing allotments points to how the clothing reflected the hierarchies within the enslaved workforce and the relationships between slave and master. The clothing worn by the slaves followed the theories of Veblen in becoming a visual indicator of the social and pecuniary status of the master himself.

This study looks closely at Thomas Jefferson's *Farm Book* and the records he began in 1794, and kept until 1824 that he titled *Distribution of Clothing*. Here he listed the slaves by first name, including the enslaved children. Alongside the names, he logged the fabric, accessory items and bedding allotted each. The clothing was distributed bi-annually with the major allotment in the late fall and a lesser allotment in early summer.

The initial list of 1794, by far the most detailed, reflected an imposed hierarchy within the slave community by its very organization. Jefferson set apart the 'house slaves' from what he termed the 'farm slaves'. The 'house slaves' were the most visible and expected to serve those visiting or living in the Monticello mansion. Not surprisingly, they were issued clothing superior in quality to that of the field workers. Between these two groups of 'house slaves' and 'field slaves' there was another division, in fact in later clothing distribution lists Jefferson added a third category for 'tradesmen'. These were men and women who were trained in occupations that supported life in the house or were vital to the workings of the plantation, such as the cook, blacksmith, joiner, or those assigned to supervise various operations. These were positions of responsibility and recognized with clothing superior to that of slaves working in the fields and further from the master. Within each of these groups gender and age were factors in the distribution of clothing and accessories.

2   'House Slaves'

Placed at the head of the 1794 list was Jefferson's personal servant, Jupiter, who had attended Jefferson since their youth. Both men were born in 1743 on Jefferson's father's plantation, and following custom, Jupiter had been assigned as Jefferson's personal servant when both were quite young. Jupiter accompanied Jefferson when he attended the College of William and Mary in Williamsburg, Virginia. The two traveled together with Jupiter often serving as coachman. He performed a variety of duties both as Jefferson's personal attendant and in the functioning of the plantation and was often in a position visible to the public. In addition to his ten and one-half yards of Irish linen for shirts and accessories, Jupiter was allotted 'coat, waistcoat, breeches of cloth' with '2 pr. worsted stockings & 1 pr. cotton'.[4] When Jefferson used the term 'cloth', for his own clothing, he was indicating wool suiting, such as wool broadcloth. There is no indication as to color and how Jupiter's suit may have been trimmed.

Following Jupiter in the list were two brothers, James and Peter Hemings, who were stationed in the Monticello kitchen. When Jefferson left for Paris in 1784 to assume duties as American Minister Plenipotentiary, he took James Hemings along to have him trained in the art of French cooking. Hemings must have done well, as following their return to the United States, he served as chef to Secretary of State Jefferson in New York and Philadelphia from 1790 to 1793. Prior to their return to Monticello after Jefferson resigned as Secretary of State, they reached an agreement that Hemings would become a free man after he trained the person that Jefferson would appoint to assume James' duties.[5] In 1794 James was training his brother Peter to take over the Monticello kitchen upon his manumission and leaving the plantation as a free man. Jefferson enjoyed a reputation as host and appreciated fine food himself, which made these two men, James and Peter Hemings, important to his household staff and the lifestyle he enjoyed. It is not surprising that they followed immediately behind Jupiter in the list of clothing allotments.

The Hemings brothers received an issue similar to Jupiter's in the Irish linen for shirts, a coat, and waistcoat but instead of breeches they were to receive 'overalls of cloth'. A surviving pair of Jefferson's own overalls that he as often called sherryvallies were cut much like regular knee breeches but with the distinguishing feature of buttons along the outside of each leg. Jefferson's were made of sturdy cotton, and ample enough to be worn over a pair of breeches. Monticello overseer, Edmund Bacon, commented of Jefferson, '[w]hen he rode on horseback he had a pair of overalls that he always put on'.[6] This describes a more utilitarian garment geared to outdoor activities, but they could be practical in the kitchen as well. According to his accounting records, Jefferson purchased

---

4   T. Jefferson, *Thomas Jefferson's Farm Book*, ed. E. M. Betts, University Press of Virginia, Charlottesville, VA, 1976, p. 41.

5   Thomas Jefferson, Agreement with James Hemings, 15 September 1793. T. Jefferson, *Papers of Thomas Jefferson* (vols. 1–41 to date), ed. J. Boyd *et al.*, Princeton University Press, Princeton, NJ, 1950, vol. 27.

6   H. W. Pierson, 'Jefferson at Monticello: The Private Life of Thomas Jefferson', in J.A. Bear, Jr. (ed.), *Jefferson at Monticello*, University Press of Virginia, Charlottesville, VA, 1967, pp. 25–138, pp. 25–138, p. 74.

overalls or sherryvallies for himself on many occasions, and a skilled white work-
man employed by Jefferson, David Watson, bargained for overalls as a part of
his salary in 1796.[7] Overalls were apparently as desirable a garment in the work-
man's wardrobe as that of the country gentleman's. An unanswered question is
whether James and Peter Hemings requested the more utilitarian overalls for
their work in the kitchen or whether the assignment was Jefferson's. Considering
James had negotiated his freedom, perhaps he was capable of negotiating preferred clothing as well. Certainly it was in Jefferson's interest to make sure their
personal needs were adequately met and that the kitchen ran smoothly.

Following these three key men in Jefferson's staff were the women who
worked in the house: Critta and Sally Hemings (sisters to James and Peter Hemings) and their niece Betsy.[8] Like their male counterparts, each woman was
issued ten and one-half yards of Irish linen that would have provided shifts and
accessories. For outerwear they received calimanco, a favored woolen fabric in
the 18th century described as having, 'a fine gloss upon it' that could appear
in either rich solid hues or patterned with stripes and flowers.[9] There is no
hint, however, as to whether the calimanco was solid or patterned nor how the
garments may have been fashioned. Critta and Sally were issued 11 yards each
and their 11 year-old niece Betsey was given eight. Each of the women received
three pair of cotton stockings. The men were issued three pairs as well but only
one pair in cotton with the other two in wool. Jefferson does not list shoes for
the house slaves, but with stockings supplied, it could be assumed that they
did receive shoes but of a quality above the plantation made shoes allotted the
field slaves and tradesmen.

Placed between the adult house slaves and the other farm slaves on the
list were four boys who had duties in the house: Joe, Wormly, Burwell and
Brown, ranging in age from 9 to 14. In quality and cost their clothing ranked
below that of the adult household slaves but superior to the majority of the
enslaved community. Instead of the finer Irish linen, they received osnaburg from the same allotment that was purchased for the farm slaves. Yet for
outerwear they were issued a more costly fabric called bearskin, a durable,
napped woolen, and according to Jefferson's notes, blue in color.[10] As the

7   T. Jefferson, *Jefferson's Memorandum Books*, ed. J.A. Bear, Jr., and L. Stanton, Princeton
      University Press, Princeton, NJ, 1997. See index under 'clothing' for purchases of overalls;
      for overalls for Watson, see ibid., vol. 2, p. 936.

8   For more on the Hemings family, see A. Gordon-Reed, *Hemings of Monticello: An Ameri-
      can Family*, W.W. Norton & Company, New York, NY, 2008.

9   F. M. Montgomery, *Textiles in America, 1650–1870*, W.W. Norton & Company, New York, NY,
      1984, p.185. Note: in Montgomery the fabric is spelled 'calimanco'.

10   Ibid.

only slaves on the plantation wearing this particular fabric, their clothing would have given them a visual identity that functioned very much as livery. Jefferson used livery at the President's House (today's White House) while serving as president from 1801 to 1809, but there is no substantial evidence that he used a traditional livery on a regular basis at Monticello. The blue suits of the house boys came closest, as they served in the dining room, as messengers and carried out other miscellaneous assignments. Former Monticello slave, Peter Fossett, who served in the house as a youth, recalled in his memoirs, '[a]s a boy I was not only brought up differently, but dressed unlike the plantation boys'.[11] Fossett recognized the visual distinction made by the clothing he was issued; a distinction that parallels Veblen's assertion that within industrial society, those who stood closest to the master/owner received marks of status above their peers and in return served to enhance the image of the master.

One of the houseboys listed in the 1794 clothing list, Burwell Colbert, would grow up to be Jefferson's personal servant and the carrier of the keys at Monticello – an important and trusted position. Burwell and his uncle, John Hemings, a highly skilled carpenter and brother to James and Peter Hemings, were ultimately allowed to select their own clothing. Jefferson addressed notes to a local merchant with whom he maintained an account to allow the bearer [Burwell Colbert or John Hemings] to choose their own clothing items: '[c]lothes for the bearer Burwell such as he may chuse',[12] dated 1812 and again in 1815, '[a] ny clothing which the bearer Burwell may chuse for himself'.[13] In 1819 Jefferson recorded, '[g]ave John Hemings an order ... for clothes to the amount of 12.D. instead of his annual clothing'.[14] Though notes are not extant for each year, Burwell Colbert and John Hemings' names disappear from the regular clothing roles. These two men obviously had acquired Jefferson's trust and favoritism. Clothing of their own choosing was far beyond the uniform issue given the field slaves working and living some distance from the main house – and the master.

11   P. Fossett, *Memoirs*, as cited in L. Stanton, *'Those Who Labor for My Happiness'– Slavery at Thomas Jefferson's Monticello*, University of Virginia Press, Charlottesville, VA, 2012, p. 171.

12   Thomas Jefferson to James Leitch, 15 February 1813 and 25 March 1813. T. Jefferson, *Papers of Thomas Jefferson: Retirement Series* (vols. 1–12 to date), ed. J. Jefferson Looney, Princeton University Press, Princeton, NJ, 2004, vol. 4, p. 496;

13   Ibid., vol. 8, p. 830.

14   Jefferson, *Memorandum Books*, vol. 2, p. 1352.

3   'Field Slaves' and 'Tradesmen'

The greatest portion of the 1794 clothing distribution list pertains to the 93 slaves working outside the house. For men's shirts and women's shifts there was no Irish-linen but rather German osnaburg, which in the late 18th century would likely be of a coarse grade of flax, unbleached and a natural brownish color. For outer garments Jefferson provided two types of woolen fabrics called knaps and half-thicks in red, blue, and green. Florence Montgomery in her work *Textiles in America, 1650–1870* identified both as heavy, coarse woolens, but Jefferson's records show the knaps as slightly more expensive. It was the issue to key slaves that worked outside the house but in the group that Jefferson identified as tradesmen.

Monticello slave foreman Big George and his family led the list of these outside workers. George Granger was unique, as he would be the only slave within Jefferson's farm operation ever to rise to the position of overseer and manage one of the quarter-farms that composed the Monticello plantation. George's wife Ursula Granger held key roles including nursemaid to the children of Jefferson and his wife Martha and supervised many of the household activities. Their son George was the plantation blacksmith and younger son Isaac was trained as a tinsmith and blacksmith.[15] This family was given the more expensive knaps, and Big George and Ursula were allotted an additional yard of osnaburg and of wool than that given the other slaves.

Lucy, the cook, and the kitchen staff working under James and Peter Hemings were issued the knaps as well. A survey of the clothing records from 1794 to 1812 shows that the allotments to the cooks consistently placed them in this middle tier of slaves who had developed special skills. They played a significant role in Monticello's reputation for food above the usual plantation fare. Kitchen staff changed, yet as late as 1824 when Daniel Webster visited Monticello, he pronounced that '[d]inner was served in half Virginian, half French style, in good taste and abundance'.[16]

The farm slaves ('field workers') were allotted seven yards of osnaburg and eight of wool, one pair of stockings and a pair of shoes. A total of 60 pairs of shoes were assigned in 1794 that appear to have been made at Monticello, as no purchases of shoes are recorded, rather Jefferson purchased leather for soles and uppers. He had a shoemaker on the slave work force, whose name, Phill Shoemaker, identified his trade. Jefferson apparently saw the importance

---

15   Stanton, *'Those Who Labor for My Happiness'*.

16   D. Webster, *The Private Correspondence of Daniel Webster* (vol.1), ed. F. Webster and E.D. Sanborn, Little, Brown & Company, Boston, MA, 1857, p. 365.

of this craft and instructed that two of the younger slaves train with Phill. He wrote, '[w]hen Phill proceeds to the making shoes for the people, Barnaby & Shepherd should join him, as they have heretofore done, in order to perfect themselves in shoemaking'.[17] How well Barnaby and Shepherd 'perfected themselves in shoemaking' is questionable as in 1810, the year following Phill's death, Jefferson purchased 112 pairs of shoes and was seeking to hire – or purchase a shoemaker.

4   Clothing for the Slave Children

Excluded from the shoe allotment were slaves either too old or too young to be active in the work force, which in 1794 was Old Aggey and Juno, and children under 10. With the Virginia climate moderate, the children could go barefoot much of the year but how might they manage in the coldest winter months? A possible explanation comes from an incident in the winter of 1795 when Jefferson's grandchildren, Anne and Jeff Randolph, both toddlers, were staying with their grandfather. Jefferson's letter to his daughter Martha had a tone of exasperation as he explained that two-year-old Jeff, 'has not worn his shoes an hour this winter. If put on him, he takes them off immediately'.[18] But the problem was resolved: '... we have put both him and Anne into mockassens, which being made of soft leather, fitting well and lacing up, they have never been able to take them off'.[19] Jefferson was not explicit as to the source of this idea, but if it came from Anne and Jeff's slave nanny, it would follow that moccasins could have been the solution used by slave parents for their own children.

Not only did the enslaved children not receive shoes, they were given a lesser quality fabric. Attached to his 1794 fabric order was an entry for 60 yards that Jefferson listed as 'white cotton'. The term cotton can be deceiving, as it was actually a wool fabric with a napped surface that was achieved through a process called cottoning.[20] Left undyed and of poorer quality, it was less in cost and frequently assigned the enslaved children. In 1813, however, due to the war with Britain, cheap, imported fabrics were limited, which pushed Jefferson to increase his home manufacture of textiles in order to clothe his slaves. He

17   Thomas Jefferson to Edmund Bacon, 6 October 1806. *Coolidge Collection of Thomas Jefferson Manuscripts* [microfilm], Massachusetts Historical Society, reel 5, 1806–1807.

18   Jefferson to Martha Jefferson Randolph, 22 January 1795. Jefferson, *Papers of Thomas Jefferson*, vol. 28, p. 249.

19   Ibid.

20   Montgomery, *Textiles in America*.

wrote of one of his weavers that her work was so bad that the stuff she was producing, 'will not be worth giving the children'.[21] Two years later when they were short on wool, Jefferson decided that 'we will try a mixture of hemp & cotton for the negro children'.[22] This was not just Jefferson's practice. In an 1806 article in a Virginia newspaper proposing a cure for the 'scab' in sheep, the farmer wrote that his flock was so diseased that the quality of the wool was, 'so sorry as to be barely fit to make clothing for the young negroes'.[23]

5   Images of Virginia Slaves

There are no images of Monticello slaves made during Jefferson's lifetime to give an idea of how the clothing may have looked, but a series of watercolor sketches by architect Benjamin Henry Latrobe during a trip through Virginia in 1797–1798 capture snapshots of slaves in the central Virginia region. His watercolor titled *An overseer doing his duty. Sketched from life near Fredericsburg*, illustrates two female agricultural slaves wearing short, tabbed bodices over ankle-length petticoats. The upper body garment for the women slaves working outside the main house was referred to as a 'waist' in Jefferson's records, however it might also be called a waistcoat, jacket or short gown. It could be cut to end at the waist but often extended below the waist with either a peplum or tabs and might be loose or fitted. In her article, 'Short Gowns', Claudia Kidwell begins by stating, '[t]he short gown, worn with a petticoat, was serviceable garb used in America in the 18th and early 19th centuries'.[24] Linda Baumgaten concurs when writing about the 18th century clothing collection at Colonial Williamsburg and states, '[s]uch bodices and petticoats formed a kind of two-piece working suit for many slave women in Virginia'.[25] Latrobe's women appear barefoot and the color of their clothing is uniform (Figure 18.1).

Latrobe offers possibilities for the men's clothing in a sketch titled, *Preparations for the enjoyment of a fine Sunday among the Blacks, Norfolk* (Figure 18.2).

21   Jefferson to Jeremiah Goodman, 5 March 1813. Jefferson, *Papers of Thomas Jefferson: Retirement Series*, vol. 5, p. 663.

22   Jefferson to Jeremiah Goodman, 6 January 1815. Ibid., vol. 8, p. 185.

23   Mr. Pleasants, 'Attention Farmers', a newspaper clipping in T. Jefferson, 'Thomas Jefferson's Commonplace Scrapbook' [unpublished manuscript], *Jefferson Papers, Special Collections*, University of Virginia Library, Charlottesville, VA.

24   C. Kidwell, 'Short Gowns', *Dress: The Journal of the Costume Society of America*, vol. 4, no. 1, 1978, pp. 30–65, p. 30.

25   L. Baumgarten, *Eighteenth-Century Clothing at Colonial Williamsburg*, Colonial Williamsburg Foundation, Williamsburg, 1993, p. 31.

FIGURE 18.1 Benjamin Henry Latrobe, "An overseer dong his duty. Sketched from life near
Fredericsburg," watercolor on paper, 1798.
USED WITH KIND PERMISSION MARYLAND HISTORICAL SOCIETY.

FIGURE 18.2 Benjamin Henry Latrobe, "Preparations for the enjoyment of a fine Sunday
Evening," watercolor on paper, 1797.
USED WITH KIND PERMISSION MARYLAND HISTORICAL SOCIETY.

The two figures in the background are wearing jackets that are approximately hip-length and without the shaping of the fashionable 18th century coat, as they hang straight from the shoulder. The figure sitting atop the barrel wears ankle-length pantaloons rather than knee-breeches that are not unlike those traditionally worn by sailors and lower class working men that needed service-able garments that moved easily. Ironically, at the close of the 18th century the trend was favoring the longer pantaloons, although the fashion conscious elite would have his fitted snugly, making them less practical as far as movement but defining the shape of the leg. Latrobe's figure is wearing lower cut shoes that were coming into vogue and has a low-crowned round hat.

In another sketch from this same series, Latrobe recorded *Alic, a faithful and humorous servant* (Figure 18.3). He shows Alic in a coat that reaches to the back of his knees and has collar and lapel, sleeve cuffs and pocket flaps that appears much like the fashionable late 18th century man's coat except it does not fit Alic as smartly, as it hangs straighter from the shoulders with less shaping. Per-haps this is simply Latrobe's quick rendering, or possibly it was a coat handed down from master to servant, as this was not an uncommon practice. In 1792 Jefferson was arranging clothing for the house slaves and noted for slave, Rob-ert Hemings, 'I had promised to send him a new suit of clothes. Instead of this I send a suit of superfine ratteen of my own, which I have scarcely ever worn'.[26]

This practice of handing on clothing to house slaves was used among the women as well. Jefferson's granddaughter Ellen was on a visit to Richmond and wrote her mother requesting, 'send me some of the dresses that I left to make presents of to the servants'. She especially wanted, 'my purple striped gingham. I do not recollect any thing else, but it is possible you may find something'.[27] In this instance the gift clothing was reclaimed, but it could be presumed that such presentations were not uncommon and that such second-hand dresses would be finer than the regular allotment, allowing the house slaves some variety in their wardrobes. The dresses must have been in reasonably good condition and still fashionable or else they would no longer have been of interest to Ellen.

Moving into the early 19th century the silhouette for women had become nar-row with the waist line high. Jefferson's calculations for 1810 appeared to take this change into account, as he reduced the yardage allotment by three yards, with two yards for a waist and three yards for a petticoat. For men he used the

---

26   Jefferson to Martha Jefferson Randolph. Jefferson, *Papers of Thomas Jefferson*, vol. 24, p. 741.

27   Ellen Randolph to Martha Jefferson Randolph, 29 March 1819. 'Jefferson Family Letters', *Ellen Wayles Randolph Coolidge Correspondence*, University of Virginia Library, Special Collections, MS 9090, Box 1, 1810–1825.

FIGURE 18.3 Benjamin Henry Latrobe, "Alic, a faithful and humorous servant," watercolor and
pen on paper, 1797.
USED WITH KIND PERMISSION MARYLAND HISTORICAL SOCIETY.

newer term, 'pantaloons' and reduced yardage by one and one-half yards of fabric, though the motivation for this reduction is not as obvious as that reassigned
the women.[28] A drawing by Baroness Hyde de Neuville made in Washington in
1810–11 of a scrub woman shows her wearing a short gown or waist and petticoat,
but in the narrow, high-waist style that followed the fashion trend (Figure 18.4).

6   Conclusion

In his critical study of the industrial-age leisure class, Thorstein Veblen argued that wealth or power must be placed in evidence in order to be believed

---

28   Jefferson, *Jefferson's Farm Book*, p. 137.

FIGURE 18.4 Baroness Hyde de Neuville, "Scrubwoman," watercolor on paper, before 1822.
USED WITH KIND PERMISSION NEW YORK HISTORICAL SOCIETY.

and to gain the esteem of others. He named fashion as an immediate visual symbol that signalled status and identified social relationships, even those between owner/master and those working on his behalf. Veblen's analogies were directed at a different time and social structure yet offer a framework for considering the role of clothing issued the enslaved on the Monticello plantation. The clothing functioned on a dual level: first, it identified the hierarchies and revealed the status of individuals or groups within the Monticello's enslaved and secondly, a decently-clothed slave community added to the status of the patriarch and master, Thomas Jefferson, by affording evidence of his pecuniary means and resources to adequately provide for those under his ownership.

As Veblen noted, the presence and appearance of the personal servant was an integral part of the status image of the master himself. In 1794 Jefferson's personal servant Jupiter was given a three-piece suit with linen for his shirts and accessories. Later, from 1812 to 1825, Jefferson allowed his personal servant Burwell Colbert to choose his own clothing from a local merchant and sometimes gave this privilege as well to his valued carpenter John Hemings. Jupiter's three-piece suit and the personal choices of Colbert and Hemings would instantly set them apart visually from the uniforms of the majority of the slaves on the plantation. The women who worked inside the house were allotted calimancoes and linen as opposed to the osnaburg and half-thicks of those working in the fields. When sent on an errand, the house boys in their blue suits could be recognized immediately as representing Monticello's patriarch or someone who stood very close to him in authority. Big George was a slave but also an overseer and needed the respect from other workers. The clothing issued him and his family was of a slightly higher quality and could support George Granger's need for respect from the slave workers in order to make Jefferson's plantation run smoothly. In the broader view a well-clothed workforce awarded Thomas Jefferson the esteem that Veblen maintained could only come from putting wealth or power in evidence. The slave clothing became this evidence and as such fulfilled some of the duties of fashion.

Bibliography

Baumgarten, L., *Eighteenth-Century Clothing at Colonial Williamsburg*. Colonial Williamsburg Foundation, Williamsburg, 1993.

Baumgarten, L., *What Clothes Reveal: The Language of Clothing in Colonial and Federal America*. Yale University Press, New Haven (CT) and London, 2002.

Coolidge Collection of Thomas Jefferson Manuscripts [microfilm], Massachusetts Historical Society, reel 5, 1806–1807.

Gordon-Reed, A., *The Hemingses of Monticello: An American Family*. W. W. Norton & Company, New York, NY, 2008.

'Jefferson Family Letters', *Ellen Wayles Randolph Coolidge Correspondence*. University of Virginia Library, Special Collections, MS 9090, Box 1, 1810–1825.

Jefferson, T., 'Thomas Jefferson's Commonplace Scrapbook' [unpublished manuscript], *Jefferson Papers, Special Collections*. University of Virginia Library, Charlottesville, VA.

Jefferson, T., *Thomas Jefferson's Farm Book*. Ed. E. M. Betts. University Press of Virginia, Charlottesville, VA, 1976.

Jefferson, T., *Jefferson's Memorandum Books*. Ed. J.A. Bear, Jr., and L. Stanton. Princeton University Press, Princeton, NJ, 1997.

Jefferson, T., *Papers of Thomas Jefferson* (vols. 1–41 to date). Ed. J. Boyd *et al.* Princeton University Press, Princeton, NJ, 1950.

Jefferson, T., *Papers of Thomas Jefferson: Retirement Series* (vols. 1–12 to date). Ed. J. Jefferson Looney. Princeton University Press, Princeton, NJ, 2004.

Kidwell, C., 'Short Gowns', *Dress: The Journal of the Costume Society of America*, vol. 4, no. 1, 1978, pp. 30–65.

Montgomery, F. M., *Textiles in America, 1650–1870*. W. W. Norton & Company, New York, NY, 1984.

Pierson, H. W., 'Jefferson at Monticello: The Private Life of Thomas Jefferson', in J.A. Bear, Jr. (ed.), *Jefferson at Monticello*. University Press of Virginia, Charlottesville, VA, 1967, pp. 25–138.

Stanton, L., *'Those Who Labor for My Happiness' – Slavery at Thomas Jefferson's Monticello*. University of Virginia Press, Charlottesville, VA, 2012.

Veblen, T., *The Theory of the Leisure Class*. Modern Library, New York, NY, 2001 [1899].

Webster, D., *The Private Correspondence of Daniel Webster*. Ed. F. Webster and E.D. Sanborn. Little, Brown & Company, Boston, MA, 1857.

CHAPTER 19

The Metamorphosis of Dress in Cyprus during the British Period

Noly Moyssi and Maria Patsalosavvi

Abstract

When the administration of Cyprus was passed over to Britain, in 1878, the island entered a new, 'European' phase. The ceding of the administration of Cyprus to Britain resulted in a deep social transformation of the island. The British period (1878–1960), characterized by rapid change in urban life style in contrast to much slower progress in rural areas, also opened the way to more travellers, mostly of higher social classes, from around the world, especially from Britain.

The European dress became prevalent in towns and gradually penetrated the countryside with a more provincial fashion style. Younger town people readily adopted modern lifestyle and elegant fashion ways. One consequence of the change in attire was the introduction of new occupations, such as tailors, seamstresses and dressmakers. The new upper class created a different lifestyle, while Cyprus moved gradually but steadily towards its Europeanization. In the towns, the people of higher classes, who in earlier times would wear oriental Ottoman dress, now wore contemporary European clothing. Upper classes members, typically the first to adopt new fashion, comprised only a small portion of the Cypriot population; yet, they represented a new dynamic element in the society, which gave further impetus to economic and social transformations.

The wider strata of the population proudly wore traditional costume, which by the end of the 19th century had become the national dress of the Cypriots. Traditional costumes would continue to be worn by ordinary people. Various types of traditional village dress would still echo 18th century or earlier urban styles.

Keywords

British colony – society transformation – lifestyle – European dress – traditional costume

1　　Introduction

Modes of dress are determined and influenced by considerations such as the economic structure and prosperity of a place, the moral and spiritual values in a society. Fashions do not arise on their own but result from broader changes, e.g. urban, economic, social or cultural.[1] Nevertheless, fashion does not remain stationary but changes through the years, following the trends of times. In this sense it is pertinent to briefly review certain events that occurred during that time and shaped dress in the island of Cyprus.

In the 18th and 19th century Cypriot dress underwent a transformation from traditional to modern, from local to cosmopolitan. This transition, from one kind of attire to the other occurred gradually, always depending on the speed of urban growth of each region.

As was common in an era when empires would disintegrate or transform into nations, national dress would come into existence as a means of ethnically unifying the national population; what is more accurately described as 'ethnic' or 'regional dress', the 'national dress' helped to unify diverse populations and to define national borders. Though 'national dress' was short lived as a way of dressing, it paved the way towards international fashion and westernization of the local population; most Cypriots abandoned the traditional/national dress in favor of styles inspired by Western European fashion.

2　　The Ottoman Rule

Through the centuries, Cyprus, an island in the Eastern Mediterranean, became property of various nations who left their mark on the local culture and dress. After the Lusignans (1191–1489) and the Venetians (1489–1570), Cyprus became part of the Ottoman Empire (1571–1878). For the three centuries that followed, the island was transformed: new administration, new systems of taxation, different use of land, resources and economy. For the duration of this period, Cyprus was part of a multicultural empire, centered on its capital,

---

1　'Taking as its starting point the idea that fashions do not arise on their own but are result of a broader changes, e.g. urban, economic, social, cultural'. A. Falierou, 'From the Ottoman Empire to the Turkish Republic: Women's Clothing Between Tradition and Modernity', in C. Vintil-Ghitulescu (ed.), *From Traditional Attire to Modern Dress, Modes of Identification, Modes of Recognition in the Balkans (XVIth–XXth Centuries)*, Cambridge Scholar Publishing, Cambridge, 2011, pp. 175–192, p. 176.

Istanbul (Constantinople), which was the focus of fashion, economy and political power.[2]

When Cyprus became part of the Ottoman Empire, the urban higher social classes responded by fostering the contemporary Ottoman trends in dress. The Cypriot Dragomans (interpreters) would, from then on, wear the *tzoupe* and the *calpac*. The *tzoupe* was a sleeved over-garment, open all the way down at the front. The best samples were lined with fur, such as sable. The *calpac* was a large fur hat. The female dress was composed of a long-sleeved caftan called *anteri* with a large, oval neckline. Women wore a chemise underneath, large pantaloons and a headdress. Cypriot Dragomans Chatzigeorgakis Kornesios and Christophakis Constantinou who engaged in bourgeois professions, both wore the typical Ottoman dress.[3]

During the centuries of Ottoman rule, oriental dress became fashionable, not only in Cyprus, but throughout the Empire. In 1738 Richard Pococke noticed:

> [t]he common people here dress much in the same manner as they do in the other islands of the Levant; but those who value themselves on being somewhat above the vulgar, dress like the Turks...[4]

Oriental dress was promptly adopted by the upper classes, by privileged persons who could afford to buy high quality imported items. Similar remarks were made by Giovanni Mariti, who lived on the island from 1760 to 1767:

> [t]he men dress 'alla Turca', like those of Constantinople, and so too the women of any position, except as to the adornment of the head, which is high and striking ... Their head dress consists of a collection of various handkerchiefs of muslin, prettily shaped, so that they form a kind of casque of a palm's height...[5]

---

2   The social hierarchy during the Ottoman rule is described in great detail in E. Rizopoulou-Egoumenidou, 'From Oriental (Ottoman) to European (Frankish) Dress: Dress as a Key Indicator of the Lifestyle and the Role of the Elite of Cyprus during the 18th and 19th Centuries', in C. Vintil-Ghitulescu (ed.), *From Traditional Attire to Modern Dress, Modes of Identification, Modes of Recognition in the Balkans (XVIth–XXth Centuries)*, Cambridge Scholar Publishing, Cambridge, 2011, pp. 129–143.

3   Analytical description of Ottoman Dress in Cyprus upper class. I. Papantoniou, *Greek Dress, From Ancient Times to the Early 20th Century*, Commercial Bank of Greece, Athens, 2000.

4   Quot. in C.D. Cobham, *Excerpta Cypria. Materials for a History of Cyprus*, Cambridge University Press, Cambridge, 1908, p. 268.

5   G. Mariti, *Travels in the Island of Cyprus*, trans. C.D. Cobham, Cambridge University Press, Cambridge, 1909, pp. 4–5.

However, the Ottoman dress code would soon begin to change. Despite strong objections by the Janissary and the Ulema (religious and judicial elite), whose dress preferences remained strictly traditional, Selim III (1761–1808) applied European changes to the military dress code, adopting Western-styled tight pants and short jackets for the army uniforms. Selim's military uniforms did not find success and died with him in 1808. According to Otto Friedrich von Richter who visited Cyprus in 1816, '[t]he attractions that Larnaca offers to a European returning from Asia are the various traces of Europeanism in the local dress code; here, the hat has pushed the turban aside'.[6] Sultan Mahmud II (1785 -1839) applied reforms to cover various aspects of individual life. In 1827, Sultan Mahmud designed a new military uniform, replacing the turban with the *fez*, a cylindrical cap of red felt wool with silk tassel hanging from the top. Later, the *fez*, together with a shirt with a collar, and frock coat was a standard dress for governmental employees.[7] European fashion was adopted by non-Muslim Ottoman women, especially Greek and Armenian. Non-Muslims were the first to adopt the Western fashion in clothing, while the Muslim community adopted changes more slowly or partially.

In 1821 the Greeks declared independence. Anticipating an insurrection movement in Cyprus, its Governor, Küçük Mehmet, adopted strict measures and tactics. The independent kingdom of Greece was established in 1833. The bonds between the Greeks of Cyprus and mainland Greece were strengthened, which also resulted in dress habits, since the Cypriot elite attempted to follow the trends set by the Greeks.

King Othon and Queen Amalia arrived from Bavaria to Greece in 1837. Upon arrival, they adopted a different interpretation of Greek popular costumes, such as the romantic folkloric dress worn at the court, known to Greeks as the 'Amalia' national Greek costume. The 'Amalia dress' was inspired by contemporary European fashion and the Greek traditional costume. Its composition was based on a combination of Eastern and Western dress elements. This was both a motion for a 'national dress' and a statement that the newly formed Greek kingdom had made the transition from its Oriental past to Western

---

6   R. C. Severis, 'Where the Turban is Substituted by the Hat. Otto Friedrich von Richter and Cyprus', *Thetis. Mannheimer Beiträge zur Klassischen Archäologie und Geschichte Griechenlands und Zyperns*, vol. 3, 1996, pp. 157–164, p. 160.

7   An approach of the reforms of the Sultans related to dress culture. O. Inal, 'Women's Fashions in Transition: Ottoman Borderlands and the Anglo-Ottoman Exchange of Costumes', in C. Vintil-Ghitulescu (ed.), *From Traditional Attire to Modern Dress, Modes of Identification, Modes of Recognition in the Balkans (XVIth–XXth Centuries)*, Cambridge Scholar Publishing, Cambridge, 2011, pp. 144–174.

modernity.[8] The 'Amalia dress' influenced both the independent as well as the Ottoman urban centers in the Balkans as well as in the islands, even in Cyprus.

In 1878, Cyprus was an undeveloped rural country lacking infrastructure and serious industrial production; however, progress was gradual and that was especially obvious in the urban centers. Europeanization trends were apparent before Cyprus was ceded to Great Britain.

3   The First Years of British Rule

The Cyprus Convention was ratified in Berlin the summer of 1878, between the Ottoman Empire and Great Britain. Great Britain would guarantee the military support of the Ottoman Empire against the threat of the Russian Empire, in exchange for the administration of the island of Cyprus for an annual fixed payment (tribute). Lieutenant-General Sir Garnet Wolseley was the first High Commissioner of Cyprus; the first Municipal Committee was established in 1882. By 1914, the Ottoman Empire had joined Germany in the first World War and Cyprus was annexed to the Great Britain. In 1923 Turkey waved its rights on Cyprus with the Treaty of Lausanne; in 1925 Cyprus was proclaimed a Crown Colony of the Great Britain.[9]

The British rule (1878–1960) was characterized by rapid social and economic growth in the urban districts, by contrast to slow development in the rural areas. The new status quo manifested as developments in the technical, political and social sectors, which would define both the setup and the character of urban Cyprus, as well as the Cypriots' way of life. The private and public spheres in Nicosia were to take shape against the background of the establishment of the new, British administration of Cyprus.

Soon after the British rule was established in 1878, the first female travelers began arriving on the island, describing in their notes the local dress attires. These were mostly English women, interested in getting to know the new

---

8   'The Amalia costume served as an elaborate language of symbolic practice and communication...Its composition was based on an extremely well-judged marriage of Eastern and Western sartorial elements'. See N. Macha-Bizoumi, 'The Amalia Costume: The Visual Symbol of the Transition from the Oriental Past to Western Modernity (19th Century)', in N. Lemos (ed.), *Patterns of Magnificence, Traditional and Reinvention in Greek Women's Costume*, The Hellenic Centre, London, 2014, pp. 48–55, p. 50. See also N. Macha-Bizoumi, 'Amalia Dress: The Invention of a New Costume Tradition in the Service of Greek National Identity', *Catwalk: The Journal of Fashion, Beauty and Style*, vol. 1, 2012, pp. 65–90.

9   W. Malinson, *Cyprus: A Historical Overview*, Press and Information Office, Nicosia, 2011.

British colony. Foreign travelers provided information about the costume worn by the inhabitants of the island in the opening years of the 19th century.[10]

Among all the women who travelled to Cyprus, the best known were Esme Scott-Stevenson and Annie Brassey in 1878 and Mrs. Lewis in 1893. In 1894, Magda Helena Schonherr accompanied her husband, German Archaeologist Max Ohnefalsch-Richter, to Cyprus. Having studied the customs and mores of the island and being able to make comparisons with those of antiquity, Magda Helena Schonherr was different from typical British women travelers of the time.[11] Older types of traditional village dress reminiscent of 18th century or earlier urban styles. The Oriental-looking type of long dress, open, with sleeves, low cut on the bosom, secured at the waist and worn over a white chemise and pantaloons, survived until the mid 20th century in the form of traditional costumes with the *saya*, in the most conservative regions of rural Cyprus.

Alongside the traditional costume there was a newer type of dress; the skirt which was European in form, arrived in Cyprus via the independent Greek mainland as a variation of the 'Amalia dress' of the late 19th century. This ensemble consisted of a pleated white cotton petticoat, a short off-white silk chemise with low sleeves and a long skirt. There is a black felt velvet jacket, the *sarka*, with two types of gold ornamentation. A *fez* was worn on the head, adorned with various cotton laces which formed flowers in relief.[12] Women in the cities wore different types of headdresses, including embroidered scarves made of silk or printed kerchiefs. In urban centers the way a woman was dressed and her jewelry was an indication of her social status.[13] References of men's costumes are few; however, Magda Ohnefalsch-Richter noted the most typical characteristics of the traditional Cypriot costume. This featured a shirt, a *vraka*

---

10   'Foreign travellers provide information about the costume worn by the inhabitants... they all concentrate on women's ensembles, ensembles that survived virtually unchanged till the beginning of 20th century'. D. Fotopoulos, *Athenians Fashions, at the Return of the 19th Century*, Hellenic Literary and Historical Archive (EΛΙΑ), Athens, 1999, p. 47.

11   The article refers to the description of both the attires and related costumes. E. Rizopoulou-Egoumenidou, 'Cypriot Costumes as Seen by Women Travelers during the First Decades of British Rule: Impressions and Reality', *Folk Life*, vol. 44, 2005, pp. 48–62.

12   'On the ensemble, there were two types of gold ornamentation. One is a local, Cypriot type, the other was perhaps brought over from Asia Minor or from the islands of the Eastern Aegean'. I. Papantoniou, *Greek Regional Costumes*, Peloponnesian Folklore Foundation, Nafplion, 1996, p. 154.

13   The book describes all the elements of Intangible Cultural Heritage related with information of local topography and social structure. A. Pouradier-Loizidou (ed.), *Elements of the Intangible Cultural Heritage of Cyprus*, Cyprus Research Centre, Cyprus National Committee for UNESCO, Nicosia, 2012.

(baggy trousers), *zimbouni* (waistcoat), *zostra* (a belt at the waist), a *fez* with or without a headscarf and boots.

4   British Innovations

A number of various small industries developed in Cyprus in the first half of the 20th century; they were however dependent on raw materials produced locally. A great variety of excellent quality silk, cotton and flax fabrics, manufactured on hand-looms were produced and sold in European, near Eastern and local markets. In 1926 a silk factory was established in Geroskipou, in the Pafos district. It operated till 1931, during World War II and occasionally later on. A flax-processing plant was founded in 1932 also in Geroskipou, which operated until 1956.[14]

The sewing machine was the hallmark of the industrial revolution at the end of the 19th century; this gave a huge push to illustrated fashion publications and patterns for embroidery. Sewing machines were sold in the countryside while schools taught professional cutting and tailoring and formal classroom training became more common.[15] The sewing machine made it possible for the amateur sewer to keep up with current fashions; paper patterns allowed women to make fashionable garments and brought fashion closer to the common people.[16]

The trend towards Europeanization is reflected in the increasing numbers of these new occupations, dressmakers, sewers and seamstresses, tailors, costumiers hat-makers, stocking-makers, hand knitters *etc.*[17]

---

14   C. Aristidou, 'Household Production-Industry-Occupations', in M. Chatzikosti (ed.), *Geroskipou: From Antiquity to Modern Times*, Municipality of Geroskipou, Geroskipou, 2008 [Χ. Αριστείδου, 'Οικοτεχνία – Βιομηχανία – Ασχολίες', *Γεροσκήπου: από την Αρχαιότητα μέχρι Σήμερα*, Μ. Χατζηκωστή (ed.), Δήμος Γεροσκήπου, 2008, Γεροσκήπου. This title is only available in Greek].

15   'Family members were largely responsible for teaching the next generation sewing skills throughout the nineteenth century. But the rise of women's education and home economics programs in women's colleges, formal classroom training, correspondence courses were offered...' In E.J. Spanabel, *A History of the Paper Pattern Industry, the Home Dressmaking Fashion Revolution*, Bloomsbury, London, 2014, p. 88.

16   'The sewing machine had a significant impact on fashions. Ready-made garments such as the hoop skirt and capes and cloaks for outdoors could be made rapidly, mass produced, and therefore were much less expensive than if they had to be hand-sewn. This contributed to their acceptance as current fashions'. P.G. Tortora, *Dress and Technology, from Prehistory to the Present*, Bloomsbury, London, 2015, p. 134.

17   'In 1901, dressmakers and seamstresses, all female, numbered 759, and tailors 420 male and 72 female. In 1911, the following were recorded: sewers and dressmakers 134 male

5   Lifestyle Changes during British Rule

Urbanization was one of the characteristics of the 20th century; urban centers were the staging ground upon which a new growing middle class with people involved in many new occupations was formed. This led to the emergence of a new upper class, different from the past. Members of the new elite founded the first industries, promoted trade and occupied high administrative posts. They created a 'modern' lifestyle and were the first who donned 'Frankish' attire.[18] This new era was reflected in the appearance and behavior of the inhabitants of urban environments. British rule enhanced the Europeanization of Cyprus to a large degree.

Europeanization reflects upon pastimes and leisure activities, sports and culture. The first football club was founded in Nicosia in 1900. Several football clubs were founded around 1924 when dealing with football was gaining popularity. Clubs, set up mainly by students and unions, begun appearing; such was the mixed group of the Pancyprian Gymnasium students and teaching, the English School group, the Turkish School in Nicosia, the Panergatikos Association (PS 11.), The English Club, the team of the Association 'Youth Union Trust', the 'People's Compound' etc.[19]

---

and 1,935 female; tailors, costumiers 423 male and 126 female; hat-makers 8 male and 16 female; stocking-makers 3 male and 353 female. By 1921, numbers in the above occupations had increased: sewers and dressmakers 14 male and 3,408 female; tailors, costumiers 650 male; stocking-makers 61 male and 228 female. In 1931, the following are recorded: dressmaker's employers 5 male and 2,886 female, dressmakers' assistants 2 male and 466 female; tailor's employers 563 male, and tailor's assistants 462 male and 2 female; hosiery knitters (machine) 85 female, and hand knitters 2 male and 44 female; makers of head-covers for ladies 30 female, all in Nicosia; sock-makers 2 male and 130 female ... By 1930, the making of stockings by machinery mainly for local use had spread considerably and the industry of hat-making, for ladies, was gaining ground ...' It is interesting to notice the differentiation that gender brings in the above recorded specialized occupations. E. Rizopoulou-Egoumenidou and A. Damdelen (eds.), *Turkish Cypriot Dress – The Aziz Damdelen Collection*, Cultural Heritage Series No. 6, Ministry of Education and Culture – Cultural Services, Nicosia, 2012, p. 78.

18   'An attachment to French and English styles of urban dress was now apparent. Initially it was men's dress, copying the Frankish, that was affected since women were excluded at the time for commercial transactions'. D. Fotopoulos, *Athenians Fashions*, p. 472.

19   M. Vrionidou-Giangou (ed.), *With Strings and Instruments, Pleasure and Entertainment in Cyprus from Antiquity to Independence*, Cultural Centre of Marfin Laiki Bank, Nicosia, 2008 [Μ. Βρυωνίδου-Γιάγκου (ed.), *Εν Χορδαίς και Οργάνοις. Διασκέδαση και Ψυχαγωγία στην Κύπρο από την Αρχαιότητα μέχρι την Ανεξαρτησία*, Cultural Centre of Marfin Laiki Bank, Nicosia, 2008. This title is only available in Greek].

Around 1900 the theatre also starts to become popular. The Nicosia Papado-poulou Theatre was a very elegant building, Italian in design, modern, the prime reference point of the capital. There, beyond the performances of local, Greek and foreign troupes, concerts were held, events, charity evenings, patriotic perfor-mances *etc.* It was a place where the original events were held and people enjoyed a dose of European culture.[20] The movie makes its appearance in 1907. The danc-es again were something that began to spread in the city; the most well-known of them all were the 'Bal Rouge', masked dances. The carnival was a popular custom of Limassol and Nicosia, while other events, parades, competitions, were taking place in the cultural urban activities lists of the time.[21]

These new social events created the need for a new type of clothing. The common dress consisted of two parts: a bodice and a skirt. The bodice was mounted on a boned silk foundation; it had a high neck, long sleeves, and it fastened with metal eyelets and hooks. There could be a handmade lace trim made on net with silk thread. The skirt could have been pleated for better ap-plication. The dress could be accompanied with gloves and a hat decorated with flowers. The bags and the hats were definitely imported due to the dif-ficulty of manufacturing them. The two most common bag types of the era were the tapestry bag and the sterling purse. The tapestry bag was ground with fabric decorated commonly with flowers; the sterling purse comprised of a silver frame with chain and a ball clasp. So, at that time people had started to systematically follow fashion trends and use imported goods, mainly from Great Britain.

6   Towards a New European Dress Country

With World War II breaking out and as Greece entered the war in 1940, the British authorities urged Greek Cypriots to fight on the side of Greece for free-dom. Many Cypriot volunteers took part in World War II, fighting on the side of the Allies. After the end of war, Cypriots were hoping that Cyprus' unification with Greece would be allowed; however, their demand for union with Greece was denied. This resulted to the launch of an armed struggle for independence in 1955, which was to carry on until 1959.[22]

---

20   Ibid.

21   Ibid.

22   A. Pavlides, *History of the Island of Cyprus. From the Beginning until Today*, Epifaniou, Nicosia, 2013 ['Α. Παυλίδης, *Ιστορία της Νήσου Κύπρου. Από την Αρχή έως Σήμερα*, Επιφανίου, Λευκωσία, 2013. This title is only available in Greek].

Cypriots tried to find many ways to protest apart from the armed struggle. Their boycott movement against imported fabrics and clothes was the most popular action. The *alatzietina* cotton dresses and costumes were originally meant as an act of 'passive resistance' of the Cypriots against the British rule during the 1955–1959 anti-colonial struggles. These clothes and fabrics were made in Cyprus, utilizing only locally made materials; given the fact that the island produced first class cotton it was suggested that cotton cloth be woven and used. Dresses were made by *alatzia* and were decorated with traditional embroidery or needlework.[23]

The concept behind 'passive resistance' was a policy of non-violent economic warfare, following the example of India; this movement would make a systematic effort to financially weaken the government by refraining from buying and consuming British goods. The boycott targeted the material, and not the tailoring and the design of the garments; this was strong indication that the Europeanization had been accomplished to a great extent.

The signing of the London and Zurich Treaty in February 1959 heralded a new period of changes. On 13 December 1959, Archbishop Makarios III was elected first President of the newly independent state, with Fazil Küçük as Vice-President. On 15 August 1960, the island was officially proclaimed the Independent Republic of Cyprus; Nicosia has been its capital city since.[24] Under this new idea of liberation and democracy people could now express themselves as Europeans and freely choose attire closer to their preference. Eponymous tailors begun appearing, creating fashionable dresses and suits. The full-length dress with short sleeves, round neckline, bearing colorful prints, was a European way to celebrate this new beginning.

---

23   As noted by Georgios Grivas-Digenis, EOKA's military leader, '[t]he youth of Cyprus, the first to conform to EOKA's institutions regarding the support of Greek goods, is dressed in Cypriot Alatzia, woven by the hands of their mothers, and Cypriot loom is revived. Hundreds of Cypriot maidens find work at the loom... Alatzias is becoming Cyprus national dress'. A. Hamatsou, 'Politicization of Dress: Dress as a Means of Resistance in Early Morden and Contemporary Cyprus', *Endyesthai – Towards a Costume Culture Museum*, Peloponnesian Folklore Foundation, Nafplion, 2010, pp. 131–135, pp. 134–135.

24   This book aims to be a comprehensive analysis of the constitutional development of Cyprus during the period of British rule; this constitutional development was limited and distorted to a dramatic extent as a result of British political priorities. It also integrates a broader discussion on the basic peculiarities of Cypriot constitutional development, reflecting upon the internationalization of the issue in the 1950s. E. Chatzivasiliou, *The Cyprus Issue 1878–1960. The Constitutional Aspect*, Ellinika Grammata, Athens, 1998 [E. Χατζηβασιλείου, *Το Κυπριακό Ζήτημα 1878–1960. Η Συνταγματική Πτυχή* Ελληνικά Γράμματα, Αθήνα, 1998. This title is only available in Greek].

7 Conclusion

The development and modernization of the urban environment reflect upon constant changes in all kinds of social interactions; such changes emerge slowly after the 19th century, shaping a new universal language for the interaction of people, now that travelling and exchanging goods and ideas is easier than ever before. The importance of class, financial status, age, background, begins to fade in contrast to fashion and creativity which represent the next evolutionary step for the social interaction of individuals.[25]

In Cyprus, as in the rest of Europe, trends become fashion with a strong notion of multiculturalism and cosmopolitanism. These trends become lifestyle and trading commodities. The need for fashion and intellectualism derives from the growth of urbanization. The urban environment is no longer being utilized as a protective barrier against elements of nature or invading forces; it is now the launching pad for the human expression and creativity. It is used as an interaction platform for different cultures and trends.

For Cyprus, the Europeanization opened new horizons and brought in accelerated progress and evolution. Through a multi-cultural environment, a new identity was formed, integrating the population of the island.

Bibliography

Aristidou, C., 'Household Production-Industry-Occupations', in M. Chatzikosti (ed.), *Geroskipou: From Antiquity to Modern Times*. Municipality of Geroskipou, Geroskipou, 2008 [orig. Αριστείδου, Χ., 'Οικοτεχνία – Βιομηχανία – Ασχολίες', Μ. Χατζηκωστή (eds), *Γεροσκήπου: από την Αρχαιότητα μέχρι Σήμερα, Δήμος Γεροσκήπου,* Γεροσκήπου, 2008].

Breward, C., *Fashioning London, Clothing and the Modern Metropolis*. Berg, Oxford and New York, NY, 2000.

Chatzivasiliou, E., *The Cyprus Issue 1878–1960. The Constitutional Aspect*. Ellinika Grammata, Athens, 1998 [orig: Χατζηβασιλείου, Ε., *Το Κυπριακό Ζήτημα 1878–1960. Η Συνταγματική Πτυχή. Ελληνικά Γράμματα, Αθήνα, 1998*].

---

25   'The growing commodification of fashionable trends and interests, emphasized the worldly and the cosmopolitan. As Breward observes, the growing importance of the city as a focus of social interaction and display and a sense of cosmopolitism'. A. Yagou, 'Dress Modernity and Theories of Biological Evolution in the 19th Century Greece', in C. Vintil-Ghitulescu (ed.) *From Traditional Attire to Modern Dress, Modes of Identification, Modes of Recognition in the Balkans (XVIth–XXth Centuries)*, Cambridge Scholar Publishing, Cambridge, 2011, pp. 194–211, p. 197.

Cobham, C. D., *Excerpta Cypria. Materials for a History of Cyprus.* Cambridge University Press, Cambridge, 1908.

Dimitriou, M., *The Treasures of Ethnographic Museum of Cyprus.* Ethnographic Museum of Cyprus & Society of Cypriot Studies, Nicosia, 2002 [orig: Δημητρίου, Μ., *Θησαυροί του Εθνογραφικού Μουσείου Κύπρου,* Εθνογραφικό Μουσείο Κύπρου & Εταιρεία Κυπριακών Σπουδών, Λευκωσία, 2002].

Falierou, A., 'From the Ottoman Empire to the Turkish Republic: Women's Clothing Between Tradition and Modernity', in C. Vintil-Ghitulescu (ed.), *From Traditional Attire to Modern Dress, Modes of Identification, Modes of Recognition in the Balkans (XVIth–XXth Centuries).* Cambridge Scholar Publishing, Cambridge, 2011, pp. 175–192.

Fotopoulos, D., *Athenians Fashions, at the Return of the 19th Century.* Hellenic Literary and Historical Archive (ΕΛΙΑ), Athens, 1999.

Hamatsou, A., 'Politicization of Dress: Dress as a Means of Resistance in Early Morden and Contemporary Cyprus', *Endyesthai – Towards a Costume Culture Museum,* Peloponnesian Folklore Foundation, Nafplion, 2010, pp. 131–135.

Inal, O., 'Women's Fashions in Transition: Ottoman Borderlands and the Anglo-Ottoman Exchange of Costumes', in C. Vintil-Ghitulescu (ed.), *From Traditional Attire to Modern Dress, Modes of Identification, Modes of Recognition in the Balkans (XVIth–XXth Centuries).* Cambridge Scholar Publishing, Cambridge, 2011, pp. 144–174.

Ipek, S., 'Women's Fashion at the Ottoman Court in the 18th and 19th Centuries' [proceedings], in X. Politou (ed.), *Endyesthai (To Dress): Historical, Sociological and Methodological Approaches,* Peloponnesian Folklore Foundation, Nafplion, 2012, pp. 30–34.

Macha-Bizoumi, N., 'Amalia Dress: The Invention of a New Costume Tradition in the Service of Greek National Identity', *Catwalk: The Journal of Fashion, Beauty and Style,* vol. 1, 2012, pp. 65–90.

Macha-Bizoumi, N., 'The Amalia Costume: The Visual Symbol of the Transition from the Oriental Past to Western Modernity (19th Century)', in N. Lemos (ed.), *Patterns of Magnificence, Traditional and Reinvention in Greek Women's Costume.* The Hellenic Centre, London, 2014, pp. 48–55.

Malinson, W., *Cyprus: A Historical Overview.* Press and Information Office, Nicosia, 2011.

Mariti, G., *Travels in the Island of Cyprus.* Trans. C.D. Cobham. Cambridge University Press, Cambridge, 1909.

Oikonomidou-Mpotsiou, F. (ed.), *People and Objects: Life Relations, New additions to the Museum from Grants.* Folklore and Ethnological Museum of Macedonia – Thrace, Thessaloniki, 2009 [orig: Οικονομίδου – Μπότσιου, Φ. (ed.), *Άνθρωποι και Αντικείμενα: Σχέσεις Ζωής, Νέα Αποκτήματα από Δωρεές στο Μουσείο,* Λαογραφικό και Εθνολογικό Μουσείο Μακεδονίας – Θράκης, Θεσσαλονίκη, 2009].

Papadimitriou, E., *Cypriot Costumes*. Peloponnesian Folklore Foundation & Folk Art Museum of the Society of Cypriot Studies, Athens, 1991.

Papantoniou, I., 'Cypriot Costume', in K. Kanelopoulos (ed.), *Proceedings of the 3rd Symposium of Cypriot Folklore Culture*. Peloponnesian Folklore Foundation, Nafplio, 1999, pp. 39–44 [orig: Παπαντωνίου, I., 'Κυπριακή Ενδυμασιολογία', K. Κανελόπουλος (ed.), *Πρακτικά Γ' Συμποσίου Κυπριακής Λαογραφίας*, Πελοποννησιακό Λαογραφικό Ίδρυμα, Ναύπλιο, 1999, pp. 39–44].

Papantoniou, I., *Greek Dress, From Ancient Times to the Early 20th Century*. Commercial Bank of Greece, Athens, 2000, pp. 130–138.

Papantoniou, I., *Greek Regional Costumes*. Peloponnesian Folklore Foundation, Nafplion, 1996.

Papantoniou, I., *Greek Women's Dress and Jewellery Past and Present*. Ministry of Culture and Sciences & Peloponnesian Folklore Foundation, Nafplion, 1985.

Papantoniou, I., 'The Development of Costume in the Sphere of Influence of Greek Civilisation', in N. Lemos (ed.), *Patterns of Magnificence, Traditional and Reinvention in Greek Women's Costume*. The Hellenic Centre, London, 2014, pp.16–27.

Pavlides, A., *History of the Island of Cyprus. From the Beginning until Today*. Epifaniou, Nicosia, 2013 [orig: Ά. Παυλίδης, *Ιστορία της Νήσου Κύπρου. Από την Αρχή έως Σήμερα*, Επιφανίου, Λευκωσία, 2013].

Pieridi, A., *Cypriot Folklore Art*. Publications of the Society of Cypriot Studies, Nicosia, 1991 [orig: Πιερίδη, Α., *Κυπριακή Λαϊκή Τέχνη*, Δημοσιεύματα της Εταιρείας Κυπριακών Σπουδών, Λευκωσία, 1991].

Politou, X., 'The Costume of the Ladies-in-Waiting to Queen Olga: Court Elegance Using Local Materials', in N. Lemos (ed.), *Patterns of Magnificence, Traditional and Reinvention in Greek Women's Costume*. The Hellenic Centre, London, 2014, pp. 56–63.

Pouradier-Loizidou, A. (ed.), *Elements of the Intangible Cultural Heritage of Cyprus*. Cyprus Research Centre, Cyprus National Committee for UNESCO, Nicosia, 2012.

Rizopoulou-Egoumenidou, E., 'Cypriot Costumes as Seen by Women Travelers during the First Decades of British Rule: Impressions and Reality', *Folk Life*, vol. 44, 2005, pp. 48–62.

Rizopoulou-Egoumenidou, E., 'Cypriot Costume at the End of the 19th Century', *The Cypriot Costumes of the National Historical Museum. A Flashback to the World of Cyprus on the Dawn of the 20th Century*. KAPON, Athens, 1999, pp. 50–79 [orig: Ριζοπούλου – Ηγουμενίδου, Ε., 'Η Κυπριακή Ενδυμασία στα Τέλη του 19ου Αιώνα', *Οι Κυπριακές Φορεσιές του Εθνικού Ιστορικού Μουσείου. Μια Αναδρομή στον Κόσμο της Κύπρου την Αυγή του 20ου Αιώνα*, ΚΑΠΟΝ, Αθήνα, 1999, pp. 50–79].

Rizopoulou-Egoumenidou, E., 'From Oriental (Ottoman) to European (Frankish) Dress: Dress as a Key Indicator of the Lifestyle and the Role of the Elite of Cyprus during the 18th and 19th Centuries', in C. Vintil-Ghitulescu (ed.), *From Traditional Attire to Modern Dress, Modes of Identification, Modes of Recognition in the Balkans*

(*XVIth–XXth Centuries*). Cambridge Scholar Publishing, Cambridge, 2011, pp. 129–143.

Rizopoulou-Egoumenidou, E., 'Lifestyle and Social Behaviour of the Elite of Cyprus, 1775–1821', *Folk Life*, vol. 48, 2010, pp. 48–62.

Rizopoulou-Egoumenidou, E., *The Urban Apparel of Cyprus in the 18th and 19th Century*. Cyprus Bank Cultural Foundation, Nicosia, 1996 [orig: Ριζοπούλου-Ηγουμενίδου, Ε., *Η Αστική Ενδυμασία της Κύπρου κατά τον 18ο και 19ο Αιώνα*, Πολιτιστικό Ίδρυμα Τραπέζης Κύπρου, Λευκωσία, 1996].

Rizopoulou-Egoumenidou, E., and A. Damdelen (eds.), *Turkish Cypriot Dress – The Aziz Damdelen Collection*, Cultural Heritage Series No. 6, Ministry of Education and Culture – Cultural Services, Nicosia, 2012.

Severis, R.C., 'Where the Turban is Substituted by the Hat. Otto Friedrich von Richter and Cyprus', *Thetis. Mannheimer Beiträge zur Klassischen Archäologie und Geschichte Griechenlands und Zyperns*, vol. 3, 1996, pp. 157–164.

Spanabel, E.J., *A History of the Paper Pattern Industry, the Home Dressmaking Fashion Revolution*. Bloomsbury, London, 2014.

The Leventis Municipal Museum of Nicosia [official website] <http://www.nicosia.org.cy/en-GB/discover/museums/leventis-municipal-museum> (Accessed 20 June 2015).

Tortora, P. G., *Dress and Technology, from Prehistory to the Present*. Bloomsbury, London, 2015.

Vrionidou-Giangou, M. (ed.), *With Strings and Instruments, Pleasure and Entertainment in Cyprus from Antiquity to Independence*. Cultural Centre of Marfin Laiki Bank, Nicosia, 2008 [orig. Βρυωνίδου-Γιάγκου, Μ., (eds.) *Εν Χορδαίς και Οργάνοις. Διασκέδαση και Ψυχαγωγία στην Κύπρο από την Αρχαιότητα μέχρι την Ανεξαρτησία*, Cultural Centre of Marfin Laiki Bank, Λευκωσία, 2008].

Welters, L., 'Ethnicity in Greek Dress', in J. B. Eicher (ed.), *Dress and Ethnicity, Change Across Space and Time*. Berg, Oxford and New York, NY, 1999, pp. 53–77.

Welters, L., 'Dress and Community' [proceeding], in X. Politou (ed.), *Endymatologika* vol. 4, Peloponnesian Folklore Foundation, Nafplion, 2010, pp. 67–75.

Yagou, A., 'Dress Modernity and Theories of Biological Evolution in the 19th Century Greece', in C. Vintil-Ghitulescu (ed.), *From Traditional Attire to Modern Dress, Modes of Identification, Modes of Recognition in the Balkans (XVIth–XXth Centuries)*. Cambridge Scholar Publishing, Cambridge, 201, pp. 194–211.

Xristodoulou, D., 'Greek Tailors and Biedermeier: Othon's Foustanela and Amalia's Costume', *Archaeology and Arts*, vol. 84, 2002, pp. 30–36 [Χριστοδούλου, Δ., Ελληνορράπται και Biedermeier: η Φουστανέλα του Όθωνα και Στολή της Αμαλίας', *Αρχαιολογία και Τέχνες*, vol. 84, 2002, pp. 30–36].

CHAPTER 20

Process and *Mani Sapienti*: Arte Povera and the Default to Order

Laura Petican

Abstract

In the late 1960s, Arte Povera artist Marisa Merz asserted a process-based object as the foundation of a practice rooted in the politics of artistic labor. Her *Scarpette*, tiny shoes knitted with copper wire or nylon thread, were neither functional nor coldly conceptual. Her colleague Alighiero Boetti contemporaneously launched a geopolitical project that left aesthetic decisions up to his Afghan and Pakistani collaborators, women highly skilled in the craft of embroidery. Both Merz and Boetti had defaulted to a predetermined order, a repetitive action, a system, as a way of marking their engagement with the transhistorical and universal processes of everyday life. Their works evoke the *mani sapienti* of fashion and design ateliers – the painstaking handiwork hierarchically positioned somewhere beneath the maestro's vision – and align the 1960s Italian avant-garde with concurrent advances in craft and design. What is to distinguish Merz's knitting and Boetti's outsourced embroidery from Ottavio Missoni's zigzagging knitting machines? Largely unbeknownst to contemporary fashion consumers, Missoni's iconic knitwear was born of found machinery, capable of generating one motif that by default, became its hallmark. The repetitive, systematic processes of hand-stitching, sewing, and embroidery associated with the fashion industry became the mechanisms of radical aesthetic engagement. In the post-World War II era, Italian artists and artisans alike had 'opted out' of a trickle-down dynamic in aesthetic experimentation. Conceding to a predetermined system – knitting, embroidery, machines – they defaulted to order and revered the *mani sapienti* processes of Italy's fashion industry in an interdisciplinary, non-hierarchical socio-cultural practice.

Keywords

Marisa Merz – Alighiero Boetti – Missoni – *mani sapienti /petites mains* – process – fashion – design – art – radicalism – aesthetics – experimentation – interdisciplinary

1   Introduction

In 1976, the renowned Italian art critic and art historian Achille Bonito Oliva proclaimed in an article titled 'Process, Concept and Behaviour in Italian Art' that art is not '[...] a specialized activity but an adventure involving all levels of existence, enabling man as artist to live through an experience which has nothing to do with art as a so-called profession'.[1] What Bonito Oliva seemed to be referring to was a radical conception of aesthetic engagement that moved beyond the object fetish of art historiography, toward a journey centred in a democratic experience, free of hierarchy and convention, and with the goal of deploying all the matter of existence for the total autonomy of art. Through non-specialization, Bonito Oliva prescribed the conditions for indiscriminate participation in aesthetic and political processes; those of the artist, the philosopher, the craftsperson, the artisan, the politician, the seamstress, the builder, the mathematician, the mason, and the technician. In doing so, Bonito Oliva also foretold the interdisciplinary practices of the late 20th and 21st centuries' art, design, and fashion movements, those particularly in Italy, where members of Arte Povera,[2] Missoni, and innumerable other designers forged thorough investigations of the very tenets of their disciplines. While critics such as Germano Celant proclaimed that 'animals, vegetables and minerals take part in the world of art',[3] artists and designers were entrenched in investigations that would overturn ways in which materials were understood and experienced, in which aesthetic experience and everyday life were consolidated, and in which the realms of industry and the domestic, of fine art, craft, and design were integrated toward an expression of social and political engagement.

Within this climate of radical experimentation, artists such as Marisa Merz (b. 1926) and Alighiero Boetti (1940–1994), both members of the Italian art movement Arte Povera, constructed aesthetic practices as embodiments of the immersive experience of the 'poor theatre'.[4] Their works, often rendered in materials that reached beyond the confines of fine art conventions, made use of industrial processes and practices, defaulting to the rote mechanics of

1   A. Bonito Oliva, 'Process, Concept and Behaviour in Italian Art', *Studio International*, vol. 191, no. 979, 1976, pp. 3–9, p. 3.

2   Arte Povera is the name given to an Italian art movement that emerged in the late 1960s in the north of Italy. The term was coined by Italian art critic Germano Celant on the occasion of an exhibition at Galleria La Bertesca in Genoa (Italy) in 1967.

3   G. Celant, 'Introduction', *Arte Povera*, Praeger, New York, NY, 1969, pp. 225–230, p. 225.

4   The concept of the 'poor theater' is credited to the Polish theatre director and theorist Jerzy Grotowski (1933–1999). See J. Grotowski, *Towards a Poor Theatre*, ed. E. Barba, Routledge, New York, NY, 1968.

patterns, systems, and matrices. It was here where copper, metal, found wood, wool, yarn, and embroidery and knitting needles found their way from the artists' hands to the hands of various collaborators, from artist to maker, and from Bonito Oliva's 'so-called profession' to the skilled professions of craftspeople. In the process, Italian artists and designers breached the limits of their respective disciplines and engaged with the dynamics of everyday life, transgressing the margins of their fields of practice toward an inclusive and engaged encounter.

From this perspective, this chapter will examine the radical practices of Merz, Boetti, and the Italian fashion house Missoni in order to demonstrate the non-hierarchical and democratic approaches taken by each in efforts to circumvent the elitist, detached aspects of their disciplines, as evidence of their interests in navigating the political and economic climate of post-World War II Italy. The chapter will examine selected works by each that demonstrate a reverence for craft and the *mani sapienti*[5] that play an integral role in the process-oriented, participatory, and socially transformative aesthetic experiences of Italy's 20th and 21st century art, fashion, and design. Merz, Boetti, and Missoni engaged in craft processes that combined aspects of conceptual abstraction and technical experimentation that facilitated adaption to the post-World War II environment and the geopolitics of object-based practices. These developments not only allowed for economic survival during the *miracolo italiano*,[6] they engendered cultural dialogue within a contemporary existence precariously balanced between nature and culture during the post-war economic boom and ensuing decades. The paper will offer a holistic and interdisciplinary interpretation of these cultural figures regarding their use of craft, the technical expertise of craftspeople, and an experimental approach to artistic activity wherein materials are used to enact intellectual, political, and social processes.

2   *Mani Sapienti* and Found Machines

At the presentation of Karl Lagerfeld's Chanel Haute Couture Fall/Winter 2016/2017 show in Paris at the Grand Palais on 5 July 2016, notions of craft and process were on full display to the discerning eyes of fashion's cognoscenti.

---

5   The term *mani sapienti* is used here somewhat interchangeably with *petites mains*, as an expression that refers to the skilled artisans employed in a couture atelier who are responsible for the fine handiwork and detailing in the finishing of couture garments. Roughly translated, it is understood as 'knowledgeable hands'.

6   The *miracolo italiano* is a term given to the era of post-World War II economic recovery and regeneration in Italy that was aided by the Marshall Plan.

Featured alongside Lagerfeld's masterful couture creations rendered in the house's signature tweed, elaborate embroidery and beading, were not only bolts of fabric and mannequins, sketches, sewing machines and cutting tables, but the *petites mains* themselves, the often overlooked, though highly skilled and revered craftspeople responsible for the fine handiwork that finishes and embellishes the garments. Lagerfeld's vision for this show was inspired by and indeed dedicated to these artisans, with whom the maestro posed for a photo toward the end.[7] That Lagerfeld holds the *petites mains* in such high estimation is testament not only to his own appreciation for their skills and contributions to the house's esteem, but also to the fact that recently, according to *The Daily Telegraph*'s Lisa Armstrong, ateliers are busier than they have been for years, in light of the era of fast fashion and its overtly mechanized nature. In this sense, Lagerfeld's gesture is understood as a nod to 'the human aspect' of couture,[8] a sentiment echoed in Dior artistic director Maria Grazia Chiuri's recent endorsement of the *petites mains* as an integral component of Dior's legacy, providing a 'human touch' to the realm of couture, and contributing to the atelier's collective spirit of 'teamwork'.[9]

The *petites mains* are known as such to the wider realm of fashion ateliers beyond Paris; in Italy, they are known as *mani sapienti* – knowledgeable or expert hands similarly skilled in the delicate embroidery, beading, and finishing techniques of couture and luxury goods.[10] The term is not as widely used in

7   M.-L. Gumuchian, 'Lagerfeld Pays Tribute to Atelier Seamstresses at Chanel Show', *Reuters Entertainment News*, 5 July 2016 <https://www.reuters.com/article/us-fashion-paris-chanel/lagerfeld-pays-tribute-to-atelier-seamstresses-at-chanel-show-idUSKCN0ZL25O> (Accessed 16 November 2017).

8   L. Armstrong, 'Inside the Haute Couture Atelier at Chanel – At Yesterday's Chanel Haute Couture Show in Paris, Karl Lagerfeld Unveiled his Latest Collection in Front of the Talented Hands That Create it', *The Daily Telegraph*, 6 July 2016, p. 23.

9   In an online video titled 'Dior's Les Petites Mains/The Little Hands' presented by *The Business of Fashion* and sponsored by Christian Dior Couture, 'les petites mains' are defined as (i) '[t]he appellation for seamstresses that work in Paris' haute couture ateliers', and (ii) '[t]he first professional rank in an atelier workforce'. 'Dior's Les Petites Mains/The Little Hands' [video], *The Business of Fashion* (sponsored by Christian Dior Couture) <https://www.businessoffashion.com/articles/video/les-petites-mains?utm_source=Subscribers&utm_campaign=5b93d65fac-the-trouble-with-topshop-nike-launches-flyleather-&utm_medium=email&utm_term=0_d2191372b3-5b93d65fac-419439753> (Accessed 8 September 2017).

10   Enrico Matzeu translates directly from the French term as *piccole mani* ('little hands'), although the present author has been advised that there is no such direct translation in Italian; rather, the term *mani sapienti* is used to connote a similar notion of knowledgeable/talented hands, as per an e-mail correspondence (8 September 2017) with Prof. Dr. Luca Lo Sicco di Leonvago, Associate Chair and Professor of Fashion Marketing and Management, School of Fashion, SCAD, Atlanta, Georgia. See E. Matzeu, 'Piccola guida alla haute

Italy, although the traditions of craftsmanship and technical expertise in the Italian fashion industry have in fact been those employed by the French fashion industry since its formalization at the outset of the Industrial Revolution in the late 19th century.

The *mani sapienti* of Italy's fashion design industry in the mid 20th century were presented with a unique set of circumstances however, that led to a tradition of experimentation and openness where materials and technique are concerned. While the rise of Fascism promoted an appreciation of local craftsmanship earlier in the century, heightened by increasing nationalist sentiment, traditional techniques such as embroidery and lacework were revived with the help of new vocational schools.[11] As fashion historian Bonizza Giordani Aragno writes, Benito Mussolini's declaration in 1935 of national autarchy caused a shortage of traditional materials, which provoked experimentation with alternative, sometimes more humble materials such as rope, flax, raffia, and various by-products.[12] The 'inventiveness' of this new needs-based approach to fashion design contributed to an environment of experimentation that saw the combination of elevated skill with as yet-unrefined materials in new fashion forms. As Giordani Aragno writes, '[...] the skilled application of unusual materials and the bold juxtaposition of "poor" and precious materials was certainly striking', and that '[t]his authentic Italian style did not aspire to embody either haute couture or prêt-à-porter, but rather stood as a reality of its own, and came to be known as Boutique fashion'.[13]

This make-do spirit was also to be observed in the founding of the Italian fashion house Missoni by Ottavio Missoni in 1953. Missoni's discovery of abandoned knitting machines was in fact the starting point of a fashion empire constructed upon these very notions of experimentation and necessity, culminating is what is known as the 'Missoni alphabet'.[14] This dynamic is what Giordani Aragno characterizes as 'the inventiveness of poverty',[15] and locates

couture', *Il Post Moda*, 26 January 2016 <http://www.ilpost.it/2016/01/26/piccola-guida-alla-haute-couture/> (Accessed 16 November 2017).

11   B. Giordani Aragno, 'Boutique Fashion, a Sum of Concepts and Innovations', in A. Ellis (ed.), *Italian Glamour: the Essence of Italian Fashion From the Postwar Years to the Present Day: the Enrico Quinto and Paolo Tinarelli Collection*, Skira, Milan, 2014, pp. 11–15.

12   Ibid.

13   Ibid., p.11. Boutique fashion was officially launched with a fashion show in Florence held on 12 February 1951, organized by Emilio Pucci, Marquise Olga de Gresy, Baroness Clarette Galloti, and Franco Bertoli.

14   E. Zanella, 'They are Museum Pieces, but You Can Still Wear Them', *Missoni Art Colour* [exhibition catalogue], Skira Rizzoli, New York, NY, 2016, pp. 25–39, p. 29.

15   Giordani Aragno, 'Boutique Fashion', p. 11.

its products in several boutiques in Italy which became new locales for intellectual activity, claiming that

> items of different provenance and different functions 'coexisted', at the crossroads between art and fashion. Here one could find everything that craftsmanship and the avant-garde had to offer.[16]

The founding of Missoni was recently commemorated in the exhibition catalogue *Missoni Art Colour*, published by Skira Rizzoli in 2016 on the occasion of the exhibitions at the Fashion and Textile Museum in London and Museo MA*GA Gallarate.[17] In it, the notion of 'roots' is used to evoke the genesis of an interdisciplinary aesthetic practice centred in both fashion and the visual arts, with the historical avant-garde as its birthright. Delaunay, Kandinsky, Klee, and the Futurists Balla and Severini, are credited with establishing the foundation of an 'expressive language' articulated on the 'rhythmic composition of shapes and colours used with purity', that Missoni has translated as 'central motifs' in their designs.[18] The Italian art critic and art historian Luciano Caramel wrote of this interdisciplinary tendency in the history of Missoni's legacy, stating that

> the restrictive distinction between on the one hand art, such as painting, sculpture, architecture and also music, literature and poetry, and on the other the applied arts, sometimes still known as the 'minor' arts, is, fortunately, more and more a thing of the past, the relic of a palaeoideologist philosophical aesthetic.[19]

A 1975 exhibition titled *Missoni and the Machine-Magician*[20] included a text by the art critic Guido Ballo, Chair of Art History at the Brera Academy of Fine Arts in Milan in the 1970s, who discussed the 'creative diligence' with which Missoni rendered works on a machine, that conveyed '[...] the value of knitted

---

16   Ibid.

17   The exhibition at the Museo MA*GA Gallarate took place from 19 April to 24 January 2016, and at the Fashion and Textile Museum (London), from 6 May to 4 September 2016.

18   See 'Le radici/Roots', *Missoni Art Colour*, Skira Rizzoli Publications, Inc., New York, NY, 2016, p. 49.

19   L. Caramel, 'Missoni, Art and Colour. Between Visible and Invisible', *Missoni Art Colour* [exhibition catalogue], Skira Rizzoli, New York, NY, 2016, pp.17–23, p. 17.

20   The exhibition was originally titled *Missoni e la macchina-mago* and was held in September 1975 at the Navigliovenezia Art Gallery in Venice (Italy). See L. Missoni, 'Macchina mago/The Machine-Magician', *Missoni Art Colour* [exhibition catalogue], Skira Rizzoli, New York, NY, 2016, pp. 41–43.

fabric, almost though it had been hand-made'.[21] According to Caramel, Missoni had embraced 'the precepts of craftsmanship' in what Ballo described as 'an often loose weave, without the anonymous pedantry of the machine', suggesting that for Missoni 'the machine itself is another continuation of the hand [...], the Machine-Magician'.[22] Caramel continues to quote Ballo regarding Missoni's 'intelligently open attitude to contemporary reality, also in artistic production.'[23]

> [...] at a time when aesthetic manifestations have expanded to the point of overflowing, this value of the hand-and-mind and of the Machine-Magician is not a return to the past or a step backwards: it is simply a matter of realizing the possibilities that artistic precepts can still offer so naturally in the midst of a technological civilization.[24]

For Missoni, the knitting machines were another incarnation of the *mani sapienti* of earlier couture and Boutique fashion ateliers which afforded the opportunity to experiment with process toward a simultaneously ordered yet unpredictable outcome.

In describing the layout of the *Missoni Art Colour* exhibition, Caramel notes its curatorial approach in displaying works by Ottavio Missoni alongside other Modern masters. He writes that the artists in this exhibition, 'numerous and of high quality', are aligned in such a way to produce 'an enlightening dialogue' centred on 'research into colour, space, rhythm, sign and matter'.[25] The result is that visitors are invited to 'evaluate assonances and contrasts, stepping outside of static academic schemata and purely, or prevalently, theoretical and technical considerations'.[26] Emma Zanella, Director of the Museo MA*GA Gallarate, writes of the ongoing debate surrounding the nature of the relationship between the arts and their respective 'limits', proposing that a shift in focus to the subject and one's senses encourages a fluidity of experience that points out the 'temporary nature of the limits set'.[27] She argues for a contemporaneity in Missoni's *oeuvre* situated within a 'great history' of culture and the arts wherein 'the language of art is no longer perceived as a tool of representation,

---

21   Guido Ballo, cited in L. Caramel, 'Missoni, Art and Colour', p. 18.
22   Ibid.
23   Ibid.
24   Ibid.
25   Ibid., p. 23.
26   Ibid.
27   E. Zanella. 'They Are Museum Pieces', p. 26.

but itself becomes representation'.[28] These elements of process, or the 'liquid alphabet' found in Missoni's studies for garments underlines his osmotic relationship with the environment, drawing as he did on 'the vitality and the energy of nature, of plants, of flowers, of the undergrowth, of the sea and sky in unfettered liberty'.[29]

It was this sense of fluidity that fueled the Missonis' approach to design, centred on a process of 'action and reaction',[30] guided by the practical considerations necessary to their equipment. Citing Ottavio Missoni, Zanella recounts the story of how the limits of the early knitting machines contributed to what are now iconic designs:

> [...] the truth is that we had machines that could only make stripes. We can certainly say that we made stripes of all colours and sizes, using them not only horizontally and vertically, but also diagonally and even in zigzag. And when we got our hands on a machine that could do horizontal and vertical stripes at the same time we plunged headlong into the huge range of Scottish tartan fabrics.[31]

The resulting designs, neither intentional nor random, were, as described by Zanella, consistent in their infinite variety[32] and greatly influenced by the abstract art movement of the 1930s that had taken hold in Milan.

Missoni's experiments with form, colour, and technique took his practice toward the purely decorative as well. His tapestries, described as a 'short-circuit between art and design', push the boundaries of his creative process beyond the functionality of the garments, 'blending their research into the material, into colour and into sign with the compositional freedom of artistic making ...'.[33] In the introduction to an exhibition catalogue of 1981, gallerist Renato Cardazzo is quoted as writing, 'Missoni is not a factory, he is not a designer but simply an artist'.[34] Principles of measure, rhythm, and method provided the foundation of Missoni's process, as they had done for the avant-garde

---

28   Ibid., p. 27.
29   Ibid., p. 30.
30   Ibid., p. 33.
31   Ibid., p. 34.
32   Ibid.
33   Ibid., p. 37.
34   R. Cardazzo, cit. in O. Missoni, 'L'emozione della materia/Passion for Materials', *Missoni Art Colour* [exhibition catalogue], Skira Rizzoli, New York, NY, 2016, pp.152–153, p. 153. Ottavio Missoni elaborates on this notion, asking: '[a]re we designers? Artisans? Fashion creators? Maybe a bit of all these things and more'. Ibid.

movements of the early 20th century. What had endured in particular, was a mode of experimentation that opened the aesthetic object up to the principles of an external order – the repetitive machinations of the knitting apparatus, the skilled yet individual temperaments of the *mani sapienti*. These aspects of social engagement and the embrace of rote processes not only indicated a predilection toward freedom and coincidence, they manifested an intersection of nature and culture indicative of a democratic aesthetic act.

3   Marisa Merz's *Scarpette* and the Process of Knitting

In 1966, Marisa Merz painstakingly assembled a work that came to be known as *Living Sculpture*, a suspended arrangement of coiled and intertwined aluminum tubes, described as a configuration in which 'disorder couples itself with the openly declared absence of control'.[35] Merz worked on the piece within the confines of her home, often seated at her kitchen table, intermittently attending to her daughter Bea, as the work grew to inhabit the domestic space. While the aluminum forms seemed to infinitely proliferate in space and organize themselves according to some internal logic, the realms of nature and culture intersected and essentialized the processes and practices of everyday life. The repetitive, quotidian nature of maintaining a household and caring for a family – eating, cleaning *etc.* – intertwined with the organic forms of the *Living Sculpture* in a way that suggested a communal environment between art and life. The curator Connie Butler has described Merz's actions as 'literally breathing life and action into form', within 'an alien culture in which the domestic and the material are conflated, digested even, and reconfigured into a living, breathing environment'[36] that counters a hierarchy of materials and artistic convention. Christopher G. Bennett has observed ways in which other artists associated with Arte Povera also used materials and techniques associated with knitting, embroidery, and sewing. He explains that these processes were understood as indistinguishable from those which populated her daily life in various roles as artist, mother, *etc.*, and that these projects (and some by Pino Pascali) 'stem from an interest in blurring conventional distinctions between "high art" and craft'.[37]

35   T. Trini cit. in C. Butler, 'Marisa Merz: Alien Culture', *Marisa Merz: The Sky is a Great Space*, DelMonico Books/Prestel, New York, NY, 2017, pp. 13–35, p. 16.
36   Ibid., p. 29.
37   C. G. Bennett, ' "For Lasting Beauty": Alighiero e Boetti and Afghanistan', *Order and Disorder: Alighiero Boetti by Afghan Women* [exhibition catalogue], Fowler Museum of Art, University of California, Los Angeles, CA, 2012, pp. 32–61, p. 55.

While Lagerfeld and Chiuri have referred to the *petites mains/mani sapienti* as being representative of 'the human aspect' or the 'human touch' within the realm of the couture atelier, a similar sentiment has been used to describe Merz's contribution to Arte Povera. According to Butler, Celant has used the expression 'new humanism' to describe her particular mode of expression, taking as she has 'the movement of the activities and stuff of the studio into the realm of the exhibition space'[38] and in doing so, refashioned the artistic act into one of social participation. To speak of the social aspect of her work however, is not to suggest an extroverted inclination; rather, an interest in what it means to embody the essence of being alive and in touch with one's own reality. For Merz, this has meant a resolute stance on maintaining her own individual existence within a guarded, private realm; as she has stated, 'there has never been any division between my life and my work'.[39] Life, in this sense, is understood as a process through which change and evolution take place and in which the work of art is an enactment of that vital force.

Her process, in fact, has been likened to that of 'maternal labor',[40] specifically those in which she uses copper wire in knitted works, such as the *Scarpette* or 'little shoes'. These knitted shoes, exhibited variously in gallery spaces, in domestic environments, and photographed on a beach, appearing as some floating, metallic sea creature, live simultaneously as aesthetic objects and as mental processes materialized. They ring of the slippers worn by housebound women and yet due to their industrial composition, are non-functional in this regard. Their mechanical technique separates them from the realm of fine art, rendered as they are in a simple knitting stitch, yet evokes the craft, technical skill, and humanness of the *mani sapienti*. Merz's materials have been tied to the industrial environment of Turin in the post-World War II era, the *miracolo italiano* and the mechanized existence associated with the city's FIAT factory.[41] This environment, however, is realized upon the dynamics of process and individual, intellectual being, what the art historian Corinna Criticos describes as 'mental processes and sensual experiences that are given form through an action and the transformation of materials'.[42]

---

38   Butler, 'Marisa Merz: Alien Culture', p. 15.

39   P. Roberts, 'Marisa Merz. Untitled (Living Sculpture) 1966', *Tate*, June 2016 <http://www.tate.org.uk/art/artworks/merz-untitled-living-sculpture-t12950> (Accessed 30 November 2017).

40   Butler, 'Marisa Merz: Alien Culture', p. 17.

41   Ibid.

42   C. Criticos, 'Reading Arte Povera', *Zero to Infinity: Arte Povera 1962–1972*, Tate Modern, London, 2001, pp. 67–88, p. 84.

These processes are intricately connected to the notion of environment in both intimate and universal terms. The 'lunar spheres of influence', as described by Criticos, that helped to determine the installation of Merz's *Scarpette* at the Galleria L'Attico in Rome in 1975, indicated something of the rote nature of Missoni's knitting machines in that the manual labor had been taken over by the repetitive actions of Merz's knitting needles, but then subjected to the patterns of the solar system. That is, with Merz wearing a pair of the *Scarpette*, she sat upon a chair, looking out a window at the moon with her feet resting on the wall; her husband, Arte Povera artist Mario Merz, attached one slipper to the wall where Marisa's foot had been resting, while the other was attached the next night as she watched the moon again, yet in a slightly different position.[43] The art historian and curator Carolyn Christov-Bakargiev writes: '[i]ntuitively, to the scale of her minute body, she exercises the art of infinite repetition, variation, and echo to mark the time from sunrise to sunset, day after day'.[44]

Merz seemed intent on asserting her actions on unrelentingly personal terms contingent only upon the particularities of her own environment, and yet, open to the multitude of ways in which her works could change and evolve outside of that environment. There is an entropic inclination firstly in Merz's defaulting to a preexisting system in the repetitive knitting actions, and secondly, in her willingness to let the works react beyond her. Butler writes that

> [t]he simultaneous drive toward entropy, the permission to allow an object or heap of materials to alter and change over time, and the new notion of remaking it in response to site and situation were an international phenomenon in art making in the late 1960s.[45]

The *Scarpette* and other knitted works such as *Coperte* of 1967 and *Bea* of 1968 were subject to various realms of nature and culture, photographed on the sand and on gallery walls, and as Butler writes, this was 'a way of performing them' and having them 'activated' in a process that is both 'nomadic' and intuitive,[46]

43   Ibid. Criticos' account of this particular installation of the *Scarpette* originally appeared in A.-M. Sauzeau-Boetti, 'Lo specchio ardente, Interview with Carla Accardi, Marisa Merz, and Iole de Freitas', *Data*, no. 18 (September-October), 1975, pp. 51–53.

44   C. Christov-Bakargiev, 'You Can Make Shoes Out of Brains', *Marisa Merz: The Sky is a Great Space*, DelMonico Books/Prestel, New York, NY, 2017, pp. 273–279, p. 273.

45   Butler, 'Marisa Merz: Alien Culture', p. 25.

46   Ibid.

subject to rote process and accumulating meaning beyond the concrete limits of its material. Butler contends that

> Merz – her work and her own narration of life as an artist – requires a different set of actions, a less fixed kind of history making, indeed a refutation of the gesture of art history.[47]

Merz's use of knitting, of forging her practice within the confines of her own domestic environment, enforce a non-hierarchical understanding of aesthetic experience rooted in ancient craft. As with her drawings, which have a quality of prefiguration,[48] Merz's *Scarpette* transcend the objecthood of their recognizable iconography and exist in a much longer view of cultural history. If, as Merz states '[t]his work already existed before it was made because mankind is ancient',[49] the *Scarpette* occupy a place that is at once contemporary and historical, ephemeral and enduring, avant-garde and artisanal.

4   Alighiero Boetti's *Mappe* and Afghani Embroidery

The linear historicism of Western art is also conjured in reference to Boetti's work; in particular, in his use of craft traditions, which were being rediscovered in the realms of Italian design in the 1960s and 1970s.[50] While Merz's *Living Sculpture* share with the *Scarpette* a fluidity that allows an ongoing permutation in space that is experience-based and subject to an open-ended process of becoming, so too are Boetti's *Mappe* and tapestry works, known as *arazzi*. Begun as a collaborative initiative with artisans working in Afghanistan, the *Mappe* project is one conceived upon a social contract and understanding, but also on a defaulting to rote process reliant on the skilled labor of others. Described as a process that 'organizes itself as materiality' through the 'reiteration of a single gesture',[51] one imagines Boetti's Afghani collaborators as the *mani sapienti* of an avant-garde artistic practice. As with Merz's *Scarpette*

---

47   Ibid., p. 17.

48   Pier Giovanni Castagnoli credits Tommaso Trini for the term 'prefigures', regarding Merz's figurative drawings and sculptures. See P.G. Castagnoli, 'Marisa Merz', in P.G. Castangoli and D. Eccher (eds.), *Marisa Merz* [exhibition catalogue], Hopefulmonster, Torino, 1998, pp. 82–90, p. 90.

49   Marisa Merz, cit. in Christov-Bakargiev, 'You Can Make Shoes Out of Brains', p. 274.

50   P.L. Tazzi, cit. in L. Cerizza, *Alighiero e Boetti: Mappa*, Afterall Books, Central Saint Martins College of Art and Design, London, 2008.

51   T. Trini, cit. in Christov-Bakargiev, 'You Can Make Shoes Out of Brains', p. 276.

rendered in a craft process and open to an evolving existence in space, Boetti's role as author and producer of objects became, according to Tommaso Trini, '[...] open to the inherent self-determination of the materials'.[52] Aligned with Arte Povera's interest in industrial and pre-existing forms, Boetti's process involved using '[...] preexisting systems of representation and reworking them'.[53]

The *Mappe*, a series of approximately 200 works initiated by Boetti following his first trip to Afghanistan in 1971, were begun as part of a process that involved the participation of numerous unknown individuals skilled in the art of embroidery. The subject, according to Bennett, stems from a previous work by Boetti titled *Planisfero politico* of 1969, which involved Boetti colouring over a pre-existing world map with the flags representing each country.[54] They evolved to an on going collaborative project with Afghani women from whom Boetti commissioned embroideries on a similar scale over the next several years. According to Roy W. Hamilton, Boetti's interest in the embroidery of Afghanistan began earlier in his career as part of his interest in textile when in 1969 he asked his wife Anne-Marie to do a cross-stitch embroidered map reflecting Israeli-occupied territories in 1967.[55] Upon Boetti's first trip to Kabul, Hamilton writes that '[s]urrounded by some of the most colourful embroidery in the world, he was inspired to think about the possibility of using this technique – and those who created it – as a means for extending his own art'.[56] Over the next few years, Boetti managed a collaborative project with these female artisans, mediated by their male counterparts, in a process that demonstrated his appreciation for their skill and aesthetic sensibilities, while developing 'quality-control measures'[57] that simultaneously gave direction to the project, but also allowed for the 'human aspect' to partly determine their outcome. What is important about this process was that, despite communicating a somewhat defined vision for the *Mappe*, Boetti's role was not that of the sole author, but as collaborator. His process embraced chance, interpretation, and in turn, evinced a lived experience that included many *mani sapienti* beyond his own, ascribing 'ononimo'[58] to works not made directly by his hand.

---

52   Ibid.
53   Bennett, ' "For Lasting Beauty" ', p. 32.
54   Ibid.
55   R. W. Hamilton, 'Introduction: Alighiero Boetti and Embroidery in Afghanistan', *Order and Disorder: Alighiero Boetti by Afghan Women* [exhibition catalogue], Fowler Museum of Art, University of California, Los Angeles, CA, 2012, pp. 10–17.
56   Ibid.
57   Ibid., pp. 14–15.
58   Luca Cerizza explains that 'ononimo' is a combination of *omonimo* ('with the same name') and *anonimo* ('without name'). Cerizza, *Alighiero e Boetti*, p. 61.

As an 'abstract thought process' based in 'physical materiality',[59] the *Mappe* function on the very 'human aspect' so valued by Lagerfeld and Chiuri regarding the *petites mains*. In this sense, the human aspect symbolizes a certain communal function that not only allows for interpretation but embraces the so-called idiosyncracies engendered by a collaborative process. Andrea Marescalchi, a former assistant to Boetti, also comments on the relative 'freedom' inherent in this process as

> one of checking the adherence to that system but also allowing a necessary autonomy so that the sensibility for color choices – as given by the tradition of embroidery by women in Afghan families – could fully manifest itself, according to the qualities that Alighiero knew so well and appreciated.[60]

Christian Rattemeyer explains that initially the colour choices were determined by the type of thread that was available in Afghanistan – Anchor brand – and that on one occasion, Boetti had forgotten to specify the colour the ocean should be. It turned out green and as Rattemeyer explains, ensuing works that presented the ocean in hues ranging from pink to gold, purple and yellow, rendered the design of the *Mappe* 'an aesthetic decision'[61] on the part of the embroiderers rather than an empirical one.

Cerizza explains that Boetti was interested in grasping the 'difference in repetition' which allowed a countering of the 'rhetoric of the artist-individual, the trap of subjectivity and the "inner necessity" of Romantic origin',[62] what Bennett describes a restoration of autonomy for the Afghani artisans. By allowing for an element of chance to determine the outcome of the *Mappe*, Boetti rebutted the industrial, commercial process of mass production that would have eliminated this variation – the very 'human' presence in these works.[63] This was in fact Boetti's 'system', an arrangement of processes Alessandra Bonomo describes as a 'series of casual events, coincidences ...'[64] In fact, Boetti

59   Bennett,' "For Lasting Beauty" ', p. 32.
60   A. Marescalchi, 'Notes for a Book Project', in R. M. Steinberger (ed.), *Boetti by Afghan People*, Ram Publications, Santa Monica, CA, 2015, pp. 104–105, p. 105.
61   C. Rattemeyer, 'From Alighiero to Boetti', in L. Cooke, M. Godfrey, and C. Rattemeyer (eds.), *Alighiero Boetti: Game Plan*, The Museum of Modern Art, New York, NY, 2012, pp. 29–37, p. 36.
62   Cerizza, *Alighiero e Boetti*, pp. 62–63.
63   Bennett, ' "For Lasting Beauty" ', p. 47.
64   A. Bonomo and R.M. Steinberger, 'Randi Malkin Steinberger & Alessandra Bonomo: A Conversation', in R. M. Steinberger (ed.), *Boetti by Afghan People*, Ram Publications, Santa Monica, CA, 2015, pp.107–121, p. 107.

described the resulting colour schemes as a matter of 'surprise', stating that it was like '... the disorder invading the formal order of the grid'.[65] The irregularities were a product of having different people work on the same *Mappa* over a period of time; however, as Bonomo points out, there is a consistency that remains, as all of the women worked in the same style, [66] with similar training, so the effect is one of heterogeneity within homogeneity, a 'personal collective'[67] that Bennett characterizes as 'an unresolved co-presence of seemingly antithetical concepts'.[68]

As a collaborative process then, the *Mappe* become social surfaces[69] that are products of aesthetic and philosophical vision, artisanal skill, and political engagement. In their particular time and place, the project resonated with political significance and became sites of heterogeneous political voices.[70] While Bonomo argues that the project may have provided the women an outlet '[...] from a tradition of subordination',[71] perhaps a more broadly conceived political gesture is enacted whereby the *Mappe* are the surfaces upon which a multitude of voices and hands participate, not only those of women. The *Mappe* as social surfaces exist in a similar spatial-temporal realm as Merz's *Scarpette*; they rely on a practice rooted in ancient craft and are subject to accumulated and shifting meaning, composed as they are of repetitive actions, rote process, and dynamics/decisions external to the artist/author. Bennett describes Boetti's process as follows:

> [t]o summarize, while retaining the work of art as a factual vehicle of engagement, Boetti anchored his practice in an experiential framework that cut past any particular artefact. Paradoxically, then, when looked at, the object becomes that much more vivid, with the main goal here being to suspend oneself like salt and water in the sea.[72]

---

65 Boetti, cit. in M. Godfrey, 'Boetti and Afghanistan', in L. Cooke, M. Godfrey, and C. Rattemeyer (eds.), *Alighiero Boetti: Game Plan*, The Museum of Modern Art, New York, NY, 2012, pp. 155–175, p. 166. Quote originally from an interview by Kazuo Akao Art Agency, Tokyo, 1980.

66 Bonomo and Steinberger, 'Randi Malkin Steinberger & Alessandra Bonomo'.

67 Boetti, cit. in Cerizza, *Alighiero e Boetti*, p. 56.

68 C. G. Bennett, 'With Alighiero Boetti: Eight Turns of the Hourglass, Approximately', in R. M. Steinberger (ed.), *Boetti by Afghan People*, Ram Publications, Santa Monica, CA, 2015, pp. 123–126, p. 123.

69 Bennett, ' "For Lasting Beauty" '.

70 Godfrey, 'Boetti and Afghanistan'.

71 Bonomo and Steinberger, 'Randi Malkin Steinberger & Alessandra Bonomo', p. 114.

72 Bennett, 'With Alighiero Boetti', p. 125.

Boetti's social practice regarding the *Mappe* and other tapestry-oriented works opens onto a measure of uncertainty,[73] seen as a productive aspect of their making. In his conscious giving over to the intricacies of a daily work dynamic far removed from his own, situated as he was in his apartment in Rome for much of the production of these works, Boetti steered the direction of his artistic vision and defaulted to the order of an external system of craft process and collaboration. This was Boetti's political act against the primacy of the object, relying on the 'inviolability of materials and rudimentary gesture',[74] in the image of Missoni's knitting machines and the *mani sapienti* of Italy's fashion industry.

5   Conclusion

The relationship between process and product lies at the basis of radical artistic experimentation and is what problematizes the alienating dynamics of industrial production. In this regard, Criticos evokes John Dewey's 1934 *Art as Experience*, which, in a chapter titled 'The Expressive Object', argues for the significance of this relation (between 'action' and 'product'), stressing the aspect of their coexistence:

> [i]f the two meanings are separated, the object is viewed in isolation from the operation which produced it, and therefore apart from the individuality of vision, since the act proceeds from an individual live creature ... A poem and picture present material passed through the alembic of personal experience. They have no precedents in existence or in universal being. But, nonetheless, their material came from the public world and so has qualities in common with the material of other experiences, while the product awakens in other persons new perceptions of the meanings of the common world. The oppositions of individual and universal, of subjective and objective, of freedom and order, in which philosophers have reveled, have no place in the work of art. Expression as personal act and as objective result are organically connected with each other.[75]

---

73   Ibid.
74   C. Gilman, 'Figuring Boetti', in L. Cooke, M. Godfrey, and C. Rattemeyer (eds.), *Alighiero Boetti: Game Plan*, The Museum of Modern Art, New York, NY, 2012, pp. 133–141, p. 133.
75   Criticos, 'Reading Arte Povera', p. 87. See J. Dewey, *Art as Experience*, Perigee, New York, NY, 1980.

Dewey stresses the commonality between process and material, between materials and other experiences, a sentiment pronounced in Merz's *Scarpette*, Boetti's *Mappe*, and in Missoni's knitted garments-as-artforms. What these works accomplish is what Pier Giovanni Castagnoli describes as '... a threshold that is neither a border nor a separation, but a place, a passageway permeable to comings and goings',[76] a type of continuum in which works, differently assembled at points over time, evolve in ongoing relationships with each other and with viewers. The works could not have been realized if not for the participation of a multitude of collaborators,[77] a cooperative initiative of skilled partners committed to enacting a 'transnational process' responsible for what have become Boetti's most iconic works.[78]

By allowing the assistants, the embroiderers, and the calligraphers to add their sentiments to the borders of some of the works, Boetti was enacting a political process that democratically relied on the voices of a community. As Hamilton writes, Boetti

> must have appreciated how the messages borne on the surface of his own work had been taken out of his hands to be disordered and then reordered into something new and unpredictable beyond his control.[79]

Echoing the words of Celant, Boetti has commented on the order and disorder harmoniously present in aesthetic processes:

> [t]here are extraordinary things which derive from the mineral world, the vegetable world and the animal world. These worlds have been separated and placed in a hierarchy, but it is my view that ultimately there is not hierarchy: what we have before us is always the same thing, the same manifestation of a *design* in things.[80]

---

76   Castagnoli, 'Marisa Merz', p. 82.

77   Hamilton notes that, as pointed out by Randi Malkin Steinberger, Boetti acknowledged his collaborators, often by including lettering in the embroideries that indicated that they were created by 'unknown Afghan women'. Hamilton, 'Introduction', p. 15. The employment he provided to these Afghan women was not considered a make-work project or as charity; rather, he '[...] was simply engaging the skilled workers he needed to fulfill his vision.' Ibid., p. 16.

78   Ibid.

79   Ibid., p. 17.

80   A. Boetti, 'Overnight', in C. Christov-Bakargiev, *Arte Povera*, Phaidon Press Ltd., London, 1999, pp. 237–239, p. 239. The present excerpt of 'Overnight' of 1986 was translated into English by Liz Heron and was originally published as an artist's statement titled 'Dall'oggi al domani'. A. Boetti, 'Dall'oggi al domani', ed. S. Lombardi, Associazione Edizioni L'Obliquo, Rome, 1988, pp. 13–29.

The coexistence of order and disorder is present in the iconography of the maps themselves as subject to constant geopolitical dynamics, as well as in the participation of various collaborators, in the ancient and predetermined patterns of knitting and embroidery, and in the unknown capacities of knitting machines. As Luca Cerizza writes, '[t]hrough the different versions and variations of the maps, he harnessed disorder in the guise of order that constantly revealed its continuous, potentially infinite regeneration',[81] and in the process, called into question conventions surrounding authorial dominance and 'global realities'.[82]

What Lagerfeld and Chiuri proposed with their expression of reverence for their *mani sapienti* was an upholding of craft traditions alongside the multitude of processes involved in realizing an artistic vision, avant-garde or otherwise. Like Dewey, they put forth the conditions for an experience-based aesthetic act that was democratic, inclusive, and entrenched in the practices of everyday life. Regarding Boetti's international project, the philosopher Fabrizio Scrivano writes that

> [o]n the verge of globalization, Boetti seems to have realized that art must follow its own distinctive formal themes and languages in order to construct models for perceiving political and social reality.[83]

For Scrivano, the 'meaning of surface' is rooted in the senses, emotions, and being 'bodily involved' in the process of ideological experience. This process-based route to aesthetic action is realized in Merz's knitted *Scarpette*, in Boetti's embroidered *Mappe*, and in Missoni's mechanically produced garments – all processes of a democratic, non-hierarchical, and participatory vision of aesthetic engagement.

Acknowledgements

I would like to thank The Italian Art Society and Dr. Tenley Bick for the opportunity to present aspects of this research at the College Art Association's 2018 annual conference in Los Angeles, California. Thanks also to Texas A&M

---

81   Cerizza, *Alighiero e Boetti*, p. 64.
82   Bennett, ' "For Lasting Beauty" ', p. 59.
83   F. Scrivano, 'Getting to the Bottom of the Issue of Surface', in G. Maffei and M. Picciau (eds.), *Alighiero e Boetti: Oltre il libro/Beyond books*, Maurizio Corraini S.r.l., Mantova, 2001, pp. 94–103, p. 103.

University-Corpus Christi, Office of the Dean of the College of Liberal Arts, and the Center for Faculty Excellence for their support of this research.

Bibliography

Armstrong, L., 'Inside the Haute Couture Atelier at Chanel – At Yesterday's Chanel Haute Couture Show in Paris, Karl Lagerfeld Unveiled His Latest Collection in Front of the Talented Hands That Create It', *The Daily Telegraph*, 6 July 2016, p. 23.

Bennett, C. G., ' "For Lasting Beauty": Alighiero e Boetti and Afghanistan', *Order and Disorder: Alighiero Boetti by Afghan Women* [exhibition catalogue]. Fowler Museum of Art, University of California, Los Angeles, CA, 2012, pp. 32–61.

Bennett, C. G., 'With Alighiero Boetti: Eight Turns of the Hourglass, Approximately', in R. Malkin Steinberger (ed.), *Boetti by Afghan People*. Ram Publications, Santa Monica, CA, 2015, pp. 123–126.

Boetti, A., 'Overnight', in C. Christov-Bakargiev (ed.), *Arte Povera*. Phaidon Press Ltd., London, 1999, pp. 237–239.

Boetti, A., 'Dall'oggi al domani'. Ed. S. Lombardi. Associazione Edizioni L'Obliquo, Rome, 1988, pp. 13–29.

Bonito Oliva, A., 'Process, Concept and Behaviour in Italian Art', *Studio International*, vol. 191, no. 979, 1976, pp. 3–9.

Bonomo, A., and R.M. Steinberger, 'Randi Malkin Steinberger & Alessandra Bonomo: A Conversation', in R. M. Steinberger (ed.), *Boetti by Afghan People*. Ram Publications, Santa Monica, MA, 2015, pp. 107–121.

Butler, C., 'Marisa Merz: Alien Culture', *Marisa Merz: The Sky is a Great Space*. DelMonico Books/Prestel, New York, NY, 2017, pp. 13–35.

Caramel, L., 'Missoni, Art and Colour. Between Visible and Invisible', *Missoni Art Colour* [exhibition catalogue]. Skira Rizzoli, New York, NY, 2016, pp. 17–23.

Castagnoli P. G., 'Marisa Merz', in P.G. Castangoli and D. Eccher (eds.) *Marisa Merz* [exhibition catalogue]. Hopefulmonster, Torino, 1998, pp. 82–90.

Celant, G., 'Introduction', *Art Povera*. Praeger, New York, NY, 1969, pp. 225–230.

Cerizza, L., *Alighiero e Boetti: Mappa*. Afterall Books, Central Saint Martins College of Art and Design, London, 2008.

Christov-Bakargiev, C., 'You Can Make Shoes Out of Brains', *Marisa Merz: The Sky is a Great Space*. DelMonico Books/Prestel, New York, NY, 2017, pp. 273–279.

Cooke, L., M. Godfrey, and C. Rattemeyer (eds.), *Alighiero Boetti – Game Plan*. The Museum of Modern Art, NY, 2012.

Criticos, C., 'Reading Arte Povera', *Zero to Infinity: Arte Povera 1962–1972*. Tate Modern, London, 2001, pp. 67–88.

Dewey, J., *Art as Experience*. Perigee, New York, 1980.

'Dior's Les Petites Mains/The Little Hands' [video], *The Business of Fashion* (sponsored by Christian Dior Couture) <https://www.businessoffashion.com/articles/video/les-petites-mains?utm_source=Subscribers&utm_campaign=5b93d65fac-the-trouble-with-topshop-nike-launches-flyleather-&utm_medium=email&utm_term=0_d2191372b3-5b93d65fac-419439753> (Accessed 8 September 2017).

Gilman, C., 'Figuring Boetti', in L. Cooke, M. Godfrey and C. Rattemeyer (eds.), *Alighiero Boetti: Game Plan*. The Museum of Modern Art, New York, NY, 2012, pp. 133–141.

Giordani Aragno, B., 'Boutique Fashion, a Sum of Concepts and Innovations', in A. Ellis (ed.), *Italian Glamour: the Essence of Italian Fashion From the Postwar Years to the Present Day: the Enrico Quinto and Paolo Tinarelli Collection*. Skira, Milan, 2014, pp. 11–15.

Godfrey, M., *Alighiero e Boetti*. Yale University Press, New Haven (CT) and London, 2011.

Godfrey, M., 'Boetti and Afghanistan', in L. Cooke, M. Godfrey and C. Rattemeyer (eds.), *Alighiero Boetti: Game Plan*. The Museum of Modern Art, New York, NY, 2012, pp. 155–175.

Gregotti, V., 'Italian Design, 1945–1971', in E. Ambasz (ed.), *Italy: The New Domestic Landscape. Achievements and Problems of Italian Design*. The Museum of Modern Art, New York, NY, 1972, pp. 315–340.

Grotowski, J., *Towards a Poor Theatre*. Ed. E. Barba. Routledge, New York, NY, 1968.

Gumuchian, M.-L., 'Lagerfeld Pays Tribute to Atelier Seamstresses at Chanel Show', *Reuters Entertainment News*, 5 July 2016 <https://www.reuters.com/article/us-fashion-paris-chanel/lagerfeld-pays-tribute-to-atelier-seamstresses-at-chanel-show-idUSKCN0ZL25O> (Accessed 16 November 2017).

Gute, C., *Boetti by Afghan People. Pesharwar, Pakiston, 1990*. Ram Publications + Distribution, Santa Monica, CA, 2011.

Hamilton, R. W., 'Introduction: Alighiero Boetti and Embroidery in Afghanistan', *Order and Disorder: Alighiero Boetti by Afghan Women* [exhibition catalogue]. Fowler Museum of Art, University of California, Los Angeles, CA, 2012, pp. 10–17.

'Le radici/Roots', *Missoni Art Colour*. Skira Rizzoli Publications, Inc., New York, NY, 2016.

Marescalchi, A., 'Notes for a Book Project', in R. M. Steinberger, *Boetti by Afghan People*. Ram Publications, Santa Monica, CA, 2015, pp. 104–105.

Matzeu, E., 'Piccola guida alla haute couture', *Il Post Moda*, 26 January 2016 <http://www.ilpost.it/2016/01/26/piccola-guida-alla-haute-couture/> (Accessed 16 November 2017).

Missoni Art Colour [exhibition catalogue]. Skira Rizzoli, New York, NY, 2016.

Missoni, L., 'Macchina mago/The Machine-Magician', *Missoni Art Colour* [exhibition catalogue]. Skira Rizzoli, New York, NY, 2016, pp. 41–43.

Missoni, O., 'L'emozione della materia/Passion for Materials', *Missoni Art Colour* [exhibition catalogue]. Skira Rizzoli, New York, NY, 2016, pp. 152–153.

Rattemeyer, C., 'From Alighiero to Boetti', in L. Cooke, M. Godfrey, and C. Rattemeyer (eds.), *Alighiero Boetti: Game Plan*. The Museum of Modern Art, New York, NY, 2012, pp. 29–37.

Roberts, P., 'Marisa Merz. Untitled (Living Sculpture) 1966', *Tate*, June 2016 <http://www.tate.org.uk/art/artworks/merz-untitled-living-sculpture-t12950> (Accessed 30 November 2017).

Sauzeau-Boetti, A.-M., 'Lo specchio ardente, Interview with Carla Accardi, Marisa Merz, and Iole de Freitas', *Data*, no. 18 (September-October), 1975, pp. 51–53.

Scrivano, F., 'Getting to the Bottom of the Issue of Surface', in G. Maffei and M. Picciau (eds.), *Alighiero e Boetti: Oltre il libro/Beyond books*. Maurizio Corraini S.r.l., Mantova, 2001, pp. 94–103.

Zanella, E., 'They Are Museum Pieces, but You Can Still Wear Them', *Missoni Art Colour* [exhibition catalogue]. Skira Rizzoli, New York, NY, 2016, pp. 25–39.

Index of Names

Index of Subjects